Y. Ohno (Ed.)

DISTRIBUTED ENVIRONMENTS

Software Paradigms and Workstations

With 135 Illustrations and 4 in Color

Springer-Verlag
Tokyo Berlin Heidelberg
New York London Paris
Hong Kong Barcelona

EDITOR

Professor Dr. *Yutaka Ohno*
Department of Computer Science and System Engineering, Ritsumeikan University, Tojiin,
Kitamachi, Kita-ku, Kyoto, 603 Japan

COEDITOR

Toshiko Matsuda
IBM Japan Ltd., 19–21, Nihonbashi Hakozaki-cho, Chuo-ku, Tokyo, 103 Japan

Cover picture: Yougao wall face; flexible view-sceen structure with half-transparent free shaped objects.
Design: Maekawa Laboratory, University of Tokyo

ISBN-13:978-4-431-68146-5   e-ISBN-13:978-4-431-68144-1
DOI: 10.1007/978-4-431-68144-1

Library of Congress Cataloging-in-Publication Data
Distributed environments: software paradigms and workstations/editor, Yutaka Ohno.
p.   cm. Includes bibliographical references and index. ISBN-13:978-4-431-68146-5
                1. Computer software—Development. I. Ono, Yutaka, 1924–
QA76.76.D47D57. 1991   005. 1—dc20. 91-15306

© Springer-Verlag Tokyo 1991
Softcover reprint of the hardcover 1st edition 1991

Typesetting: Asco Trade Typesetting Ltd., Hong Kong

Preface

The aim of this volume is to promote fundamental research in advanced software technology as a priority research area, in cooperation with key professors from the computer science departments of 12 Japanese universities. The project was proposed to the Ministry of Education of Japan in 1987 and as a result, a special research fund was established. However, this fund did not prove sufficient for the long-term support of the project. After deep consideration, we approached IBM Japan with the idea of supporting the projects since IBM has previously collaborated with academic societies worldwide including Carnegie Mellon University and MIT. IBM Japan accepted our proposal of a joint research project and after further discussion, the project was defined as the "Fundamental Research in Advanced Software Technology." This book contains the results of that project.

We would like to acknowledge the contribution made by the project members involved and we thank IBM Japan for supporting this joint research project.

Yutaka Ohno
Editor

Toshiko Matsuda
Coeditor

 *Yutaka Ohno* is a Professor Emeritus at Kyoto University, where he was formerly Professor of Information Science, and currently a Professor of Information Science and System at Ritsumeikan University. He is also President of the newly established Advanced Software Technology & Mechatronics Research Institute of Kyoto. He has been associated with many international conferences, national projects and government committees, including the Japanese Government's SIGMA project. He was President of the Information Processing Society of Japan (IPSJ) and was previously Chairman of the Japan Society of Software Science and Technology. He is the author of over thirty-five technical papers in English, and over fifty in Japanese, as well as having written and edited over ten books. He has been awarded honourable prizes by the Japanese Institutes of Electrical Engineers, Electronics and Communication Engineers, IPSJ and, in 1971, received the Order of the Purple Ribbon from the Japanese Government.

Contents

GROUP B _____

GROUP C _____

List of Contributors

DISTRIBUTED ENVIRONMENTS

1
Fundamental Research in Advanced Software Technology

Yutaka Ohno[1] *and Toshiko Matsuda*[2]

Over the past several years, workstation technology has progressed remarkably, and the number of people who use workstations for their own purposes is increasing. In accordance with the progress of computer technologies, many application systems have been developed and used in government, industry, social life, education, and research. Reviewing the history of application life-cycles, we can see that each application system has been developed for a respective purpose by utilizing centralized and/or decentralized computing facilities, and that, with changes of computing environment including machine alteration, the lives of application systems have been extended by iterative modification of old-fashioned systems. This process has required too much manpower and time, and the modified systems have had to become more productive while maintaining the quality of the systems. On the other hand, with the increase in requests by users for easily used and personalized workstations which are connected by a network and allow users to communicate freely with each other, areas of special research interest have been developing to focus on how to satisfy these requests. The required workstations must be of higher quality, more intelligent, and more reliable, with a good human-interface. From a technical viewpoint, the scope of the technologies ranges from kernel operating systems to human-interface techniques, as shown in Fig. 1.1.

In order to respond to this requirement, it is necessary to promote basic research into software development techniques, including new languages and communication software in the network environment. In addition to this, the technology of automatic generation of software parts with requirements of application specification is also important. With the increase in complexity of the computing environment, techniques and methods for the definition of software requirements and for program parts management and reuse will be very effective and important from the productivity point of view. Some of these techniques have been gradually realized.

---
[1] Department of Computer Science and Systems Engineering, Ritsumeikan University, Kyoto, 603 Japan
[2] IBM Japan, Chuo-ku, Tokyo, 103 Japan

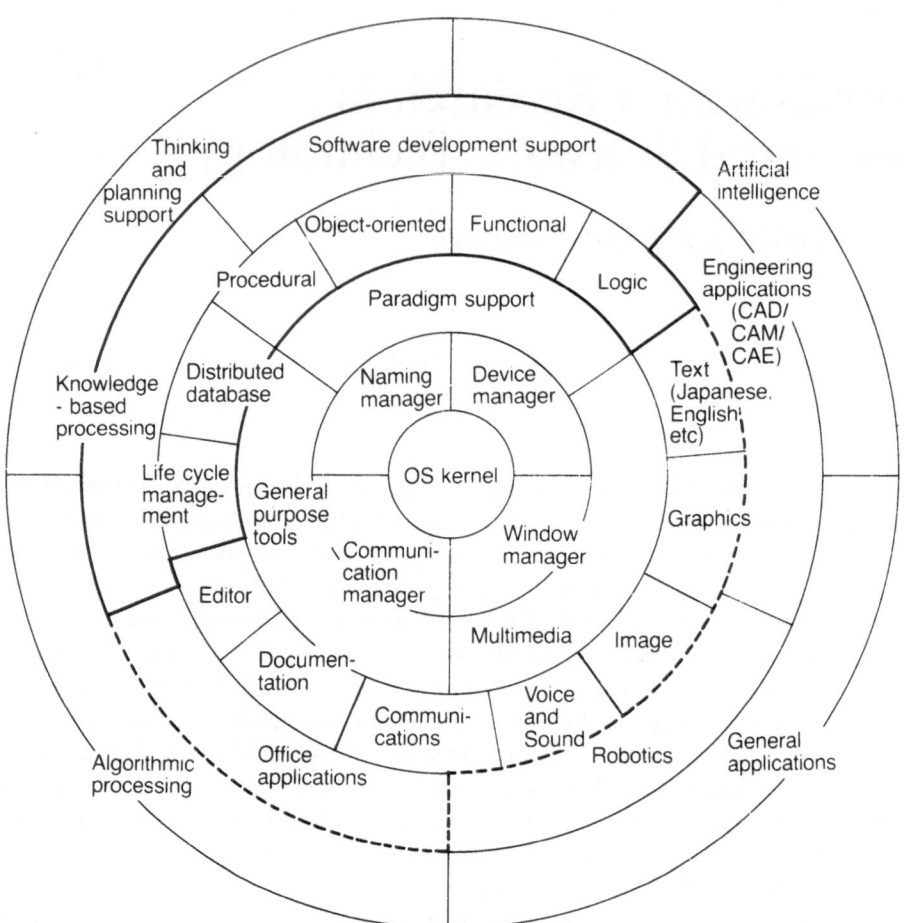

FIG. 1.1. The scope of the technologies. *OS*, operating system; *CAD*, computer-aided design; *CAM*, computer-assisted manufacture; *CAE*, computer-aided engineering

Despite the fact that many research results have been reported as papers in academic societies, real prototypes released for practical use are far fewer. Hence, our interest was to implement prototypes of some technologies which are feasible at the current research level. These technologies are shown in Fig. 1.1, enclosed by dotted lines and thick lines. Through a practical test use of a prototype and the resulting feedback to researchers, the usefulness of the prototype will be evaluated and enhancements will be encouraged. Iterating the feedback cycle of test use, evaluation and enhancement, we would like to lead the development of basic research results from the ivory tower to the practical level.

This book contains the fruits of a joint research project between IBM Japan and twelve universities. This project can be organized into three groups of subjects: (1) paradigms for software development, processing, and communication; (2) native-language interface; and (3) software development environment with related operating systems. The objectives and content of each group are as follows.

Group A: Software development on various kinds of paradigm

The objective of this group is to research the methodologies and tools of software development, processing, and communication. Research areas fall within the area enclosed by the thick line in Fig. 1.1; this area includes a variety of research from the variegated project members. The research areas consist of requirement specification, design, programming languages, communications systems, and the human interface. Programming languages include object-oriented language, functional language, and logic programming, in addition to procedural language. As a whole, the research from this group is from the standpoint of basic theory of software formation, starting from requirement analysis, and finally generating workable programs to be delivered through a workstation network.

Group B: Native-language support for workstations

This group had a very specific objective: development of a native-language support interface. Native-language support for workstations is needed when users communicate with each other through a network. The Andrew Toolkit was taken as an example of an interface tool for documentation and communication on the X-window. The key technique is the design of a uniform data model which is defined as an object which can be handled by a native language.

Group C: Software development and execution environment

The project of this group is to develop a distributed workstation system, called GALAXY. The research objective of the GALAXY project is to realize *holonic processing** in the environment of a workstation network. The target items fall within the area enclosed by the dotted line in Fig. 1.1. A multimedia workstation network environment was realized by developing experimental and kernel operating systems. A naming manager, a device manager, a window manager, and a communication manager have also been implemented in the environment. At the same time, operating system technologies were investigated, aiming at location independency, performance stability, fault tolerance, concurrency, replication, and so on. As for the interface with a multimedia workstation, *R*-language, which operates each multimedia object, was developed.

Considering the overall project, an object-oriented approach was often taken

---

* *Holonic processing* is a newly coined term representing a system which can integrate various kinds of paradigm to co-ordinate a network of resources in a wide area. *Holonic* is the adjective of "*Holon*," created by Arthur Koestler, who combined the Greek *hols* and *on* to indicate a harmonization of "a piece" with "the whole." This idea comes from a biological concept in which each cell of the human body harmonizes with other cells in order to move the whole body.

and applied to various techniques, not only in languages, but also in the man-machine interface. We hope these results will be implemented as research tools or for business use if possible, and welcome the possibility that new methodologies will be created on the basis of these ideas.

GROUP A

GROUP A

2
Japanese Software Requirements Definition Based on Requirements Frame Model

Atsushi Ohnishi[1] and Kiyoshi Agusa[2]

Summary: Many techniques for the definition of software requirements have been proposed and developed in recent years. Though some techniques have contributed to improvement in the quality of specification of requirements, there remain problems. Since such techniques are usually based on formal requirements, it is hard for many software developers to read and write the specifications. In this paper, we propose a technique for the definition of requirements, using a more natural language, i.e., a Japanese-like language. This language, named X-JRDL, is designed based on the Requirements Frame Model, which enables the detection of errors in definitions of requirements.

We describe characteristics of X-JRDL and the ease with which it allows the writing and reading of requirements. We also discuss how a requirements description with X-JRDL is utilized in the design and maintenance phase of a software life cycle.

Key words: requirements model — requirements language — SRS (software requirements specification)

2.1 Introduction

Several different models have been proposed as software requirements models, such as the Entity-Relationship model, Data Flow model, Control Flow model, Finite State Machine model, Petri Net model, Decision Table model, Predicate Logic model, and so on [1]. Each model has both advantages and disadvantages. For example, requirements based on the Data Flow model are adequate to represent functional requirements, but inadequate for performance requirements. On the other hand, the Petri Net model is adequate for performance requirements but not for functional.

---

[1] Data Processing Center, Kyoto University, Kyoto, 606 Japan
[2] Department of Electrical Engineering, Nagoya University, Nagoya, 464-01 Japan

We have developed a composite requirements model, named Requirements Frame [2]. A requirements description, based on the Requirements Frame, can be translated into other types of descriptions based on several different models, if desired. These include the Data Flow model, the Control Flow model, the Relational model, and the Predicate Logic models. This is described in Sect. 2.2.2. Derivation of descriptions is needed for the investigation of correctness, inconsistency, completeness, maintainability, and so on. It helps to improve readability of descriptions in the most appropriate form for a particular engineer [3–5]. In this paper, we discuss how to improve the ease of writing and reading of requirements descriptions.

2.2 Requirements Frame Model

2.2.1 Requirements Model

Consider the requirements for a library system. To simplify the problem, we focus on the requirements for book retrieval. That is:

> There exist users, cards for retrieval of books, and the identifier (ID) number of each book. Cards and ID numbers are data-type objects. Users are defined as objects of human type. Cards are classified into authors-cards which are sorted by author's name in alphabetical order, and title-cards, sorted by title. A user can retrieve books with these cards.

A requirements definer first identifies objects (nouns) and object types (attributes) in a target system. Secondly, he or she defines operations among objects (verbs) and roles of the operations (cases), and then constructs requirements sentences. The "cases" mean concepts about the agents, objects, and goals of the operations [6]. A particular requirements item may be defined with several sentences.

Thus, a requirements statement includes nouns and verbs as its components, and there exist roles of objects as relations among the components. From a more macro-view, a requirements description includes several requirements statements as its components. From a more micro-view, each noun has its type.

2.2.2 Requirements Frame

Our requirements model has been developed to represent easily these structures. It involves several kinds of frames. The first frame is the *Noun Frame*, a frame whose components are nouns and their types. Table 2.1 shows the noun types provided to specify file-oriented software requirements.

TABLE 2.1. Noun types of the Noun Frame

Type of noun	Meaning
Human	Active object external to the target system
Function	Active object internal to the target system
File	Passive object containing a number of instances of information set
Data	Passive object containing a single item of information
Control	Passive object to specify control transition
Device	Passive object to specify an instrument

A new noun appearing in a requirements description will be classified into one of the types.

The second frame is the *Case Frame*, a frame whose components are nouns and verbs and cases. We provide seven different cases: *agent, goal, instrument, key, object, operation,* and *source*. We also provide 16 different concepts as verbs, including data flow, control flow, data creation, file manipulation, data comparison, and structure of data/file/function. There are several verbs to represent one of these concepts. For example, to specify a verb type *data flow*, we use *input, output, print out, display, send,* and so on. A requirements definer can use any verbs which can be categorized in these 16 concepts provided.

The frame defines the case structure of a verb. For example, the verb *data flow* has agent, source, goal, and instrument cases. The agent case corresponds to data which are transferred from source case object to goal case object. So, an object assigned to the agent case should be a data type object. An object in the source or goal cases should be either a human or a function type object. If and only if a human type object is assigned to source or goal cases, some instrument should be specified as a device case. This is illustrated in Fig. 2.1.

The Case Frame enables the detection of illegal usages of data and lack of cases.

The third frame is the *Function Frame*, a frame whose components are requirements sentences. Let us consider a function, "output a result of retrieval," which consists of subfunctions, file retrieval and data output. These two subfunctions are

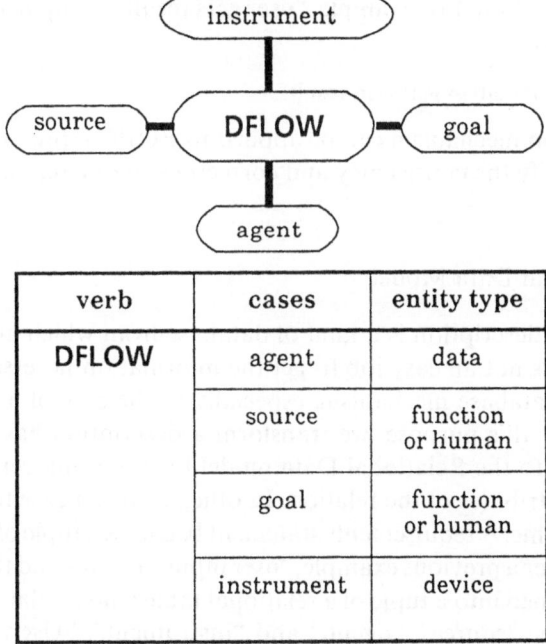

verb	cases	entity type
DFLOW	agent	data
	source	function or human
	goal	function or human
	instrument	device

If type of "source" is human or type of "goal" is human, then "instrument" case is indispensable else "instrument" should not be assigned.

FIG. 2.1. Case Frame of verb, "DFLOW"

connected to each other by the fact that the same data type object is used in the goal case of file retrieval and in the agent case of data output. By providing "output a result of retrieval" as an indispensable function, we can point out an error when this function is absent. In the Function Frame, there are ten essential functions, such as data processing, data input, data output, file definition, file manipulation, and so on [2]. We can check the absence of them in a certain requirements description.

2.2.3 Requirements Models from Requirements Frame

The Requirements Frame can be transformed into several models. In this sense we regard the Requirements Frame as a composite requirements model.

2.2.3.1 Logic Model

A requirements description consists of facts, such as, "user inputs a command through a terminal." Each fact can be represented with the first-order predicate calculus (FOPC) by introducing a predicate corresponding to the verb used in the description. This becomes

input(user, command, terminal).

We transform a requirement based on the Requirements Frame into FOPC form by regarding a verb as a predicate, nouns as terms, and the sequence between two facts as an implication. For example, "user gets result by inquiring with terminal" is transformed into

inquire(user, terminal) → get(user, result)

The resolution mechanism can be applied to FOPC representation. This model is utilized to verify the consistency and correctness of the requirements description [3, 4].

2.2.3.2 Relational Data Model

A requirements description is a kind of database from which all engineers retrieve information. It is not an easy job to get the information necessary for a particular use without a database mechanism, especially in the case of a large requirements description. For this purpose, we transform a description based on the Requirements Frame into the Relational Data model by regarding verbs as relations and their cases as attributes of the relation. In other words, a case frame is regarded as a relational scheme. A requirements statement becomes a tuple of a relational table.

Let us consider a previous example, "user inputs a command through a terminal." This is transformed into a tuple of a relational table whose relation name is "input". It has attributes: "source," "agent," and "instrument." "User," "command," and "terminal" are attribute values of these attributes, respectively. In this way we store a requirements description with some relational database management system (DBMS). It helps to retrieve information easily and quickly for system design [5, 7].

2.2.3.3 Control/Data Flow Model

A requirements description can be described from several viewpoints, such as data flow, control flow, function structure, data structure, and so on. A requirements description based on the Control/Data Flow model is suitable for rapid prototyping. We can get these flow models from requirements on the Requirements Frame, and have developed a prototyping method/system with the derived description [5].

2.3 Japanese Requirements Language: X-JRDL

2.3.1 JRDL and X-JRDL

We developed two requirements languages, JRDL and GRDL, on the basis of the Requirements Frame model. JRDL (Japanese Requirements Description Language) allows flexible word order in conformity with Japanese grammar. For elimination of the ambiguity of requirements description with natural Japanese, the syntax of JRDL is more limited and simpler, and its semantics is defined more exactly.

1. A JRDL statement is a simple sentence in principle.
2. Demonstrative pronouns cannot be used.
3. Omission of cases is not permissible.

JRDL supports 16 essential concepts (10 verb type concepts and 6 adjective type concepts) as shown in Table 2.2. One JRDL statement is transformed into the internal expression named CRDL (Conceptual Requirements Description Language) statement. The CRDL is based exactly on the Case Frame model.

X-JRDL (eXtended JRDL) is a version of JRDL extended to achieve more naturalness and flexibility. The three listed limitations of JRDL are eliminated in

TABLE 2.2. Concept of CRDL (Conceptual Requirements Description Language)

Concept	Meaning
DFLOW	Data flow
CFLOW	Control flow
ANDSUB	And-tree structure of function, file, or data type object
ORSUB	Or-tree structure of function, file, or data type object
GEN	Data creation
RET	Retrieve a record in a file
UPDATE	Update a record in a file
DEL	Deletion of a record in a file
INS	Insertion of a record in a file
MANIP	File manipulation
EQ, NE, LT, GT, LE, GE	Logic operators

X-JRDL. Requirements description with X-JRDL is also transformed into CRDL expressions.

2.3.2 Interpretation of X-JRDL Description

An X-JRDL description is analyzed through three interpreters [8]. Since X-JRDL allows compound sentences and complex sentences, a surface interpreter divides them into a set of simple sentences. Another interpreter, a word interpreter, fulfills a Case Frame, consulting with dictionaries. Since a noun is interpreted with its type, a noun dictionary holds a name and its type. A verb (or an adjective) is interpreted with its corresponding concept. In the case of a pronoun or an omission, we guess its type with Case Frame. By a sentence interpreter, a simple sentence is transformed into a CRDL expression with checking of absences of indispensable cases.

X-JRDL allows the use of pronouns and the omission of nouns. We frequently come across such features in Japanese sentences. The X-JRDL analyzer automatically assigns a concrete word into a pronoun or an absent case. The following Japanese pronouns are supported by X-JRDL:

それ(it)、これ(this)、あれ(that)、彼(he)、彼女(she)、彼ら(they)、ここ(here)、そこ(there)、前者(the former)、後者(the latter)

Conjunctions are used to write down compound sentences and complex sentences. The analyzer divides such a sentence into a set of simple sentences with conjunctions. The following Japanese conjunctions are supported by X-JRDL:

後(after)、時(when)、もし(if)、そして(then)、かつ(and)、または(or)、しかし(but)

The X-JRDL analyzer has a dictionary of nouns, verbs, and adjectives. When a requirements definer uses a word which does not appear in the dictionary, the analyzer guesses a type for a new noun and a concept for a new verb and adjective with the Requirements Frame. Table 2.3 shows registered verbs. It can also inflect these verbs.

Table 2.4 shows a prototype outline for *software requirements specification* (SRS) [9]. An X-JRDL user can write requirements with a similar format.

TABLE 2.3. Verbs in dictionary

Concept	Verbs (in Japanese)
DFLOW, CFLOW	Pass, move, transfer, receive, input, output
ANDSUB, ORSUB	Subpart, part, construct
GEN	Generate, produce, make
RET	Retrieve
INS	Insert, add
UPDATE	Update
DEL	Delete

TABLE 2.4. Prototype outline for software requirements specification (SRS) taken from [9]

Table of Contents:
1 Introduction
  1.1 Purpose
  1.2 Scope
  1.3 Definitions, Acronyms, Abbreviations
  1.4 References
  1.5 Overview
2 General Description
  2.1 Product Perspective
  2.2 Product Function
  2.3 User Characteristics
  2.4 Assumptions and Dependencies
3 Specific Requirements
  3.1 Functional Requirements
    3.1.1 Functional Requirement 1
      3.1.1.1 Introduction
      3.1.1.2 Inputs
      3.1.1.3 Processing
      3.1.1.4 Outputs
    3.1.2 Functional Requirements 2
      ⋮
    3.1.n Functional Requirements n
  3.2 External Interface Requirements
    3.2.1 User Interface
    3.2.2 Hardware Interface
    3.2.3 Software Interface
    3.2.4 Communication Interface
  3.3 Performance Requirements
    3.3.1 Real Time
    3.3.2 Other Time Constraints
    3.3.3 Resource Utilization
  3.4 Design Constraints
    3.4.1 Standards Compliance
    3.4.2 Hardware Limitations
    3.4.3 Operating Constraints
  3.5 Attributes
    3.5.1 Security
    3.5.2 Maintainability
    3.5.3 Reliability
      3.5.3.1 Availability
      3.5.3.2 Integrity
  3.6 Other Requirements
Appendices
Index

TABLE 2.5. CRDL representation
of simple sentences (Sect.2.4.1)

Relation	ANDSUB
Agent	System
Object	Command analyzer
Object	Processing unit
Object	Report unit

Relation	GEN
Agent	**undefined**
Source	Input command
Goal	Analysis result

2.4 Analysis of Requirements Description with X-JRDL

This chapter shows how to analyze and interpret requirements description with the
Requirements Frame.

2.4.1 Analysis with Case Frame

Suppose we have these simple requirements:

> A system consists of a command analyzer, a processing unit, and a report unit, and
> generates the analysis result upon an input command.

The analyzer first divides this sentence into two simple sentences:

1. System consists of command analyzer, processing unit, and report unit.
2. **undefined subject** generates analysis result upon an input command.

CRDL representations of them are shown in Table 2.5.

The Case Frame of GEN, which is a concept corresponding to the verb *generates*,
says the agent case of GEN should be a noun of function type. There are four nouns
of function type: *system, command analyzer, processing unit,* and *report unit.*

Given the fact that when a subject is undefined, it may be the same as the subject
of the last sentence, *system* is the first candidate for the subject of the second
sentence. The analyzer will ask the definer if the omitted subject is *system.* If there
is only one candidate word, the analyzer will simply make a confirmation.

If a pronoun appears in a statement such as the following, the pronoun is
determined in a similar way:

> A system consists of a command analyzer, processing unit, and report unit, and *this*
> generates the analysis result upon an input command.

In this way, compound sentences and complex sentences with pronouns are
analyzed and divided into simple statements supplementing some indispensable
cases. These sentences are just sentences in JRDL.

TABLE 2.6. Function Frame

Function	Properties
Data creation	For any data defined in **ANDSUB** or **ORSUB**, or appearing in "source" of an **INS, DEL**, or **UPDATE** statement, there should exist either a **DFLOW** statement whose "agent" is the data or a **GEN** statement whose "goal" is the data.
Data processing	For any data identified in "goal" of **GEN** or **RET**, there should exist either a **DFLOW** statement whose "agent" is the data or a **GEN** statement whose "goal" is the data.
External input	For at least one item of data, there should exist a **DFLOW** statement whose "agent" is the data and whose "source" is a human type object.
External output	For at least one item of data, there should exist a **DFLOW** statement whose "agent" is the data and whose "goal" is a human type object.
File definition	For any file, there should exist an **ANDSUB** statement whose "agent" is the file.
File manipulation	For any file appearing in "source" or "goal" of a **MANIP** statement, there should exist an **ANDSUB** statement which defines the same file scheme.
File retrieval	For any data in "key" of a **RET** statement, there should exist an **ANDSUB** statement whose "object" is the data and whose "agent" is the object specified in the "source" of the **RET**.
Deletion of a record	For any file specified in "goal" of **DEL**, there exists a **RET** statement whose "source" is the file.
Insertion of a record	For any file specified in "goal" of **INS**, there exists a **RET** statement whose "source" is the file.
Update of a record	For any file specified in "goal" of **UPDATE**, there exists a **RET** statement whose "source" is the file.

2.4.2 Analysis with Function Frame

Derived simple sentences are checked as to whether they satisfy properties according to the Function Frame, shown in Table 2.6. This table holds 10 essential functions. With this frame we can detect the absence of indispensable functions. For example, the first function, *data creation*, insists that every data item used in the target system should be defined somewhere. By investigating whether all data specified in a description satisfy this property, we can detect the lack of a data definition statement.

With these Requirements Frames, we can eliminate both ambiguity and the lack of indispensable requirements. Then, we will achieve a correct requirements description.

2.5 Example

Let us consider the requirements of a stock-management system, using X-JRDL. The following is a portion of the requirements specified with X-JRDL. Since X-JRDL is based on Japanese, we will show parallel requirements description translated into English.

在庫管理システムは入庫管理部、出庫管理部、在庫管理部から構成される。
　1. 入庫管理部
　　在庫管理係から制御を受け取り、彼からキーボードを通して品名と数量からなる入庫票を受け取る。そして、それを用いて在庫マスタファイルを更新し、在庫管理係に制御を返す。

Stock management system consists of a stock-in manager, a stock-out manager, and a stock file manager.

　1. Stock-in manager
　　Receives control from the stock managing officer and also gest stock-in data including item name and amount via keyboard. Then, using them, updates stock master file and returns the control to the stock managing officer.

First of all, the X-JRDL analyzer finds out unknown words. If there exist such words, the analyzer queries the definer as follows:

"在庫管理係" の型は何ですか。

　　1: HUMAN 2: FUNCTION 3: DEVICE 4: FILE 5: DATA 6: CONTROL
　　==> 1

Please give me the type of "stock managing officer"

　　1: HUMAN 2: FUNCTION 3: DEVICE 4: FILE 5: DATA 6: CONTROL
　　==> 1

If there exist some unknown verbs, the X-JRDL analyzer asks the correspondence between the new verbs and CRDL concepts:

"返す" は辞書にない動詞です。
この動詞は次のどのCRD動詞に対応しますか。

　　1: DFLOW 2: CFLOW 3: FLOW 4: SUB 5: RET 6: INS 7: UPDATE
　　8: DEL 9: GEN 10: 新動詞
　　==> 2

この動詞の終止形を入力してください。〔"返す"〕

　　==>

"そしてそれを用いて在庫マスタファイルを更新し在庫管理係に制御を返す。" の "返す" は次のどの文型で用いられていますか。

　　1: function/human は function/human に control を返す。
　　2: control は function/human から function/human に返す。
　　3: function/human は function/human から control を返す。

　　==>

"returns" is not registered in the system dictionary. Please give me the concept of "returns".

> 1: DFLOW 2: CFLOW 3: FLOW 4: SUB 5: RET 6: INS 7: UPDATE
> 8: DEL 9: GEN 10: 新概念
> ==>

What is the normal form of "returns"? [default: "returns"]

Then, compound sentences and complex sentences are divided into simple sentences. The following shows this process:

これから単文に分解します。
　在庫管理システムは入庫管理部と出庫管理部と在庫管理部から構成
　される。
見出し語：入庫管理部
　在庫管理係から制御を受け取る。
　　"入庫管理部" が "受け取る" のですね。
　入庫票は品名と数量からなる。
　彼から入庫票をキーボードで受け取る。
　　"彼" の指す名詞は "在庫管理係" ですね。
　　"入庫管理部" が "受け取る" のですね。
　在庫マスタファイルをそれで更新する。
　　"入庫管理部" が "更新する" のですね。
　　"それ" の指す名詞は何ですか。
　　RET："入庫票" 1："数量" 2："品名"
　　2
　在庫管理係へ制御を返す。
　　"入庫管理部" が "返す" のですね。

In this step, pronouns and absence of nouns are confirmed. If there are a few candidates, the analyzer queries the definer.

これから確認します。
　在庫管理システムは入庫管理部と出庫管理部と在庫管理部から構成さ
　れる。
見出し語：入庫管理部
　入庫管理部は在庫管理係から制御を受け取る。
　入庫票は品名と数量からなる。
　入庫管理部は在庫管理係から入庫票をキーボードで受け取る。
　入庫管理部は在庫マスタファイルを品名で更新する。
　入庫管理部は在庫管理係へ制御を返す。

Lastly, new words are registered into the system dictionary as shown in the following:

解析した記述中に現れた新出名詞を以下に示します。

　　1："在庫管理係"

辞書に登録しますか？

n

解析した記述中に現れた新出動詞を以下に示します。

　　1："返す"

辞書に登録しますか？

y

A part of the CRDL expression is as follows:

```
#S(FRAME2 VERB (VERB "受け取る" FLOW3 NIL) CRD CFLOW IFAG
   NIL IFOB NIL IFV NIL AGENT ((NOUN "制御" CNT "を" OBJ))
   SOURCE ((NOUN "在庫管理係" HUMAN "から" FROM)) GOAL
   ((NOUN "入庫管理部" FUNC)) OBJECT NIL INST NIL KEY NIL SKIP
   NIL)
#S(FRAME2 VERB (VERB "なる" SUB1 T) CRD ANDSUB IFAG NIL
   IFOB NIL IFV NIL AGENT ((NOUN "入庫票" DATA "を" OBJ))
   SOURCE NIL GOAL NIL OBJECT ((NOUN "品名" DATA "と" AND)
   (NOUN "数量" DATA "から" FROM)) INST NIL KEY NIL SKIP T)
#S(FRAME2 VERB (VERB "受け取る" FLOW3 T) CRD DFLOW IFAG
   NIL IFOB NIL IFV NIL AGENT ((NOUN "入庫票" DATA "を" OBJ))
   SOURCE ((NOUN "在庫管理係" HUMAN)) GOAL ((NOUN
   "入庫管理部" FUNC)) OBJECT NIL INST ((NOUN "キーボード" DEV
   "を通して" BY3)) KEY NIL SKIP NIL)
```

2.6 Concluding Remarks

We have developed a more natural Japanese requirements language (X-JRDL), and its analyzer. With this language, a requirements definer can write down requirements quite naturally and flexibly. Besides, the absence of indispensable functions can be detected with the Requirements Frame. The ease of reading/writing of requirements and the completeness of requirements description are improved with the X-JRDL [2, 8]. X-JRDL is now working on a KCL (Kyoto Common Lisp) environment.

The description with X-JRDL is translated into CRDL expressions by its analyzer. The CRDL representation can be transformed into several different representations, such as representations based on Predicate Logic, Relational Data, or Flow models. Based on these models, we have also developed several methods supporting the definition of requirements [3, 4, 7]. These methods have contributed to the improvement of the correctness, traceability, feasibility, and maintainability of requirements description [10].

The future work will be to integrate subsystems, each of which supports one of our requirements definition supporting methods, as a Requirements Definition Environment: CARD (Computer-Aided Requirements Definition) [5]. We hope our methods and system will be a powerful aid to software developers.

References

1. Ramamoorthy CV, So HH (1978) Software requirement and specifications: status and perspective. IEEE Tutorial, Software Methodology
2. Ohnishi A, Agusa K, Ohno Y (1987) Requirements frame for requirements definition (in Japanese). Trans IPS Japan 367–375
3. Agusa K, Ohnishi A, Ohno Y (1984) A verification method for formal requirements description. J. Inf Process 7: 223–229
4. Agusa K, Ohno Y (1986) A supporting system for software maintenance—ripple effect analysis of requirements description modification. J Inf Process 8: 179–189
5. Ohnishi A, Agusa K, Ohno Y (1986) A technique/environment for software requirements definition, CARD (in Japanese). Proc CASE Environment Symp, IPS Japan, pp 19–28
6. Shank R (1977) Representation and understanding of text. Machine intelligence 8, Ellis Horwood, Cambridge, pp 575–607
7. Ohnishi A, Agusa K, Ohno Y (1985) Requirements model and method of requirements definition. Proc COMPSAC, pp 26–32
8. Ohnishi A, Agusa K, Ohno Y (1990) Software requirements specification technique based on requirements frame (in Japanese). Trans IPS Japan 31: 175–181
9. ANSI/IEEE (1984) Guide to software requirements specification. ANSI/IEEE Std. 830-1984
10. Ohnishi A (1987) Studies on software requirements definition environment. Doctoral thesis, Kyoto University

3
A Computer-Aided Software Requirements Engineering Environment: KyotoDB-I

Yoshihiro Matsumoto and Tsuneo Ajisaka[1]

Summary: **KyotoDB-I** is a computer-aided environment to support software requirements engineering. It consists of a user interface, a set of tools, and an object environment which allows project members to create a project model (object-oriented model), interprets the described model, and manages a set of persistent objects. Each of the objects included in the project model represents (1) a model/view of one individual software configuration item, (2) a plan (process program) to elaborate this software configuration item, and (3) relations between data in one model/view/plan and data in another model/view/plan.

In software requirements engineering, and especially in system integration engineering, we need to organize many different aspects of input from members from different organizations and to create one final prototype model. The user interface includes a function called "collaborator" which supports collaboration between members. A collaborator is defined as a function of KyotoDB-I which can organize a common session on many individual workstations, and which enables project members to talk to one another through workstations and to achieve consistent software configuration items. In the collaboration, relation objects stated in (3) are used to check dependencies between data of different members.

Key words: requirements engineering — system integration — computer-aided environment — object-oriented model — process program

3.1 Introduction

The objective of this research project is to develop a computer-aided software requirements engineering environment called **KyotoDB-I**. While KyotoDB (Kyoto University Software Engineering Database) is the name of the project which aims to develop a computer-aided environment to support software engineering activities for a whole life cycle model, KyotoDB-I is the name of the environment which

---

[1] Department of Information Science, Kyoto University, Sakyo-Ku, Kyoto, 606 Japan

focuses its scope on the software processes and products only for the stage of requirements engineering.

KyotoDB-I consists of a user interface, an object environment, and a set of tools. The object environment allows users to describe a connected set of objects, which will be called the *object model*, interprets the object model and manages persistent objects. Each object included in the object model is used for one of the following purposes:

1. To encapsulate important data, which are included in each software artifact or configuration item, in the object which represents this artifact. These data are assigned to the instance variables of the object.
2. To encapsulate the relations between data included in the different artifact objects in the relation object. This relation object is shared by the artifact objects which include the related data. The relations are assigned to the instance variables of the relation object.
3. To enable project members to trace up and down through different software artifacts using relation objects.
4. To enable collaboration between many participating members who are responsible for different software artifacts using relation objects. The collaborations are required to enable members to talk one another to implement consistent products.
5. To encapsulate the process plan used in elaborating an artifact in the object which represents the artifact. The plan (we understand that the plan will be used as a process program) is assigned to the instance variables of the artifact object.

The architecture of KyotoDB-I is presented in Sect. 3.2. The object environment we use is the experimental system called COB, which has been developed by IBM Japan [1]. It provides the language COB, with which we can describe object models.

The object model which we developed for the purpose of KyotoDB-I has the structure that the instance variables of an n-th layer object include $(n - 1)$-th layer objects. Each object layer has one-to-one correspondence with the layer of the process program (plan), that is, the structure of the engineering process discussed in Sect. 3.3.

Some earlier research on software engineering environments provided process programming support. Systems which support process programming for creating specification and design, based on methodology specific to each system, are PAISLey [2], RSL/REVS [3], SARA [4] Data Flow Diagram Designs [5], and USE [6]. Other systems such as Interlisp [7], Cornell Synthesizer [8], Gandalf [9], and Mentor [10] are environments to support process programming in programming.

Arcadia [11] is a research project to develop environments to support no fixed, predetermined process or product. KyotoDB-I takes an approach similar to Arcadia in the sense that process programming aims to be a general process. However, what characterizes our research is that we classify the process program in a multi-layer model, and encapsulate each layered process program into objects of the corresponding layer as explained in Sect. 3.3.

A typical requirements engineering process model which has been applied to our real-time application systems is introduced in Sect. 3.4. This model is used in Sect. 3.5 to describe the behavior of KyotoDB-I concretely. At the stage of requirements engineering, especially in engineering jobs to accomplish contracts calling for system integration, many different aspects must be organized in order to build an optimum prototype model. The aspects to be taken into account at this stage are those of customers (system engineers, system operators, maintenance members, etc.) and manufacturers (system designers, software designers, programmers, test members, etc.). In order to build a correct prototype model, we have to collect as many different aspects as possible, organize and optimize them. Here, "correct" means the degree to which the prototype satisfies user needs and value constraints. In order to facilitate cooperation between participating members through workstations, KyotoDB-I provides the facility called "collaborator." The collaboration is discussed in Sect. 3.5 using the example of the process model discussed in Sect. 3.4. The concluding remarks are given in Sect. 3.6.

3.2 KyotoDB-I

KyotoDB-I includes:

1. the environment which allows users to describe object models, interprets described object models, and manages persistent objects,
2. user interface, and
3. a set of tools.

The architecture of KyotoDB-I is presented in Sect. 3.2.1.

Internally, an object is divided into two parts: the declaration part and the implementation part. The internal structure of object class is discussed in Sect. 3.2.2.

3.2.1 Architecture

KyotoDB-I runs on a distributed system which consists of workstations W_1, $W_2, \ldots, W_p$, a local area network, and a host computer H. UNIX (UNIX is a registered trademark of AT&T Bell Laboratories) is used on all computers. We assume that the workstations $W_1, W_2, \ldots, W_p$ are used for one particular project in which p project members participate, and that each project member uses one individual workstation. The host computer H may be shared by any project member and by other projects.

The basic software configuration of KyotoDB-I is shown in Fig. 3.1. The box on the upper right is the environment provided by COB, which allows members to describe object models, interprets the described object models, and manages persistent objects.

The object description is produced by project members through the user interface shown on the upper left. We use the experimental user interface called CANAE which has been developed by NEC Corporation [12]. CANAE is also used to interact with KyotoDB-I while members are developing their software products. The software of CANAE itself is a client process of X-Window Version 11 Release

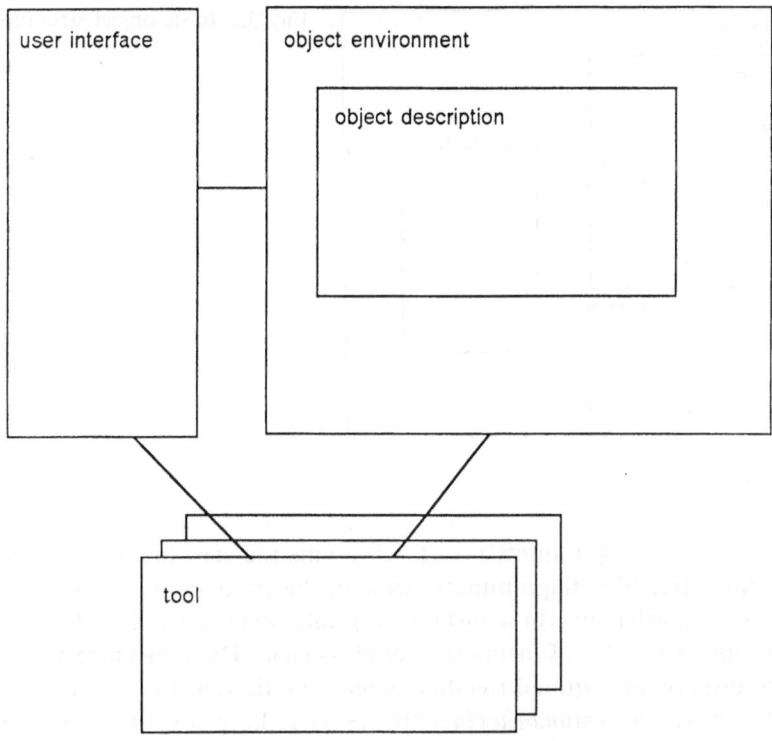

FIG. 3.1. Basic architecture of KyotoDB

2. It provides toolkits and the environment to develop dialogs using a language called script programming language. Some of the documentation tools, such as text editor, table editor, and graph editors, are included in CANAE. However, most of the tools which are used for system integration (e.g., clustering tool, decision support systems) are included in the boxes shown at the bottom of Fig. 3.1.

The objects in the box labelled "object description" are produced project-by-project. Each object is described based on the pattern shown as *standard class* in Fig. 3.2. A standard class includes four instance variables: *model, view, plan*, and *relation*. The standard class also includes many methods. Though *model, view, plan*, and *relation* are instance variables of *standard class*, each of these is also a class. The methods of *standard class* use these classes. The purposes of these classes are described in the following:

– Object *standard class*, if it is instantiated to *A*, represents the product *A*, where "product" means a software configuration item, an artifact, or a description to be elaborated as a commercial product.
– Object *model*, if it is instantiated to *A*, represents the data model of product *A*. If product *A* is a text-like specification written in a Natural-like language, the text is converted to a set of formatized records of data, as discussed in Sect. 3.5, and these formatized records are assigned to the instance variables of instance *A* of class *model*.

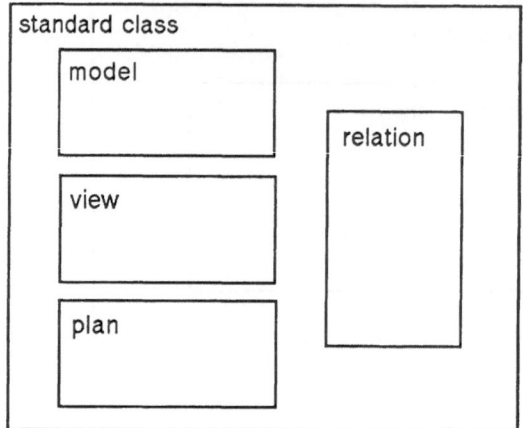

FIG. 3.2. Basic object structure

– Object *view*, if it is instantiated to *A*, represents the view model of product *A*. If you want a tree-like diagrammatic view of the product *A*, instance *A* of class *standard class* will convert the instance variables of instance *A* of class *model* into the instance variables of instance *A* of class *view*. These instance variables are used to display the required tree-like diagrammatic view through the user interface. The methods in *standard class* always try to keep consistency between data in *model* and the data in *view*.
– Object *plan*, if it is instantiated to *A*, represents the process program for elaborating product *A*. This will be discussed in Sect. 3.3.
– Object *relation*, if it is instantiated to *A*, maintains the relationships between each elementary data item included in the instance variables of instance *A* of class *model*.
– Object *relation*, if it is instantiated to *A−X*, maintains the relationships between each elementary data item included in the instance variables of instance *A* of class *model* and elementary data included in the instance variables of instance *X* of class *model*. This *relation* will be stored in host computer *H*, and it is accessed by any *model* objects using virtual pointers. How to access is discussed in Sect. 3.5.

3.2.2 Objects

In this section, details of the basic object structure shown in Fig. 3.2 are explained. The object named *standard class* in Fig. 3.2 is programmed using language COB. The program shown in Fig. 3.3, class stdobj, is the implementation of *standard class*. This class may be instantiated to all real project instances shown in Fig. 3.5. We will discuss Fig. 3.5 in Sect. 3.3.

Only major program lines of class stdobj are shown in Fig. 3.3. The class denotation consists of two parts: the declaration part and the implementation part. Shown in Fig. 3.3 are only declaration parts.

Included in the figure are the declarations of class stdobj, class model, and class tree_view. The four classes shown in lines 2, 3, 4, and 5 are the instance variables of class stdobj. However, the declarations of *plan* and *relation* are not shown in this figure. Only tree_view is used in this example. If you need another view, such as a text-like view, another class, text_view, should be added.

The implementation parts of these objects, not shown in Fig. 3.3, describe the codes to implement each method. From line 6 to line 12, instance methods are declared. Only four of these are shown in the figure. Method mtov is the method to transform the model data, which are described in the portion from line 102 to 110, to the tree_view data, which are described in the portion from line 204 to line 208. The next method vtom is the method to transform the tree_view data to the model data.

These methods are used when we transform tree_view data to model data, or when we reuse existing model data, which have been made in the past, and transform them to tree_view data.

If, for example, you want to insert or delete elementary data included in the instance variables of instance *A* of class model, you will enter your request to the "user interface" while you watch an image produced by instance *A* of class tree_view. Receiving this request, the "user interface" will call method insert or delete of instance *A* of class stdobj. Then the implementation of the called method executes insert or delete of instance *A* of class tree_view. If the data that you want to change has no dependency on data in some other different products, the said method of instance *A* of class stdobj will change also the instance variables of instance *A* of class model. (The said method refers to instances of class relation to check dependencies). In this way, we maintain consistency between model data and tree_view data.

The idea of keeping consistency between model and view in the way described has been presented previously [13]. However, most of elementary data included in *model* have some dependencies to other data included in other *models*. Therefore, we must first establish consistencies between coupled data in different *models* before we rewrite our *model* data. KyotoDB-I does this consistency maintenance in the following way:

1. If a member wants to change some data included in the *model* which represents the artifact for which the member is responsible, the member will enter the request to the "user interface". When the request is entered, the "user interface" may be displaying the view data in one type of view, as previously explained.
2. One of the methods in stdobj is invoked by the "user interface". The invoked method will change only view data by invoking one of the methods in class view.
3. The method in stdobj invoked by the "user interface" also makes access to relations which are the classes that maintain dependencies between the data to be changed and the related data in other objects. If any related data are found, the change of *model* data is postponed.
4. If the change of the data in the *model* is postponed, the "user interface" goes into the session called "collaboration." Through this session, the members responsible for the related data talk to one another. After the change is approved by all responsible members, the method in class stdobj makes class model change the model data. An example of a collaborating session is described in Sect. 3.5.

```
        /* class definition of standard object */
000 class decl stdobj {
001 instvar:
        /* standard object has 4 classes, see figure 2 */
002     class model      *modelp;
003     class view       *viewp;
004     class plan       *planp;
005     class relation   *relationp;
006 instmethod:
007     int     mtov(class model *modelp, class view *viewp);
                        /* transform model to view */
008     int     vtom(class view *viewp, class model *modelp):
                        /* transform view to model */
009     int     insert_view(class view *viewp, int p);
                        /* calls insert of view class */
010     void    move_view(class view *viewp, int p);
                        /* calls move of view class */
011     /* other methods to invoke every method in model and
           tree_view come here */
012 }

        /* class definition of Model Object */
100 class decl model {
101 instvar:
        /* model of software configuration item described
           in case-grammar, see figure 7 and 9 */
102     struct CASE {
103             char    id[IDSIZ];      /* S0000, d0000, ... */
104             char    subject[STRMAX];
105             char    verb[STRMAX];
106             struct {
107                     char    caselabel[STRMAX];
108                     int     tag;    /* indicates if caseterm is
                                           char * in fact or not */
109                     struct CASE *caseterm;
                        /* if no other case expression is nested,
                           it should be casted for char * */
110             } terms[TERMMAX];
111     } *sci;         /* root pointer of item */
112     int     saved;  /* flag indicating if saved to file */
a
```

FIG. 3.3a, b. Class definitions

Going back to Fig. 3.3, the lines from 100 to 125 describe the object model. The instance variables described from line 101 to line 112 store values of the data included in the software product (artifact or software configuration item). For example, the data included in Fig. 3.7 or Fig. 3.9 are assigned to each instance variable of the model. These instance variables include the real content of the software product which object stdobj represents. The values assigned to these instance variables must be persistent. These values are saved in the file system using the method described in line 119. The name of the file, which is a persistent-data name, must be orthogonal to the instance name of model that we assigned at the instantiation. Persistent-data names will be used in retrieving persistent data.

```
113 instmethod:
114      void    init(struct CASE *sci); /* initialize instance */
115      int     destroy(int forced);     /* destroy instance */
116      int     insert(char *id, struct CASE *sci);
                              /* insert a part of this model */
117      int     modify(char *id, struct CASE *sci);
                              /* as above */
118      int     delete(char *id);        /* as above */
119      int     write_data(char *scheme, char *attribute);
                              /* write on database */
120      int     read_data(FILE *infd);  /* get from database */
121      int     find_influence(char *id, FILE *inf_file) deferred;
                              /* find influence on other model */
122      int     get_part(char *id, struct CASE *sci);
                          /* get a part of this Model Object */
123 classmethod
124      class model *create(struct CASE *sci);  /* create instance */
125 };

     /* class definition of tree structured view */
200 class decl tree_view
201 superclass view
202 {
203 instvar
204      int     next;    /* node id to be inserted next */
205      struct tree {
206              node            desc;
207              struct tree     *children[DEGMAX];
208      } *document;
         /* root pointer to tree structured document */
209 instmethod
210      /* init and destroy come here */
211      int     insert(struct tree *document);
212      /* modify, ..., get_part customized for tree come here */
213      struct tree *lookup(int p_num, struct tree *p_from);
                              /* find subtree */
214      void    move(strct tree *treep);        /* move view */
215      /* ...... */
216 classmethod
217      class tree_view *create(char *viewname);
218 };
```

b

FIG. 3.3 (*continued*)

The method shown in line 121 is used to find data of other objects which are dependent on designated data.

3.3 Process Program

A Unit Workload (UW) is defined as the smallest unit of work process assigned to a project member. The software process for a project can be modeled as a network of UW's, in which UW's are connected to one another through some relationships.

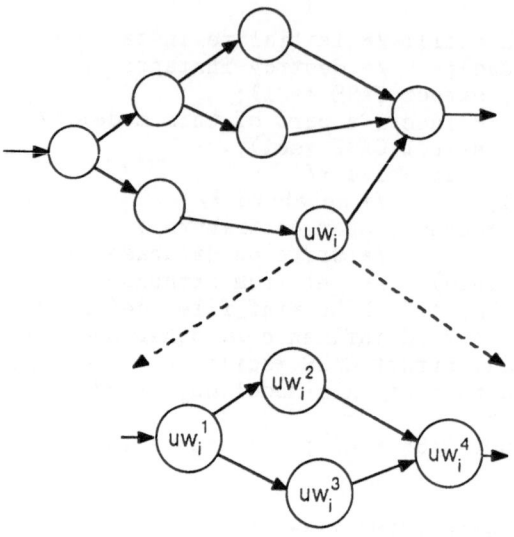

Fig. 3.4. Unit workload network

Each node in the network, shown in Fig. 3.4, is a UW or a subnetwork. A UW is assumed to be performed by one project member, and is defined by the following attributes:

1. Name of the UW
2. Features of the products (software configuration items or artifacts) to be produced by the UW
3. References (e.g., standards, internal guidelines) to be followed in the UW
4. Preconditions which must be satisfied before starting the UW (e.g., data to be passed from the preceding UW's)
5. Intermediate conditions which must be satisfied at some points during the UW
6. Post-conditions which must be satisfied before finishing the UW
7. Objective productivity which should be accomplished by the member responsible for the UW
8. Objective reusing rate which should be accomplished by the member responsible for the UW
9. Objective time schedule which must be followed by the member responsible

The use of the UW network for a project is divided into the planning phase, execution phase, and modification phase. In the planning phase, UW's which should be included in the network are planned and the following values are calculated under the constraints of project start/end timing and designated project cost, using the attributes of each planned UW (we use a tool [14] for doing this planning):

1. The date to satisfy each condition (pre-, intermediate-, and post-)
2. Suggestions of the person who is responsible for each UW. (We have a file which includes work schedule, career, and capability of every project member.)

After we finish a plan of the UW network, we transform the calculated attributes of each UW in the instance variables of each instance of class plan. These plans encapsulated in each plan object are the process programs in KyotoDB-I. In the execution phase of the UW network, project members can use these instance variables of the plan object through the "user interface." The data included in pre-, intermediate- and post-conditions are a subset of the data included in the model object of the same class. The consistency of the data between model and plan is maintained by the methods in the same instance of class stdobj. During the project, the plans may be rewritten using the same procedures that are used in the planning phase.

As the UW network has the hierarchical structure which was shown in Fig. 3.4, the object model of a project has a nest shown in Fig. 3.5. This figure is drawn with the semantics that the name of the inner object is equivalent to data of instance variables included in the model object of the nearest outer object. If you want to define the process program for producing products to finer granularity, you can refine the UW network to the level that you need and increase the layers of the nested objects to the desired depth.

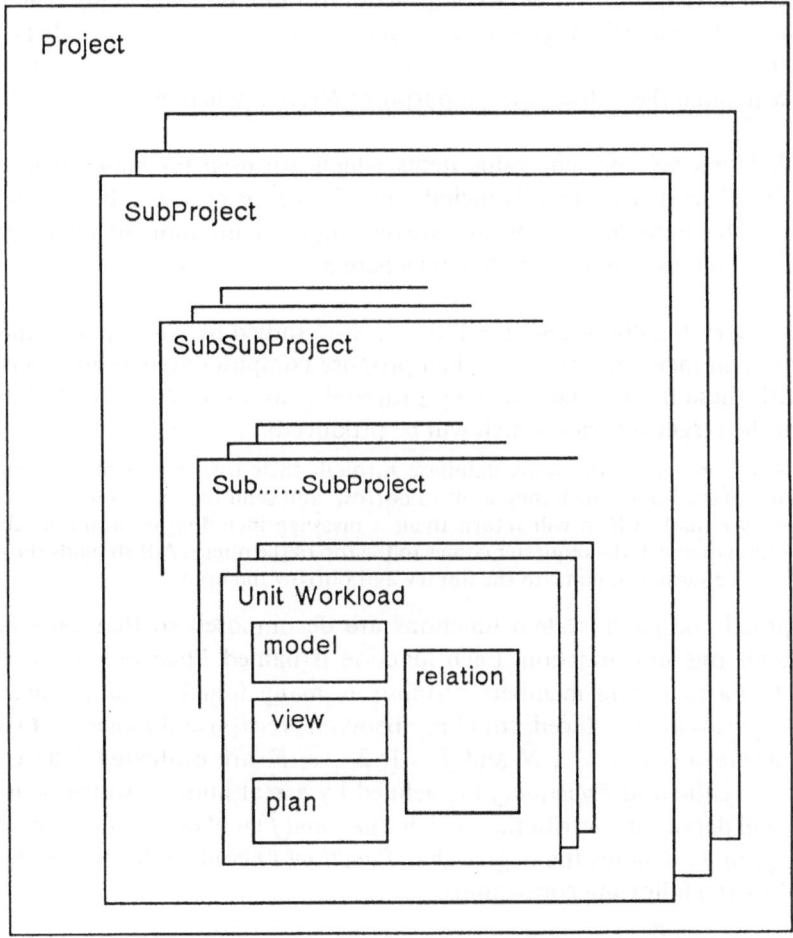

FIG. 3.5. Object structure for a project

3.4 Process Model

A typical process model, which is normally used in our real time application software project in a system-integration type contract, is introduced. Shown in Fig. 3.6 is a typical model. The model starts when users start to deliver initial purposes/needs (in box 1) and values/constraints for the target software (in box 2). The model ends when requirements are finally specified (in box 11). KyotoDB-I aims to support the activities shown in each box. An example to show how KyotoDB-I supports participating members is described in Sect. 3.5. The details of each box of Fig. 3.6 are given in the following.

Block 1: Users specify why the target software is needed and what purposes the target software should attain. An example of the initial description may be:

"We want to improve the efficiency of the library by introducing an information system to improve serviceability and to reduce the cost of operation of the library."

This initial description will be decomposed into more detailed items. The decomposition will be made through cooperation by many participating members, mostly user members.

We will name these decomposed purposes $Need(n)$ where $n = 1, 2, ..., N$.

Block 2: Users also present value items which are used for value analysis, and constraints. The items generally include such factors as cost, reliability, safety, and security. Value items and constraints are decomposed into more detailed items. We will call decomposed items $ValuItem(v)$ where $v = 1, 2, ..., V$.

Block 3: Every $Need(n)$ where $n = 1, 2, ..., N$ is studied by participating members, mostly design members, and they then propose computer system functions which cope with these needs. The following proposal is an example (note: AdLib is the name of the target software which will be produced):

"Students can search the book-database through their own workstation, identify the existence of the book which they want to borrow, and send the request for reservation to AdLib by e-mail. AdLib will return them a message including information about the reservation queue. If the requester comes to the top of the queue, AdLib sends the message to ask the requester to come to the library and borrow the book."

Proposed computer system functions are decomposed so that each function implements one unit function. Each function is named $Function(f)$ where $f = 1$ 2, ..., F. Participating members propose as many functions as possible. After these proposals are produced, couplings between $Need(n)$ and $Function(f)$ for all n and f, where $n = 1, 2, ..., N$ and $f = 1, 2, ..., F$, are evaluated. The coupling between $Need(n)$ and $Function(f)$ is defined by a real number which denotes the normalized degree of contribution which $Function(f)$ makes for satisfying $Need(n)$. $Coupling_{nf}(n, f)$ denotes the degree that $Function(f)$ contributes to $Need(n)$, normalized by the following constraints:

$$\sum_{f=1}^{F} Coupling_{nf}(n, f) = 1 \quad where \quad n = 1, 2, ..., N$$

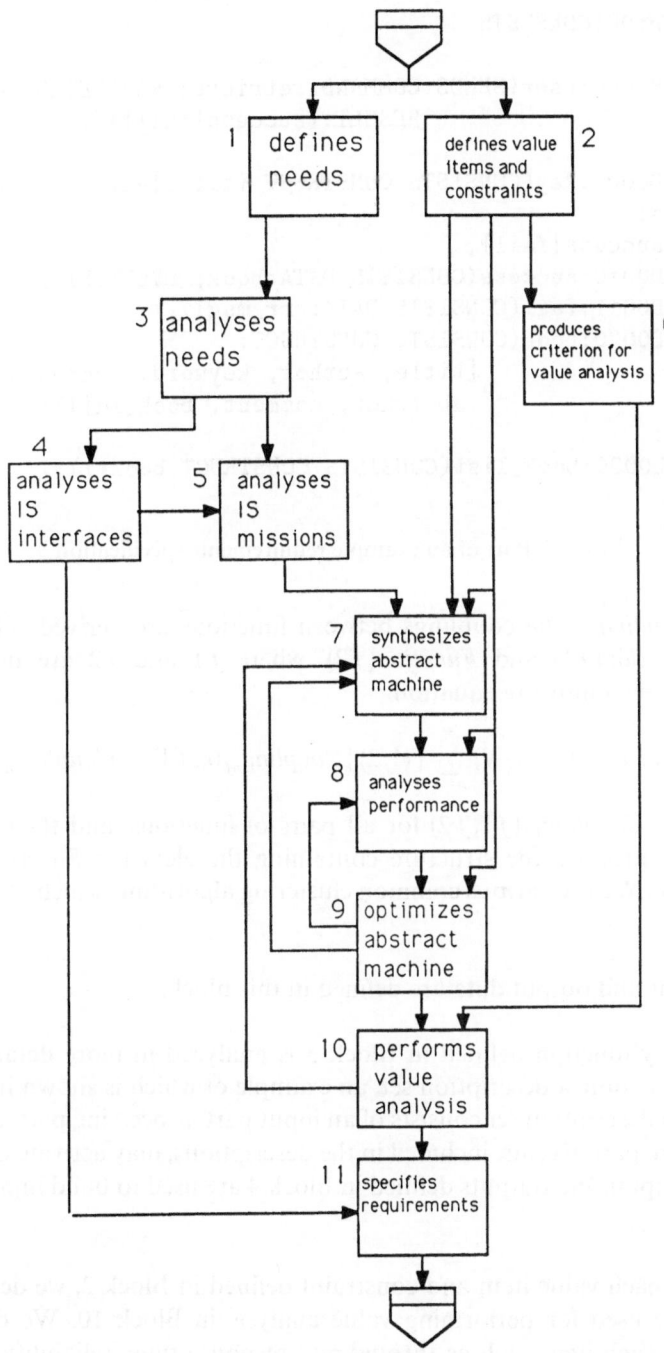

FIG. 3.6. A typical process model of requirements engineering

```
Requirement00(CONSISTS
Process:
        (S0000:user(SENDS COMMAND:retrieve; PARAMETER:key;
                            RESULT:{success|fail}));
InputData:
        (D0000:key(CONSISTS CONSTRUCT:{title|author|keyword*}));
OutputData:
        {success|fail},
        (D0010:success(CONSISTS DATA:book; EVENT:hit)),
        (D0011:fail(CONSISTS DATA:err_msg)),
        (D0020:book(CONSISTS CONSTRUCT:
                        [title, author, keyword, contents,
                         abstract, comment, book_id]));
DataStore:
        (D0030:book_list(CONSISTS CONSTRUCT:book*));
)
```

FIG. 3.7. Part of an example requirements specification

Using $Coupling_{nf}$, the couplings between functions are derived. The coupling between $Function(f1)$ and $Function(f2)$, where $f1$ and $f2$ are not equal, is computed by the following equation:

$$Coupling_{ff}(f1, f2) = (1/N) \sum_{n=1}^{N} [(1/2)\{Coupling_{nf}(n, f1) + Coupling_{nf}(n, f2)\}]$$

We obtain $Coupling_{ff}(f1, f2)$ for all pairs of functions, and then using these couplings we produce the structure containing the elements $Function(f)$ where $f = 1, 2, \ldots, F$. We use various common clustering algorithms which fit the purpose [15, 16].

Block 4: Input and output data are defined in this block.

Block 5: Every function defined in Block 3 is analyzed in more detail. For each elementary function, a description set, an example of which is shown in Fig. 3.7, is written. Each description set consists of an input part, processing part, output part, and data-store part. Events, included in the descriptions, may activate or terminate processing. Inputs and outputs defined in Block 4 are used to build input parts and output parts.

Block 6: For each value item and constraint defined in Block 2, we define criteria which will be used for performing value analysis in Block 10. We define value functions for each item such as throughput, response time, reliability, size of the information system, cost, and development schedule.

Block 7: Using descriptions produced in Block 5 and constraints defined in Block 2, we plan configuration of the target information system. Then we create one prototype or several alternative prototypes if necessary. The prototype only

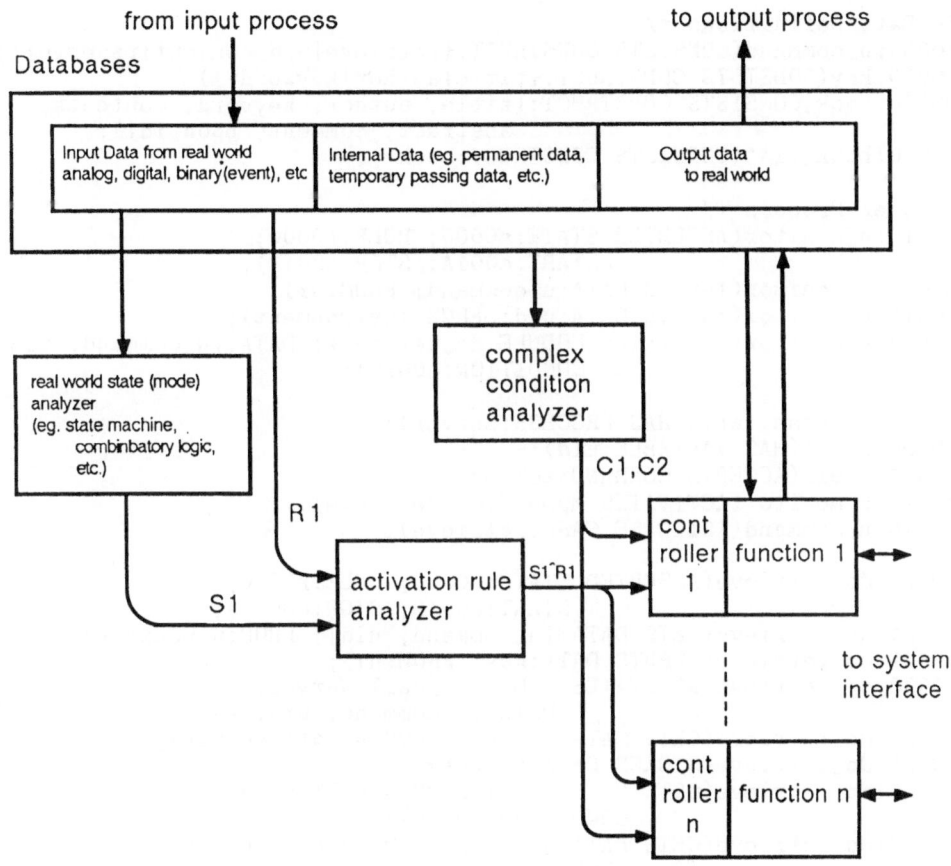

FIG. 3.8. Typical prototype model

describes the logical behavior of the target software. A typical prototype model is shown in Fig. 3.8. Major objects included in the prototype are in a database including input data, output data, and internal data passed from function to function, a real-world state analyzer, activation rule analyzer, complex condition synthesizer, function-controllers, and functions. Each function is enabled to act or terminate by the function-controller. The output from the function-controller is a result of logical operations performed using the outputs from complex condition synthesizer and activation rule analyzer. The complex condition synthesizer outputs the results of logical operations performed using input data and internal data. The activation rule analyzer computes conditions in which function controllers are enabled to act. Let us assume, for example, the symbols shown in Fig. 3.8 are given. If real world is in state S and the database condition makes R true, controller 1 is activated. If, at the same moment, complex condition $C1$ is true, function 1 is made to run as long as $S \wedge R \wedge (\neg C2)$ is true. The function is made to terminate when condition $C2$ becomes true. The function is made to be aborted if S and/or R become such that $S \wedge R \wedge (\neg C2)$ is false.

```
/* Data Definitions */
d0000:u_command(CONSISTS CONSTRUCT:{retrieve|upd_comment|reserve});
D0000:key(CONSISTS CONSTRUCT:{title|author|keyword*});
D0020:book(CONSISTS CONSTRUCT:[title, author, keyword, contents,
                                 abstract, comment, book_id]);
D0030:book_list(CONSISTS CONSTRUCT:book*);

/* User Process */
m0010:u_monitor(ASSERTED STATE:s0000; RULE:r0000;
                           START:c001A; STOP:c001B);
m0011:u_monitor(INPUTS DATA:u_command; FROM:ui);
m0012:u_monitor(INPUTS DATA:uid; FROM:environment);
m0013:u_monitor(ACTIVATES MODULE:do_retrieve; DATA:[u_command, uid];
                           CONDITION:c0010);

s0000:process_table(HAS PROCESS:server);
r0000:shell(HAS VARIABLE:uid);
c001A:shell(ACCEPTS COMMAND:adlib);
c001B:u_monitor(ACTIVATES MODULE:do_retrieve);
c0010:u_command(ISINCASE CASE:retrieve);

m0020:do_retrieve(ASSERTED STATE:s0000; RULE:r0000;
                           START:c001B; STOP:c002B);
m0021:do_retrieve(GETS DATA:[u_command, uid]; FROM:u_monitor);
m0022:do_retrieve(INPUTS DATA:key; FROM:ui);
m0023:do_retrieve(ACTIVATES MODULE:u_call_server;
                           DATA:[u_command, uid, key);
m0024:do_retrieve(GETS DATA:rc_ret; FROM:u_call_server);
m0025:do_retrieve(STORES DATA:rc_ret);
m0026:do_retrieve(GETS DATA:book; FROM:u_call_server;
                           CONDITION:c0020);
m0027:do_retrieve(GETS DATA:err_msg; FROM:u_call_server;
                           CONDITION:c0021);
m0028:do_retrieve(STORES DATA:book.book_id; CONDITION:c0020);
m0029:do_retrieve(OUTPUTS DATA:book; TO:ui; CONDITION:c0020);
m002A:do_retrieve(OUTPUTS DATA:err_msg; TO:ui; CONDITION:c0021);

c002B:do_retrieve(OUTPUTS DATA:(|| book err_msg);
c0020:rc_ret(ISINCASE CASE:0);
c0021:rc_ret(ISINCASE CASE:1);
```

FIG. 3.9. Part of an example design specification

The databases shown in Fig. 3.8 periodically receive inputs and send outputs. Other boxes are driven by these inputs and outputs.

The prototype model is specified with descriptions, an example of which is shown in Fig. 3.9. This specification was implemented using an object-oriented language which was described in [17]. The model implemented is connected to the object environment stated in Fig. 3.1, and made to be executed. At each execution of the prototype model, every Requirement described in Fig. 3.7 is confirmed.

Blocks 8 and 9: The prototype model used in Block 5 includes, as its partial function, a performance monitor, which virtually computes performance parameters such as response time, utilization of major resources, and throughput. Using this function, participating members can plan the best resource allocation for each function.

Block 10: Using the criteria for each of *ValuItem(v)* where $v = 1, 2, \ldots, V$, defined in Block 6, the behavior of the prototype is evaluated. If the prototype does not satisfy the objective level, Block 7 is resumed again.

Block 11: If the prototype attains the quality of the objective level, requirements specification is produced using the completed prototype.

3.5 Example of the Use of KyotoDB-I

One of the major roles of KyotoDB-I in supporting system integration engineering is to keep consistency between software configuration items produced during the process shown in Fig. 3.6. The consistency is maintained by cooperation/collaboration support. The example described here is a scenario to show how we change the requirements specification shown in Fig. 3.7. Should the specification that is produced in box 5 of Fig. 3.6 change, we also have to change the prototype specification, shown in Fig. 3.9, and which is produced in box 7 of Fig. 3.6.

The specification of Fig. 3.7 is a result of needs analysis (box 3 in Fig. 3.6), interface definition (box 4), and function definition (box 5). Now the specification includes descriptions of input/output data, data storage, and a function unit which satisfies some user needs. The specification of Fig. 3.9 is transformed to a prototype model shown in Fig. 3.8. Then it includes input data (d0000 and D0000 in Fig. 3.9), output data (D0020), internal data (D0030), real world state (s0000), activation rule (r0000), complex condition (c001A, c001B, and c002B), function-controller (m0010 and m0020), and functions (m0011, m0012, etc.).

The requirements specification in Fig. 3.7 is formatized using simple grammar which is denoted in the following:

[⟨label⟩]:⟨subject⟩ (⟨verb⟩ ⟨case-label 1⟩:⟨case-term 1⟩;
... ⟨case-label n⟩:⟨case-term n⟩);

Each case-term may be an atomic element or a new case-expression. The prototype description shown in Fig. 3.9 is also formatized using the same grammar. We have a tool to convert a specification description written in a Natural-like language into a formatized description based on this grammar. This tool also converts the latter to the former.

We adopted this format to describe every software configuration item, in order to identify distinguishable units of data included. A distinguishable unit is the data which has some semantic relationships with other distinguishable units in different software configuration items. The distinguishable units are mapped to the instance variables of each instance of class model to which the data of the units are assigned. Shown in lines 102 through 111 of class model in Fig. 3.3 are the instance variables mapped from the formatized description written in the said grammar.

Distinguishable units included in the different software configuration items have some semantic relationships with one another. The semantic relationships are formatized using the same grammar. Figure 3.10 shows part of such a relation. The first line of Fig. 3.10, read as d0000.CONSTRUCT.retrieve, is the implementation

```
d0000.CONSTRUCT.retrieve(IMPLEMENTS ENTITY:S0000.COMMAND.retrieve);
m0022.DATA.key(IMPLEMENTS ENTITY:S0000.PARAMETER.key);
c0020.CASE.0(IMPLEMENTS ENTITY:S0000.RESULT.success);
c0020.CASE.1(IMPLEMENTS ENTITY:S0000.RESULT.fail);
c0020.CASE.0(IMPLEMENTS ENTITY:D0010.EVENT.hit);
m0010(DERIVED FROM:design_paradigm15);
      ......
m001*.u_monitor->m002*.do_retrieve(ACCOMPLISHES Requirement00)
```

FIG. 3.10. Part of a relation description

of ENTITY:S0000.COMMAND.retrieve. The last line, read as Requirement00 shown in Fig. 3.7, is accomplished by the catenation of u_monitor and do_retrieve.

Let us assume that we are going to change the requirements specification of Fig. 3.7 in the following way:

> In the line beginning with D0000:key, we want to change {title | author | keyword*} to [title, author, keyword*]. This means the new key should be read as a sequential set of title, author, and a sequence of keywords, instead of a selection from title, author, and a sequence of keywords.

A project member, say M, who is responsible for the requirements specification will open a session in KyotoDB-I and call CANAE to adopt this change to the *view* of the specification using the CANAE graph editor.

Once M enters this change to the *view*, method modify of class stdobj is activated and searches for any side-effect using *relation* objects. Then KyotoDB-I refers to the relation object which includes the description of Fig. 3.10. In the second line of Fig. 3.10, KyotoDB-I finds that key is related to the following line of the prototype description:

> S0000:user(SENDS COMMAND:retrieve; PARAMETER:key;
> RESULT:{success|fail});

Let us assume the member responsible for this prototype description is N.

At this point, a collaboration session is triggered. Collaboration windows are opened on M's and N's workstations. A realtime duplex talk program is allocated to each window, and M and N can talk about this change using these windows. If M and N succeed in the negotiation on this change, N modifies the data, which undergoes the change. After the completion of N's work, M can complete the intended change by copying the values of the instance variables in *view* to those in *model* using method vtom.

3.6 Concluding Remarks

KyotoDB-I is a computer-aided environment to support requirements engineering. Many members, who have responsibility for different aspects of the target software to be produced, cooperate to produce one final prototype which satisfies the requirements. KyotoDB-I works on a distributed system in which each project member uses an individual workstation. KyotoDB-I manages dependencies between specified atomic data included in every artifact or product produced during the project. Through a "user interface," participating members generate their products. By defining relationships between atomic data included in every product, we can improve the completeness of the prototype produced. The coverage rate of the relationships is used as the measure of completeness.

The defined relations are used for navigating from product to product. Also, relations are used to check consistencies between products. If one of the members should find that data produced by other members is inconsistent with the member's own product, this member can send messages to the members responsible and talk about the problem using the collaboration system provided by KyotoDB-I. The behavior of the produced prototype, which we assess by the execution of the prototype, is tested by comparing it with the requirements specification, item by item, using defined relations. For example, see the last line of Fig. 3.10: Requirement00 is tested by executing modules u_monitor and do_retrieve, where the second module is activated by the first module. This test is performed by the execution of the prototype referring to the relation description of Fig. 3.10. The formal description of this test will be given in a future paper. The test will promote the correctness of the prototype, where "correctness" is the degree to which the prototype satisfies the specified requirements. The coverage of the requirements specification by a successful comparison is used as the measure of correctness.

Acknowledgments. The authors thank T. Kamimura, IBM Japan, for allowing us to use COB. We also thank K. Fujino, NEC Corporation, for allowing us to use the CANAE man/machine interface environment for the purpose of this specific research work.

References

1. Kamimura T, Yokouchi H, Yoshida M, Ohira T, Lucassen JM (1989) Object oriented programming in COB (in Japanese). Computer Software, Japan Society for Software Science and Technology (1): 4–16
2. Zave P, Schell W (1986) Salient features of an executable specification language and its environment. IEEE Trans Software Eng SE-12 (2): 312–325
3. Bjorner D (1987) On the use of formal methods in software development. Proc 9th Int Conf Software Eng, pp 166–178
4. Estrin G, Fenchel RS, Razouk RR, Vernon MK (1986) SARA (System ARchitects Apprentice): modeling, analysis, and simulation support for design of concurrent systems. IEEE Trans Software Eng SE-12 (2): 293–311
5. Ward PT (1986) The transformation schema: an extension of the data flow diagram to represent control and timing. IEEE Trans Software Eng SE-12 (2): 198–210
6. Wasserman AI, Pircher PA, Shewmake DT, Kersten ML (1986) Developing interactive information systems with the user software engineering methodology. IEEE Trans Software Eng SE-12 (2): 326–345
7. Teitelman W, Masinter L (1981) The Interlisp programming environment. Computer 14 (4): 25–33

8. Teitelbaum T, Reps T (1981) The Cornell Program Synthesiser: a syntax directed programming environment. Commun ACM 24 (9): 563–573
9. Habermann AN, Notkin D (1986) Gandalf: software development environments. IEEE Trans Software Eng SE-12 (12): 1117–1127
10. Donzeau-Gouge V, Huet G, Kahn G, Lang B (1984) Programming environments based on structured editors: the Mentor experience. In: interactive programming environments. McGraw-Hill, New York, pp 128–140
11. Taylor RN, Belz FC, Clarke LA, Osterweil L, Selby RW, Weilden JC, Wolf AL, Young M (1988) Foundations for the Arcadia environment architecture. ACM 0-89791-290-X, pp 1–13
12. Rekimoto J, Sugai M, Mori T, Uchiyama A, Tarumi H, Sugiyama T, Akiguchi C, Yamazaki G (1989) CANAE: a multi-media user-interface development platform on X-window. Proc 30th Programming Symposium, Information Processing Society of Japan, pp 105–115
13. Myers BA (1983) Incense: a system for displaying data structures. Comput Graphics 17: 115–125
14. Matsumoto Y, Agusa K, Ajisaka T (1989) A software process model based on unit workload network. Proc 5th Int Software Process Workshop
15. Matsumoto Y (1982) Application of a clustering technique to program development. Proc COMPSAC82, IEEE, pp 167–174
16. Matsumura K, Mizutani H, Arai M (1987) An application of structural modeling to software requirements analysis and design. IEEE Trans Software Eng SE-13 (4): 461–471
17. Matsumoto Y (1989) Requirements specification in a new software development paradigm. In: Matsumoto Y, Ohno Y (eds) Japanese perspectives in software engineering. Addison-Wesley, pp 21–40

4
Implementation of an Object-Oriented Concurrent Programming Language on a Multiprocessor System

Hiroaki Nakamura[1]

Summary: In this paper, the design of an object-oriented concurrent programming language, ConcurrentCOB, and its implementation on a multiprocessor system are described. ConcurrentCOB is a concurrency extension to the object-oriented programming language COB. The design principle is that ConcurrentCOB should be a minimal extension to COB. The main feature of its runtime system is that it has a two-layered structure. The first layer provides concurrency of objects and communication between them. The second layer provides extra functions, such as memory management, based on the first layer. Results of an evaluation of the runtime system are discussed.

Key words: object-oriented programming — concurrent programming — parallel programming — implementation — multiprocess

4.1 Introduction

VLSI technology in recent years has made it possible to construct practical parallel computers. Although these can achieve more throughout by running multiple tasks, it is not so easy to parallelize and accelerate a single task. One reason for this is that no suitable programming languages exist.

Object-oriented concurrent programming is an appropriate methodology for describing parallel processing, because parallelism and synchronization are embedded as objects and message passing, respectively, in object-oriented concurrent programs. Researchers on concurrent objects have given much thought to the expressiveness of objects but there have been few studies on how to implement objects in parallel environments or on how to acquire sufficient performance for practical use.

For these reasons, we designed an object-oriented concurrent programming language, ConcurrentCOB, which is a concurrency extension to a C-based object-oriented language called COB [1], and implemented it on a multi-processor system

[1] IBM Research, Tokyo Research Laboratory, 5–19, Sanbancho, Chiyoda-ku, Tokyo, 102 Japan

called TOP-1 [2] in order to study ways of making object-oriented concurrent programming practical.

The rest of this paper is organized as follows. Features of ConcurrentCOB are discussed in Section 4.2. Section 4.3 describes the implementation of ConcurrentCOB on TOP-1. Section 4.4 describes the results of the evaluation of its performance. Section 4.5 discusses ConcurrentCOB in the context of related work. Section 4.6 summarizes the paper and outlines our future plans.

4.2 ConcurrentCOB Language Features

4.2.1 Design Principles

ConcurrentCOB is an object-oriented concurrent programming language that is a concurrency extension to COB. The objectives of the original language COB are as follows:

- To maintain compatibility with C
- To increase the modularity and reusability of program components
- To decrease the number of error sources by providing safe language constructs
- To achieve good run-time performance by extensive optimization.

COB's simple and consistent semantics, which is based on the strategy that objects are allocated only in the heap area, is especially suitable for parallelization.

In designing ConcurrentCOB, we emphasized its closeness to COB. Our aim, other than to introduce the listed features of COB into ConcurrentCOB, were as follows:

- To allow COB programs to be rewritten easily in ConcurrentCOB. This generally makes it possible to parallelize existing COB programs and to debug concurrent programs sequentially in the previous stage.
- To allow mixed use of COB and Concurrent COB programs. This helps users to reuse COB programs such as libraries when programming in ConcurrentCOB, and to reduce the overheads of synchronization when it is not essential.

4.2.2 Communication Between Objects

The objects of ConcurrentCOB are units of concurrency. They have their own individual activities. We adopted only synchronous communication between objects for the following reasons:

- Similarity to function calls of C and COB
- Adaptability for communication of request-and-reply sets
- Minimum language extension to COB
- Ease of handling errors and exceptions [1]
- Capacity for simulating asynchronous communication with buffer objects.

Synchronous communication can be seen as a remote procedure call (RPC). A defect of RPC as a facility for communication between concurrent objects is that it reduces potential concurrency by unifying the locus of execution of the sender object

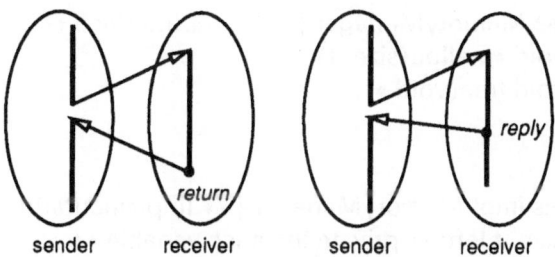

Fig. 4.1. Two ways of returning results. [By permission of Japan Society for Software Science and Technology]

and that of the receiver. To cope with this problem, we introduced two ways of returning results (Fig. 4.1). One, indicated by return, is the same as an RPC in the sense that it terminates execution when returning the results. The other, indicated by reply, returns the results to the sender but continues execution of the receiver's method. Incidentally, return can be implemented as a special case of reply.

4.2.3 Modularization of Synchronization

Inheritance plays an important role in introducing flexibility into strongly typed programming languages. However, the adaptation of inheritance to object-oriented concurrent languages has created several problems [4]. The method of receiving messages during execution of a certain procedure, seen for example in Ada's rendezvous, requires users to rewrite the synchronizing parts of a program each time a new procedure is added to the program. In many object-oriented concurrent languages, therefore, synchronization is realized as a component that determines whether or not the execution of a procedure should be started. Still, synchronization can be said to be modularized, because describing a subclass requires knowledge of the implementation of the superclass if the user specifies by their names which messages can be accepted [5].

We avoided this difficulty by attaching predicates to each method. These predicates are formed by the arguments of messages, instance variables, and private functions. Only messages that satisfy the predicates can be accepted. These predicates are called guards and are indicated by when(⟨expression⟩) between the method's head and definition part. We achieved modularization of synchronization by means of guards.

4.2.4 Example of a Program

Figure 4.2 shows a description of a memory manager class in ConcurrentCOB. A class is defined by an interface part and an implementation part. The class interface part is a construct of a type, and the implementation part represents how the class is realized. Private instance variables as well as function definitions are placed in the implementation part. These features of ConcurrentCOB are identical to those of COB.

A memory manager object evaluates its guard when it receives a malloc message requesting a memory area. The value of the guard is true if there are memory areas

```
class MemoryManager {          /* Interface */
  void *malloc(size_t);
  void free(void *);
  ...
};

class impl MemoryManager { /* Implementation */
  size_t left; /* private instance variable */
  ...
definition:
  void *malloc(size_t req) when (left > = req) {
    ⟨calculate 'addr' to be allocated⟩
    reply addr;
    ⟨update 'left'⟩
  }
  void free (void *p) {
    ...
  }
  ...
};
```

FIG. 4.2. Examples of ConcurrentCOB program

left. In the malloc method, the object calculates the initial address of the area to be allocated, returns the address to the sender object, and updates its internal states. If the message malloc is suspended, it will be accepted when sufficient areas are restored by the message free.

4.3 Implementation

4.3.1 Overview of the Implementation on TOP-1

TOP-1 is a shared-memory multiprocessor workstation. Attached to the bus are ten processing units, each equipped with an Intel 80386, a 128-Kbyte snoop cache, and a system bus interface. It runs a multiprocessor operating system called TOP-1 OS, which is based on AIX* [6]. We implemented the runtime system of ConcurrentCOB on TOP-1 OS.

The major feature of the runtime system of ConcurrentCOB is that it consists of two layers (Fig. 4.3). The first layer described in COB implements concurrency of objects and communication between them. The second layer provides the following facilities:

1. Memory management (Fig. 4.2)
2. Input/output (I/O) management
3. Communication between domains.

---

*Trademark of IBM Corporation.

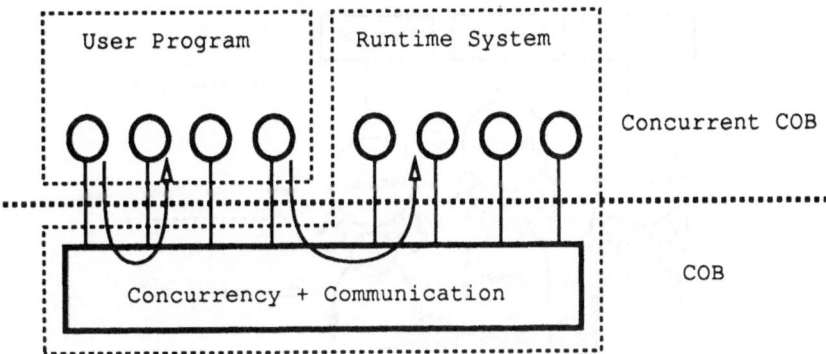

FIG. 4.3. Structure of the runtime system. [By permission of Japan Society for Software Science and Technology]

We chose the layered structure because it is

- Easy to restructure and extend this structure
- Easy to extract concurrency from the runtime system as well as from user programs
- Easy to tune up and to increase the performance.

Ease of restructuring is a common advantage of not only ConcurrentCOB but of most layered systems.

The second of the listed reasons was considered important because it is desirable that the runtime system of a concurrent language on a multiprocessor system should run in parallel as far possible. However, it is not easy to implement a fine mutual exclusion mechanism for each resource on multi-processor systems. The difficult part of the runtime system can be written with concurrent objects and the parallelism of the runtime system can be extracted quite naturally.

The performance of layered structured systems often seems to be poor. However, it is easy to localize the bottleneck of a layered system, and to tune up its performance. We will describe our experience of performance tuning in Sect. 4.4.

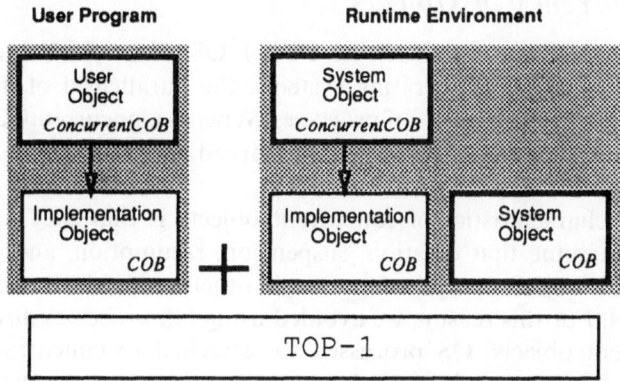

FIG. 4.4. Execution of a user program. [By permission of Japan Society for Software Science and Technology]

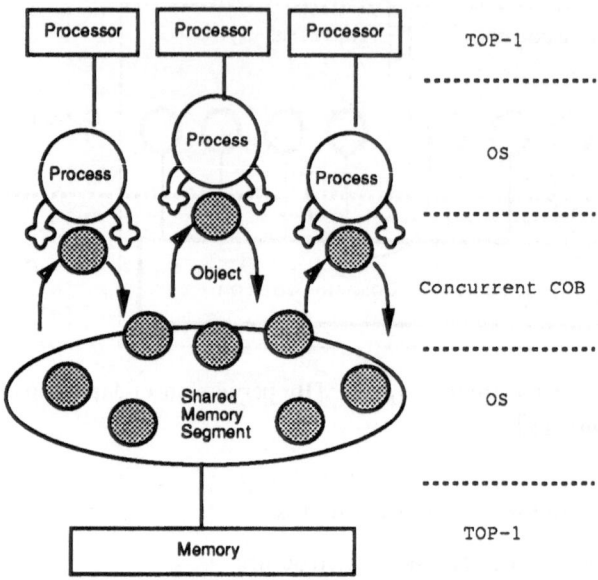

Fig. 4.5. Implementation of concurrency in objects. [By permission of Japan Society for Software Science and Technology]

Objects in user programs in ConcurrentCOB are translated into implementation objects. They are linked with the runtime system and then executed on TOP-1 (Fig. 4.4). An implementation object in COB is a composite one, and includes an object that assigns an activity to the implementation object. As already mentioned, the runtime system is divided into a COB part and a ConcurrentCOB part. The latter is translated into implementation objects of COB in the same way as user programs.

The rest of this section describes the functions provided by the first layer of the runtime system. Section 4.3.2 describes the implementation of concurrency in objects. Section 4.3.3 describes the communication between them.

4.3.2 Concurrency of Objects

We implemented ConcurrentCOB on TOP-1 OS. Since TOP-1 uses the same process model as existing operating systems, the parallelism of its hardware is provided to users as the number of processes. When a ConcurrentCOB program is invoked, a specified number of processes are forked, and from then on, they behave as virtual processors (Fig. 4.5).

One of the characteristics of concurrent objects is that they have their own activities. We assume that creation, suspension, resumption, and destruction of ConcurrentCOB objects are quite frequent; in other words, that concurrent objects are rather light. For this reason, we avoided using OS processes directly to implement concurrent objects. OS processes are attached to concurrent objects dynamically. Creation and switching of concurrent objects are executed at the user level of TOP-1 OS.

Black [7] classifies the execution policies of parallel programs on multiprocessor systems with operating systems into four categories, according to which our policy is called 'user concurrency'. The number of processors is the same as that of the parallelism provided by the OS, and the parallelism of the user program is much greater than that of processes. Parallelism is, therefore, controlled not by the OS itself but in the user level.

Concurrent objects are allocated on a shared memory segment that is attached to all processes, so that every object is accessible by all processes. An object has not only its own original instance variables, but also a context for execution, including processor registers, a stack area, and a work area. These are used to interact with other objects. Each process selects an object from the shared memory, executes some instructions of a method of that object, and releases it. Processes iterate these actions. From the objects' point of view, on the other hand, the objects float from one process to another during execution.

4.3.3 Communication Between Objects

Concurrent objects cannot directly invoke methods of another object, because synchronization is needed for them to communicate. We put some system objects that manage communication in processes. In implementing a parallel programming system with multiple processes, it is important to decide the role of the shared area and that of the private area of each process; in other words, the serialization and replication of system objects [7].

Figure 4.6 shows the arrangement of the main system objects of the Concurrent-COB runtime system. Mailers and Schedulers are in the private areas of processes, and an ObjectPool is in the shared area of each process. A ConcurrentCOB object makes requests for communication to the Mailer of the process in which it exists,

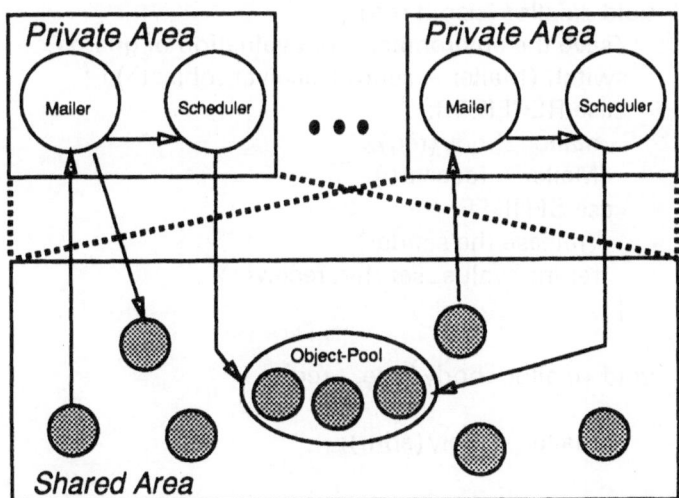

FIG. 4.6. Implementation of communication between objects. [By permission of Japan Society for Software Science and Technology]

whenever it tries to communicate with another object. When the Mailer accepts a request, it investigates whether the object should be switched. A Scheduler, which is invoked by a Mailer, switches objects. The ObjectPool manages all executable objects in the system. Because private areas are accessed by one fixed process, synchronization is not necessary for accessing Mailers and Schedulers. A hardware-level mutual exclusion mechanism is utilized only when Mailers and Schedulers access shared areas of processes. In order to avoid unnecessary invalidation or update of the cache memory, we utilize the spin lock algorithm, which requires few atomic instructions [9].

A method call between ConcurrentCOB objects is translated into a method call between an implementation object and a Mailer. The Mailer, which plays the intermediary role of communication, has three methods: receive, send, and reply.

receive Invoked by a receiver object when the receiver completes execution of a method. If there are messages for the receiver object at that time, the Mailer makes the receiver start execution of the method corresponding to the message. Otherwise, it suspends execution of the receiver.

send Invoked by a sender object when it comes to communicate with another object. If the receiver object has been suspended as a result of an invocation of receive, it is released from suspension, and execution of the method is started. If the receiver is executing a method or has been suspended as a result of an invocation of send, the sender is suspended and registered to the sender. In any case, execution of the receiver is suspended.

reply Invoked by a receiver. It releases the sender from suspension and allocates the return value to the sender object.

In addition to those listed, these methods switch the contexts of objects, invoke a˙ Scheduler to resume other objects, and evaluate the guards of methods.

```
void *malloc(size_t req) {
  ⟨save the environment for evaluation of guards⟩
  switch (Mailer → send(⟨receiver_object⟩)) {
  case RECEIVER:
    malloc_body(req);
    Mailer → receive();
  case SENDER:
    ⟨release the sender⟩
    return ⟨value_set_by_receiver⟩
  }
}
void *malloc_body(size_t req) {
  . . .
  Mailer → reply(addr);
  . . .
}
```

FIG. 4.7. Translated method

We select the method malloc in the memory manager (Fig. 4.2) as an example and show in Fig. 4.7 how it is translated into a method of an implementation object that communicates by using a Mailer.

4.4 Performance Evaluation

4.4.1 Overhead of Communication

Before implementing the ConcurrentCOB runtime system on TOP-1, we implemented it on a single-processor workstation [9]. Our experience with the early version indicated that most of the execution time of a ConcurrentCOB program was consumed in communication betwen objects. We therefore improved the runtime system of the early version, as a result of which the performance was increased by a factor of 4.4. This experience led us to adopt the following criteria for achieving good performance of the runtime system:

1. System objects that function as intermediaries for communication between objects must not be created whenever a request for communication is raised. The runtime system must manage them so that they can be reused.
2. The message search algorithm must be efficient.
3. The system must be constructed so that it is easy to tune up the performance.

As we have already explained, we implemented the TOP-1 version of the ConcurrentCOB runtime system in a layered structure in order to make it easy to tune up the performance. Because the mechanism for synchronization of user programs and that for the runtime system itself are unified in the first layer, we can concentrate on this layer in order to tune up the performance. We made the following additional improvements to reduce the overheads of the runtime system:

- Rewrote heavy routines in machine code (20 lines).
- Changed the algorithm.

As a result, the runtime system was 2.4 times as fast as the first TOP-1 implementation.

We measured the time required for primitive operations on TOP-1. A method call of COB (1), which is implemented as an 1-level indirect function call, is much faster than a method call of ConcurrentCOB (3), which needs a context switch with a method call (Table 4.1).

TABLE 4.1. Execution time of primitive operations

Operation	Time
(1) method-call (COB)	5.2 μs
(2) context-switch + schedule	28.8 μs
(3) method-call (ConcurrentCOB)	104 μs

However, since synchronous communication inevitably requires rescheduling (2) twice, and since a method call of ConcurrentCOB also provides conditional synchronization with guards, we believe that the performance of a method call in ConcurrentCOB is acceptable. This result implies that ConcurrentCOB objects must be used where concurrency and synchronization are necessary but that otherwise COB objects should be used in order to execute programs efficiently.

4.4.2 Speedup by Multiprocessing

We were able to achieve the expected linear speedup for programs with little dependency between objects. However, practical programs usually have more dependency between objects, so we measured how much speedup is possible by using a distributed quick sort program that has many objects closely connected to each other. The results of running the distributed quick sort program using one to eight processors are shown in Fig. 4.8. The speedup for eight processors is about 3.5.

We roughly model execution of a program, that is, divide it into a part that can be executed completed in parallel and a part that must be executed sequentially. Let the parallelism in a program be p and let the number of processes be N. The speedup ratio S_p is

$$S_p = \frac{1}{(1 - p) + \dfrac{p}{N}}$$

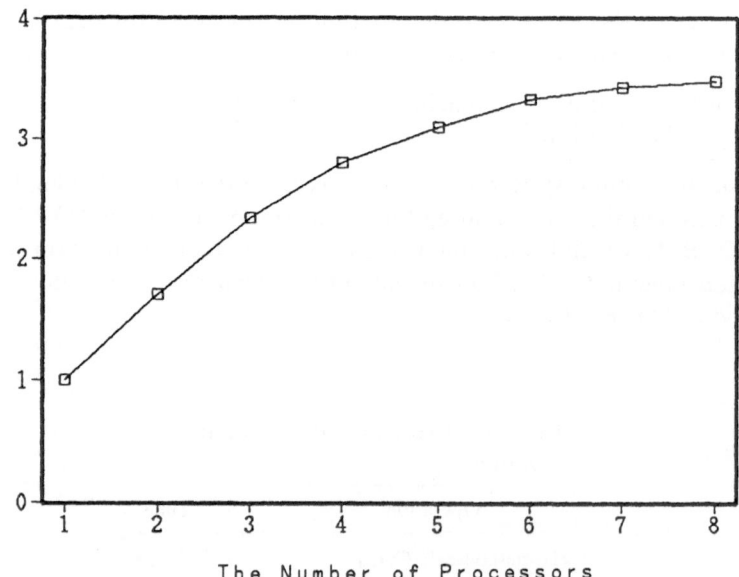

FIG. 4.8. Speedup ratio. [By permission of Japan Society for Software Science and Technology]

p is calculated at about 85% for every N. The factors that restrict parallelism are categorized into two types:

1. Serialization at the front gates of objects (software-level synchronization)
2. Collisions during access to objects (hardware-level synchronization).

Because p in this example is almost a constant, we can recognize that the overhead of hardware-level synchronization can be ignored in this implementation.

4.5 Related Work

The function provided by the ConcurrentCOB runtime system resembles the mechanism for concurrent programming called a thread or light-weight process. There are two kinds of thread implementation. One is implemented in the system space and the other in the user space of the OS. However, when implemented on multiprocessors, both types of thread have defects. The threads implemented in the kernel space are quite heavy to create and to switch, so this overhead limits the adaptability of threads to various programs. On the other hand, threads implemented in the user space cannot be executed in parallel, because they are realized in one process.

Portable Common Runtime (PCR) [11] solved this difficulty by implementing threads in the user space, using multiple processes. The implementation of ConcurrentCOB on TOP-1, which we have described, is the same as that of PCR. PCR is also intended to be a C++ library. However, it may be more redundant and slower than a thread library, which was originally designed to have an object-oriented interface, because the object-oriented interface must be implemented as a combination of synchronization mechanisms already provided in PCR.

The task system of C++ [12] is a thread library with an interface to an object-oriented language. PRESTO [13] is a concurrent programming environment for C++ programming on multiprocessors. The C++ task system and PRESTO provide concurrency and synchronization as libraries, while ConcurrentCOB provides them as language specifications.

An advantage of languages with built-in concurrency is that they can reduce the complexity of concurrent programs by uniting data, procedure, and concurrency. It is easy to modularize programs in ConcurrentCOB, because synchronization is encapsulated in each object, whereas it is difficult to modularize programs with concurrency libraries, because synchronization in libraries depends on how they are used. Moreover, in programs written in concurrent languages such as Concurrent-COB, errors can be detected in compile time by using type checking, and synchronization can be optimized by compilers, which is quite important for constructing concurrent systems.

4.6 Conclusion

We designed and implemented an object-oriented concurrent programming language, called ConcurrentCOB, on a multiprocessor system. After some improvements, we verified that the runtime system of ConcurrentCOB gave an acceptable performance. In the future, we hope to study a methodology for its effective use. We are also planning to implement it in a distributed environment as an extension to this system.

References

1. Onodera T, Kuse K, Kamimura T (1990) Increasing safety and modularity of C-based objects. Proc 3rd Int Conf TOOLS 3.
2. Oba N, Moriwaki A, Shimizu S (1990) TOP-1: A snoop-cache-based multiprocessor. Proc IEEE Int Phoenix Conf Computer Communication.
3. Bal HE, Steiner JG, Tanenbaum AS (1989) Programming languages for distributed computing systems. ACM Comput Surv 21 (3)
4. Kafura DG, Lee KH (1989) Inheritance in actor-based concurrent object-oriented languages. Proc ECOOP'89. Cambridge University Press
5. Tomlinson C, Singh V (1989) Inheritance and synchronization with enabled-sets. Proc OOPSLA'89. ACM
6. International Business Machines Corporation (1988) IBM advanced interactive executive for the Personal System/2 (AIX PS/2) general information manual (GC23-2055-00). International Business Machines Corporation
7. Black DL (1990) Scheduling support for concurrency and parallelism in the Mach Operating System. IEEE Comput 23 (5)
8. Pallas J, Ungar D (1988) Multiprocessor Smalltalk: A case study of a multiprocessor based programming environment. Proc Conf Programming Language Design Implementation. ACM
9. Yamanouchi N (1990) Performance effects of program structure on a snoop-cached multiprocessor system. Proc InfoJapan '90 Computer Conf. IPSJ
10. Hosokawa K, Kamimura T (1989) Concurrent programming in COB. 2nd UK/Japan Workshop on Computer Science
11. Weiser M, Demers A, Hauser C (1989) The portable common runtime approach to interoperability. Proc Twelfth ACM Symp Operating System Principles.
12. Stroustrup B, Shopiro JE (1987) A set of C++ classes for co-routine style programming. Proc C++ Workshop. USENIX
13. Bershad BN, Lazowska ED, Levy HM, Wagner DB (1988) An open environment for building parallel programming systems. Proc Symp Parallel Programming. ACM

5
A Garbage Collecting Method for Object-Oriented Concurrent Languages

Tomohiro Takeda, Toshiyuki Kamada, Norihisa Doi[1],
and Yasushi Kodama[2]

Summary: We propose a simple and efficient method for garbage collection based on the mark and sweep technique, which is suitable for object-oriented concurrent languages. In order for an object to send a message to another object, the object has to be known to the other object. So in object-oriented concurrent language, we can define an object that is not known to any object as garbage. By introducing a mechanism to support the "knows"-relation between objects which change dynamically, we implemented the proposed method in the object-oriented concurrent language $A_B CL/_{c+}$. This method is applicable to distributed systems.

Key words: garbage collection — object-oriented concurrent language

5.1 Introduction

Garbage collection is extremely useful for object-oriented concurrent languages because objects are created dynamically and may become unneeded during execution. Since in object-oriented concurrent languages, such as ABCL [1–4], a created object is an independent unit of execution and corresponds to a process, such languages need to have a storage management mechanism different from the ones for Smalltalk and Lisp. In object-oriented concurrent languages, we can define an object that is not known to any object as garbage, because computation and information processing are done by exchanging messages among objects that are made active in parallel and act in parallel, and in order for an object to send a message to another object, the object must know the other object.

Three kinds of garbage collection techniques are proposed and implemented: (1) reference counting [5–7], (2) mark and sweep [6, 7], and (3) a moving (copying) technique (such as "generation scavenging" [7–10]). Among these techniques, reference counting is not suitable for an object-oriented concurrent language because garbage that forms cyclic structures cannot be collected. Generation scaveng-

[1] Department of Computer Science, Graduate School of Science and Technology, Keio University, Yokohama, 223 Japan
[2] Graduate School of Systems Management, University of Tsukuba, Tsukuba, 305 Japan

ing is effective for Smalltalk in which a large number of objects are created. But when a process is a unit, it is unsuitable for object-oriented concurrent languages like ABCL because there are not as many created objects as there are in Smalltalk. We propose a garbage collection method that is suitable for object-oriented concurrent languages by using the mark and sweep technique. This method is also applicable to distributed systems.

5.2 Outline of the Method

The objects we will be discussing have the following functions:

1. An object can be created by defining the object with syntax structure. (This object exists from the beginning of the execution. We call this object a *defined object*.)
2. An object can be created during execution. (For instance, a new object can be created by sending a message which requests an object to create objects.)
3. An object can commit suicide. (One object can make another object commit suicide by sending a message. Of course, to do so, the object must be able to accept the message.)
4. Each object has a list of objects that it knows. (This list corresponds to the acquaintances [11] in the ACTORS model. We call this list an *acquaintance list*.)
5. An object can always forget objects that it knows.
6. When two or more messages arrive at an object, the object accepts only one message at a time.

Because an object may be sent as an argument and the object which has created an object does not have to know the created object, when all of the objects are connected by the "*knows*"-relation, generally the structure proves to be a directed cyclic graph. When object "*A*" knows object "*B*," we connect *A* with *B* by an arrow which heads from *A* to *B*. An object which is known to another object but does not know any objects is called the *terminal object*.

Because objects (processes) cannot link with each other through memory like Lisp and Smalltalk, we have to introduce a mechanism to decide if the object has been marked or not. To do so, we introduce an object called the *GC-object*, to manage the garbage collection. The GC-object manages all of the objects that are alive by using a table called the *object table*. (Whether the object table is managed in the distributed state or in the centralized state in a distributed environment is an implementation issue beyond the scope of this paper.) When an object (including a defined object) is created, the object registers itself on the object table by sending a message to the GC-object. When an object commits suicide, it removes itself from the table by sending a message to the GC-object.

The GC-object starts collecting garbage by sending a *marker* to the defined objects. During this time, active objects keep executing. An object which has accepted a marker sends the marker to all of the objects which it knows and waits for their replies. If a terminal object accepts the marker, it returns the reply, including its ID, to the object from which it accepted the marker. The object which waits for the replies makes a list called the *marked object list* by appending the objectIDs in the replies to its own objectID. When the object receives replies from all of the objects to which it has sent the marker, it returns the complete marked object list to the object from which it accepted the marker. When the GC-object accepts a reply, marked objects are remembered by raising a flag called the *marked flag* in the object table for all of the objects in the marked object list. In this way, the marking is finished when the GC-object has received the replies from all of the objects to which it had sent the marker. Because the "knows"-relation forms a directed cyclic graph, the following issues arise:

1. How is the end of the marking decided when the "knows"-relation forms a cycle?
2. What does the object do if it accepts a request for marking when it has already sent a marker and is waiting for replies?

In our method, we have solved these problems by introducing the following:

1. the marking flag
2. the null reply

The marking flag indicates whether or not the object has already accepted a marker. When an object receives a marker after it has already accepted another one, the null reply (which has an empty marked object list) is returned. That is, an object that has already accepted a marker is regarded as the last object of marking in the cycle, and the null reply signifies the end of marking in the cycle.

Now, if a terminal object commits suicide, the objects that knew only it may become new terminal objects. That is, there is a chance that an object which was not a terminal object may become one. So, when each object accepts a marker, it has to make sure whether it is a terminal object or not. (An object can be determined to be a new terminal object as follows: when an object sends a marker to an object, if the receiving object has already committed suicide, the system sends an error message, such as "message could not be sent." When the error message is received, the object is deleted from the acquaintance list. If the list becomes empty, the object is known to be a terminal object.)

If an object is created during the marking, the object registers itself on the object table by sending a message to the GC-object an the GC-object raises the marked flag of the object. In this way, we can prevent the objects created during the marking from being regarded as garbage.

The sweeping is done by sending the "suicide" message to the objects which have become unknown to all other objects. But if we collect such objects as garbage, the following problem arises.

Assume that objects A and B know each other, but B is known only to A. Furthermore, assume that B has accepted a message from A, and while B deals with it, A forgets B. According to our definition of garbage, B is garbage because it is not known to any objects. But while B is dealing with a message and is in the active mode, B may return a reply to A. So if we collect B as garbage, the reply that should reach A, will not.

To solve this problem, we make each object know whether it is active or not. If an object does not know any other objects when the garbage collection starts, the object accepts the "suicide" message from the GC-object. At this time if it is active, it does not do anything, i.e., it does not commit suicide. In this way we prevent the object from being collected as garbage.

Furthermore, the objects of the sweeping are only the ones that exist up to the end of the marking. In this way, the objects created during the sweeping and as yet have no set marking flag will not be swept.

5.3 Mark and Sweep Algorithm

The following is a mark and sweep algorithm based on the strategy discussed in Sect. 5.2.

5.3.1 Marking Algorithm

The actions of the object which has accepted a marker are as follows:

if the marking flag has already been raised **then**
  • return the null reply to the object which sent the marker.
else
  • raise the marking flag.
  • register itself on the marked object list.
  if the object is a terminal object **then**
    • return the reply including its marked object list to the object which sent the marker.
  else
    • send the marker to all of the objects that it knows.
    while the object does not accept replies from any of the objects that it knows **do**
      on receipt
        of reply **do**
          • append the marked object list in the reply to its own marked object list.
        od
        of marker **do**
          • return the null reply to the object which sent the marker.
        od
    od
    • return the reply including its marked object list to the object which sent the marker.
  fi
fi

The exchange of the marker and the reply is done by sending and receiving messages. The phrase **on receipt** is the syntax structure which signifies that if an object accepts either "reply" or "marker" specified by the phrase **of** reply **do** ... **od** or **of** marker **do** ... **od**, the action **do** ... **od** is executed according to "reply" or "marker." When execution arrives at the **on receipt** statement, if neither a reply nor a marker has arrived yet, the object has to wait until either a reply or a marker arrives. Because the exchange of the marker and the reply is done even while normal messages are being dealt with, unless this sending and receiving are done at a mode which has a higher priority than the normal mode, garbage collection may take a long time.

5.3.2 Sweeping Algorithm

The sweeping algorithm for the GC-object is as follows:

> **while** scanning the object table from the beginning,
>> there is an object to be swept **do**
>> **if** the marked flag has been raised **then**
>> - reset the marked flag.
>> - make the object reset the marking flag by sending a message.
>> **else**
>> - remove the object from the object table and collect it as garbage.
>> - make the object commit suicide by sending a message.
>> **fi**
> od

5.4 Proof for the Correctness of the Algorithm

We will informally prove the correctness of the marking algorithm. To do so, we will show that a reply or a null reply will never be sent more than twice, and that both replies will never be sent from the same object, and that the algorithm will terminate. As for the first two, we will show that the exchange of the marker and the reply (a reply or a null reply) will always be done only once. The following observations can be made about the algorithm:

1. An object sends a marker to all of the channels (all of the objects which it knows) only when it accepts a marker and the marking flag has not been raised yet. If the marking flag has already been raised and it accepts the marker, it does not send the marker again.
2. If an object accepts a marker when the marking flag has already been raised, it sends a null reply to the object from which it accepted the marker.
3. If the terminal object accepts a marker, it returns the reply to the object from which it accepted the marker, only once.
4. If an object, excluding a terminal object, accepts the replies from all of the channels to which it sent markers, it returns the reply only to the object from which it accepted the marker.
5. When the GC-object accepts the replies from all of the channels to which it sent the marker, the marking finishes.

Suppose there is an object "O." We will assume that there are m channels coming into object O (the object O is known to m different objects) and n channels going

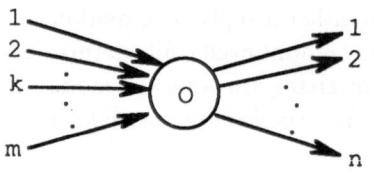

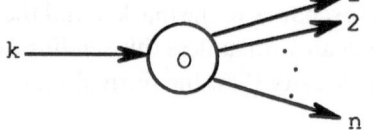

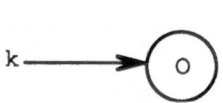

FIG. 5.1. Object O   FIG. 5.2. Non-terminal object   FIG. 5.3. Terminal object

out of the object O (the object O knows n objects) (Fig. 5.1). We will also assume
that k is the channel which sent the marker first. Because an object accepts only
one message at a time, the marker from k raises the marking flag of object O.

From postulate (1), it is guaranteed that a marker goes through a channel only
once. Because the marking flag has already been raised when the object accepts the
marker from channels other than k, from postulate (2) the object O returns the null
reply to those channels only once. So, the exchange of the marker and the reply (the
null reply) is always done for only one sending and receiving cycle on the channels
excluding k.

Because it is guaranteed that the exchange of the marker and the reply (the null
reply) is always done for only one sending and receiving cycle on the channels
excluding k, we can remove these channels from the object O. Then, the state of the
channel of object O is reduced to the state shown in Fig. 5.2 and Fig. 5.3. Then, from
postulates (3) and (4), the reply through k is returned only once for all channels.
Thus, the exchange of the marker and the reply (the reply or the null reply) will
always be done only once.

Because we have not been discussing a specific type of object, this holds for all
objects. Moreover, when a structure, as in Fig. 5.2 and Fig. 5.3, is catenated
recursively a definite number of times, it will have a tree structure. That is, it will
have a tree structure whose root is the GC-object. So from postulates (3), (4), and
(5), the reply to the GC-object is returned only once and the marking will terminate.

5.5 Implementation

We implemented the proposed algorithm in the object-oriented concurrent language $A_BCL/_{c+}$ [3, 4]. In order to improve the efficiency of execution, the sending
and receiving of messages for collecting garbage needs to be done at a mode which
has higher priority than the normal mode. $A_BCL/_{c+}$ has two modes, normal mode
and express mode, for sending and receiving messages. A message sent in express
mode will be accepted by interrupting the action being done for a message in normal
mode. So, the implementation is done using this express mode. The algorithm
written in $A_BCL/_{c+}$ will be found in Appendix B. This algorithm is automatically
incorporated into objects by the compiler.

We will discuss the implementation of the acquaintance list in $A_BCL/_{c+}$ in this
section.

5.5.1 *"Knows"-Relation Between Objects and Garbage Collection*

$A_BCL/_{c+}$ is a language will types based on the language C. We introduce a new type called object-ID-type (oid-type) to distinguish an object from other data. The object-ID-type is realized as a pointer to an agent (structure in the language C) of an object. The constituent elements of an agent are as follows:

1. port-ID
2. host-name
3. reference counter

The port-ID is information (i.e., a number) for communicating with the object. The host-name makes possible the delivery of objects on distributed systems. The reference-counter indicates the number of object-ID-type pointers pointing to the agent of an object.

We also introduce a new type called object-list-type to deal with objects collectively, as when marked objects are sent as an argument of a reply in the aforementioned marking algorithm. The object-list-type is implemented as a pointer to the structure which has an object (object-ID-type variable) as its member.

By delivering an object or object-list as an argument of a message, a situation may arise where an object is known for the first time. Also, sometimes objects that were known may be forgotten by assigning a new object to the object-ID-type variable which had been pointing to the object, or by creating a new object. Therefore, the "knows"-relation between objects changes dynamically. So, we need a mechanism to cope with these changes so that the marker can be delivered smoothly during garbage collection.

Next, we describe a method for maintaining the acquaintance list, and the timing for increasing or decreasing the reference counter, which form the nucleus of this mechanism.

5.5.2 *Implementation of the Acquaintance List and the Registration and Removal of Objects*

The acquaintance list of each object is declared as an object-list-type in the include file.

When an object is registered on an object-list-type list, the reference counter of the object is increased by one. So, when an object is registered on the acquaintance list, the reference counter is increased by one.

Next, we will describe the increase and decrease of the reference counter, and the registration and removal of objects on the acquaintance list, as automatically incorporated into an object by the compiler.

An object is removed from an acquaintance list when the reference counter is decreased to one, or in other words when only the acquaintance list knows the object.

1. When a creator-object (an object which creates an object) accepts a "New" message and returns a newly created object:

a) When the newly created object has the name ObjectO:

```
[object Creator
   script{
     (==> :New #oid
          ! [object ObjectO
          . . .
```

The object "ObjectO" is registered to the acquaintance list of object "Creator." The reference counter of ObjectO is set to 2. The counter is first increased by assigning the new object to ObjectO and then increased again by registering the object on the acquaintance list, for a total of 2.

When Creator creates a new object by accepting the message "New" again, the object "ObjectO" which had been created is removed from the acquaintance list.

b) When the newly created object does not have a name:

```
[object Creator
   script{
     (==> :New #oid
          ! [object
          . . .
```

Because the newly created object does not have a name, Creator does not know this object. Therefore, the object is not registered on the acquaintance list.

2. When a message is sent to a new object which was created by sending a message to a creator-object:

```
[[Creator <== :New #oid] <= :Message];
```

When the object accepts an oid-type value as a reply, the object registers it to the acquaintance list and its reference counter is set to 1.

When it finishes sending the message, it removes the object from the acquaintance list.

3. When a new object created by sending a message to a creator-object is assigned to a variable:

```
oid NewObject;
NewObject := [Creator <== :New #oid];
```

When the object accepts an oid-type value as a reply, it registers it to its acquaintance list and its reference counter is set to 1. When it is assigned to NewObject, its reference counter is increased.

4. When an object or object-list is assigned to a variable:

```
oid A, B;            olist A, B;
A := B;              A := B;
```

a) When both agents pointed to from A and B exist:

In the case of an object, the reference counter of the agent pointed to from **A** is decreased and the reference counter of the agent pointed to from B is increased.

In the case of an object-list, the reference counters of all of the objects registered to the object-list point to from A are decreased. A copy is made of the agent of the object-list pointed to from B and its pointer is assigned to A. At that time, the reference counters of all of the objects registered to the object-list are increased.

b) When an agent pointed to from B exists but A does not point to one:

In the case of an object, the reference counter of the agent pointed to from B is increased.

In the case of an object-list, a copy is made of the agent of the object-list pointed to from B and its pointer is assigned to A. At that time, the reference counters of all of the objects registered to the object-list are increased.

c) When an agent pointed to from A exists but B does not point to one:

NULL is assigned to A, then in the case of an object, the reference counter of the agent pointed to from A is decreased.

In the case of an object-list, the reference counters of all of the objects registered to the object-list pointed to from A are decreased.

d) When neither A nor B point to an agent, nothing is done.

5. When an object or object-list is assigned to an auto-variable[3]:

```
(=> :Message X                  (=> :Message L
     oid X;                          olist L;
     {                               {
          oid A;                          olist A;
          A := X;                         A := L;
          . . .                           . . .
})                              })
```

When actions corresponding to an accepted message are finished, NULL is assigned to A. If an object is assigned, the reference counter of the agent pointed to from A is decreased. If an object-list is assigned, the reference counters of all of the objects registered to the object-list pointed to from A are decreased.

6. When an object or an object-list is delivered as an argument of a message:

For the receiver of a message:

a) When an object is accepted as an argument of a message:

```
(=> :Message ObjectID
     oid ObjectID;
```

The accepting object is registered on the acquaintance list and its reference counter is set to 1. And when it is assigned to a variable "ObjectID," its reference counter is increased.

When actions corresponding to an accepted message are finished, NULL is

---

[3] An auto-variable is a variable stored on the stack (the temporary memory). It is effective only in a declared execution unit and its value is not retained after the execution is finished.

assigned to ObjectID and the reference counter of the agent pointed to from ObjectID is decreased.

b) When an object-list is accepted as an argument of a message:

(=> :Message ObjectList
olist ObjectList;

All of the objects registered in the accepted object-list are registered to the acquaintance list and their reference counters are set to 1. And when it is assigned to a variable "ObjectList," the reference counters of all of the objects are increased.

When actions corresponding to an accepted message are finished, NULL is assigned to ObjectList and each reference counter of the agent pointed to from ObjectList is decreased.

For the sender of a message:

A copy is made of the agent pointed to from the object or object-list. Before being sent as an argument, in the case of an object, its reference counter is reset to 0, and in the case of an object-list, the reference counters of all of the objects registered to it are reset to 0. This is because the reference counters of the agents (objects) of the sender and receiver need to be independent of each other.

7. When an object is defined with syntax structure:

Objects defined with syntax structure (defined objects) are managed by the *name-server*. By managing all of the defined objects, this name-server makes possible the sending of a message to objects by name. The existence of this server is invisible to users.

5.6 Conclusion

We proposed a simple and efficient method for garbage collection which is extremely useful for object-oriented concurrent languages, and which is based on the mark and sweep technique. Also, we described the incorporation into the object-oriented concurrent language $A_BCL/_{c+}$ of a method for maintaining the acquaintance list and the timing for increasing and decreasing the reference counter. These form the nucleus of the mechanism to support the "knows"-relation between objects which changes dynamically and to enable the marker to be delivered smoothly during garbage collection. This method is also applicable to distributed systems.

References

1. Yonezawa A, Briot JP, Shibayama E (1986) Object-oriented concurrent programming in ABCL/1. Proc OOPSLA'86, pp 258–269
2. Yonezawa A, Shibayama E, Takada T, Honda Y (1987) Modelling and programming in an object-oriented concurrent language ABCL/1. In: Yonezawa A, Tokoro M (eds) Object-oriented concurrent programming. MIT Press
3. Yonezawa A (ed) ABCL: An object-oriented concurrent system. MIT Press

4. Doi N, Kodama Y, Hirose K (1988) An implementation of an operating system kernel using concurrent object-oriented language $A_BCL/_{c+}$. In: Gjessing S, Nygaard K (eds) Proc ECOOP, pp 250–266
5. Cohen J (1981) Garbage collection of linked data structures. Comput Surv 13 (3): 340–367
6. Goldberg A (1983) Smalltalk-80: The language and its implementation. Addison-Wesley
7. Ungar D (1984) Generation scavenging: a non-disruptive high performance storage reclamation algorithm. Proc ACM SIGSOFT/SIGPLAN Software Eng Symp Practical Software Development Environments
8. Ballard S, Shirron S (1982) The design and implementation of VAX/Smalltalk-80. In: Smalltalk-80: bits of history, words of advance. Addison-Wesley, pp 127–150
9. Lieberman H, Hewitt C (1983) A real-time garbage collector based on the life-time of objects. Commun ACM 26 (6): 419–429
10. Ungar D, Jackson F (1988) Tenuring policies for generation-based storage reclamation. Proc OOPSLA'88, pp 1–17
11. Agha G (1986) ACTORS: A model of concurrent computation in distributed systems. MIT Press

Appendix A: Object-Oriented Concurrent Language $A_BCL/_{c+}$

A.1 Object

Each object has its own processing power and a private memory which only it accesses and changes. The *state* of an object is defined according to the contents of its private memory. The procedures for referring to and changing the private memory are called the *script*.

Objects exchange information by sending and receiving messages. When an object accepts a message, it chooses one of the procedures in the script and executes it. Generally, an object that accepts a message executes a combination of the following 4 basic actions:

1. Computation of values storeable in the private memory
2. Reference to and change of contents in the private memory
3. Message passing
4. Dynamic production of objects

The messages that an object can accept are determined by its pattern, the values in the message, the state of the object on acceptance, etc. When defining an object, we must specify the expression of the private memory, message patterns, constraints for accepting a message, and the actions to be performed on accepting a message. In $A_BCL/_{c+}$, an object is defined as follows:

```
[object object-name
   state{
           type-of-state-variable
             state-variable := initial value;
                 ⋮
        }
   script{
             (=> message-pattern @ destination variable
```

      where constraint # type
     type-declaration-of-pattern-variable; ... ;
     {
       declaration-of-temporary-variable; ... ;
       description-of-action; ... ;
     })
               ⋮

}]

When a message arrives, the first set (from the top of the script) of "message-pattern," "constraint," and "type" in "script ..." that is satisfied is chosen, and the actions in "description-of-action" are performed.

A.2 Message Passing

A.2.1 The Three Types

There are three types of message passing: past, now, and future. We assume in the following that message M is sent from object O to object T.

– Past type
   After sending M, O can continue executing without waiting for a reply. The past-type message passing is denoted as follows:

$$[T <= M]$$

– Now type
   After sending M, O stops executing until the reply is returned. T may send the reply either while it is executing the actions corresponding to the message or when it is done. The now-type message passing is denoted as follows:

$$[T <== M]$$

This notation not only represents the sending of a message but it also denotes the reply. In $A_BCL/_{c+}$, the assignment of a value to a variable is denoted by $\langle variable \rangle := \langle value \rangle$. Thus, by writing $\langle variable \rangle := [T <== M]$, we can assign the reply to $\langle variable \rangle$.

– Future type
   O specifies a reply destination and continues its actions without waiting for the reply. A reply that arrives at the reply destination can be accessed only by O. The future-type message passing is denoted as:

$$[T <== M \$ x]$$

where x is the reply destination.

A.2.2 The Two Modes

Messages are sent in either "normal" mode or "express" mode. Messages sent in express mode have a higher priority than those in normal mode. Express mode is one of the simplest forms of interruption.

The condition for accepting an interruption can be specified by changing part of the notation of the object's definition.

(= > message-pattern @ destination-variable
    where constraint # type

is the form for messages sent in normal mode. By changing "= >" to "= ≫", the form for messages sent in express mode can be written as follows:

(= ≫ message-pattern @ destination-variable
    where constraint # type

Appendix B: Algorithm

```
state{
 int MarkingFlag := 0;
 int ReplyCounter := 0;
 int AcquaintanceListNumber := 0;
 olist MarkedObjectList := ONEW;
}
script{
 (=>> :Mark @ ReplyTo
  oid ReplyTo;
  {
   oid KnownObject := NULL;
   olist EmptyList := ONEW;
   if(MarkingFlag == 0){
    MarkingFlag := 1;
    ReplyCounter := AcquaintanceListNumber;
    ObjectEnqueue(MarkedObjectList, Me);
    if(ReplyCounter == 0)
     [ReplyTo <<= [:EndOfMarking MarkedObjectList]];
    else{
     [AcquaintanceList <<= :Mark @ Me];
     [select-loop
     (=>> [:EndOfMarking ReplyList]
      olist ReplyList;
      {
       olist CopyList;
       if(ObjectDequeue(ReplyList, NON_REMOVE)
          != (oid)NULL){
        CopyList := CopyObjectList(ReplyList);
        MarkedObjectList :=
        AppendObjectList(MarkedObjectList, CopyList);
       }
       ReplyCounter--;
       if(ReplyCounter == 0){
        [ReplyTo
              <<= [:EndOfMarking MarkedObjectList]];
        ResetObjectList(MarkedObjectList);
        ResetObjectList(ReplyList);
        Exit();
```

(Continued next page)

```
      }})
      (=>> :Mark @ ReplyObject
      oid ReplyObject;
      {
       ![:EndOfMarking EmptyList];
       })]}}
    else
     [ReplyTo <<= [:EndOfMarking EmptyList]];
     })
   (=>> :ResetTheFlage
   {
    MarkingFlag := 0;
    !:EndOfProcessing;
   })
   (=>> :Quit
   {
    Suicide();
   })}
```

6
Hybrid Language
of C and Equations C==

Takahiro Yamamoto, Toshiki Sakabe, and Yasuyoshi Inagaki[1]

Summary: In this paper, we present a hybrid language C==. The language has the feature for hierarchically specifying ADTs by equations, in addition to all the features of C, a practical procedural language. Two extreme programming styles are possible in C==. One is a fully algebraic programming style, in which a programmer can write all programs as specifications in equations. The other is a purely procedural one, in which a programmer can write C programs. That is, programmers can stay in C== throughout all developing phases from specification to implementation.

The compiler of C== consists of Cdimple, which is a translator of algebraic specifications or term rewriting systems into C programs, and ordinary C compiler, and allows to do separate compilation. This construction can be applied to other combinations of procedural languages and algebraic specifications.

An application of C== to line-drawing software is presented, and the experience shows that a hybrid language such as C== is useful in developing the event-driven programs.

Key words: algebraic specification — procedural language — separate compilation — event-driven programming

6.1 Introduction

An abstract data type (ADT) is the concept abstracted from a collection of functions related to each other, and provides a conceptual tool for hierarchical, modular programming. One of the most popular specification techniques for ADTs is the algebraic one [1]. The algebraic specification of an ADT, which consists of equations, makes it possible to verify formally properties of the ADT based on equational logic, and also to prototype the ADT by using the symbolic execution mechanism.

In the current computer technology, symbolic execution of algebraic specifications is inefficient in time and memory. Therefore, it is desired that algebraic

---

[1] Department of Electrical Engineering, Nagoya University, Nagoya, 464 Japan

specifications are transformed to efficient programs in a practical programming language, automatically if possible. However, automatic transformation from algebraic specifications to efficient implementations does not seem to be realized. Therefore, programmers should conduct almost all parts of the transformation process.

This fact motivates designing a hybrid language which combines a practical procedural language and algebraic specifications. Such a language allows programmers to work in a single language from specification phase to coding phase.

In this paper, we present a hybrid language C==. It has a feature for hierarchically specifying ADTs by equations, in addition to all the features of C, a practical procedural language.

There are two extreme programming styles in C==. It is well-known that any computable function can be specified by equations. Therefore, in principle, we can write programs in C== by using the algebraic specification feature only, except for the input/output behavior of programs, obtaining fully algebraic or equational programs. On the other hand, it is obvious that any program can be written without using the algebraic specification feature of C==, resulting in purely procedural programs in C. Thus, a programmer can develop programs in any programming style desired between these two extreme styles.

In the fully algebraic programming style, almost all parts of the program can be investigated in the algebraic framework, so that we can obtain high reliability of the program at the cost of inefficiency of symbolic execution. In the purely procedural programming style, we can write in C== programs as efficient as in C, though we can only use ordinal techniques for assuring high reliability of programs.

The gap between fully algebraic and purely procedural programs can be bridged by transforming ADTs to purely procedural programs part by part. If the transformation is proved correct, the resulting program has not only high efficiency but also as high reliability as the original fully algebraic programs. Such steps of stepwise transformation may be stopped when the required efficiency of programs is achieved.

The compiler of C== should offer a separate compilation facility in order to support this stepwise transformation. We present an implementation of the C== compiler which enables separate compilation. This implementation suggests a general method for developing compilers of procedural and equational hybrid languages.

In the rest of this paper, we present the grammar and compiler of C==, and an application of C== to line-drawing software.

6.2 C== Equals C+ Equations

C== is a hybrid of C and algebraic specifications of ADTs. Its purpose is to allow programmers to work in a single language throughout all the steps of transformational software development, from the highly abstract specification level to the concrete level of C programs.

Design goals of C= = are as follows:

1. Algebraically specified abstract data types can be used in the same way as the built-in data types of C such as integer, float, character, and so on.
2. Hierarchical specifications can be written.
3. Required change in syntax is minimal for C to include the algebraic specification feature.
4. Separate compilation is possible.

To achieve the goals we introduce new reserved words into C. They are "package," "parameter," "instance," and "use". In the following sections, the syntax and semantics related to these new reserved words are presented.

6.2.1 Package and Parameter

Package is the feature for algebraically specifying ADTs in C= =. In a package block, a parameterized algebraic specification is written in the usual way. Of course, a package denotes a parameterized ADT.

The main part of the syntax rules for package blocks is as follows:

⟨PACKAGE-BLOCK⟩ ::=
  [extern] package ⟨PACKAGE-NAME⟩ {
  [⟨PARAMETER-SORTS⟩]
  ⟨FUNCTION-DECLARATIONS⟩
  ⟨EQUATIONS⟩ }

⟨PARAMETER-SORTS⟩ ::=
  parameter ⟨SORT⟩, ..., ⟨SORT⟩;

⟨FUNCTION-DECLARATIONS⟩ ::=
  ⟨FUNCTION-DECLARATION⟩ ... ⟨FUNCTION-DECLARATION⟩

⟨FUNCTION-DECLARATION⟩ ::=
  [extern] ⟨SORT-OF-RETURNED-VALUE⟩
    ⟨FUNCTION⟩, ..., ⟨FUNCTION⟩;

⟨FUNCTION⟩ ::=
  ⟨FUNCTION-NAME⟩
    (⟨SORT-OF-ARGUMENT⟩, ..., ⟨SORT-OF-ARGUMENT⟩)

⟨EQUATIONS⟩ ::=
  { ⟨EQUATION⟩ ... ⟨EQUATION⟩ }

⟨EQUATION⟩ ::=
  ⟨TERM⟩ = = ⟨TERM⟩;

Parameter declaration is optional. If this option exists, it means that the sorts following "parameter" are formal parameters of the specified parameterized ADT. Substitution of actual parameters by formal parameters is declared in an instance block. Actual parameters should be sorts instantiated already, or data types of C.

An optional prefix, "**extern**," of "**package**" means that this package is declared in another source file and should not be compiled.

A function declaration may also have an optional **extern** preceding the sort of returned value. It means that the function with **extern** is declared in another package. This feature, together with "instance," enables the programmer to write packages in a hierarchical or modularized way.

Typical examples of packages are as follows:

```
package boolean {
  bool TRUE(), FALSE();
  bool NOT(bool), AND(bool, bool);
  {
    AND(b1, FALSE()) == FALSE();
    AND(FALSE(), b2) == FALSE();
    AND(b1, TRUE()) == b1;
    AND(TRUE(), b2) == b2;
    NOT(TRUE()) == FALSE();
    NOT(FALSE()) == TRUE();
  }
};

package stack_of_data {
  parameter data;
  extern bool TRUE(), FALSE();
  extern bool NOT(bool), AND(bool, bool);
  stack NEW(), PUSH(stack, data), POP(stack);
  data TOP(stack);
  bool   ISNEW(stack);
  {
    POP(PUSH(sO, dO)) == sO;
    TOP(PUSH(sO, dO)) == dO;
    POP(NEW()) == NEW();
    ISNEW(NEW()) == TRUE();
    ISNEW(PUSH(sO, dO)) == FALSE();
  }
};
```

6.2.2 *Instance* and *Use*

Since packages denote parameterized ADTs, actual parameters should be substituted for formal parameters before using specified ADTs. In C==, parameter substitution is declared by an instance block. That is, an instance block denotes the ADT which is obtained by instantiating parameters of a parameterized ADT. The sorts of such an ADT are called defined types.

In an instance block, a package name and an instance name are specified, and parameter sorts of a package are associated with data types of original C or defined types by using "**typedef**."

The main part of the syntax rules concerning "instance" and "use" is as follows:

⟨INSTANCE-BLOCK⟩ ::=
  instance ⟨PACKAGE-NAME⟩ ⟨INSTANCE-NAME⟩ {
    [⟨PARAMETER-INSTANTIATION⟩ ...
     ⟨ PARAMETER-INSTANTIATION⟩]
    [⟨USE-DECLARATION⟩] }

⟨PARAMETER-INSTANTIATION⟩ ::=
  typedef ⟨DATA-TYPE⟩ ⟨SORT⟩;

⟨DATA-TYPE⟩ ::=
  ⟨DATA-TYPE-OF-C⟩ | ⟨DEFINED-TYPE⟩

⟨DEFINED-TYPE⟩ :: =
  ⟨INSTANCE-NAME⟩ . ⟨SORT⟩

⟨USE-DECLARATION⟩ ::=
  use ⟨INSTANCE-NAME⟩ ,..., ⟨INSTANCE-NAME⟩;

As stated in the previous section, a function declaration in a package may have extern as option, which means that the function belongs to the ADT defined by another package and instance. Thus, when instantiating a package which includes extern functions, we have to determine which ADT the function belongs to. This is done by using "use." The following example shows the usage of **use**:

```
instance boolean BOOLEAN {
}

instance stack_of_data STACK_OF_FLOAT {
    typedef float data;
    use BOOLEAN;
}
```

6.2.3 Interface with C

To interface C with the ADT defined by a package and an instance, some notation for defined types and functions of the ADT is introduced.

A defined type is written by juxtaposing an instance name, a period ("."), and a sort. Variables of a defined type are declared as usual. An example of variable declarations is:

```
STACK-OF-FLOAT . stack a;
STACK-OF-FLOAT . data x;
```

When calling a function of an ADT (i.e., an instantiated package), the function name is preceded by the instance name and a period. Such a function can be called in the same way as the ordinal functions of C. The following are examples of assignment statements of C= = including calls of functions of an ADT:

```
a = STACK-OF-FLOAT . PUSH (STACK-OF-FLOAT . NEW ( ), 3.14);
x = STACK-OF-FLOAT . TOP (a);
```

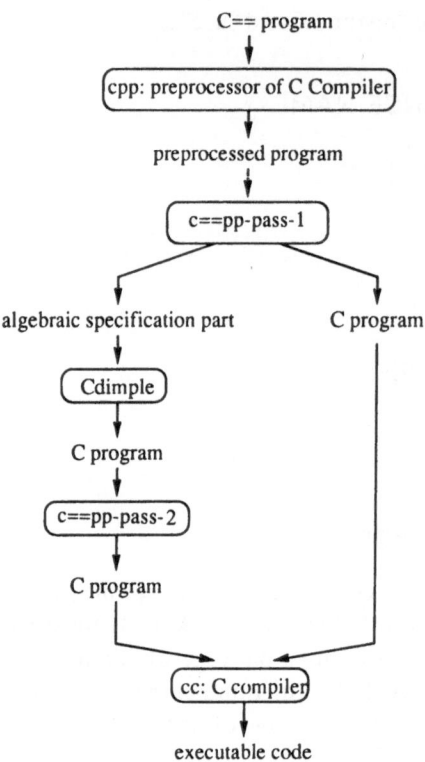

Fig. 6.1. Construction of C== compiler

6.3 Compiler of C==

The C== compiler is implemented as the preprocessor plus the C compiler. Figure 6.1 shows the construction of the C== compiler. The preprocessor transforms package blocks and instance blocks of a source program in C== into C programs, and then the C compiler translates them to executable codes together with the C program part of the source.

Such an implementation is easily modified to adapt to combinations of algebraic specifications and procedural languages other than C.

6.3.1 Preprocessor of C==

The preprocessor of C== is the whole of Fig. 6.1 except for cpp and cc, i.e., it consists of c==pp-pass-1, c==pp-pass-2, and Cdimple. The kernel of the pre-processor is Cdimple, a direct implementation system of algebraic specifications, which was developed by [2]. Given an algebraic specification, Cdimple translates it to a set of function programs of C, each of which corresponds to a function of the specification. Cdimple regards the equations of the specification as a term rewriting system (TRS) and the C function programs generated by Cdimple simulate inner-most term rewriting. That is, if an expression of C corresponding to a term composed of the functions is evaluated, the normal form of the term is returned by using the innermost term rewriting strategy.

C==pp-pass-1 separates the input program from cpp into two parts: the algebraic specification part and the C program part. The algebraic specification part is passed to Cdimple, and the C program part to cc, the C-compiler.

C==pp-pass-2 receives the C program from Cdimple and modifies it so that separate compilation is possible.

6.3.2 Data Structures for Separate Compilation

Cdimple treats the algebraic specification written in a C== program as a TRS and generates the program that evaluates expressions of the specified ADT by symbolic execution based on the TRS. In the program generated by Cdimple, terms of an ADT are represented by a tree structure. The data structure for representing the tree nodes is illustrated in Fig. 6.2. The contents of the symbolid slot is the number assigned to a function symbol of an ADT. This number is determined by Cdimple to be unique in the given source program file. Thus, separate compilation may cause collisions between the function numbers that are equationally defined in different source files. Therefore, the data structure for terms must be changed to allow separate compilation of C== programs.

The data structure for terms used in C== is shown in Fig. 6.3. In this data structure, the slot of the instance address is the pointer to the instance block that instantiates the function of the node. A trick is used to represent right hand sides of equations. That is, if a right hand side of an equation contains a function symbol which belongs to another instance, then a dummy tree node is inserted between the node of the function symbol and its parent node (see Fig. 6.3). By this mechanism, separate compilation is enabled, with minimal change to Cdimple.

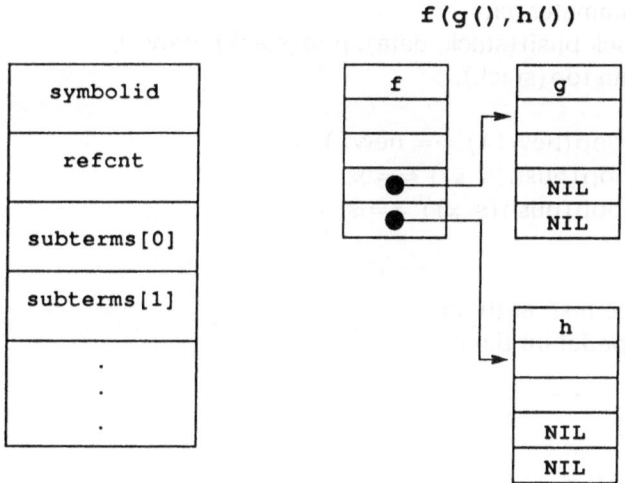

FIG. 6.2. Data structure for terms in Cdimple

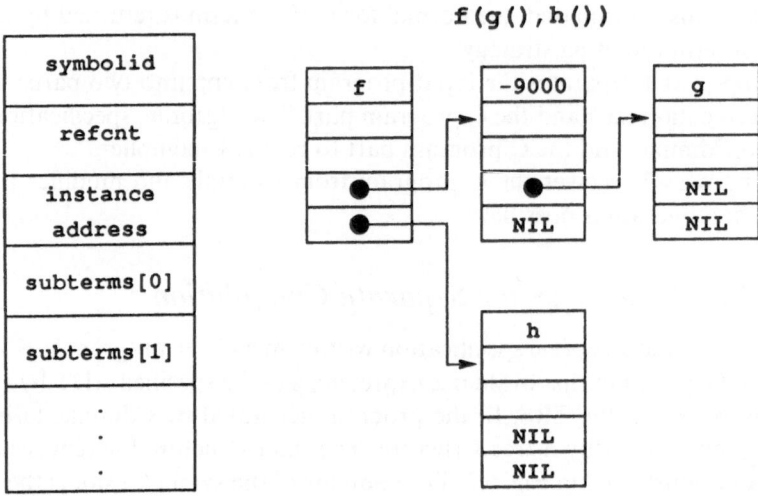

FIG. 6.3. Data structure for terms in C==

6.3.3 *Performance of* C== *Compiler*

To evaluate the performance of the C== compiler, we use the following two programs: test 1.c== and test2.c. Both programs do the same job, that is, repeat push, top, and pop operations 100,000 times. The difference is that in test 1.c== the stack data type is defined algebraically, while in test2.c it is written in pure C. Thus, they are compiled with the C== compiler and the ordinal C compiler, respectively.

```
/****************** test1.c== ******************/
    #include <stdio.h>
    package test_ar {
        parameter data;
        stack push(stack, data), pop(stack), new();
        data top(stack);
        {
            pop(new()) == new();
            top(push(s, x)) == x;
            pop(push(s, x)) == s;
        }
    };
    instance test_ar tb_ar {
        typedef int data;
    };

    main()
    {
    tb_ar.stack b;
    tb_ar.data x, a;
        b = tb_ar.new();
```

```
      for (x = 0; x < 100000; x++) {
          b = tb_ar . push (b, x);
      }
      for (x = 0, x < 100000; x++) {
          a = tb_ar . top (b);
          b = tb_ar . pop (b);
      }
```

```
/****************** test2.c= = ******************/
    # include ⟨stdio . h⟩
    # define STACKSIZE 100000

    struct stack_base {
      int data [STACKSIZE];
      int stack_point;
    };

    typedef struct stack_base *STACK;

    STACK new ( );
    STACK push ( ), pop ( );
    int top ( );

    main ( )
    {
      int i, x;
      STACK a;

      a = new ( );
      for (i = 0; i < 100000; i++) {
        a = push (a, i);
      }
      for (i = 0; i < 100000; i++) {
        x = top (a);
        a = pop (a);
      }
    }

    STACK new ( )
    {
      STACK spoint;

      spoint = (STACK) calloc (1, sizeof (struct stack_base));
      spoint −⟩ stack_point = 0;
      return spoint;
    }

    STACK push (s, data)
        STACK s;
        int     data;
```

```
{
    s −> data [s −> stack_point] = data;
    s −> stack_point+ +;
    return s;
}
int top (s)
    STACK s;
{
    return s −> data [s −> stack_point];
}
STACK pop (s)
    STACK s;
{
    s −> stack_point− −;
    return s;
}
```

The execution time is 26.5 seconds for test1.c== and 1.3 seconds for test2.c. Thus, test1.c== is about 20 times slower than test2.c. Incidentally, the compile time of C== is comparable to that of C, i.e., the overhead for preprocessing algebraic specifications in C== programs is not so heavy.

This experiment implies that fully algebraic programs are impractical. But, by appropriately restricting the algebraic specification part, C== programs can be used for prototypical purposes and even for practical purposes in cases where efficiency is not so critical. Such a case is shown in the next section.

6.4 Application to Line-Drawing Software

Application software on a multi-window system is often developed based on the idea of "event-driven" routines [3]. A typical event-driven program consists of an initialization routine, an event loop, and a termination routine. In the event loop, event-processing routines are triggered according to which event happens. The role of catching events caused by the operation of a mouse, keyboard, and so on is done by the event manager, which is a part of the multi-window system.

In this section, we show an event-driven implementation of the basic part of a line-drawing program in C==. The basic features implemented are:

1. Drawing lines and saving their vector data in memory
2. Moving lines around
3. Deleting lines

An outline of the flow of event processing is illustrated in Fig. 6.4. In the implementation, the event-processing routines are algebraically described by equations, and the rest are written in C. Specifically for algebraic description, the data structure for storing vector data of lines is specified by the package

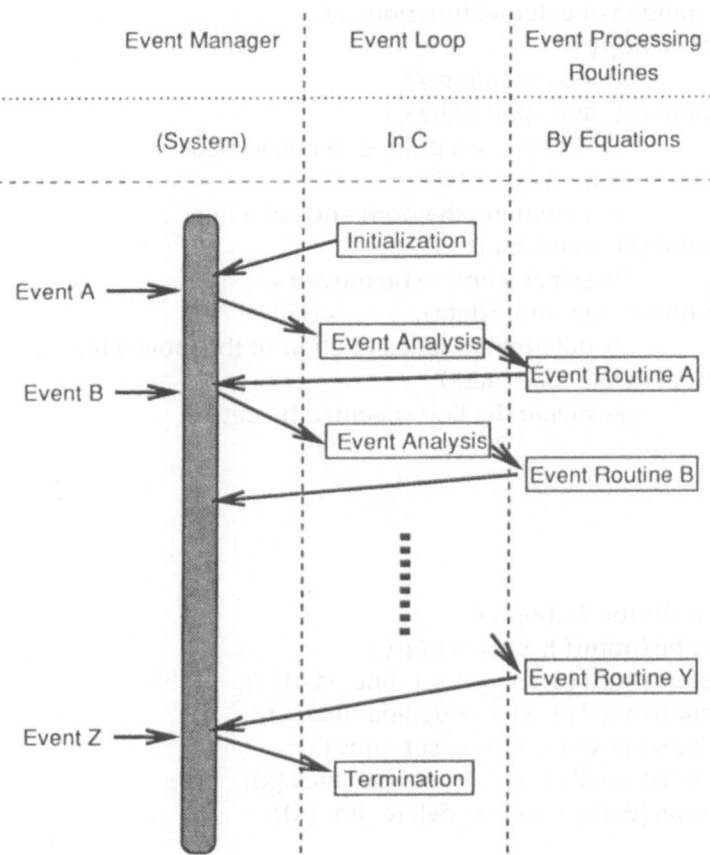

FIG. 6.4. Flow of event processing

abs_line_data, and the state transition caused by mouse events is specified by the package abstract_state. For example, the state transition caused when the left-button is pushed is written in abstract_state as follows:

package abstract_state {

    parameter bool, data;

    /* state declaration */
    state line1 ( );   /* when one end of the line to be drawn is pointed */
    state mov1 ( );   /* when a line is pointed in moving mode */
    state del1 ( );   /* when a line is pointed in deleting mode */
    state norm( );   /* neither in drawing, moving nor deleting mode */
    state line2( );   /* when the other end of the line to be drawn is pointed */
    state mov2( );   /* when the destination position is point */
    . . . .
    . . . .

```
/* declarations of external functions */
extern bool nop();
                 /* no operation */
extern bool set_line_start(data);
                 /* set the start point of a line to data */
extern bool decide_line(data);
                 /* determine the both ends of a line */
extern bool set_mov(data);
                 /* select a line to be moved */
extern bool decide_mov(data);
                 /* determine the destination of the moved line */
extern bool delete_line(data);
                 /* delete the line specified by data */
. . . .
. . . .
{
  . . . .

  . . . .
  /* Left Button Action */
  lb_action(norm(), x) == nop();
  lb_action(line1(), x) == set_line_start(x);
  lb_action(line2(), x) == decide_line(x);
  lb_action(mov1(), x) == set_mov(x);
  lb_action(mov2(), x) == decide_mov(x);
  lb_action(del1(), x) == delete_line(x);
  . . . .
  . . . .
}
}
```

The performance is sufficient for prototype use, that is, drawing, moving, and deleting lines are done in almost real time. A hard copy of the display when running the line-drawing software is shown in Fig. 6.5.

The total size of the implementation is 217 source code lines for the algebraic specification part and 524 for the rest. If we write C programs for the event routines, its size will be greater than that of the algebraic specifications.

This experiment suggests that C== is matched well to event-driven programming.

6.5 Conclusion

In this paper, we have presented a hybrid language C== that is C plus algebraic specifications, a technique for constructing a compiler for such a hybrid language, and an application of C== to line-drawing software.

FIG. 6.5. Window running the line-drawing software

It is possible for programmers to stay in C== throughout all the steps of stepwise transformational development of software.

The C== compiler is constructed as a reprocessor plus C compiler, so that the idea of this construction is easily applied to other combinations of procedural languages and algebraic specifications. The core of the preprocessor is Cdimple, the system which translates algebraic specifications into the C program that simulates the TRS corresponding to the specification. The technique to make separate compilation possible is very simple and it imposes only small changes to the original Cdimple.

The line-drawing software was developed in a very short period by the idea of "event-driven" routines and using C==. This application suggests that a hybrid of procedural and equational languages is useful for event-driven programming.

It is left as a future problem to establish a programming style that combines the idea of event-driven routines and C==. To remove the restrictions imposed on the syntax of C== is another problem to be addressed in the future.

Acknowledgments. We would like to thank Prof. Hirata, Prof. Toyama, Dr. Naoi, Mr. Sakai, Mr. Yuen, and other colleagues of Nagoya University for valuable comments and discussion.

References

1. Inagaki Y, Sakabe T (1984) Foundation of abstract data types and their algebraic specifications (1)—many sorted algebra and equational logic J Inf Process 25 (1): 47–53
2. Sakai M, Sakabe T, Inagaki Y (1987) Direct implementation system for algebraic specifications of abstract data types: Cdimple. Comput Software (Japan) 4 (4): 16–27
3. Sun Microsystems (1986) Sun View programmer's guide

7
An Application of Term Rewriting Systems for Functional Programming

Yutaka Kikuchi and Takuya Katayama[1]

Summary: Term rewriting systems have some excellent properties as a functional computation model. However, their programming is similar to logical programming rather than functional programming. This paper proposes the use of term rewriting systems as a mechanism of execution and verification, and the use of a functional programming language as syntax sugar which hides the underlying layer.

We show how to translate functional programs into term rewriting systems derived from techniques of conditional term rewriting systems. Selectors in programs, which are obstacles at the stage of development of programs, can be eliminated at the same time.

As an example of this concept, we describe a graph rewriting system and its application for functional programming. The graph grammar and its rewriting system are similar to term rewriting systems, except that the graph rewriting system can treat naturally both multiple output functions and call-by-name evaluation. We define properties, termination and confluency, for equational reasoning on this system, and then we show that this system is useful for evaluating and verifying programs which have multiple output functions.

Key words: term rewriting system — attribute grammar — lazy evaluation — verification — graph rewriting

7.1 Introduction

The concept of a *term rewriting system* (TRS) is a kind of reduction system known as *λ-calculus* and *combinatory logic*. TRSs provide a model of computation which has simple syntax and semantics. They are used for analyzing consistency of algebraic specifications, automatic theorem proving, and computation mechanisms of functional programming languages.

2-12-1 O-okayama, Meguro, Tokyo, 152 Japan
[1] Department of Computer Science, Tokyo Institute of Technology, Meguro-ku, Tokyo, 152 Japan

A TRS consists of rewriting rules on equivalent classes of terms defined by a set of equations. A TRS gives an algebraic semantics because all of its rules come from underlying equations, and also gives an operational semantics because the rules are considered as concrete computation rules.

There is an interesting property, *completeness*, which means that a TRS has termination and confluency. A completion algorithm, which was originally developed by Knuth and Bendix to solve the word problem of the group theory [1], makes TRSs complete. The completion algorithm is able to prove an equation inductively without explicit induction mechanisms [2–4].

We have been developing a functional programming language AG and its programming environment SAGE [5]. AG is based on a computation model derived from attribute grammar [6]. AG modules which are units of AG computation are highly independent of other modules and free from side effects. SAGE provides an integrated programming environment to allow programmers to make AG programs in many aspects of programming.

Requirements for the interpreter of SAGE become strict, as SAGE has been used for large applications. First, a program should be executed even if it is not yet written completely. However, SAGE does not take symbolic values, but only concrete values. This is an obstacle when evaluating incomplete specifications in the situation of developing programs. Second, the interpreter should be able to use programming techniques based on lazy evaluations. For example, on computing the number of Fibonacci's sequence, it is common to make a combination of an infinite Fibonacci sequence generator and an nth filter. But there is no infinite data structure allowed in AG, because the interpreter based on attribute grammar supports only eager evaluation.

On the other hand, it forces users to learn one more language to use the verifier of SAGE. Because the verifier takes two languages as its inputs, one is AG itself to be executed and another is an assertion language to describe behaviors of programs. The existence of an assertion language is one of the obstacles to the utilization of the verifier for a programming tool.

We have had an idea for applying TRS to the evaluation subsystem and the verification subsystem in SAGE. Our aim is to give AG another semantics using TRS, and then to provide new evaluation and verification methods for SAGE. TRSs take values symbolically and can evaluate them lazily. The completion algorithm on TRSs checks consistency between two programs. This means that it is not necessary to prepare any assertion languages.

TRS cannot be applied to SAGE directly. One of the problems is how to translate programs in a functional language into TRS. There are selection constructs to determine one of conditional alternatives in functional languages. TRSs select a rule to be applied to an evaluating term by unification of the term and the left-hand sides of the rules, but functional languages do not. Another problem is that a term expresses only one value in TRS, but functions in AG can return multiple values.

We show a method to translate a subset of programs in a functional language into rewriting rules by syntactical manipulations. Also, as an extension of this method, we show a method to eliminate selectors from rewriting rules. Rewriting rules including selectors behave worse than rules without selectors in stages of execution of wrong programs during program developing.

In addition, we have developed an extended version of TRS, named *AGRS*, to handle multiple values. This is a kind of Graph grammar with a rewriting system on it. AGRS can solve a problem by means of interpreting nodes as functions, incoming arcs to a node as inputs of the function corresponding to the node, and outgoing arcs from a node as outputs of the function. Many properties of TRSs hold also on AGRS, such as confluency, termination, and completion.

A subset of the AG programs can be translated into AGRS. *Call by need* evaluation is described and applied in AGRS more naturally than TRS. AGRS allows lazy evaluation, symbolic execution, and verification without an extra assertion language.

7.2 Term Rewriting Systems (TRSs)

In this section, we introduce the terminology of TRSs briefly. TRSs are reduction systems, which are defined on the congruence relation over terms with variables. A formal specification in TRS is considered as an algebraic specification, because a model of initial algebra is defined by the set of equations from rewriting congruence of the specification. On the other hand, it is considered as an operational specification, because TRS defined with the specification produces a resulting value by the reduction procedure. Therefore, we can use the TRS as executable specifications. TRSs are discussed further in [7–9].

7.2.1 Reduction Systems

Definition 1: (reduction system) is a pair $(A, \rightarrow)$ where A is an arbitrary set and $\rightarrow$ is an arbitrary binary relation on A.

Notation 1: a reduction step $a \rightarrow b$ is an infix notation of a relation of $\rightarrow$ where a, $b \in A$.

In intuitive understanding, $a \rightarrow b$ means that a is equal to b in a sense, and that b is simpler than a in another sense.

Definition 2: (reducible) $a(\in A)$ is reducible if there exists $b(\in A)$ such that $a \rightarrow b$.

Definition 3: (irreducible) $a(\in A)$ is irreducible if $\neg(a \rightarrow b)$ holds for all $b(\in A)$.

Note that every element of A is either reducible or irreducible.

Notation 2: $\xrightarrow{*}$ is a reflexive transitive closure of $\rightarrow$.

Theorem 1: A pair $(A, \xrightarrow{*})$ is a preordered set.

7.2.1.1 Termination

Definition 4: (normal form) a' is a normal form (canonical form) of a such that $a \xrightarrow{*} a'$ and a' is irreducible.

Notation 3: (normal form) $a \downarrow$ denotes a normal form (canonical form) of a.

Definition 5: (weak termination) a reduction system has weak termination if there exists $a \downarrow$ for all $a(\in A)$.

Notation 4: $|\vec{a}|$ is the length of the reduction sequence $\vec{a}$.

For example, $|a \rightarrow b \rightarrow c| = 2$.

Definition 6: (termination) a reduction system has termination (noetherian) if $|\vec{a}| \leq n_a$ holds where there exists a normal form $a \downarrow$ and a natural number (zero or more) n_a for all $a (\in A)$.

Theorem 2: $(A, \overset{*}{\rightarrow})$ is a partially ordered set if $(A, \overset{*}{\rightarrow})$ has termination.

7.2.1.2 Confluency

Definition 7: (confluency) a reduction system has confluency if there exists b for all a, a_1, a_2 such that $a \overset{*}{\rightarrow} a_1$, $a \overset{*}{\rightarrow} a_2$, $a_1 \overset{*}{\rightarrow} b$, and $a_2 \overset{*}{\rightarrow} b$.

Notation 5: $(\overset{*}{\leftrightarrow})$ is a reflexive transitive symmetric closure of $\rightarrow$.

Definition 8: (equivalence relation) is a relation over $\overset{*}{\leftrightarrow}$.

Notation 6: $a_1 = a_2$ denotes that they are in an equivalence relation.

Note that $a_1 = a_2$ iff $a_1 \overset{*}{\leftrightarrow} a_2$.

Definition 9: (Church-Rosser) a reduction system has the Church-Rosser property if there exists b for all a_1 and a_2 such that $a_1 = a_2$ and $a_1 \overset{*}{\rightarrow} b$, $a_2 \overset{*}{\rightarrow} b$.

Theorem 3: a reduction system has confluency iff it has Church-Rosser.

7.2.1.3 Complete Reduction Systems

Theorem 4: If a reduction system has both weak termination and confluency, the following holds:

$$a = b \Leftrightarrow a \downarrow \equiv b \downarrow .$$

Definition 10: A reduction system is complete (canonical, convergent) if it has both termination and confluency.

7.2.2 Terms and Reduction Systems

7.2.2.1 Terms

Here we define variables and functions first, and then define terms.

1. *Variables*: there are enumerable infinite variables. V denotes an enumerable infinite set of variables.
2. *Functions*: there are finite functions in a system under consideration. F denotes a finite set of functions. *Arity* is the number of inputs of a function. *Constants* are functions whose arity is 0.

Terms are defined as follows:

1. The variables are terms.
2. $f(\tau_1, \tau_2, \ldots, \tau_n)$ is a term where the arity of a function f is n and $\tau_1, \tau_2, \ldots, \tau_n$ are terms.

$T(V, F)$ denotes a set of the terms on V and F. Terms which do not have any variables are *ground terms*.

$T(F)$ denotes a set of the ground terms on F.

7.2.2.2 Reduction Systems on Terms

A term rewriting system is a reduction system over $T(V, F)$. $\tau \Rightarrow \sigma$ is a rewriting rule where τ and σ are elements of $T(V, F)$. $\mathscr{R}$ denotes a set of the rewriting rules.

The equivalence relationship introduced from the reduction $\rightarrow$ over the term rewriting system $\mathscr{R}$ is called *congruence*. Note that we get an equation system by substituting '$=$' for '$\Rightarrow$' in the term rewriting system $\mathscr{R}$.

Definition 11: (left-linear (rewriting rules)) a rewriting rule is left-linear if there is no more than one occurrence of each variable in a left-hand-side of the rule.

Definition 12: (left-linear (TRSs)) a TRS is left-linear if all rewriting rules are left-linear in the TRS.

Definition 13: (non-overlapping) a TRS is nonoverlapping if there is no ambiguity of rules to be applied for all terms.

Definition 14: (regular) a TRS is regular if it is left-linear and nonoverlapping.

Theorem 5: regular TRSs are confluent.

Note that this is a useful theorem and one of the well-known theorems on TRS. The restriction class of TRS here, i.e., *regular*, is stronger than that in the original theorem proved in [7].

7.3 Translation of Functional Programs into TRSs

In this section, we show how to translate functional programs into TRSs. As mentioned in the previous section, regular TRSs are confluent. There is great scope for translation because ordinal functional programs are similar to regular TRSs in the following respects:

1. Declarations of argument variables may be in the top of function definitions. There is only one occurrence of every argument in each function.
2. Function definitions must be deterministic. There is no ambiguity of execution behavior.

CTRSs are extended TRSs, which have conditional rewriting rules rather than nonconditional rewriting rules [10]. We use a *conditional term rewriting system* (CTRS) as an intermediate language between functional programs and TRS, because conditional branches in functional programs directly correspond to rewriting rules in CTRS.

At first, programs are translated into CTRS. In the next step, CTRS is translated into TRS [10, 11]. The method of eliminating conditions takes only syntactical manipulation. As an additional manipulation of this, we show the method to eliminate selectors from given TRSs.

cardinal function sub(x, y)

    cardinal x, y ;

begin

    if (y == 0)

        return x ;

    else

        sub(pred(x), pred(y)) ;

end

FIG. 7.1. An example program for translation

We will fail to accomplish translation when a condition of a conditional branch in the functional program breaks the left-linearity of TRS. Therefore, we can not translate all functional programs, only a subset of them.

Figure 7.1 is a sample functional program as a source program for translation. We translate this step-by-step in the rest of this section.

7.3.1 *Conditional Term Rewriting Systems (CTRSs)*

Selections of rules are determined by a pattern-matching algorithm in the traditional TRSs. Recently, CTRSs have been studied with the aim of describing specifications naturally. There are three types of CTRSs [10]. Forms (1), (2), and (3) are categorized as TYPE I, TYPE II, and TYPE III. Bergstra and Klop studied confluency of these types and showed an efficient condition of confluency:

$$t \Rightarrow s: -t_1 = s_1 \wedge \cdots \wedge t_n = s_n \tag{1}$$

Rule (1) rewrites t into s is all equations hold.

$$t \Rightarrow s: -t_1 \downarrow s_1 \wedge \cdots \wedge t_n \downarrow s_n \tag{2}$$

where $t_i = s_i$ means that t_i and s_i have a common reduct.

$$t \Rightarrow s: -t_1 \xrightarrow{*} s_1 \wedge \cdots \wedge t_n \xrightarrow{*} s_n \tag{3}$$

where $t_i = s_i$ means that t_i is reduced into s_i.

Functional programs are translated into TYPE II easily, but TYPE II is not confluent in general. We cannot use TYPE II for translation.

7.3.1.1 Translating Functional Programs into TRS

CTRSs are confluent in the case that $s_1, \ldots, s_n$ are normal forms of TYPE III, called TYPE III$_n$. This result means that a restricted set of functional programs is translated into TRS safely.

function f(x)

This program can be translated into CTRS (4)
and TRS (5) where s is a compound function
of constructors.

begin

  if (t(x) == s)

    return g(x);

end

$$f(x) \Rightarrow g(x): -t(x) \xrightarrow{*} s \qquad (4)$$

$$\left.\begin{array}{l} f(x) \Rightarrow f'(x, t(x)) \\ f'(x, s) \Rightarrow g(x) \end{array}\right\} \qquad (5)$$

The example program can be translated into TRS (6) in the same way:

$$sub(x, y) \Rightarrow sub'(x, y, y)$$

$$sub'(x, y, 0) \Rightarrow x$$

$$sub'(x, y, succ(z)) \Rightarrow sub(pred(x), pred(y)) \qquad (6)$$

Note that the number of function symbols does not increase, because every appearance of the function symbol *sub* in all rewriting rules will be rewritten to *sub'*.

7.3.1.2 Optimization

Products of the translation discussed will be simpler in a special case such as TRS (7):

$$t \Rightarrow s: -t \xrightarrow{*} t[x_1/s_1, \ldots, x_n/s_n] \qquad (7)$$

where $x_1, \ldots, x_n$ are all variables appearing in a term t. In this case, the conditional rewriting rules can be translated into a simple rule:

$$t[x_1/s_1, \ldots, x_n/s_n] \Rightarrow s[x_1/s_1, \ldots, x_n/s_n] \qquad (8)$$

This program can be translated into TRS (9) without any auxiliary functions.

```
function f(x)
begin
  if (x == s)
    return g(x);
end
```

$$f(s) \Rightarrow g(s) \qquad (9)$$

The example program can be translated into TRS (10) which does not use *sub'*:

$$sub(x, 0) \Rightarrow x$$

$$sub(x, succ(z)) \Rightarrow sub(pred(x), pred(succ(z))) \qquad (10)$$

7.3.1.3 TRSs with Rule Priorities

Generally, it is not easy to find the condition according to the '**else**' construct in the program. It is necessary to attach priorities in rewriting rules. This was studied in [12], where it was named the *priority rewrite system* (PRS), and *specificity ordering* was defined as the property of priorities. The authors conclude that left-linear PRS with specificity ordering is confluent.

The example program 1 (Fig. 7.1) can be translated into PRS (11):

$$sub(x, y) \Rightarrow sub'(x, y, y)$$

$$\left.\begin{array}{l} sub'(x, y, 0) \Rightarrow x \\ sub'(x, y, z) \Rightarrow sub(pred(x), pred(y)) \end{array}\right. \qquad (11)$$

The vertical arrow indicates the priority of the two rules, the former of which is a first target of pattern matching.

If the condition part is a special case the same as in Sect. 7.3.1.2, the example program can be translated into PRS (12) without the auxiliary function symbol sub'.

$$\left\downarrow \begin{array}{l} sub(x, 0) \Rightarrow x \\ sub(x, y) \Rightarrow sub(pred(x), pred(y)) \end{array} \right. \qquad (12)$$

7.3.2 Constructors and Selectors

Functions in programs consist of constructors and other functions. Constructors of a program construct a data structure of the program. Functions which are not constructors consist of selectors and functions defined by the user.

Selectors are not desirable in a stage of program development. Consider TRS (13) which has constructor '0' and $succ$, a selector $pred$, and defined functions '+' and '−'.

$$pred(succ(x)) \Rightarrow x$$
$$+(x, 0) \Rightarrow x$$
$$+(x, succ(y)) \Rightarrow succ(+(x, y))$$
$$-(x, 0) \Rightarrow x$$
$$-(x, succ(y)) \Rightarrow -(pred(x), y) \qquad (13)$$

TRS (13) may produce terms with the selector as concrete values in the data structure, because it does not expect that the first argument is less than the second argument.

$$-(succ(0), succ(succ(0))) \overset{*}{\to} pred(0) \qquad (14)$$

If the system is more complicated, it is difficult to identify the cause of the trouble after the spread of the illegal execution.

TRS (15), which does not use the selector, behaves the same as TRS (13) when the first argument is greater than or equal to the second.

$$+(x, 0) \Rightarrow x$$
$$+(x, succ(y)) \Rightarrow succ(+(x, y))$$
$$-(x, 0) \Rightarrow x$$
$$-(succ(x), succ(y)) \Rightarrow -(x, y) \qquad (15)$$

If arguments for the TRS are insufficient for the requirement, reduction will stop without producing an unexpected value (16). It is easy to realize that the problem is the application of wrong arguments to the function '−'.

$$-(s(0), s(s(0))) \to -(0, s(0)) \qquad (16)$$

7.3.2.1 Eliminating Selectors

Selectors in the rewriting rules can be eliminated by an auxiliary function symbol, as in the case of eliminating conditions.

Let *sel* be a selector of the constructor *con*.

$$sel(con(x)) \Rightarrow x$$

If there is a rewriting rule which uses the selector *sel*,

$$f(x) \Rightarrow h(sel(g(x))),$$

it can be translated into rewriting rules without the selector which keeps regularity:

$$f(x) \Rightarrow f'(g(x))$$
$$f'(con(x)) \Rightarrow h(x) \tag{17}$$

If the function *pred* is a selector of the constructor *succ*,

$$pred(succ(x)) \Rightarrow x,$$

and the example program can be translated into TRS (18).

$$sub(x, y) \Rightarrow sub'(x, y, y)$$
$$sub'(x, y, 0) \Rightarrow x$$
$$sub'(succ(x), succ(y), succ(z)) \Rightarrow sub(x, y) \tag{18}$$

Here we have a target program in TRS from the source code.

7.3.2.2 Optimization

If the function *g* is the identity function in Sect. 7.3.1.2 such that:

$$f(x) \Rightarrow h(sel(x)),$$

it can be translated into a more simple one without any auxiliary functions:

$$f(con(x)) \Rightarrow h(x)$$

The example program can be translated into TRS (19).

$$sub(x, 0) \Rightarrow x$$
$$sub(succ(x), succ(y)) \Rightarrow sub(x, y) \tag{19}$$

7.4 The Language AG and its Environment

AG is a functional programming language based on *absolute noncircular attribute grammar* as a functional and hierarchical computation model. AG is developed as a general purpose computation language, and it provides a good solution where substantial determination of values on the hierarchical structure is required.

SAGE, *Support for AG Environment*, is a programming environment designed to help produce programs correctly written in AG. SAGE aims to:

1. Confirm that AG is powerful enough to express general computational processes
2. Provide the basis for application of attribute grammars into various application areas
3. Establish programming methodologies that are effective with programming based on attribute grammar
4. Provide a test bed for various support tools for these methodologies
5. Establish a systematic way of composing the programming environment

7.4.1 The Computation Model HFP

Hierarchical Functional Programming (HFP) [13] is a computation model based on attribute grammar. HFP has two concepts, *modules* and *module decompositions*.

A *module* is a unit of processing. Its functionality is defined by a relation between its inputs and outputs. A module M is denoted as follows

$$M(M_{in_1}, \ldots, M_{in_m} | M_{out_1}, \ldots, M_{out_n})$$

where $M_{in_1}, \ldots, M_{in_m}$ are inputs and $M_{out_1}, \ldots, M_{out_n}$ are outputs. Inputs and outputs are also called *attributes*. Intuitively, modules can be interpreted as multiple valued functions. Let $D_{M_{in_1}}, \ldots, D_{M_{in_m}}$ be the domains of $M_{in_1}, \ldots, M_{in_m}$; and $R_{M_{out_1}}, \ldots, R_{M_{out_n}}$ be the ranges of $M_{out_1}, \ldots, M_{out_n}$,

$$M: D_{M_{in_1}} \times \cdots \times D_{M_{in_m}} \to R_{M_{out_1}} \times \cdots \times R_{M_{out_n}}$$

is the type of M.

If the functionality of M is simple enough, the outputs $M_{out_1}, \ldots, M_{out_n}$ will be directly expressed in terms of the inputs $M_{in_1}, \ldots, M_{in_m}$. Otherwise the module M must be decomposed into submodules. M may be decomposed into submodules $M1, \ldots, Ml$ as

$$M \Rightarrow M1, \ldots, Ml$$

associated with a set of *attribute relation definitions*. Attribute relation definitions are equations between attributes in a module. Equations in a module hold the following properties:

- Equations must not make any circular dependency.
- The output attribute of the module must appear only once in the module description.
- Each input attribute of submodules must appear only once in the module description.

Figure 7.2 shows a simple example of a decomposition of M into $M1 \ldots M2$.

HFP differs from pure attribute grammar in the sense of absence of a precomputed abstract syntax tree. In HFP, the virtual computation tree is generated as computation proceeds by repeated application of decompositions, whereas pure attribute grammar does not do this.

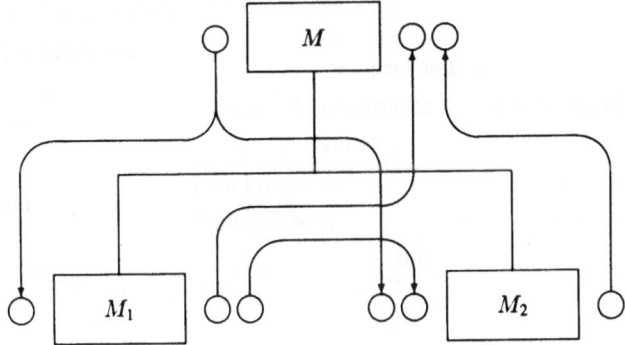

FIG. 7.2. A decomposition example

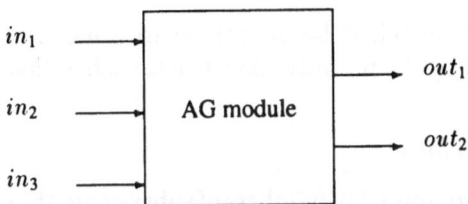

FIG. 7.3. An AG module as a blackbox

There is no side effect in HFP because any attributes must be substituted with values only once. Also, there is no concept of global variables which effect the execution behavior of modules implicitly. Therefore, a module is considered as a blackbox which has a relation between input and output attributes (Fig. 7.3). This feature allows us to verify modules at the point of relations between inputs and outputs.

7.4.2 *The Language AG*

AG is based on the computation model HFP, and designed as a general purpose and strictly typed functional language. The units of processing in AG are modules, the same as in HFP.

Simple modules must not be decomposed. The outputs of a simple module can be derived from just its inputs. Composite modules are decomposed into other modules. Switch modules are decomposed into one or more sets of submodules within a 'switch' construct. A set of submodules is selected according to 'case' and 'otherwise' conditions. The former must be selected if two or more conditions hold. Figure 7.4 shows program examples of modules in AG.

AG has primitive data types such as boolean and integer, and methods to construct complex data types over any types recursively. There are complex types such as Cartesian product and set. Recently, abstract data types have been allowed in AG.

There are some constructs to make programs easily, such as 'for' and 'while',

```
                                                   define dec=
                                                     module( in | out )
  define dup=                define incdec=           switch
    module( in | out1, out2 )   module( in | inc, dec )   case in == 0
      where                       where                     zero( | out )
        out1 = in                   succ( in | inc )      otherwise
        out2 = in                   pred( in | dec )        pred( in | out )
  end                         end                         end
                                                     end
```

FIG. 7.4. Simple, composite, and switch modules

but we do not explain them here because these are not essential for our discussion, and can be simulated by the primitive constructs such as '**switch**'.

7.4.3 SAGE Overview

The SAGE system is composed of numbers of subsystems, the editor, the interpreter, the debugger, the compiler, the verifier, and other miscellaneous support modules.

7.4.3.1 Editor

The editor is responsible for composing the programs written in AG, creating internal representations of these programs, and passing them to other components for their use. It is a syntax-directed editor for AG. It detects not only syntax errors but semantic errors which are statically detectable such as type incompatibilities between their declaration and their use. It is written in *Synthesizer Specification Language* (SSL) and generated by *Cornell Synthesizer Generator* (CSG) [14, 15], an editor generator based on the attribute grammar

7.4.3.2 Interpreter, Debugger, and Compiler

The interpreter performs evaluation of AG programs by traversing the internal representation of the program prepared by the editor. It is capable of executing a program which is a mixture of compiled modules and not compiled ones, because the mechanism for attribute evaluation by the interpreter is designed to be equivalent to that of compiler-generated codes.

The debugger is an execution monitor for the interpreter. It does not have any mechanism for evaluation but merely manipulates execution contexts of the interpreter. It is very independent of features of the language such as internal representation in SAGE.

The compiler generates target codes in the C language as a native object language of AG. It concentrates on generating efficient codes, and performs less error checking, since errors are supposed to be corrected before compilation by the cooperation of the interpreter, the debugger, and the verifier.

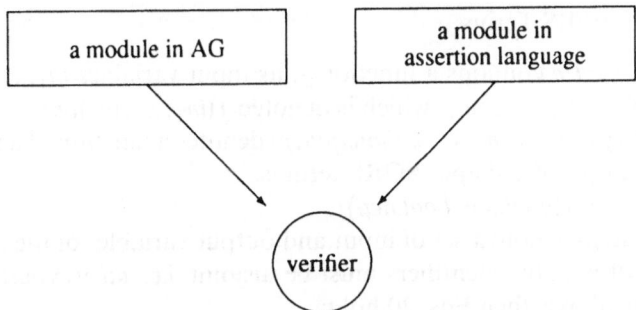

FIG. 7.5. Verification with an assertion language

7.4.3.3 Verifier

The verifier checks the consistency of a module and its assertion (Fig. 7.5). An assertion of a module describes a relation between inputs and outputs of the module in a language based on first-order predicate logic, rather than in AG.

The verifier subsystem is composed of VCG (Verification Condition Generator) and a theorem prover. VCG generates verification conditions for each module decomposition from assertions and programs in the form of clauses of the first-order logic.

These verification conditions are passed to the theorem prover. If all verification conditions are proven to be true, it is concluded that the program is partially correct about the given assertions.

VCG is written in SSL [16] and generated by CSG, the same as the editor. We adopted *intthp* [17, 18] as a theorem prover.

7.5 Attribute Grammatical Rewriting Systems (AGRS)

We introduce the definition of a graph grammar and a rewriting system on it, named the *Attribute Grammatical Rewriting System*, or *AGRS*. AGRS is an extended term rewriting system to allow functions with multiple values. Any graphs of AGRS must not be made circular, to be consistent with the absolutely noncircular attribute grammar. This system is similar to *hyperedge* [19] rather than the ordinal graph grammar frameworks.

7.5.1 Syntax of Graph

7.5.1.1 Functions and Variables

There is a set of certain finite functions $\mathscr{F}$ in the system under consideration. *Arity* is the number of inputs of a function. *Coarity* is the number of outputs respectively. There is a set of enumerable infinite variables $\mathscr{V}$ to denote inputs and outputs of AGRS terms described below. Functions and variables refer to nodes of a graph on AGRS and directed edges between them, respectively.

7.5.1.2 Simple AGRS Terms

A *simple AGRS term* contains a function f, its input variables $in_1, \ldots, in_m$, and its output variables $out_1, \ldots, out_n$, which is denoted $f(in_1, \ldots, in_m | out_1, \ldots, out_n)$ where arity and coarity of f are m and n. *Function*(ρ) denotes a function of a simple AGRS term ρ. An example of a simple AGRS term is:

$foo(card.x, card.y | bool.pos, bool.neg)$

$in(\rho)$ and $out(\rho)$ denote a set of input and output variables of the AGRS term ρ respectively. All variable identifiers must be disjoint, i.e., $in(\rho) \cap out(\rho) = \phi$. Let ρ be the example above; then Eqs. 20 hold:

$$
\begin{aligned}
foo &= function(\rho) \\
\{card.x, card.y\} &= in(\rho) \\
\{bool.pos, bool.neg\} &= out(\rho)
\end{aligned}
\tag{20}
$$

An AGRS simple term means a node with directed edges graphically.

7.5.1.3 AGRS Terms

An *AGRS term* is a set of simple AGRS terms. Here is an example of an AGRS term. A pair of braces means a set.

$$
\left\{
\begin{array}{c}
afo(card.x | card.tmp1) \\
bar(card.y | card.tmp2) \\
foo(card.tmp1, card.tmp2 | card.out)
\end{array}
\right\}
\tag{21}
$$

Input variables in an AGRS term τ do not appear in any output variables of the simple AGRS terms in τ. Similarly, *output variables* in τ do not appear in any input variables of the simple AGRS terms in τ. All output variables of the simple AGRS terms in an AGRS term must be disjoint. $In(\tau)$ and $Out(\tau)$ denote input and output variables of τ respectively. Equations (22) hold in the example (21).

$$
\begin{aligned}
\{card.x, card.y\} &= In(\tau) \\
\{card.out\} &= Out(\tau)
\end{aligned}
\tag{22}
$$

AGRS terms correspond to terms in TRS.

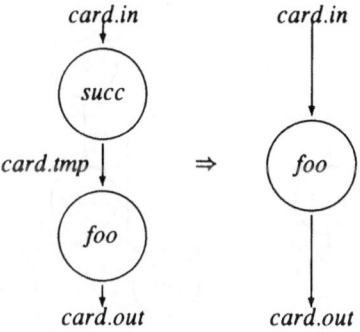

FIG. 7.6. An *AGRS term rewriting rule* as a graph rewriting rule

7.5.1.4 AGRS Ground Term

An *AGRS ground term* τ is an AGRS term which does not have any input variable, i.e. $In(\tau) = \phi$. An example is:

$$\left\{ \begin{array}{c} zero(|card.zero) \\ succ(card.zero|card.one) \\ foo(card.one|card.out) \end{array} \right\} \tag{23}$$

7.5.1.5 AGRS Term Rewriting Rule

An *AGRS term rewriting rule* has a pair of AGRS terms τ and σ on both sides, denoted as $\tau \Rightarrow \sigma$. Two sets of outputs in a rule must be the same, i.e., $Out(\tau) = Out(\sigma)$. An example is:

$$\left\{ \begin{array}{l} succ(card.in|card.tmp) \\ foo(card.tmp|card.out) \end{array} \right\} \Rightarrow \{ foo(card.in|card.out) \} \tag{24}$$

Figure 7.6 is the AGRS explanation of example (24).

7.5.1.6 AGRS Term Rewriting System

The *AGRS term rewriting system* is a system $(\mathscr{F}, \mathscr{V}, \mathscr{T}(\mathscr{F}, \mathscr{V}), \mathscr{R}(\mathscr{T}))$ where $\mathscr{F}$ is a set of functions, $\mathscr{V}$ is a set of variables, and $\mathscr{T}(\mathscr{F}, \mathscr{V})$ is a set of AGRS terms which has three mapping functions.

1. $t \xrightarrow{function} f*$

2. $f \xrightarrow{In} v*$

3. $f \xrightarrow{Out} v*$

where $t \in \mathscr{T}, f \in \mathscr{F}, v*, f* \subset \mathscr{F}$

$\mathscr{R}(\mathscr{T})$ is a set of AGRS term rewriting system which has two mapping functions.

1. $r \xrightarrow{lhs} t$

2. $r \xrightarrow{rhs} t$

where $r \in \mathscr{R}$.

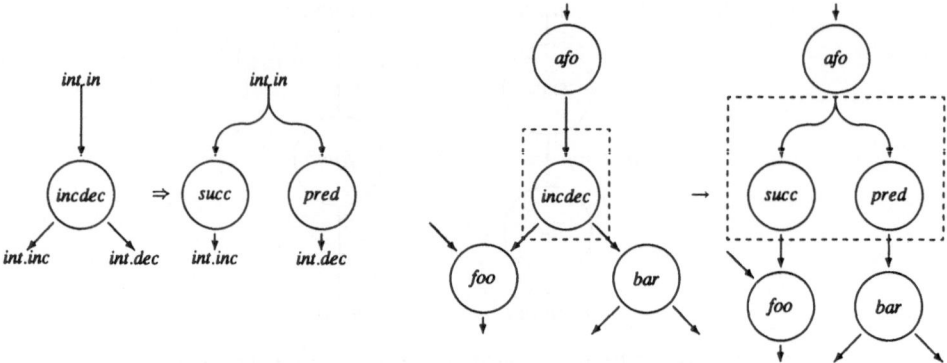

FIG. 7.7. AGRS rewriting as graph rewriting

7.5.2 Rewriting AGRS Terms

We show how to rewrite AGRS terms with a set of rewriting rules. An AGRS term τ is reduced to σ, if and only if there exists an appropriate set of substitutions s which makes a pair of AGRS terms ρ and λ to be subsets of τ and σ respectively where the rewriting rule $\rho \Rightarrow \lambda$ is a member of the given rewriting rules $\mathcal{R}$. More exactly, let s be a set of substitutions of the variable names, which does not produce any conflicting names of the inner variables in λ/s and τ. ρ/s is called a *redex*.

$\tau \to \sigma$ iff $\exists s$, $\exists r$ such that $\{\tau \supseteq \rho/s \wedge \sigma = \tau - \rho/s \cup \lambda/s\}$

where $r \in \mathcal{R}$, $lhs(r) = \rho$,

$rhs(r) = \lambda$.

An example is:

$$\{incdec(int.in|int.inc, int.dec)\} \Rightarrow \begin{Bmatrix} succ(int.in|int.inc) \\ pred(int.in|int.dec) \end{Bmatrix} \tag{25}$$

Rule (25) rewrites an AGRS term as (26):

$$\begin{Bmatrix} afo(int.x|int.y) \\ incdec(int.y|int.s, int.t) \\ foo(card.z, int.s|card.u) \\ bar(int.t|bool.v, int.w) \end{Bmatrix} \to \begin{Bmatrix} afo(int.x|int.y) \\ succ(int.y|int.inc) \\ pred(int.y|int.dec) \\ foo(card.z, int.inc|card.u) \\ bar(int.dec|bool.v, int.w) \end{Bmatrix} \tag{26}$$

Note that the node *incdec* still exists and links its input arc to the output of *afo* because any other nodes may refer to the node. Once nodes are made, the rewriting mechanism must not remove them. Only the garbage collector is allowed to remove them. Figure 7.7 shows AGRS rewriting as graph rewriting.

7.5.3 Comparison with TRSs

AGRSs are similar to TRSs from some points of view. In particular, AGRSs are equivalent to noncopying TRSs when all coarities of functions are one. Input variables of an AGRS term correspond to variables of a term in TRS. Output variables of an AGRS term also correspond to values in TRS, but the difference from TRS is that a term in AGRS has multiple values.

Here are two significant strategies (27) and (28) to rewrite redexes in AGRS:

$$x \text{ is the entering redex of } \tau \text{ iff } \exists x \forall y x \supseteq y \vee In(x) \notin y$$
$$\text{such that } x, y \text{ are redexes of } \tau \tag{27}$$

$$x \text{ is the exiting redex of } \tau \text{ iff } \exists x \forall y x \subseteq y \vee Out(x) \notin y$$
$$\text{such that } x, y \text{ are redexes of } \tau \tag{28}$$

By intuitional understanding,

- Rewriting an *entering redex* in AGRS corresponds to the *innermost reduction* in TRS.
- Rewriting an *exiting redex* in AGRS corresponds to the *outermost reduction* in TRS.

These also correspond to *call-by-value* and *call-by-name* in ALGOL, respectively.

AGRS avoids the problem of TRS in which the outermost reduction takes more reduction steps than the innermost reduction because the outermost reduction makes copies of redex. In the following case, TRS (29) takes two reduction steps to get the canonical form $g(b, b, b)$ of $f(a)$ by the innermost reduction; and TRS (29) takes four steps by the outermost reduction. AGRS (30) takes two reduction steps by each reduction.

$$\mathscr{R}_{TRS}: \begin{cases} f(x) \Rightarrow g(x, x, x) \\ a \Rightarrow b \end{cases} \tag{29}$$

$$\mathscr{R}_{AGRS}: \begin{bmatrix} \{f(in|out)\} \Rightarrow \{g(in, in, in|out)\} \\ \{a(|out)\} \Rightarrow \{b(|out)\} \end{bmatrix} \tag{30}$$

7.6 Completion Algorithm for AGRS

Considering a model of *initial algebra* defined by a set of equations, there is an efficient method to make inductive proofs by an extension of the Knuth-Bendix completion algorithm [2]. We define a new method to make proofs on equations of AGRS terms with a simple extension of the method already described. We show the extended completion algorithm over AGRS terms in Appendix B. Note that the *Definition of Principle* in [2] is naturally able to extend for AGRS.

7.6.1 Complete AGRS

A *reducible AGRS term* is an AGRS term in which there exists at least one rewriting rule to apply it. An *irreducible AGRS term* is an AGRS term to which there are no rewriting rules to apply. If there exists an irreducible AGRS term by iteration of applying rewriting rules to an AGRS term τ, it is called a *normal form* (or *canonical form*) of the AGRS term, denoted as $\tau \downarrow$.

When there are two or more AGRS terms as a result of applying different rewriting rules to one AGRS term, the AGRS has *confluency*, or the *Church-Rosser* property, if and only if there exist some rewriting rules to converge them to one AGRS term.

For an arbitrary AGRS term, the AGRS has *termination*, or the *noetherian* property, if and only if there exists a finite length sequence that rewrites the term to an irreducible one.

The AGRS is *complete*, or *canonical*, if and only if it has both confluency and termination properties.

7.6.2 AGRS Constructor Terms

We restrict AGRS here in that simple AGRS terms are either *simple AGRS constructor terms* or *simple AGRS non-constructor terms*. Simple AGRS constructor terms contain only constructors as their functions. Also, AGRS terms are either *AGRS constructor terms* or *AGRS non-constructor terms*. AGRS constructor terms contain only simple AGRS constructor terms as their elements.

7.6.2.1 Definition of Principle

We denote AGRS constructor terms, AGRS non-constructor terms, ground AGRS terms, and ground AGRS constructor terms by $\mathscr{C}$, $\mathscr{D}$, $\mathscr{G}$, and $\mathscr{GC}$ respectively. Let ε be a set of given equations, and $=_\varepsilon$ be the corresponding congruence on AGRS terms. Here is the extended principle of definition for AGRS terms as the conjunction of two properties:

1. $\forall M(\in \mathscr{G}) \exists N(\in \mathscr{GC}), M =_\varepsilon N$
2. $\forall M, N(\in \mathscr{GC})$, we have $M =_\varepsilon N$ only if $M = N$

There is a simple sufficient condition for these properties. Let ε be a set of equations defining a canonical AGRS.

1. $\forall \tau$ such that $\tau \in \mathscr{D} \wedge In(\tau) \subset \mathscr{GC}$, τ is reducible
2. $\forall \lambda$ such that $\lambda \Rightarrow \rho$, $\lambda \notin \mathscr{C}$

7.6.3 Well-Founded Set

A set of AGRS terms should be a *well-founded set* to hold the noetherian property. There are several kinds of ordering to make well-founded sets [8]. Here we will show an extension of the *generalized recursive path ordering method* which is easy for AGRS to extend.

First, we define a well-founded ordering '$\overset{\cdot}{\gg}$' over variables in arbitrary AGRS terms as follows. Here we assume a partial order relation '$>$' over the set of functions of the AGRS. We denote simple AGRS terms by τ and σ. Variables φ and ψ have a relation $\varphi \overset{\cdot}{>} \psi$, which means that the disjunction of the following four conditions (31) holds:

$$\text{if } \varphi \in out(\tau), \psi \in out(\sigma) \begin{cases} in(\tau) \overset{\cdot}{\gg} in(\sigma) & (function(\tau) = function(\sigma)) \\ \varphi \overset{\cdot}{\gg} in(\sigma) & (function(\tau) > function(\sigma)) \\ in(\tau) \overset{\cdot}{\underset{\approx}{\gg}} \psi & (function(\tau) \not\geq function(\sigma)) \end{cases} \quad (31)$$

else $in(\tau) \ni \phi$

Now, we define a well-founded relation '$\overset{*}{\gg}$' between two arbitrary AGRS terms λ and ρ as the multiset ordering between $Out(\lambda)$ and $Out(\rho)$.

7.6.4 Result of the Completion Algorithm

This algorithm results in one of following possibilities:

1. Stop with success; we get a canonical AGRS.
2. Stop with disproof.
3. Stop with failure; either the ordering '>' is inadequate or this system does not have termination.
4. Run forever, generating infinite AGRS rewriting rules.

7.7 Applications of AGRS for AG

The main purpose of developing AGRS is to make another computation model of the language AG. The new model has advantages in the aspects of evaluation and verification.

An Evaluator, or interpreter, based on AGRS evaluates AG programs lazily, partially, and symbolically, even if they are not completely specified. The Evaluator avoids copying redundant objects, which is one of the major problems of functional programming, especially with systems based on attribute grammar [20].

A completion algorithm of AGRS may solve the problem of whether two program modules in AG are consistent or not. This is a kind of verification system, because one of two program modules is considered as the specification, or the assertion, of the other. We need not learn any other languages to write down a specification.

7.7.1 Translating AG into AGRS

Obviously, simple modules and composite modules in AG can directly be translated into rules in AGRS. For example, the result of translation of the composite module *incdec*, shown as program (4), is the rewriting rule (25).

When there are '**switch**' modules in the program, conditional parts of them should be eliminated. Also, we eliminate selectors of them if necessary.

7.7.1.1 Eliminating Conditions and Selectors

As in Sect. 7.2, we use an auxiliary function to eliminate a condition of each module. The input to an auxiliary function has two parts. The first is the same as the inputs of an original function. The second takes the output of a function which tests the given condition. Here is the example program (4) used in Sect. 7.4 again. This program can be translated into three rules, as in Fig. 7.8. Then, these rules can be translated into rules without constructors, as in Fig. 7.9.

```
define dec =
   module (in | out)
      switch
         case in == 0
            zero ( | out)
         otherwise
            pred (in | out)
      end
   end
```

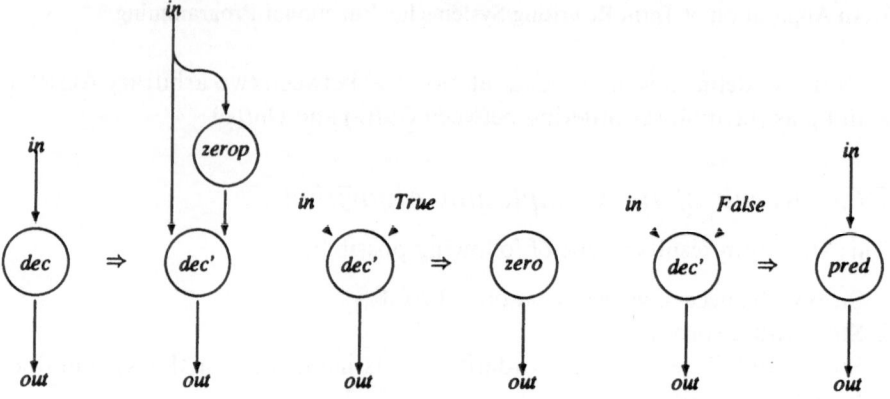

FIG. 7.8. Eliminating conditions

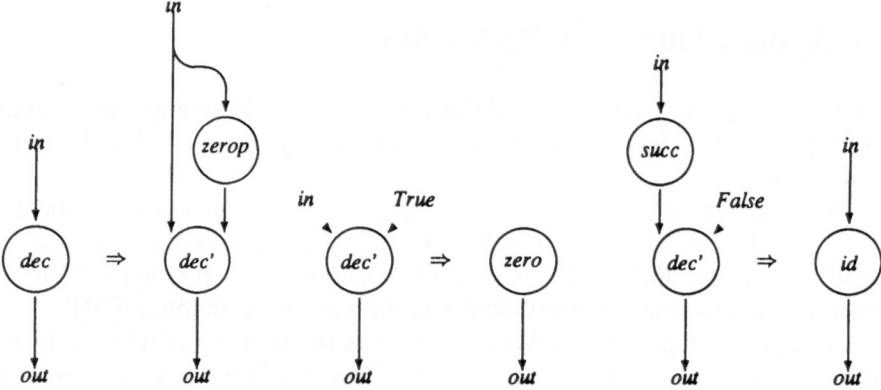

FIG. 7.9. Eliminating selectors

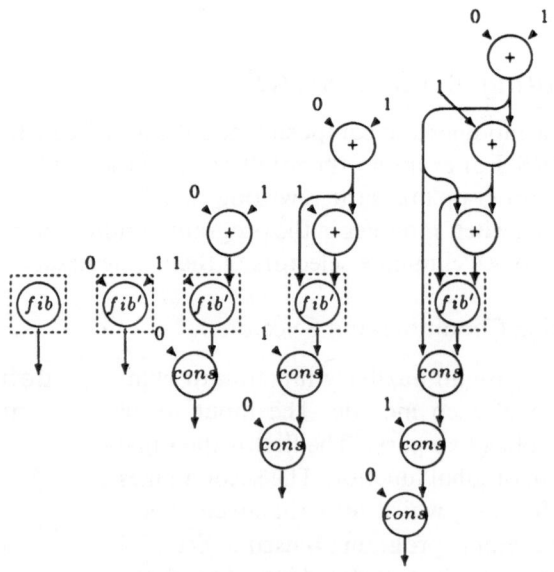

FIG. 7.10. Infinite evaluation of *fib*

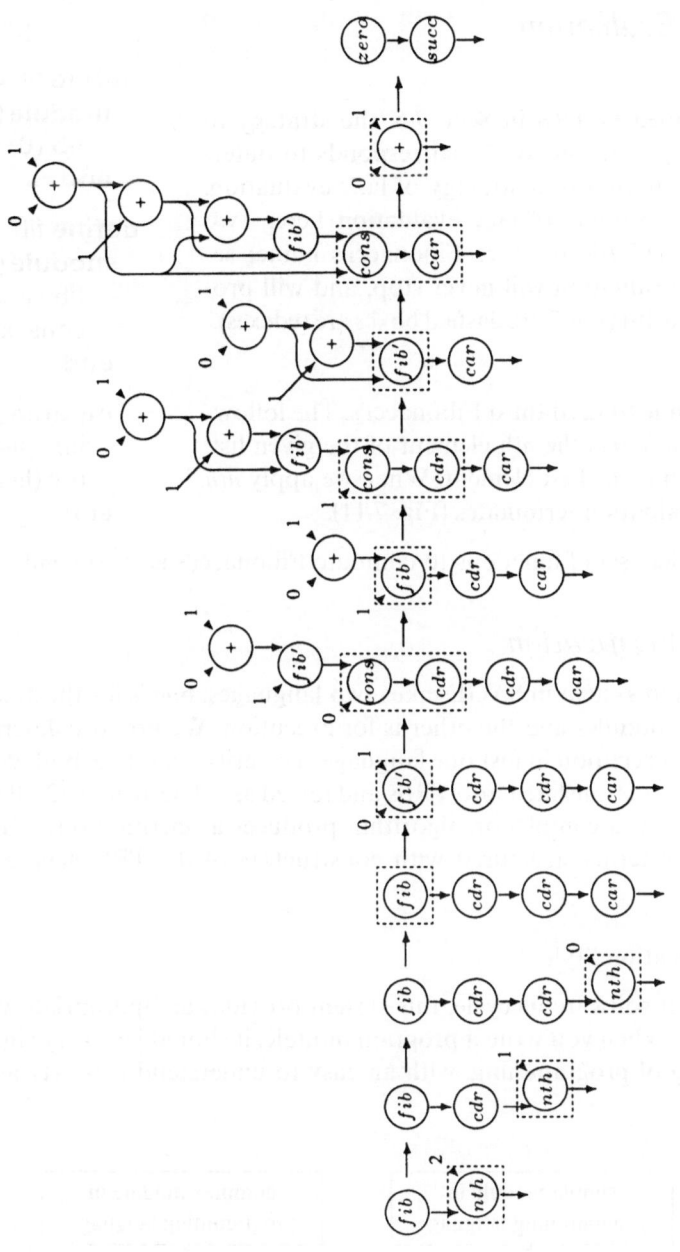

Fig. 7.11. Evaluation of *fib* with *nth*

7.7.2 *AG Evaluation*

As we described in TRS in Sect. 7.5, the strategy to rewrite exiting redex in AGRS corresponds to outermost reduction, that is, a strategy of lazy evaluation. We show an example of lazy evaluation here. Two modules *fib* and *fib'* produce Fibonacci's numer sequence. The evaluation will never stop, and will produce an infinite list (Fig. 7.10, dashed boxes are redexes).

Here we assume to need third Fibonacci's. The following function *nth* gets the *n*th element of the given list. Note that 0'th is the first element. When we apply *nth* to *fib*, the evaluation terminates (Fig. 7.11).

```
define fib =
  module(|out)
    fib'(0, 1|out)
  end

define fib' =
  module(x, y|out)
    fib'(y, x + y|tmp)
    cons(x, tmp|out)
  end

module(|out)
  fib'(|list)
  nth(list, 2|out)
end
```

The complete set of functions to compute Fibonacci's is in Appendix A.

7.7.3 *AG Verification*

The verification system in SAGE takes two languages: one is for the description of properties of modules and the other is for execution. We propose describing both assertion and execution in just one language. To verify a module, both descriptions of the module are translated into TRSs and mixed as a TRS (Fig. 7.12). If it contains an inconsistency, a completion algorithm produces a rewriting rule which breaks the domain of terms structured with constructors of the TRS, such as $1 \Rightarrow 0$ or $True \Rightarrow False$.

7.7.3.1 Verification Style

In the sense of software lifecycle, this system provides an appropriate verification environment. When you write a program module, it should be a very simple one at the beginning of programming, with an easy-to-understand property as an asser-

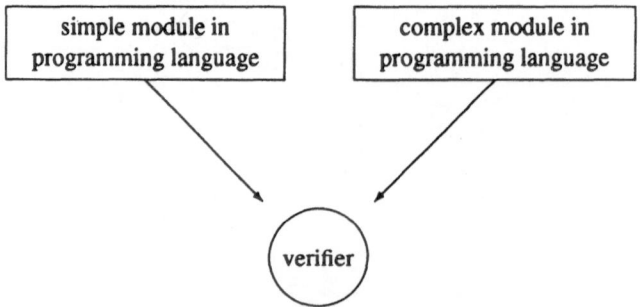

FIG. 7.12. Verification without an assertion language

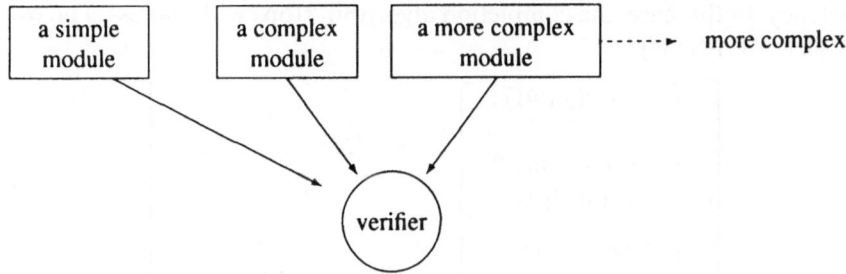

FIG. 7.13. A new verification style in SAGE

tion. Then, you will improve the program for execution efficiency. The verifier checks the consistency, i.e., equivalency, between the simplest module and the effective one. You can use the verifier at each step of the gradual modifications (Fig. 7.13).

7.7.3.2 Verification Example

Here is an AG program *mc*. An expression (32) defines *mc* which is modified from McCarthy's 91 function. Note that we do not use an inequality to avoid complication in the AG program.

$$mc = \begin{cases} x - 10 & (x \geq 10) \\ mc(mc(x + 11)) & (x < 10) \end{cases}$$

```
define mc =
  module(in|out)
    switch
      case in == 0
        ⋮
      case in == 9
        add(in, 11|tmp1)
        mc(tmp1|tmp2)
        mc(tmp2|out)
      otherwise                    (32)
        sub(in, 10|out)
    end
  end
```

```
define mc =
  module(in|out)
    switch
      case in == 0
        where out = 0
        ⋮
      case in == 9
        where out = 0
      otherwise
        sub(in, 10|out)
    end
  end
```

Soon we can guess *mc* is equal to a simpler module, as (33):

$$mc = \begin{cases} x - 10 & (x \geq 10) \\ 0 & (x < 10) \end{cases} \qquad (33)$$

Use the completion algorithm to verify that both programs are consistent. First we translate two AG programs into AGRS, and then, merge them and check the consistency. In this case, the completion algorithm stops with success. The result is a complete AGRS (34).

$$
\begin{bmatrix}
\left\{\begin{array}{c} succ(in|in1) \\ \vdots \\ succ(in9|in10) \\ mc(in10|out) \end{array}\right\} \Rightarrow \{identical(in|out)\} \\[3em]
\left\{\begin{array}{c} zero(|zero) \\ succ(zero|one) \\ mc(one|out) \end{array}\right\} \Rightarrow \{zero(|out)\} \\[3em]
\left\{\begin{array}{c} zero(|zero) \\ succ(zero|one) \\ \vdots \\ succ(eight|nine) \\ mc(nine|out) \end{array}\right\} \Rightarrow \{zero(|out)\}
\end{bmatrix} \qquad (34)
$$

Next, we intend to make a mistake to guess the nature of *mc*, as in (35):

$$
mc = \begin{cases} x - 10 & (x \geq 10) \\ 1 & (x < 10) \end{cases}
$$

```
define mc =
  module (in|out)
    switch
      case in == 0
        where out = 1
          ⋮
      case in == 9
        where out = 1          (35)
      otherwise
        sub (in, 10|out)
    end
end
```

The completion algorithm stops with failure, because the algorithm cannot make a rewriting rule that converges two AGRS constructor ground terms, such as rule (36).

$$
\{zero(|zero)\} \quad \overset{\Rightarrow}{\underset{\Leftarrow}{???}} \quad \left\{\begin{array}{c} zero(|zero) \\ succ(zero|one) \end{array}\right\} \qquad (36)
$$

7.8 Discussion

In this paper, we have shown an approach using TRSs for evaluation and verification of functional programs which are not based on TRSs originally. This method is based on the property of regular TRSs, the Knuth-Bendix completion algorithm, and the method of translating functional programs into TRSs. This approach is new, in the sense of applying TRSs to a language which already exists.

At first, we investigated properties of CTRSs, and transferred techniques for translating CTRSs to TRSs into the field of translation of functional programs to TRSs as the method of eliminating conditions from functional programs. Then, we developed AGRS as an extension of TRSs to adapt to the programming language AG. AGRS is one of the graph-rewriting systems on which we can define some properties the same as TRSs, such as confluency, termination, and a well-founded relation on AGRS terms. Therefore, AGRS provides an evaluator to support lazy and symbolic evaluation for AG programs. Also, AGRS makes the assertion language unnecessary for the verification of AG programs.

Some cases of conditions of programs are sufficient for translation, but other cases are not. An idea to extend the sufficient condition is to introduce types, or sorts, to TRSs.

Consider the next strictly typed program. This function takes an argument x which contains a natural number. If a function t also returns a natural number, this is translated into a left-linear TRS (37).

```
cardinal function f(x)
  cardinal x
begin
  if (x = t(x))
    return g(x)
  else
    return h(x)
end
```

$$f(x) \Rightarrow f'(x, =_{card}(x, t(x)))$$

$$f'(x, True) \Rightarrow g(x)$$

$$f'(x, False) \Rightarrow h(x)$$

$$=_{card}(0, 0) \Rightarrow True$$

$$=_{card}(succ(x), 0) \Rightarrow False$$

$$=_{card}(0, succ(y)) \Rightarrow False$$

$$=_{card}(succ(x), succ(y)) \Rightarrow =_{card}(x, y) \tag{37}$$

In this case, an equality on natural numbers is defined by explicit rules. The method in Sect. 7.3 uses lexicographical equality which is implicitly defined as pattern matching, which may break left-linearity.

The method of eliminating selectors is considered as reducing redundancy from a system, because we can describe rewriting rules without selectors instead of ones with selectors. Considering functionalities of selectors, there may be redundant function symbols, even if not selectors. In other words, functionalities of some function symbols must not be independent of others. We intend to generalize this method as the method of eliminating redundant function symbols.

AGRS is a son of TRSs and attribute grammar. A reduction step of AGRS means a substitution of a subtree in the absolutely noncircular attribute grammar. It is interesting to adapt TRSs to different classes of attribute grammar, such as the ordered attribute grammar. Although there must not be production rules which produce an infinite subtree in HFP, the semantics of AGRS allows that some of the rules may produce an infinite AGRS term. Infinite terms become an interesting field of TRSs [21].

We will start to implement AGRS and a small AG programming environment on it. AG is a language for general purposes, and we expect that this system will be an especially strong tool for process programming, because symbolic execution on AGRS is strong enough for that field.

Acknowledgments. We wish to thank many people. Masahiko Sakai gave us helpful comments, suggestions, and his implementation of TRS **Cdimple** [22]. Osamu Watanabe provided many chances for discussions with people engaged in the field of TRS. Anil Bhatia and Takeshi Hayama helped us proofread. Finally, we thank IBM for a chance to publish the results of our research.

References

1. Knuth DE, Bendix PB (1970) Simple word problems in universal algebras. In: Leech J (ed) Computational problems in abstract algebra. Pergamon, Toyohashi, Japan, pp 263–297
2. Huet G, Hullot JM (1982) Proofs by induction in equational theories with constructors. Comput Syst Sci 25(2): 239–266
3. Hsiang J (1985) Refutational theorem proving using term-rewriting systems. Artif Intell 25: 255–300
4. Comon H (1989) Inductive proofs by specification transformations. In: Dershowitz N (ed) Rewriting techniques and applications. Springer-Verlag, Chapel Hill pp 76–91. Proceedings, 3rd International Conference, RTA-89, Lecture Notes in Computer Science, 355
5. Shinoda Y. Katayama T (1988) Attribute grammar based programming and its environment. In: Proc 21st Hawaii International Conference on System Sciences, Kona, Hawaii pp 612–620
6. Knuth DE (1968) Semantics of context-free languages. Math Syst Theory 2(2): 127–145
7. Huet G (1980) Confluent reductions: abstract properties and applications to term rewriting systems. J ACM 27(4): 797–821
8. Dershowitz N (1985) Termination. In: Jouannaud J-P (ed) Rewriting techniques and applications. Springer-Verlag, pp 180–224. Lecture Notes in Computer Science, 202
9. Klop JW (1990) Term rewriting systems. In: ICALP. Springer-Verlag, pp 350–369. Lecture Notes in Computer Science
10. Bergstra JA, Klop JW (1986) Conditional rewrite rules: confluence and termination. J Comput Syst Sci 32: 323–362
11. Giovannetti E, Moiso C (1987) Notes on the elimination of conditions. In: Kaplan S, Jouannaud J-P (eds) Conditional term rewriting systems. Springer-Verlag, pp 91–97. Proceedings, 1st International Workshop, Orsay, France, Lecture Notes in Computer Science, 308
12. Baeten JCM, Bergstra JA, Klop JW, Weijland WP (1989) Term-rewriting systems with rule priorities. Theor Comput Sci 67: 283–301
13. Katayama T (1981) Hfp, a hierarchical and functional programming. In: Proc 5th International Conference on Software Engineering, pp 343–353
14. Reps T, Teitelbaum T (1985) The Synthesizer Generator reference manual. Department of Computer Science, Cornell University, Ithaca, New York
15. Reps TW (1984) Generating language-based environments. MIT Press, Massachusetts Institute of Technology, Cambridge, Massachusetts 02142

16. Reps T, Alpern B (1984) Interactive proof checking. In: Proc 11th ACM Symp Principles of Programming Languages

17. Lusk EL, Overbeek RA (1982) An LMA-based theorem prover. Mathematics and Computer Science Division ANL-82-75, Argonne National Laboratory, 9700 South Cass Avenue, Argonne, Illinois 60439

18. Lusk EL, McCrine WW, Overbeek RA (1982) Logic machine architecture: kernel functions. In: Lecture notes in computer science 138. Springer-Verlag, pp 70–108

19. Habel A, Kreowski H-J (1986) May we introduce to you: hyperedge replacement. In: Ehrig H, Nagl M, Rozenberg G, Rosenfeld A (eds) Graph-grammars and their application to computer science. Springer-Verlag, pp 15–29. Lecture Notes in Computer Science, 291

20. Katayama T, Sasaki N (1986) Global storage allocation in attribute evaluation. In: Proc 13th ACM Symp Principles of Programming Languages, pp 26–37

21. Dershowitz N (1990) Infinite rewriting. In: Proc Toyohashi Symposium on Theoretical Computer Science. Toyohashi, Japan, pp 27–31, August 1990

22. Sakai M, Sakabe T, Inagaki Y (1987) Direct implementation system of algebraic specifications of abstract data types (in Japanese). Comput Software 4(4): 16–27

Appendix A: Functions to Compute Fibonacci's Sequence

Here is a complete program to compute the nth term of Fibonacci's sequence, where the following AGRS rules hold on the constructor '*cons*' and the selectors '*car*' and '*cdr*':

$$\left\{ \begin{array}{c} cons(x, y | temp) \\ car(temp | z) \end{array} \right\} \Rightarrow \{ identical(x | out) \}$$

$$\left\{ \begin{array}{c} cons(x, y | temp) \\ cdr(temp | z) \end{array} \right\} \Rightarrow \{ identical(y | out) \}$$

```
define fib =
   module (|out)
      fib' (0, 1 |out)
   end
define fib' =
   module (x, y|out)
      fib' (y, x + y|tmp)
      cons (x, tmp|out)
   end
```

```
define nth =
   module (list, n|out)
      switch
         case n == 0
            car (list|out)
         otherwise
            cdr (list|tmp)
            nth (tmp, n − 1|out)
      end
   end
```

Appendix B: AGRS Completion Algorithm

The following is an algorithm to check consistency of AGRS:

$\mathscr{R} := \phi$;
$\mathscr{C} := \{ \text{Constructors in the AGRS} \}$;
$\mathscr{E} := \{ \text{Equations from AGRS rules by substitution '} \Rightarrow \text{' into '} = \text{'} \}$;

while $(\mathscr{E} \neq \varnothing)$ **do**
  chose a $\{\tau = \sigma\}$ from $\mathscr{E}$;
  $\mathscr{E} := \mathscr{E} - \{\tau = \sigma\}$;
  compute $\tau \downarrow$, $\sigma \downarrow$ by $\mathscr{R}$;
  if $(\tau \downarrow \equiv \sigma \downarrow)$ **continue**
  elseif (there exists ρ such that $\rho \in \mathscr{C} \cap Out(\tau \downarrow)$)
    if $(out(\rho) = out(\lambda) \wedge \rho = \lambda)$ $\mathscr{E} := \mathscr{E} \cup \{(\tau \downarrow - \rho) = (\sigma \downarrow - \lambda)\}$;
                                                    continue
    elseif $(out(\rho) = out(\lambda) \wedge \lambda \in \mathscr{C})$ **stop** (disproof)
    elseif $(\tau \downarrow \prec \sigma \downarrow)$ $t_{left} := \sigma \downarrow$; $t_{right} := \tau \downarrow$
    else   **stop** (failure)
    endif
  elseif (there exists λ such that $\lambda \in \mathscr{C} \cap Out(\sigma \downarrow)$)
    if $(\tau \downarrow \succ \sigma \downarrow)$ $t_{left} := \tau \downarrow$; $t_{right} := \sigma \downarrow$
    else   **stop** (failure)
    endif
  elseif $(\tau \downarrow \succ \sigma \downarrow)$ $t_{left} := \tau \downarrow$; $t_{right} := \sigma \downarrow$
  elseif $(\tau \downarrow \prec \sigma \downarrow)$ $t_{left} := \sigma \downarrow$; $t_{right} := \tau \downarrow$
  else   **stop** (failure)
  endif;
  $\mathscr{R}' := \{\tau' \Rightarrow \sigma' \in \mathscr{R} | \tau'$ is able to replace $t_{left} \Rightarrow t_{right}\}$;
  $\mathscr{R} := (\mathscr{R} - \mathscr{R}') \cup \{t_{left} \Rightarrow t_{right}\}$;
  $\mathscr{E} := \mathscr{E} \cup \{\tau' = \sigma' | \tau' \Rightarrow \sigma' \in \mathscr{R}'\} \cup \{p = q | \langle p, q \rangle$ is a critical pair of $\mathscr{R}\}$
endwhile
stop (success)

8
A Qualitative Quantitative Simulator Based on Constraint Logic Programming

Hayato Ohwada and Fumio Mizoguchi[1]

Summary: Incorporating quantitative information into qualitative reasoning is a key problem for predicting and explaining the causal mechanisms of actual physical systems. In this article, we propose a framework for designing qualitative reasoning systems based on constraint logic programming. The basic idea of the framework is to amalgamate qualitative and quantitative knowledge about the domain model within a unified framework of constraint logic programming. This amalgamation can be achieved naturally by the underlying constraint solver that deals with partial ordering relations on the qualitative knowledge. Consequently, complex inference mechanisms such as maintaining the ordering relations and solving numerical constraints are committed to the constraint solver.

The resulting system, called QQS (Qualitative Quantitative Simulator) has novel features. First, QQS produces possible qualitative behaviors that match given numerical data. Second, two behaviors produced by different perturbations are comparable for desired analyses. Third, QQS obtains qualitative descriptions that correspond to the interpretations of numerical data. Since these facilities are provided within a constraint-oriented programming environment, QQS supports an interactive simulation laboratory for practical engineering applications.

Key words: Qualitative reasoning — constraint logic programming — engineering task — interactive simulation laboratory

8.1 Introduction

We have tried to explore a novel application of constraint logic programming (CLP) to qualitative reasoning which is the most useful approach to designing expert systems through the underlying first principles of a physical system [1]. In qualitative reasoning, a physical system is modeled as a set of constraints that express qualitative relations among time-varying parameters. Here, the meaning of "quali-

---

[1] Department of Industrial Administration and Intelligent System Laboratory, Science University of Tokyo, Noda, Chiba, 278 Japan

tative" comes from not requiring exact values of parameters for problem solving; inexact or estimated values are useful for obtaining qualitatively reasonable solutions in order to perform engineering tasks such as modeling, prediction, explanation, and interpretation of the physical system. Therefore, constraint solving on the qualitative relations has been one of the key concepts of qualitative reasoning in recent applied artificial intelligence paradigms. However, there has been no trial of the application of CLP to qualitative reasoning, which implies that this is a novel aspect of CLP application.

In this article, we propose a framework for designing qualitative reasoning systems based on CLP. This framework aims to provide a means of improving existing qualitative reasoners toward real world applications. For this purpose, we have developed the CLP language Triton, which was written in several Prolog systems on a UNIX workstation. The constraint solver of Triton deals with partial ordering relations among parameters [2, 3]. Therefore, complex inference mechanisms such as maintaining the ordering relations and solving numerical constraints are embedded within Triton.

The paper is organized as follows. First, the basic idea of building a qualitative reasoner in a CLP framework is described. Next, we present a constraint logic program of qualitative simulation, which produces possible qualitative behaviors of a physical system. Then, the powerful qualitative reasoner called Qualitative Quantitative Simulator (QQS) is incrementally designed without changing the original program shown in the previous section. Finally, we show that QQS supports an interactive simulation laboratory by exploiting the declarative power of CLP.

8.2 Basic Framework

We start by describing advantages of the CLP approach to qualitative reasoning.

1. *There is no distinction in description of qualitative and quantitative knowledge in CLP.* Most qualitative knowledge is in the form of partial ordering relations among parameters whose values are unspecified. In Triton, such a relation is expressed as "$X > Y$" where the variables X and Y are not instantiated to real numbers. The constraint solver of Triton automatically maintains the relation, whether the variables are instantiated or not. Thus, the CLP approach provides a unified description of knowledge about the underlying domain model.
2. *Managing quantity space is committed to the constraint solver.* In a quantity space consisting of parameter values that form a partial order, ordering relations are dynamically added over time. In order to manage the quantity space, quantity management techniques have been developed (for example, [4]). However, these techniques can be regarded as symbolic manipulation, so that they do not have a clear semantics for programming languages. In our approach, the constraint solver seeks consistency among the orderings in a CLP framework. Moreover, our constraint solver efficiently solves an equality by unification, while the previous techniques handle the equality as an ordering which must be maintained as well as inequalities.

3. *CLP supports what-if type of inference.* A constraint must be satisfied bidirectionally by the constraint solver. Since there is no input-output distinction between variables in the constraint, a *what-if* type of inference can be provided by a single CLP program. In addition, arbitrary constraints that specify the initial condition in a desired situation can be easily added into a query. Suppose that a block connecting to a spring increases the mass. If we want to simulate the behavior of the system in this situation, it is sufficient to give the goal $M > M'$ where M is the mass of the block over time and M' is the mass of the block over a distinct time period. Such a type of simulation will be described in Sect. 8.4.

4. *Different tasks in qualitative reasoning are performed within a single CLP program.* Suppose that measurement data of a system are given and we consider two qualitative reasoning tasks: simulation and interpretation. In this case, simulation corresponds to predicting behaviors that match the measurement data, while interpretation corresponds to producing qualitative descriptions of behaviors from the data. The two tasks are essentially the same; the only difference is due to the priority of performing each task. In CLP, this difference is easily made by changing the orderings of goals concerned with the tasks. Therefore, CLP provides a unified framework for performing qualitative reasoning tasks by means of the declarative character of logic programming.

5. *Constraint solving supports a means of efficient implementation.* Constraints in qualitative simulation play a role of pruning irrelevant behaviors about the system. The constraint solver seeks consistency whenever behaviors are produced. For this purpose, Triton adopts the constraint simplification mechanism which is the transformation from a set of constraints to a more simplified constraint set. This mechanism represents an active use of constraints. It is also used for implementing coroutine computation, described in Sect. 8.3.

Before describing qualitative reasoning programs having these features, we must give the CLP structure for designing Triton. The CLP scheme allows the design of various CLP languages according to given structures [5]. The proposed structure is suitable for qualitative reasoning.

Here, we introduce terminologies of qualitative reasoning in order to design the CLP structure. In general, a qualitative model consists of time-varying parameters. Each parameter has a state over an instant or a time interval. A state is specified by two components: one is the value of the parameter, and the other indicates the direction of change, that is, the derivative of the parameter. Since a parameter is regarded as a function of time, we denote the value of the parameter as follows:

$$\text{Parameter} \# \text{TemporalTerm}$$

where TemporalTerm represents either an instant or a time interval. Similarly, the derivative of the parameter is represented as:

$$\text{Parameter} @ \text{TemporalTerm}.$$

For example, the value of the position over time T is described as

$$\text{pos} \# T$$

where pos is a function for getting the state of the position.

A temporal term T has a number of parameters and their states over T. Thus, the temporal term T is formulated as follows:

$$T = \{ (parameter, Val, Dir) \,|\, Val = parameter \# T, Dir = parameter@T\}$$

Note that parameters in a temporal term are not fixed. They are dynamically added during the unification process between temporal terms, to be discussed.

It is convenient to prepare predefined predicates and functions for temporal terms. Such predicates are instant (TemporalTerm) and interval (TemporalTerm) for checking whether the temporal term is instant or interval. The function time (Instant) is built-in for getting an actual time. The functions start(Interval) and end(Interval) are used for getting the start and the end point of Interval. The function duration(Interval) = end(Interval)-start(Interval) is also predefined.

By extending Prolog according to this formulation, the CLP structure for qualitative reasoning is defined as follows:

- The domain is the union of Herbrand Universe, real numbers, and a set of temporal terms.
- The functions are the union of uninterpreted functors, arithmetic functions, temporal parameters, and a set of predefined temporal functions.
- The relations are $\{ =, \neq, <, \leq, \text{instant, interval}\}$.

Simple queries in Triton are:

$$?- X> =0, Y> =0, Z> =0, X+Y=Z, X*Y>0.$$
yes

$$?- force \# T = mass \# T * acc \# T.$$
yes

The first query indicates that Triton can handle linear equalities and inequalities. It may also solve some nonlinear inequalities when the upper or lower bounds of variables are bound to numerical values. This capability is useful for maintaining partial ordering relations in quantity space. The second query shows temporal notations. This formula corresponds to the equation $F = M*A$.

Solving arithmetic constraints is performed by the two constraint solvers: the equation solver and the inequation solver. The equation solver transforms a set of linear equations to a solved form of the original set. The solved form is a set of equations in which the left-hand sides of the equations are all distinct variables that never appear in the right-hand sides. These variables are called eliminated variables. To obtain the solved form, we use the rules: *variable elimination, tree rewriting, equation anteposition,* and *back substitution* [2]. After solving equations, the inequation solver checks the consistency of a set of inequations that have no eliminated variables. The algorithm is based on the SUP-INF method which calculates greatest lower bounds and least upper bounds for each variable [6]. We have extended the method in order to handle some nonlinear inequalities.

Unification between temporal terms is similar to that of CIL [7]. It is provided by the rule: if there exists the same parameter within the terms, unify the states of the parameters; otherwise, add the pair (parameter, val, dir) to the term which does not include the pair. This rule indicates that we do not need to pre-enumerate the parameters. We can incrementally add parameters during the simulation process. This facility is also useful for combining several physical objects and creating composite objects easily.

8.3 Architecture of Qualitative Simulation

Using this CLP structure, this section outlines a constraint logic program of qualitative simulation. This program is used for making qualitative reasoning more powerful, in the next section.

In general, qualitative simulation is governed by two rules. The first rule is concerned with interstate relations. This rule produces possible state transitions of a parameter at the next time point. The other rule is concerned with intrastate relations. It determines relevant states of the parameters at the same time. We implement the rules one by one, then combine them.

8.3.1 The Definition of State Transitions

In logic programming, rules of the form

$$A :- B_1, B_2, \ldots, B_n$$

are interpreted as procedures

$$\text{to do A, do } B_1 \text{ and so } B_2 \text{ and } \ldots \text{ do } B_n$$

This interpretation provides backward reasoning. In contrast, simulation is based on forward reasoning, and therefore the rule

$$p(T0) :- p(T1)$$

is interpreted as the statement

$$\text{given the state } p(T0), \text{ the state } p(T1) \text{ holds}$$

where T1 is the next time after T0. Based on this interpretation, state transitions are described by the rule

$$\begin{aligned}
qs\,(P, T0) :- &\; T0 < T1, \\
&\; state\_transition\,(P \# T0, P@T0, P \# T1, P@T1), \\
&\; qs\,(P, T1).
\end{aligned}$$

where the predicate state_transition generates a state at the next time. Given an initial state of the parameter p as the goal qs(p, T0), the latter rule produces an infinite sequence of state transitions. A method for preventing the infinite sequence will be described later.

Now we show the definition of state transitions in qualitative simulation. Since qualitative simulation proceeds by repeating the cycle between instant and time interval, we define two state transition rules:

```
qs (P, T) :— instant (T), !,
            start (I) = T,
            p_transition (P # T, P@T, P # I, P@I),
            qs (P, I).

qs (P, I) :— interval (I), !,
            end (I) = T,
            i_transition (P # I, P@I, P # T, P@T),
            qs (P, T).
```

where the predicate p_transition specifies the transition from an instant to an interval, and the predicate i_transition does vice versa. Note that these predicates have a nondeterministic nature which is the unique feature of qualitative simulation. This nondeterminism is due to predicting qualitatively possible states at the next time. For example, part of the definition of i_transition is as follows:

```
i_transition (in (L_i, L_{i+1}), D0, at (L_{i+1}), D1)        :— D0 > 0, D1 = 0.
i_transition (in (L_i, L_{i+1}), D0, at (L_{i+1}), D1)        :— D0 > 0, D1 > 0.
i_transition (in (L_i, L_{i+1}), D0, in (L_i, L_{i+1}), D1)   :— D0 > 0, D1 > 0.
```

where L_{i+1} denotes an adjacent landmark value that is greater than L_i, in (L_i, L_{i+1}) means the parameter value is on the interval between L_i and L_{i+1}, and at (L_i) means the value is just L_i. Note that landmark values are meaningful values for characterizing the behavior of a system.

This definition indicates possible transitions when the parameter is increasing on the interval. It is given by the condition that the parameter is continuously differentiable. The detailed explanation can be seen in [8].

8.3.2 The Definition of Constraints Among Parameters

A set of constraints among parameters is regarded as the qualitative version of a differential equation. Since the constraints must be satisfied all the time, they are described as the form

$$\forall t \text{ constraint } (p_1(t), p_2(t), \dots, p_n(t))$$

For example, a spring system is modeled as follows:

$$\forall t, \text{deriv}(\text{pos}(t), \text{vel}(t)) \wedge \text{deriv}(\text{vel}(t), \text{acc}(t)) \wedge m - (\text{acc}(t), \text{pos}(t))$$

where the constraint deriv (X, Y) means Y is the derivative of X, and the constraint m − (X, Y) specifies that the relation between X and Y is monotonically decreasing.

A general rule of constraints is of the form

```
constraint ([ ]).
constraint ([T|Ts], F_1, F_2, ..., F_n) :—
    satisfy_constraint (F_1 # T, ..., F_n # T, F_1@T, ..., F_n@T),
    constraint (Ts, F_1, F_2, ..., F_n).
```

The first argument of the predicate constraint is bound to a time sequence. Thus, the constraint satisfier performed by the goal satisfy_constraint maintains consistency among the states of the parameters each time within this recursive definition.

One of the constraint satisfiers is:

```
mon_decrease([], _, _).
mon_decrease([T|Ts], X, Y) :-
    opposite_sign(X#T, Y#T),
    opposite_sign(X@T, Y@T),
    mon_decrease(Ts, X, Y).

opposite_sign(S1, S2) :- S1 > 0, S2 < 0.
opposite_sign(S1, S2) :- S1 = 0, S2 = 0.
opposite_sign(S1, S2) :- S1 < 0, S2 > 0.
```

The constraint satisfier checks consistency even when the states of the parameters are not instantiated to numerical values. This facility indicates that qualitative constraints are naturally expressed within a CLP framework and quantity management is committed to the constraint solver of Triton. We do not need to prepare a special constraint solver for the qualitative constraints.

8.3.3 Synchronization of State Transitions and Constraint Satisfaction

The rules of state transitions and constraint satisfaction mentioned in Sects. 8.3.1 and 8.3.2 are not cooperative. Now, we provide a coroutine computation for synchronizing these rules. For this purpose, we use the extended control facility, namely the delay mechanism. This mechanism has been provided in Prolog-II [9]. In Triton, the facility is given within the goal p (X?) whose execution is delayed until the variable X is instantiated.

By using the facility, the constraint satisfier mon_decrease is rewritten into the form

```
mon_decrease([], _, _).
mon_decrease([T|Ts], X, Y) :-
    opposite_sign(X#T, Y#T),
    opposite_sign(X@T, Y@T),
    mon_decrease(Ts?, X, Y).
```

The constraint satisfier is never invoked until the first argument is bound to a temporal sequence.

Similarly, the rule of state transitions is rewritten into the form

```
qs([T, I|Ts], P) :- instant(T), !,
    p_transition(P#T, P@T, P#I, P@I),
    qs([I|Ts?], P).
qs([I, T|Ts], P) :- interval(I), !,
    i_transition(P#I, P@I, P#T, P@T),
    qs([T|Ts?], P).
```

where the first argument of the predicate qs is bound to the same time sequence as the constraint satisfier. Note that this definition does not include the declaration of temporal terms. The declaration is performed by another goal.

We combine these two rules as the representation of a qualitative model. For example, the spring system is represented by the following rule:

```
spring (Ts) :−
    deriv (Ts, pos, vel),
    deriv (Ts, vel, acc),
    mon_decrease (Ts, acc, pos),
    qs (Ts, pos),
    qs (Ts, vel),
    qs (Ts, acc).
```

Given a time sequence, the goal spring(Ts) produces a behavior by using both the state transition rule and the constraint satisfier.

On the other hand, the time sequence is constructed by the rule

```
simulate ( [T|Ts] ) :− halting_condition (T), !.
simulate ( [T|Ts] ) :−
    instant (T), start (I) = T, Ts = [I|_],
    simulate (Ts).
simulate ( [I|Ts] ) :−
    interval (I), end (I) = T, Ts = [T|_],
    simulate (Ts).
```

The goal halting_condition (T) checks whether simulation should stop or is not based on a certain rule.

Suppose that the initial position of the block connected to the spring is positive and the velocity of the block is zero. This situation is specified as the query

$$? - \text{instant}(T), \text{pos} \# T > 0, \text{pos@}T = 0, \text{spring}([T|Ts]). \qquad (Q1)$$

Then qualitative simulation is performed with the posing of the query

$$? - \text{simulate}([T|Ts]). \qquad (Q2)$$

The simulation result is obtained by the query

$$\begin{aligned} ? - &\text{Ts} = [T1, T2, \ldots], \\ &\text{pos} \# T1 = \text{Pos1}, \text{pos} \# T2 = \text{Pos2}, \ldots, \qquad (Q3) \\ &\text{vel} \# T1 = \text{Vel1}, \text{vel} \# T2 = \text{Vel2}, \ldots \end{aligned}$$

Note that the queries Q1, Q2, and Q3 are incrementally added and variables within them are treated as global. These incremental queries provide the basis for building a user-interface, as mentioned in Sect. 8.5.

8.4 QQS: A Qualitative Quantitative Simulator

This section describes a qualitative quantitative simulator, called QQS, which demonstrates the advantages of the CLP approach mentioned in Sect. 8.2. QQS is implemented by incorporating additional rules into the program described in the previous section. Figure 8.1 shows the input and output of QQS. QQS manipulates

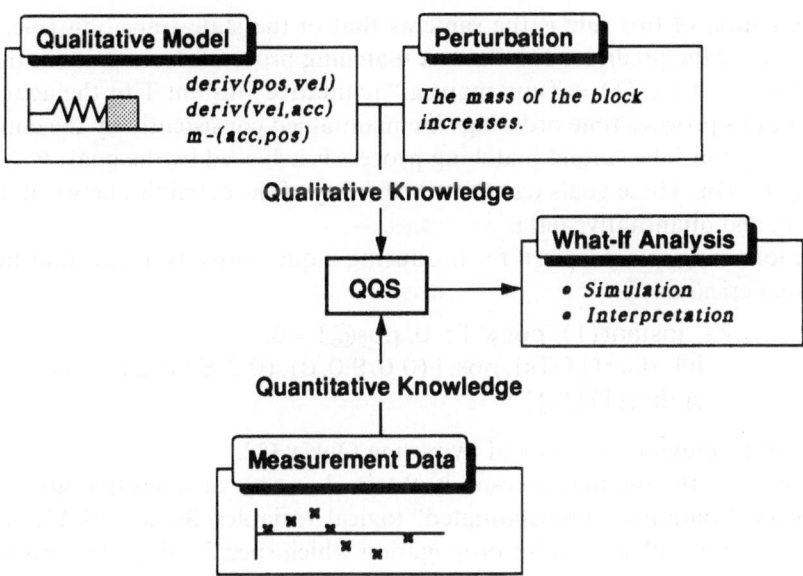

FIG. 8.1. The input and output of QQS

both qualitative and quantitative knowledge within a unified framework of CLP. This framework also supports *what-if* analysis by means of the computational and expressive power of CLP.

8.4.1 *Dealing with Quantitative Data*

It is important for performing engineering tasks to deal with quantitative data as well as qualitative data. Quantitative data indicate samples of the behavior over time. Thus, the actual behavior is given as a set of sample states of the form

$$(\text{Time, Val, Dir})$$

where Time is an observation time, Val is the value of the parameter, and Dir is the derivative of the parameter.

A qualitative behavior matching quantitative data is easily found through unification between logical variables and numerical data. The following rule unifies a qualitative description with given numerical data.

```
fill_data (_, _, [ ]).
fill_data ( [T|Ts], P, [ (Time, Val, Dir)|Data] ) :–
    time (T) = Time,
    P # T = Val,
    P @ T = Dir,
    fill_data (Ts?, P, Data).
fill_data ( [T|Ts], P, Data) :–
    fill_data (Ts?, P, Data).
```

The execution of this rule is the same as that of the state transition rule, and is controlled by the predicate simulate. A matching process occurs twice in this rule. First, the goal time (T) = Time maps a "qualitative" instant T to the actual time Time. In this process, time orderings are maintained consistently by the constraint solver of Triton. The second matching process is achieved by the goals $P \# T = Val$ and $P@T = Dir$. These goals test the satisfiability of the equalities between qualitative data and quantitative data.

The following query is used for producing a qualitative behavior that matches given numerical data.

$$?- \text{instant}(T), \text{pos} \# T > 0, \text{pos}@T = 0,$$
$$\text{fill\_data}([T|Ts], \text{pos}, [(0.0, 9.0, 0), (0.2, 5.96, \_), \dots]),$$
$$\text{spring}([T|Ts]). \qquad (Q4)$$

Qualitative simulation is invoked by posing Query Q2.

In this case, the simulation result is obtained as a set of states that are mixtures of numerical data and "uninstantiated" logical variables. Some variables may be instantiated through constraint propagation which specifies data flow from determined values to underdetermined values. The difference between quantitative and qualitative representation is whether logical variables are instantiated or not. This kind of representation is based on the standard mathematical treatment, and therefore mapping between quantitative and qualitative knowledge is straightforward. Such a facility cannot be permitted in the programming languages not amenable to CLP.

8.4.2 Differential Quantitative Analysis

Comparing two behaviors under different perturbations is an important task of qualitative reasoning. Differential quantitative analysis is a technique for solving the task [10]. This technique consists of rules that are used for explaining behaviors produced by qualitative simulation. We show that the same facility can be established within qualitative simulation.

In order to perform differential quantitative analysis, the model of the spring system connected to the block is modified as follows:

```
spring (Ts):-
    deriv(Ts, pos, vel),
    deriv(Ts, vel, acc),
    mult(Ts, mass, acc, force),
    mult(Ts, k, pos, force),
    constant(Ts, mass, positive),
    constant(Ts, k, negative),
    qs(Ts, pos),
    qs(Ts, vel),
    qs(Ts, acc),
    qs(Ts, mass),
    qs(Ts, k),
    qs(Ts, force).
```

where the predicate mult represents the multiplication constraint, and the predicate constant specifies that the parameter takes a fixed value over time.

The problem is to predict the behavior when the mass of the block is increased. Unlike the previous examples, this initial condition cannot be given as queries, because the condition indicates that there exist two spring systems having different masses. One treatment for this difficulty is to prepare two spring systems that have different initial conditions and to compare those behaviors. In this case, the initial condition is substituted with the conditions that the mass of the block in one spring system is M0 and the mass of the block in the other system is M1 where M0 < M1.

However, our program cannot represent different spring systems. Nevertheless, we can treat them by isolating each from the other with respect to time. In this treatment, two time sequences keep the behaviors of the systems.

Comparison of behaviors is performed within each parameter. The following rule helps in comparing the behaviors of two parameters:

```
compare([T1,I1|T1s], [T2,I2|T2s], P) :-
    instant(T1), instant(T2),
    P#T1 = P#T2,
    P@T1 = D1,
    P@T2 = D2,
    P#I1 = V1,
    P#I2 = V2,
    ( 0 < D1, D1 < D2, duration_rule(T1, I1, T2, I2, V1, V2) ;
      0 < D2, D2 < D1, duration_rule(T2, I2, T1, I1, V2, V1) ;
      true ),
    compare([I1|T1s?], [I2|T2s?], P).
```

where the first and second arguments of the predicate compare take different time sequences.

The main feature of differential quantitative analysis is to find the relative changes of parameters. For example, if the change rate is slower in the other system, it will take a longer time to reach the same landmark value. Therefore, two behaviors are comparable only when the values of the two parameters are the same. The latter rule applies to this case.

The rule duration_rule provides differential quantitative analysis. Two cases are shown:

```
duration_rule(T1, I1, T2, I2, V, V) :-
    ( interval(I1), interval(I2),
        duration(I1) > duration(I2) ;
      interval(T1), interval(T2),
        duration(T1) > duration(T2) ).
duration_rule(T1, I1, T2, I2, V1, V2) :-
    ( interval(I1), interval(I2),
        duration(I1) = duration(I2) ;
      interval(T1), interval(T2),
        duration(T1) = duration(T2) ),
    V1 < V2.
```

These two rules correspond to the following two cases respectively:

1. If the values at the next time are equal and the first system has the smaller derivative of the parameter, then the first system takes a longer time to change the state.
2. If the systems take the same time to change their states and the first system has the smaller derivative of the parameter, then the first system has the greater values at the next time.

To begin with, we declare two spring systems through the query

$$?- \text{instant}(T1), \text{pos}\#T1 > 0, \text{pos@T1} = 0,$$
$$\text{spring}([T1|T1s]),$$
$$\text{instant}(T2), \text{pos}\#T1 = \text{pos}\#T2, \text{pos@T2} = 0,$$
$$\text{spring}([T2|T2s]),$$
$$k\#T1 = k\#T2. \qquad (Q5)$$

The initial condition is given by the constraint

$$?- \text{mass}\#T1 > \text{mass}\#T2. \qquad (Q6)$$

To compare the behaviors of the systems, we invoke the goals that compare values of each parameter:

$$?- \text{compare}([T1|T1s], [T2|T2s], \text{pos}),$$
$$\text{compare}([T1|T1s], [T2|T2s], \text{vel}),$$
$$\text{compare}([T1|T1s], [T2|T2s], \text{acc}),$$
$$\text{compare}([T1|T1s], [T2|T2s], \text{mass}),$$
$$\text{compare}([T1|T1s], [T2|T2s], k),$$
$$\text{compare}([T1|T1s], [T2|T2s], \text{force}). \qquad (Q7)$$

Simulation starts by invoking the query

$$?- \text{simulate}([T1|T1s], [T2|T2s]) \qquad (Q8)$$

which constructs two time sequences at the same time.

Then we give the following condition:

$$?- T1s = [l1|\_], T2s = [l2|\_], \text{duration}(l1) = \text{duration}(l2). \qquad (Q9)$$

Condition Q9 indicates that the two systems take the same length of time-interval to change their states at the next time. Clearly, the condition follows the constraint propagation

$$\text{pos}\#T1 = \text{pos}\#T2, k\#T1 = k\#T2, \text{mass}\#T1 > \text{mass}\#T2$$
$$\downarrow \qquad \qquad \text{by mult}(Ts, k, \text{pos}, \text{force})$$
$$\text{force}\#T1 = \text{force}\#T2$$
$$\downarrow \qquad \qquad \text{by mult}(Ts, \text{mass}, \text{acc}, \text{force})$$
$$\text{acc}\#T1 < \text{acc}\#T2$$
$$\downarrow \qquad \qquad \text{by duration}(l1) = \text{duration}(l2)$$
$$\text{vel}\#l1 < \text{vel}\#l2$$

Suppose that we want to confirm the fact $\text{vel}\#l1 < \text{vel}\#l2$. The query

$$?- \text{vel} \# l1 < \text{vel} \# l2 \qquad (Q10)$$

is not adequate because our constraint solver is based on the active use of constraints; this query would be satisfied unless it is inconsistent. However, this problem is easily solved by introducing the rule

$$\text{provable}(C) :- \text{not}(\sim C). \qquad (R1)$$

where $\sim C$ represents, the complement of the constraint C and the predicate not provides negation by the failure rule. For example, the query

$$?- \text{not}(\text{vel} \# l1 > = \text{vel} \# l2) \qquad (Q11)$$

can be used for checking the satisfiability of the constraint only. This is due to the fact that a constraint is already satisfied if there exists sufficient information to negate the complement of the constraint. In other words, Rule R1 for checking constraint satisfiability corresponds to detecting redundancy of the constraint C.

Using Rule R1, we can confirm the fact

$$\text{vel} \# l1 < \text{vel} \# l2$$

by the query

$$?- \text{provable}(\text{vel} \# l1 < \text{vel} \# l2). \qquad (Q12)$$

Next, we show a powerful what-if type of inference in CLP by changing the orderings of the queries. In this case, we change Queries Q9 and Q12 into

$$?- T1s = [l1|\_], T2s = [l2|\_], \text{vel} \# l1 < \text{vel} \# l2. \qquad (Q13)$$

$$?- \text{provable}(\text{duration}(l1) = \text{duration}(l2)). \qquad (Q14)$$

In CLP, arbitrary constraints can be added for simulating desired situations. We do not need to care about input-output relations among arguments or the orderings of constraints to be added. This feature is due to the declarative nature of CLP.

8.4.3 Interpretation of Measurement Data

Interpreting measurement data is required for applying qualitative reasoning to diagnosis. Diagnosis is to identify faults that are derived from observed data. These faults are found by comparing the normal behavior with an abnormal behavior. Here, these behaviors are given as measurement data as shown in Sect. 8.4.1. Thus, we produce the interpretation of measurement data by combining the facilities mentioned in Sect. 8.4.1 and 8.4.2. Furthermore, this interpretation is represented as constraints that indicate the difference between the normal and abnormal behaviors.

We pose the following query and Query Q9 for detecting the difference between data from two measurements.

$$?- \text{instant}(T1), \text{pos} \# T1 > 0, \text{pos} @ T1 = 0,$$
$$\text{fill\_data}([T1|T1s], \text{pos}, [(0.0, 9.0, \_), (0.2, 5.96, \_), \ldots]),$$
$$\text{spring}([T1|T1s]),$$

instant (T2), pos#T1 = pos#T2, pos@T2 = 0,
fill_data ([T2|T2s], pos, [(0.0, 9.0, _), (0.2, 6.82, _), ...]),
spring([T2|T2s]),
k#T1 = k#T2,
compare([T1|T1s], [T2|T2s], pos),
compare([T1|T1s], [T2|T2s], vel),
compare([T1|T1s], [T2|T2s], acc),
compare([T1|T1s], [T2|T2s], mass),
compare([T1|T1s], [T2|T2s], k),
compare([T1|T1s], [T2|T2s], force),
simulate([T1|T1s], [T2|T2s]).   (Q15)

Unlike the previous case in differential quantitative analysis, the initial condition

$$mass\#T1 > mass\#T2$$

is not given. However, these measurement data derive the following inference:

pos#end(l1) < pos#end(l2)
    ↓   by pos#T1 = pos#T2
pos#l1 < pos#l2
    ↓   by pos#T1 = pos#T2 and duration(l1) = duration(l2)
vel#l1 < vel#l2
    ↓   by vel#T1 = vel#T2 and duration(l1) = duration(l2)
acc#T1 < acc#T2
    ↓   by mult(Ts, mass, acc, force)
mass#T1 > mass#T2

Therefore, the initial condition in Sect. 8.4.2 can be proved by the query

$$?-\ provable(mass\#T1 > mass\#T2).$$ (Q16)

The difference between the queries of Sects. 8.4.2 and 8.4.3 is the ordering of the queries. Queries Q5, Q6, Q7, Q8, and Q9 are posed for simulating the behaviors of the two systems under the initial condition, while Queries Q15 and Q9 perform the interpretation of the different sources of measurement data.

8.5 QQS as a Constraint-Oriented Simulation Laboratory

An interactive simulation laboratory facilitates the understanding of how a control system works by performing desired experiments. These experiments must be easily constructable in a user-friendly programming environment. This environment enables us to add and remove knowledge dynamically about the target domain model. The declarative nature of CLP has the possibility for providing such a facility, because constraints are independent of each other, and therefore we may place and remove arbitrary constraints at any place and time.

We apply the notion of incremental query [11] to CLP. Incremental query allows us interactively to add and remove queries observing the current computation state

that are described by answer substitutions. In contrast, CLP represents the computation state as a set of constraints. Therefore, QQS gives us the most simplified constraints that are of canonical form.

Here, we show examples of incremental queries in QQS. These examples have already been described.

Given Query Q1, the following constraints are displayed:

$$\rightarrow pos\#T > 0,\ pos@T = 0,\ vel\#T = 0,\ vel@T < 0,\ acc\#T < 0,\ acc@T = 0$$

QQS returns constraints associated with user input variables. Since we gave the variables T and Ts in this case, the most simplifed constraints associated with the variable are the above six constraints. The variable Ts has no constraints.

Displayed constraints help us to see the current computation state, and to place and remove queries for desired analysis. This facility is demonstrated by the following incremental queries:

Given Queries Q5 and Q7, some of the constraints returned are

$$\rightarrow vel\#T1 = 0,\ vel\#T2 = 0,\ vel@T1 < 0,\ vel@T2 < 0, \ldots$$

When we pose Query Q6, output constraints are changed as follows:

$$\rightarrow vel\#T1 = 0,\ vel\#T2 = 0,\ vel@T1 < 0,\ vel@T2 < 0,$$
$$vel@T1 < vel@T2, \ldots$$

Instead of the predicate simulate, we shall predict the behavior at the next time. This prediction is easily performed by the query

$$?-\ T1s = [l1|\_],\ T2s = [l2|\_],\ start(l1) = T1,\ start(l2) = T2.$$

Then, the following constraints appear:

$$\rightarrow vel\#T1 = 0,\ vel\#T2 = 0,\ vel@T1 < 0,\ vel@T2 < 0,\ vel@T1 < vel@T2,$$
$$vel\#l1 = vel\#l2,\ duration(l1) > duration\ (l2), \ldots$$

The new constraints $vel\#l1 = vel\#l2$ and $duration(l1) > duration\ (l2)$ are derived from the first rule of duration_rule. Here, we give the query:

$$?-\ duration(l1) = duration(l2).$$

This query is inconsistent with the current computation state. Thus, QQS generates another solution by a backtracking mechanism. The constraints produced by using the second rule of duration_rule are as follows:

$$\rightarrow vel\#T1 = 0,\ vel\#T2 = 0,\ vel@T1 < 0,\ vel@T2 < 0,\ vel@T1 < vel@T2,$$
$$vel\#end(l1) > vel\#end(l2),\ duration(l1) = duration(l2) \ldots$$

8.6 Conclusions

We have incrementally designed a qualitative reasoning system based on constraint logic programming. The system is implemented within a unified framework that is capable of manipulating both qualitative and quantitive knowledge. This capability is due to the computational and expressive power of constraint logic programming, and therefore we demonstrate the advantages of constraint logic programming application to qualitative reasoning. These advantages are useful for designing advanced qualitative reasoning systems by integrating qualitative reasoning tasks such as simulation and interpretation. Furthermore, we present a constraint-oriented simulation laboratory for providing a flexible experimental environment toward practical applications.

References

1. Ohwada H, Mizoguchi F, Kitazawa Y (1988) A method for developing diagnostic systems based on qualitative simulation. J Jap Soc Artif Intell 3 (5): 617–626
2. Kawamura T, Ohwada H, Mizoguchi F (1987) CS-Prolog: a generalized unification based constraint solver. In: Proc logic programming '87, LNCS 315, Springer-Verlag, pp 19–39
3. Ohwada H, Mizoguchi F (1990) A constraint logic programming approach for maintaining consistency in user-interface design. In: Proc 1990 North American Conference on Logic Programming
4. Simmons R (1986) Commonsense arithmetic reasoning. In: Proc AAAI-86, pp 118–124
5. Jaffar J, Lassez J-L (1987) Constraint logic programming. In: Proc 14th ACM Principles of Programming Languages Conference, Munich
6. Shostak RE (1977) On the SUP-INF method for proving Presburger formulas. J ACM 24: 529–543
7. Mukai K (1988) Partially specified term in logic programming for linguistic analysis. In: Proc Int Conf Fifth Generation Computer Systems, pp 479–488
8. Kuipers B (1986) Qualitative simulation. Artif Intell 29: 289–338
9. Colmerauer A (1982) PROLOG II: Manuel de reference et modele theorique. Tech. Report, GIA – Faculte de Sciences de Luminy
10. Weld DS (1988) Comparative analysis. Artif Intell 36: 333–373
11. van Emden MH, Ohki M, Takeuchi A (1986) Spreadsheets with incremental queries as a user interface for logic programming. New Generation Comput 4: 287–304

9
Design and Evaluation of Part-Oriented Parallel Algorithms

Katsumasa Watanabe and Tatsuo Tsuji[1]

Summary: Parallel programming aims not only to compute as fast as possible, but also to discover new areas of algorithms different from sequential ones. We introduce a "part," which performs the computation of a relatively independent task. A part is able to be treated as a unit of asynchronous and nondeterministic computation. Five programs are given, in order of increasing independence. They are written in extended C language and simulated on a single processor computer.

Key words: parallel algorithm — parallel programming language — shared variable — asynchronous computation — nondeterministic computation

9.1 Introduction

It is interesting to develop parallel algorithms, from two points of view:

1. To utilize parallel computers effectively and to obtain the results of computation as fast as possible.
2. To solve problems by developing methods different from sequential algorithms.

The key point of the first is to enlarge the degree of parallelism and to increase the possibility of running many processors efficiently. For the second point, it is important to design parallel algorithms, not by modifying the sequential methods, but from thinking in parallel originally.

Generally, we can easily find parallel methods to solve a problem which has parallelism within itself, but in practice, we need to derive parallel algorithms for problems which may or may not have parallel characteristics.

As a guide for writing parallel programs, Carriero and Gelernter classify parallelism into three conceptual classes from the point of task distribution [1]:

1. *Result parallelism* focuses on the shape of the finished products (line data structure).

---

[1] Faculty of Engineering, Fukui University, Fukui, 910 Japan

2. *Agenda parallelism* focuses on the list of tasks to be performed (distributed data structure methods).
3. *Specialist parallelism* focuses on the make-up of the work crew (message-passing methods).

Each category has the appropriate data structure for communicating among tasks.

We suggest that specialist parallelism resembles the Actor model and also the style of object-oriented parallel programming. There, each Specialist (or Actor, Object) works passively and asynchronously depending on the messages received, each local state, and the common global state.

9.2 Part-Oriented Parallel Algorithms

With this approach, we have developed parallel algorithms called "Part-Oriented Parallel Algorithms" [2, 3]. We write a program in a procedure-oriented language (such as Pascal or C) which has extended notation to activate each part as follows:

1. Simultaneous activation of multiple parts with index parameter i:

parafor $(i = 1; i <= n; i + +)$ {action (i);}

2. Conditional activation of some parts whose corresponding conditions have the logical value 'true':

```
para
   pif (condition_1) {action_1;}
    :         :              :
   pif (condition_k) {action_k;}
   [else                 {action_else;}]
endpara
```

The rules of activation are as follows:

a. When any pif_condition is true, all the corresponding actions are activated simultaneously.
b. When no pif_condition is true and para_block contains else_clause, only the action_else is activated.

Each action may contain parafor statements and/or para_pif blocks in itself; then, parallel parts are expanded in multiple levels of nesting. Parts communicate with each other through global variables (shared variables), and do not use explicit message-passing statements.

9.3 Characteristics of Part-Oriented Parallel Algorithms

In this section, we consider five well-known problems and design the part-oriented parallel algorithms, in which

1. Each part knows its own role of computation.
2. The state of each part is constrained by some common conditions.
3. The state of each part is announced to each other part using shared variables.

For each algorithm, we take notice of the following items for comparison:

a. What is a part
b. Degree of parallelism
c. Method of communication between parts
d. Mode of synchronization
e. Decision of the end of computation
f. Number of computation cycles

Each algorithm is programmed in extended C language and simulated on a single processor computer.

9.3.1 Influence of a Programming Language: Prime Numbers

Programming languages have much influence on the design of algorithms. For example, we can easily denote array-oriented computation in APL. Almasi and Gottlieb wrote an APL statement to obtain the list Z of prime numbers less than a given number D as follows [4]:

$$Z \leftarrow (\sim V \in V \circ . \times V)/V \leftarrow 1 \downarrow \iota D$$

where V is a variable. Modifying this statement, we can show a parallel algorithm implemented in Program 1, shown in Fig. 9.1 (there, D is replaced with d).

1. Make the list v which contains number 2 and odd numbers to d.
2. Make the list rt containing odd numbers to $\sqrt{d}$.
3. Make the list d3 containing odd numbers to d/3.
4. Make the table mt of outer products of rt and d3.
5. Mark the elements of v as not_prime_number if they are contained in table mt.
6. Elements of v which have no mark are prime numbers to d.

In Program 1, Step 5 is executed such that, if an element c (that is a part) of mt is less than or equal to d, then the (c/2)-th element of v is marked as not_prime_number.
   The Results of Computation 1 (Fig. 9.2) show the case of d = 111.
   The characteristics of Program 1 are as follows:

a. A part corresponds to an element of table mt (Step 5).
b. The maximum degree of parallelism is the size of table mt. If the number of processors is few, some parts are allocated to one processor.
c. Parts do not communicate with each other at all.
d. Synchronization is not necessary.
e. Computation ends when all the parts finish their own work.
f. There is only one computation cycle.

The example presented says that an appropriate parallel programming language is required in order to devise parallel algorithms.

Program 1

```
/* prime number as APL notation */
#include <math.h>
#define max      1000

main()
{
        int     d,rd,i,j,k,ni,nj,nk;
        int     v[max],rt[max/10],d3[max/3];
        int     mt[max/10][max/3];        /* multipliers table */
        int     c,nn;

        /* read d from keyboard and display it */
        rd=(int)( sqrt((double)(d)) );   /* integer part */
        printf("d=%d    and    root-d=%d\n",d,rd);
/*1*/
        v[0]=2; /* first prime number       */
        parafor(i=3,ni=1;i<=d;i=i+2){
                v[ni]=i; ni++;   /* ni is number of odd numbers */
        }
        /* print out candidate vector v */
/*2*/
        parafor(j=3,nj=0;j<=rd+1;j=j+2){
                rt[nj]=j; nj++; /* rt[0]=3,5,7...(nj*2-1) */
        }
/*3*/
        parafor(k=3,nk=0;k<=d/3+1;k=k+2){
                d3[nk]=k; nk++; /* d3[0]=3,5,7...(nk*2-1) */
        }
/*4*/
        parafor(j=0;j<nj;j++)
            for(k=0;k<nk;k++){mt[j][k]=rt[j]*d3[k];}
        /* print multiplier table mt[j][k] */
/*5*/
        parafor(j=0;j<nj;j++)    /* para for each multiplier */
            for(k=0;k<nk;k++){
                c=mt[j][k];
                if(c>d){/* over range */}
                else    {i=c/2;   /* v-entry */
                         if(v[i]==c){v[i]= -v[i];}
                }        /* end of each check */
            }
/*6*/   /* print out results from v : for v[i]>0 */
}
```

FIG. 9.1

9.3.2 Reading Neighbour's States Repeatedly: Shortest Paths

In order to find the optimal global solution on a distributed system, a method is proposed in which each node reads data from neighbours repeatedly and updates its local state [5].

For example, the length d_{ij} of the shortest path from node i to node j on the graph of n nodes is computed from the values of other nodes as follows:

1. Initially set d_{ij} with w_{ij}, which is the length of the direct path from node i to j. If there is no direct path between node i and j, w_{ij} has some large value.
2. Update d_{ij} repeatedly as follows,

Results of Computation 1

key input d as upper bound of prime
giving number d is   111
d=111   and   root-d=10

candidates of prime numbers is 56
     2   3   5   7   9   11   13   15   17   19   21   23   25   27   29   31
    33   35   37   39   41   43   45   47   49   51   53   55   57   59   61   63
    65   67   69   71   73   75   77   79   81   83   85   87   89   91   93   95
    97   99 101 103 105 107 109 111

mt .. rt[ ]=		3	5	7	9	11
d3[0]=	3	9	15	21	27	33
d3[1]=	5	15	25	35	45	55
d3[2]=	7	21	35	49	63	77
d3[3]=	9	27	45	63	81	99
d3[4]=	11	33	55	77	99	121
d3[5]=	13	39	65	91	117	143
d3[6]=	15	45	75	105	135	165
d3[7]=	17	51	85	119	153	187
d3[8]=	19	57	95	133	171	209
d3[9]=	21	63	105	147	189	231
d3[10]=	23	69	115	161	207	253
d3[11]=	25	75	125	175	225	275
d3[12]=	27	81	135	189	243	297
d3[13]=	29	87	145	203	261	319
d3[14]=	31	93	155	217	279	341
d3[15]=	33	99	165	231	297	363
d3[16]=	35	105	175	245	315	385
d3[17]=	37	111	185	259	333	407

result of prime numbers to 111
     2   3   5   7   11   13   17   19   23   29   31   37   41   43   47   53
    59   61   67   71   73   79   83   89   97 101 103 107 109
...end of result 29 numbers...

FIG. 9.2

$$d_{ij} = \min(d_{ij}, d_{ik} + d_{kj})$$

where k is any other node except i and j.

When d_{ij} is not updated, the computation is finished.

Program 2 (Fig. 9.3a) represents this simple algorithm, and the Results of Computation 2 (Fig. 9.3b) show the sample data of an 8-node graph and the calculated length of the shortest path from node i to node j.

The characteristics of Program 2 are as follows:

a. A part is the calculation of the length d_{ij}.
b. The maximum degree of parallelism is n^2 (n is the number of nodes).
c. Part(i, j) reads data from part(i, k) and part(k, j).
d. No explicit synchronization is required.
e. To know the end of computation as fast as possible, some monitoring process is required for checking the flags of updating for each part.
f. The maximum number of computation cycles (c is Program 2) is n, and each part does comparison n times in one cycle. So, the maximum total computation is n^4.

a) Program 2

```
/* shortest path for graph of pathdata.d */
#include          <stdio.h>
#define n          8

main()
{
        FILE      *fp,*fopen();
        int       i,j,k,c,m;
        int       w[n][n],d[n][n];
        int       st,by;

/*read*/fp=fopen("pathdata.d","r");
        for(i=0;i<n;i++){           /* read w[][] from pathdata.d */
                for(j=0;j<n;j++){fscanf(fp,"%d",&w[i][j]);}
        }
        fclose(fp);
/*write path cost data and set d[][] initial value*/
        printf("path cost data w[n][n]\n");
        for(i=0;i<n;i++){           /* print w[][] */
                printf("w[%d]=",i);
                for(j=0;j<n;j++){
                        printf("%4d",w[i][j]);
                        d[i][j]=w[i][j];           /* initial set d */
                }
                printf("\n");
        }
        printf("\n");

        for(c=0,m=1;m>0;c++){    /* repeat count c */
                m=0;
/*para*/        parafor(i=0;i<n;i++)
                        for(j=0;j<n;j++){
                                for(k=0;k<n;k++){
                                        st=d[i][j]; by=d[i][k]+d[k][j];
                                        if(st>by){d[i][j]=by; m++;} /* shorter path */
                                }
                        }
        }
/*out*/ printf("shortest path with set-cycle(%4d)\n",c);
        /* print out d[i][j] from node i to j */
}
```

b) Results of Computation 2

```
path cost data w[n][n]
w[0]=    0   21  999   16  999    7   25  999
w[1]= 999    0   31  999  999  999   14    6
w[2]=   10    4    0  999   11  999    8  999
w[3]= 999  999   27    0   20  999  999    9
w[4]=   12  999  999   18    0    6  999  999
w[5]= 999   16  999  999  999    0  999  999
w[6]= 999  999    5    3  999   22    0  999
w[7]= 999  999  999   16   33  999   19    0

shortest path with set-cycle(   3)
    d[0][]=    0   21   30   16   36    7   25   25
    d[1][]=   29    0   19   17   30   36   14    6
    d[2][]=   10    4    0   11   11   17    8   10
    d[3][]=   32   31   27    0   20   26   28    9
    d[4][]=   12   22   41   18    0    6   36   27
    d[5][]=   45   16   35   33   46    0   30   22
    d[6][]=   15    9    5    3   16   22    0   12
    d[7][]=   34   28   24   16   33   39   19    0
```

FIG. 9.3

This example says that we may obtain the optimal global solution by only changing each item of local data repeatedly. However, the amount of computation and communication may become large.

9.3.3 Converging Simultaneously: Algebraic Equation

Solutions of higher-order algebraic equations can be obtained one after another by the methods of Newton or Bairstow. But generally the precision would decrease and the approximation errors would increase. We can obtain all the solutions of an equation by Durand-Kerner's method [6] in which the calculation is iterated according to the formula,

$$Z_i^{k+1} = Z_i^k - P(Z_i^k) \bigg/ \prod_{\substack{j=1 \\ j \neq i}}^{n} (Z_i^k - Z_j^k),$$

where

$$P(Z) = Z^n + a_1 Z^{n-1} + \cdots + a_{n-1} Z + a_n = 0$$

or,

$$P(Z) = \prod_{i=1}^{n} (Z - \alpha_i) = 0.$$

$P(Z)$ is an nth order algebraic equation with real coefficients, Z_i^k is the approximate value of the solution α_i at iteration k, and α_1 to a_n are coefficients.

To set the initial values Z_i^0, Aberth's well-known method [6] is used:

$$Z_i^0 = -a_1/n + r_0 \exp\{[2(i-1)\pi/n + \pi/2n]\sqrt{-1}\} \quad \text{for } i = 1 \text{ to } n.$$

This means that all the solutions exist in the circle

$$\Gamma : |Z + a_1/n| <= r_0$$

whose center is $\Sigma \alpha_i/n = -a_1/n$ and whose radius is r_0. Also, r_0 is obtained from the equation

$$P(W - a_1/n) = (W^n + l_2 W^{n-2} + \cdots + l_{n-1} W + l_n) = 0$$

where w is an independent variable.

Program 3 (Fig. 9.4) is the main flow of this parallel algorithm.

1. Read dimension n, coefficients a_0 to a_n, and bound of convergence *eps*.
2. Normalize coefficients as $a_0 = 1$, and set *delta* as

$$\mathsf{max}\,(|\mathsf{coefficients}|) \times \mathsf{REL}.$$

3. Calculate radius r_0 and initialize each approximate value Z_i by Aberth's method.
4. Set up loop control variables count, endf and array convf. The flag of convergence convf [i] indicates whether the approximate value Z_i is appropriate or not, and is set when one of two conditions is satisfied:
   a. $|P(Z_i^k)| < eps$, at Step 5 in testeps (i),
   b. $|Z_i^{k+1} - Z_i^k| < delta$, at Step 6.2 in testdel (i).
   The end flag endf is set when all the convf [i] are set.

Program 3

```
/* solution of P(Z)=a0*Z^n+a1*Z^(n-1)+...+an */
#include         <math.h>
#include         <stdio.h>
#define MAX       20
#define REL       1.0e-8
#define PAI       3.14159265359
float    a[MAX][2];        /* a[i][0]:real a[i][1]:imag.     */
float    p[MAX][2],mm[MAX][2];
float    z[MAX][2],zz[MAX][2];
float    yr[MAX];          /* absolute(P(Zi))                */
float    eps,delta;        /* P(z[i])<eps,|zz[i]-z[i]|<delta */
int      n;                /* a0,a1,...,a(n-1),an            */
int      count;            /* count of repetition            */
int      endf,convf[MAX];/* end flag of repetition           */

extern   int      caddl(),csubl(),cmull(),cdivl(),cexpl(),newton();
                             /* for complex operations */

int      c[MAX][MAX];
float    l[MAX][2],q[MAX][2];
float    h[MAX];
float    thita,r0;
float    aln[2];            /* a[1]/n */

main()
{
         FILE     *fp,*fopen();
         int      i,j;

/*1*/    /* input file open and read n,eps and a[] */
/*2*/    normal();                        /* set a0=1.0 and divide*/
/*3*/    aberth();                        /* thita, r0 and Z[i]    */
/*4*/    count=0;   endf=0;
         parafor(i=0;i<=n;i++){convf[i]=0;}
/*loop*/
         for(;endf==0;count++){
/*5*/            parafor(i=1;i<=n;i++){
                     if(convf[i]==0)
                             {convf[i]=testeps(i);}
                 }                        /* P(Zi)<eps for all i   */
                 parafor(i=0,j=0;i<=n;i++){
                     if(convf[i]==1){j++;}
                 }
                 if(j==n){endf=1;}
/*6*/        if(endf==0){
                 parafor(i=1;i<=n;i++){
                     if(convf[i]==0){/* compute new zz[i]     */
/*6-1 new zz[i] */      setzz(i);
/*6-2 test delta*/      convf[i]=testdel(i);
                     }                    /* |zz[i]-z[i]|<delta    */
                 }
             }                            /* end of if             */
         }                                /* end of for            */
/*7*/    count--;
         outresult();
}

setzz(i)          /* set new zz[i]=z[i]-P(z[i])/mm[i] */
         int      i;
{        /* mm[i]=Mult(z[i]-z[j]) for j=1 to n, except i */
         /* zz[i]=z[i] - p(z[i])/mm[i]                    */
}
```

<< be continued >>

FIG. 9.4

```
<< continuation of Program 3 >>

aberth()            /* set thita,r0 and initial values of z[i] */
{
        int     k;
        float   pow[2],ex[2];

        thita=PAI/(2*n);
        aln[0]=a[1][0]/n; aln[1]=a[1][1]/n;        /* a[1]/n */
        setr0();
        parafor(k=1;k<=n;k++){
                pow[0]=0.0;          pow[1]=2*(k-1)*PAI/n+thita;
                cexpl(pow,ex);
                ex[0]=ex[0]*r0; ex[1]=ex[1]*r0;
                csubl(ex,aln,z[k]);
        }

}


setr0()             /* find r0 from n and h[] by Newton    */
{
        int     i,j;
        float   qw[2],lr;

        for(i=1;i<=n;i++){          /* binomial coefficients */
                c[i][1]=1;
                for(j=2;j<=i;j++){
                        c[i][j]=c[i-1][j-1]+c[i-1][j];
                }
                c[i][i+1]=1;
        }
/* set l[i] and q[i] */
        l[0][0]=1.0; l[0][1]=0.0;          /* l[0]=1.0 */
        l[1][0]=0.0; l[1][1]=0.0;          /* l[1]=0.0 */
        for(i=2;i<=n;i++){
                q[1][0]=aln[0]*c[n][i]; /* q[1]=nCi*a[1]/n */
                q[1][1]=aln[1]*c[n][i];
                /* q[j+1]=(q[j]+l[j]*c[n-j][i-j])*(a[1]/n) */
                for(j=1;j<i;j++){
                        qw[0]=l[j][0]*c[n-j][i-j];
                        qw[1]=l[j][1]*c[n-j][i-j];
                        caddl(q[j],qw,qw);
                        cmull(qw,aln,q[j+1]);
                }           /* q[i]=last q[j+1] */
                csubl(a[i],q[i],l[i]);
        }                   /* l[i]=a[i]-q[i] */
/* set h[i] */
        h[0]=1.0;
        parafor(i=1;i<=n;i++){
                cabsl(l[i],&lr);
                h[i]= -lr;                 /* h[i]=-|l[i]| */
        }
        newton(h,n,eps,&r0);       /* find r0 from h[0..n] */
}
```

FIG. 9.4 (*continued*)

Results of Computation 3

(3.1)   P(x)=(x-2)(x-3)(x+4)=0
source data a[ ]
 a[0][ ]=   1.000   0.000
 a[1][ ]=   -1.000   0.000
 a[2][ ]=   -14.000   0.000
 a[3][ ]=   24.000   0.000
epsilon =   0.00000100

normalized a[ ]
 a[0][ ]=   1.00000   0.00000
 a[1][ ]=   -1.00000   0.00000
 a[2][ ]=   -14.00000   0.00000
 a[3][ ]=   24.00000   0.00000
delta   =   0.00000024

l[2]=-14.33333302   0.00000000i
l[3]= 19.33333206   0.00000000i

h[ ]=   1.00000000   -0.00000000 -14.33333302 -19.33333206
thita= 0.5236   r0=   4.3351

 1   ex= 0.86602539   0.50000000i
z0[1]=   4.08763647   2.16754794i
 2   ex= -0.86602539   0.50000006i
z0[2]= -3.42096972   2.16754818i
 3   ex= 0.00000001   -1.00000000i
z0[3]=   0.33333340   -4.33509588i

loop count= 0...
z[1]=   4.08763647   2.16754794i |P(z[1])|=   61.10795212
z[2]=   -3.42096972   2.16754818i |P(z[2])|=   88.76754761
z[3]=   0.33333340   -4.33509588i |P(z[3])|=   144.89176941
loop count= 1...
z[1]=   3.61986113   1.18981028i |P(z[1])|=   20.79545212
z[2]=   -3.06093884   0.54386628i |P(z[2])|=   33.61317825
z[3]=   1.10350955   -0.62194371i |P(z[3])|=   11.19614124
loop count= 2...
z[1]=   3.21947837   0.27432513i |P(z[1])|=   3.17259264
z[2]=   -4.04954720   -0.19875711i |P(z[2])|=   8.74389744
z[3]=   1.93785346   -0.18393758i |P(z[3])|=   1.24331653
loop count= 3...
z[1]=   2.98466682   0.05694146i |P(z[1])|=   0.40626055
z[2]=   -4.00384808   0.00362110i |P(z[2])|=   0.22218803
z[3]=   2.01006198   -0.00311507i |P(z[3])|=   0.06266837
loop count= 4...
z[1]=   2.99995923   -0.00059358i |P(z[1])|=   0.00416465
z[2]=   -4.00000429   0.00000835i |P(z[2])|=   0.00039307
z[3]=   1.99999762   -0.00000592i |P(z[3])|=   0.00003792
loop count= 5...
z[1]=*   3.00000000   -0.00000000i |P(z[1])|=*   0.00000001
z[2]=*   -4.00000000   0.00000000i |P(z[2])|=*   0.00000000
z[3]=   1.99999988   0.00000000i |P(z[3])|=   0.00000191
loop count= 6...
z[1]=   3.00000000   -0.00000000i |P(z[1])|=   0.00000001
z[2]=   -4.00000000   0.00000000i |P(z[2])|=   0.00000000
z[3]=   2.00000024   0.00000000i |P(z[3])|=   0.00000000

FIG. 9.5

```
(3.2)    P(x)=(x-1)(x-1)(X^2+x+1)=0
source data a[ ]
 a[ 0][ ]=    1.000      0.000
 a[ 1][ ]=   -1.000      0.000
 a[ 2][ ]=    0.000      0.000
 a[ 3][ ]=   -1.000      0.000
 a[ 4][ ]=    1.000      0.000
epsilon =    0.00000100

normalized a[ ]
 a[ 0][ ]=    1.00000       0.00000
 a[ 1][ ]=   -1.00000       0.00000
 a[ 2][ ]=    0.00000       0.00000
 a[ 3][ ]=   -1.00000       0.00000
 a[ 4][ ]=    1.00000       0.00000
delta   =    0.00000001
l[ 2]= -0.25000000     0.00000000i
l[ 3]= -0.96875000     0.00000000i
l[ 4]=  0.77343750     0.00000000i
h[ ]=   1.00000000   -0.00000000   -0.25000000   -0.96875000   -0.77343750
thita=  0.3927   r0= -0.6886
 1   ex=  0.92387950      0.38268346i
z0[ 1]= -0.38621289     -0.26352802i
 2   ex= -0.38268340      0.92387956i
z0[ 2]=  0.51352799     -0.63621294i
 3   ex= -0.92387950     -0.38268343i
z0[ 3]=  0.88621289      0.26352802i
 4   ex=  0.38268360     -0.92387944i
z0[ 4]= -0.01352814      0.63621283i

loop count=  0...
z[ 1]=      -0.38621289     -0.26352802i   |P(z[ 1])|=        1.38593590
z[ 2]=       0.51352799     -0.63621294i   |P(z[ 2])|=        1.20799506
z[ 3]=       0.88621289      0.26352802i   |P(z[ 3])|=        0.22269277
z[ 4]=      -0.01352814      0.63621283i   |P(z[ 4])|=        1.21657646
loop count=  1...
z[ 1]=       0.28273147     -1.08709836i   |P(z[ 1])|=        2.90297151
z[ 2]=       2.29136467     -0.66466302i   |P(z[ 2])|=       18.79353333
z[ 3]=       0.83022642      0.19079071i   |P(z[ 3])|=        0.16530742
z[ 4]=      -0.15150066      0.87469894i   |P(z[ 4])|=        1.29409146
loop count=  2...
z[ 1]=      -0.16403076     -1.32532573i   |P(z[ 1])|=        3.92537141
z[ 2]=       1.00337911      0.12701195i   |P(z[ 2])|=        0.04872545
z[ 3]=       0.85342997     -0.22153574i   |P(z[ 3])|=        0.18365002
z[ 4]=      -0.43842393      0.89276636i   |P(z[ 4])|=        0.33861014
            :
loop count=  6...
z[ 1]=*     -0.49999997     -0.86602539i   |P(z[ 1])|=*       0.00000013
z[ 2]=       1.00238156      0.00505377i   |P(z[ 2])|=        0.00009392
z[ 3]=       0.99852473     -0.00312376i   |P(z[ 3])|=        0.00003569
z[ 4]=*     -0.49999994      0.86602545i   |P(z[ 4])|=*       0.00000038
loop count=  7...
z[ 1]=*     -0.49999997     -0.86602539i   |P(z[ 1])|=*       0.00000013
z[ 2]=       1.00091231      0.00192759i   |P(z[ 2])|=        0.00001367
z[ 3]=       0.99943870     -0.00119709i   |P(z[ 3])|=        0.00000524
z[ 4]=*     -0.49999994      0.86602545i   |P(z[ 4])|=*       0.00000038
loop count=  8...
z[ 1]=*     -0.49999997     -0.86602539i   |P(z[ 1])|=*       0.00000013
z[ 2]=       1.00034845      0.00073637i   |P(z[ 2])|=        0.00000202
z[ 3]=*      0.99978566     -0.00045724i   |P(z[ 3])|=*       0.00000076
z[ 4]=*     -0.49999994      0.86602545i   |P(z[ 4])|=*       0.00000038
loop count=  9...
z[ 1]=      -0.49999997     -0.86602539i   |P(z[ 1])|=        0.00000013
z[ 2]=       1.00013781      0.00027129i   |P(z[ 2])|=        0.00000025
z[ 3]=       0.99978566     -0.00045724i   |P(z[ 3])|=        0.00000076
z[ 4]=      -0.49999994      0.86602545i   |P(z[ 4])|=        0.00000038
```

FIG. 9.5 (*continued*)

Then, Steps 5 and 6 are iterated until endf becomes 1, and are executed in parallel for each Z_i.

5. Check the convergence by testeps(i) to determine the end of computation.
6. Update Z_i (by setzz( )) and check the convergence by testdel( ).
7. End the computation and output the results.

The Results of Computation 3 (Fig. 9.5) gives the intermediate and final results for equations

$$(x - 2)(x - 3)(x + 4) = 0 \qquad\qquad (3.1)$$

$$(x - 1)^2(x^2 + x + 1) = 0. \qquad\qquad (3.2)$$

There, * indicates that one of the convergent conditions is satisfied for the solution.
    The characteristics of Program 3 are as follows:

a. A part is the calculation of approximate value Z_i.
b. The maximum degree of parallelism is n (order of the equation).
c. Each part reads the current values of others.
d. The synchronization is not required explicitly.
e. The end of the computation occurs when all the parts satisfy the convergent condition.
f. The number of computation cycles cannot be determined formally, but it is known that the approximate values converge at at least second order for the equations of all the different solutions.

Given an initial value, each part could carry out computation asynchronously and independently from each other.

9.3.4 Autonomously Asynchronous Processing: the n Body Problem

When we consider the n body problem as one system wholly, it becomes complex because it requires the solution of a set of equations of movement. However, when we consider only one body as a part, it can be solved simply, such that we find stable points of each body. As in the case of an algebraic equation, each part reads the current positions of other bodies, then calculates one's potential energy, and adjusts the position to the direction of minimum energy. But they do not have any tightly bounded condition as a whole.
    As a simple example, we consider a set of n objects $\{O_i\}$ on a 2-dimensional plane, and define the potential F_i of the object O_i as the summation of all forces f from other objects,

$$F_i = \sum_{j \neq i} f_{ij} = \sum_{j \neq i} \{(r_{ij} - \sqrt{m_i m_j})^2 + m_j\} \qquad \text{(Fig. 9.6)}$$

where r_{ij} is the distance between O_i and O_j, and m_i is mass of O_i.
    Program 4 (Fig. 9.7) is the parallel program to determine the stable points of n bodies.

FIG 9.6. Potential energy of object O_i by object O_j (Program 4: n body problem)

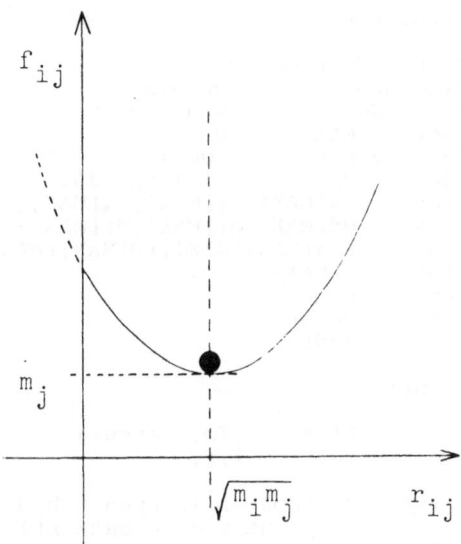

1. Read and set the position (x_i, y_i) and mass m_i of the object O_i.
2. Calculate $\sqrt{m_i m_j}$ for all i and j in parallel.
3. Inform current position of each to each other.
4. Calculate the potential and movement of each object in parallel as follows:
   a) distance r_{ij} from (x_i, y_i) and (x_j, y_j),
   b) weight of movement $w_{ij} = (r_{ij} - \sqrt{m_i m_j}) \times m_j$,
      length of movement $dx_{ij} = w_{ij} \times (x_j - x_i)/r_{ij}$,
      $$dy_{ij} = w_{ij} \times (y_j - y_i)/r_{ij},$$
      total movement $\quad dx_i = \frac{1}{2}n \sum_{j \neq i}^{n} dx_{ij}, \quad dy_i = \frac{1}{2}n \sum_{j \neq i}^{n} dy_{ij},$
   c) new position $\quad x_i = x_i + dx_i, \quad y_i = y_i + dy_i.$
5. Check each length of movement $r_i = \sqrt{(dx_i)^2 + (dy_i)^2}$ and judge the end of computation.

Steps 3, 4, and 5 are iterated until all r_i are less than the given bound value REL.

The Results of Computation 4.1 (Fig. 9.8) show the initial positions of five objects and their mass, and the number of computation cycles for $n = 2, 3, 4, 5$. (4.2) in Fig. 9.8 shows changes of positions for the case of $\{O_1, O_2, O_3, O_4\}$.

The characteristics of Program 4 are as follows:

a. A part corresponds to an object (Step 4).
b. The degree of parallelism is n (number of objects).
c. Each part needs to know the positions of all the other objects.
d. The synchronization is not required explicitly.
e. When all the movements are smaller than the bound REL, computation is over.
f. The number of computation cycles is unpredictable.

In this problem, each part is able to calculate its new position relatively autonomously.

Program 4

```
/* n-body problem         */
#include          <math.h>
#include          <stdio.h>
#define MAX      20
#define REL      0.0001
#define PAI      3.14159265359
float    x[MAX], y[MAX], m[MAX];/* position and mass      */
float    dx[MAX],dy[MAX],dr[MAX];
float    rij[MAX][MAX],r0[MAX][MAX];
float    w[MAX];
int      n;                      /* number of body         */
int      count;                  /* count of repetition    */
int      endf;                   /* end flag of repetition */

main()
{
        FILE    *fp,*fopen();
        int     i,j;

/*1*/    /* input file open "nbody.d" and read n,x[],y[],m[] */
         /* print source data x[] y[] and mass m[]            */
/*2*/    /* set sqrt(mi*mj) in r0[i][j] */
         parafor(i=1;i<=n;i++)
            for(j=1;j<=n;j++){
                r0[i][j]=sqrt(m[i]*m[j]);
         }          /* end para */
/*3*/    /* loop of step by step */
    for(count=0,endf=0;endf==0;count++){
         outposition();
/*4*/
/*4.1*/ parafor(i=1;i<=n;i++){
                for(j=1;j<=n;j++){
                    rij[i][j]=(x[i]-x[j])*(x[i]-x[j]);
                    rij[i][j]=rij[i][j]+(y[i]-y[j])*(y[i]-y[j]);
                    rij[i][j]=sqrt(rij[i][j]);
                }
         }          /* end para */
/*4.2*/ parafor(i=1;i<=n;i++){
                dx[i]=0; dy[i]=0;
                for(j=1;j<=n;j++){
                    if(j!=i){
                        w[i]=rij[i][j]-r0[i][j];
                        w[i]=w[i]*m[j];
                        dx[i]=dx[i]+w[i]*(x[j]-x[i])/rij[i][j];
                        dy[i]=dy[i]+w[i]*(y[j]-y[i])/rij[i][j];
                    }
                }          /* end of dx and dy set */
                dx[i]=dx[i]/(2*n);
                dy[i]=dy[i]/(2*n);
                dr[i]=dx[i]*dx[i]+dy[i]*dy[i];
                dr[i]=sqrt(dr[i]);
         }          /* end of each i para */
/*4.3*/ parafor(i=1;i<=n;i++){
                x[i]=x[i]+dx[i];                     /* update */
                y[i]=y[i]+dy[i];
         }          /* end para */
/*5*/    for(endf=1,i=1;(i<=n)&&(endf==1);i++){
                if(dr[i]>REL){endf=0;}
         }
    }    /* end of repetition */
        outposition();
}
```

FIG. 9.7

```
Results of Computation 4

(4.1)
source position and mass
 x[ 1]= 1.000 y[ 1]= 0.000 m[ 1]= 0.500
 x[ 2]= 3.000 y[ 2]= 0.000 m[ 2]= 2.500
 x[ 3]= 2.000 y[ 3]= 2.000 m[ 3]= 3.500
 x[ 4]=-2.000 y[ 4]= 1.000 m[ 4]= 2.000
 x[ 5]= 0.000 y[ 5]=-5.000 m[ 5]= 3.000

For Objects 1 to 2    Number of steps= 8
               1 to 3               =39
               1 to 4               =17 (as follows)
               1 to 5               =26

(4.2)
sqrt(m[i]*m[j]) in r0[i][j]
 i= 1 :    0.50000   1.11803   1.32288   1.00000
 i= 2 :    1.11803   2.50000   2.95804   2.23607
 i= 3 :    1.32288   2.95804   3.50000   2.64575
 i= 4 :    1.00000   2.23607   2.64575   2.00000

 0:( 1.0000,  0.0000)( 3.0000,  0.0000)( 2.0000,  2.0000)(-2.0000, 1.0000)
 1:( 0.9415,  0.5283)( 2.3843,-0.1421)( 1.5153,  2.0612)(-0.3674, 0.9386)
 2:( 1.0350,  0.6224)( 2.2845,-0.3038)( 1.5382,  2.2723)(-0.3063, 0.7477)
 3:( 1.1097,  0.7173)( 2.1664,-0.3509)( 1.5556,  2.3713)(-0.2078, 0.6094)
 4:( 1.1584,  0.7902)( 2.0903,-0.3751)( 1.5648,  2.4261)(-0.1409, 0.5257)
 5:( 1.1898,  0.8367)( 2.0450,-0.3873)( 1.5685,  2.4544)(-0.0986, 0.4798)
 6:( 1.2096,  0.8623)( 2.0194,-0.3940)( 1.5696,  2.4692)(-0.0736, 0.4559)
 7:( 1.2219,  0.8755)( 2.0054,-0.3979)( 1.5698,  2.4770)(-0.0593, 0.4438)
 8:( 1.2296,  0.8821)( 1.9978,-0.4002)( 1.5695,  2.4811)(-0.0514, 0.4378)
 9:( 1.2344,  0.8854)( 1.9938,-0.4016)( 1.5692,  2.4833)(-0.0470, 0.4348)
10:( 1.2375,  0.8871)( 1.9916,-0.4024)( 1.5690,  2.4845)(-0.0446, 0.4333)
11:( 1.2394,  0.8879)( 1.9904,-0.4029)( 1.5688,  2.4852)(-0.0432, 0.4326)
12:( 1.2405,  0.8883)( 1.9897,-0.4032)( 1.5687,  2.4855)(-0.0425, 0.4323)
13:( 1.2412,  0.8885)( 1.9894,-0.4034)( 1.5686,  2.4857)(-0.0421, 0.4321)
14:( 1.2417,  0.8886)( 1.9892,-0.4035)( 1.5685,  2.4858)(-0.0419, 0.4321)
15:( 1.2420,  0.8887)( 1.9891,-0.4036)( 1.5685,  2.4859)(-0.0417, 0.4320)
16:( 1.2421,  0.8887)( 1.9890,-0.4036)( 1.5685,  2.4859)(-0.0417, 0.4320)
17:( 1.2422,  0.8887)( 1.9890,-0.4037)( 1.5685,  2.4859)(-0.0416, 0.4320)
```

FIG. 9.8

9.3.5 Satisfying a Neighboring Condition: the Four-Color Problem

The four-color problem, which assigns colors to countries on a map, is treated as a tree-search problem in the area of sequential algorithms. Considering that each country is only required to have a different color from its neighbors, we are able to make a part assign some color to a country. Then, after assigning a set of colors to all countries, it is necessary to adjust the colors of some countries, according to the neighboring condition.

The part-oriented parallel algorithm is implemented in Program 5.

0. After setting the neighboring relation of countries in array conn, assign the initial color of each country in array j.
1. Clear four counters board of each country to count up colors of neighbors.
2. To inform neighbors of the color of a country, increment the counters of neighbors corresponding to the color.

Program 5

```c
/* Four color problem for map data color.d */
#include        <stdio.h>
#define BOUND    512
#define MAX      50
#define C4       4
FILE    *fp,*fopen();
int     w[MAX];                   /* number of neighbours    */
int     conn[MAX][12];           /* neighbouring countries */
int     board[MAX][C4+1];        /* count of shadow */
int     updat,movec,tryc;        /* counters */
int     nextj[MAX];              /* movable next position */
int     tryj[MAX];               /* give way position */
int     q;                       /* country number */
int     rr;                      /* other country number */
int     j[MAX];                  /* color of each country */
int     chang[MAX];              /* flag of update or not */
int     n,qn;                    /* number of countries */
int     step;                    /* step counter */
int     cycle[MAX][MAX];         /* trace of intermediate states */
int     cycp;
int     anyeq;                   /* count of eq-pattern */

main()
{
        /* read number of countries n */
        qn=n;                    /* reserve n in qn */
        rr=0; step=0;
        setconn();               /* set neighbouring relation */
        parafor(cycp=0;cycp<MAX;cycp++)
            for(  q=0;   q<MAX;   q++){cycle[cycp][q]=0;}
/*0*/   initial();               /* set initial color */
        outcolor();              /* print color of each country */
/*loop*/
        for(updat=1;(updat>0)&&(step<BOUND); ){
/*1*/           parafor(q=1;q<=qn;q++){clearline(q);}
                                 /* board clear */
/*2*/           parafor(q=1;q<=qn;q++){shadow(q);}
                                 /* shadow to neighbours */
                updat=0;         /* conflict counter */
/*3*/           parafor(q=1;q<=qn;q++){conflict(q);}
                                 /* test and count */
            if(updat>0){         /* any conflict */
                movec=0; tryc=0;
/*4*/           parafor(q=1;q<=qn;q++){moveortry(q);}
                        /* movable test and increment movec,tryc */
/*5.1*/         if(movec>0){
                        findmaxconf();  /* set rr as movable */
                }
/*5.2*/     else if(tryc>0){
                        findgiveway();  /* set rr as giving way */
                }
/*5.3*/     else {      findmaxconf();  /* set rr as compulsory */
                }
                step++;
/*6*/           loopcheck();                 /* set anyeq */
                if(anyeq>0){step=BOUND+99;}
                /* print colors if necessary */
            }   /* end of conflict  processing */
        }       /* no-conflict or over of repetition */
        if(updat==0){/* print one solution */;}
        else        {/* print step counter is over BOUND */;}
}
```

<<be continued>>

FIG. 9.9

```
<<continuation of Program 5>>

shadow(qi)
        int     qi;     /* country number */
{
        int     ii,jj,lc;

        lc=j[qi];                               /* fetch self color   */
        for(ii=1;ii<=w[qi];ii++){
                jj=conn[qi][ii];                /* neighbour country */
                board[jj][lc]++;                /* increment shadow   */
        }
}


conflict(qi)
        int     qi;     /* country number */
{
        if(board[qi][j[qi]]==0){/* shadow of same color */
                chang[qi]=0;    /* no need to change */
        }
        else{
                chang[qi]=1;    /* need to change other color */
                updat++;        /* increment update counter   */
        }
}

moveortry(qi)
        int     qi;     /* country number */
{
        int     rrj;

        nextj[qi]=-1; tryj[qi]=-1; rrj=j[qi];
    if(chang[qi]==1){                    /* scan other color */
        for(rrj=rrj % C4 +1;(board[qi][rrj]!=0)&&(rrj!=j[qi]); ){
                rrj=rrj % C4 +1;
        }
        if(rrj!=j[qi]){                 /* find other color */
                nextj[qi]=rrj;
                movec++;
        }
    }
    else{
        for(rrj=rrj % C4 +1;(board[qi][rrj]!=0)&&(rrj!=j[qi]); ){
                rrj=rrj % C4 +1;
        }
        if(rrj!=j[qi]){                 /* try possible position */
                tryj[qi]=rrj;
                tryc++;
        }
    }
}
```

FIG. 9.9 (continued)

3. Check the conflict of color with neighbours.
4. Examine the possibility of changing the color. If any color is found which will not conflict with neighbors, increment the counter movec when a country's current color is the same as the color of any neighbor, or increment the counter tryc when its current color differs from all the neighbors.
5. Change the color of one country as follows. (We can change colors of some countries at once. Then it is predicted that new conflicts occur with high probability.)

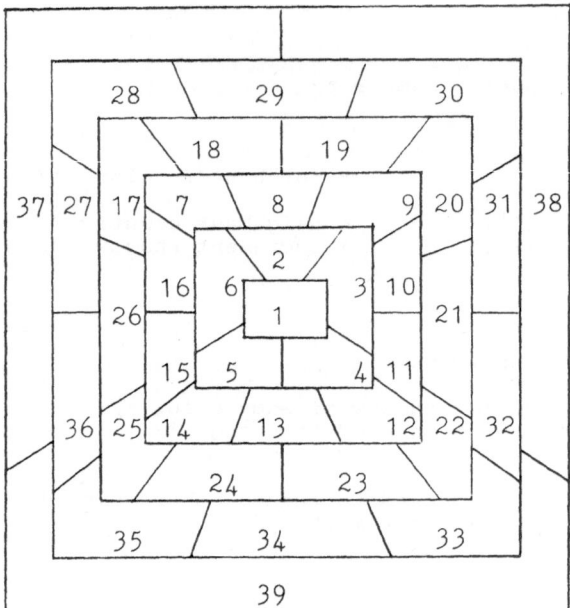

FIG. 9.10. An example of a map (Program 5: four-color problem with number of countries $n = 39$)

a) if any conflicting country is able to change color (**movec** > 0), then select the one whose conflict is the highest in degree.
b) otherwise, if some country has another non-conflicting color (**tryc** > 0), then one of them is selected in a nondeterministic manner,
c) otherwise (none of the countries has room to change color), select any one, in a nondeterministic manner, whose conflict is the highest in degree, and change its color to one whose conflict will be the lowest in degree.
6. Check for repeated assignment of the same colors, and avoid the possibility that computation will fall into an indefinite loop.

The Results of Computation 5 (Fig. 9.11) show the step-by-step assignment for 16 countries (1 to 16) of the map (Fig. 9.10). Table 9.1 denotes the number of steps to reach one assignment for n countries ($n = 30$ to 39) with four cases of initial states.
The characteristics of Program 5 are as follows:

a. One part takes care of one country.
b. The maximum degree of parallelism is n (number of countries).
c. While parallel computation is carried on (Steps 1 to 4), each part communicates only with its neighbors.
d. After any change of color, each part checks for new conflicts.
e. Computation ends when no conflict occurs, or when the number of steps exceeds the predefined number of cycles *BOUND*.
f. The number of computation cycles is unpredictable, but is bounded on $4n$ [(number of colors) × (number of countries)].

In this problem, as each part is able to change its color locally under the relation to neighbors, the whole computation would have a high possibility of nondeter-

```
Results of Computation 5

start for 16-countries with print mode p

neibouring condition is .....
index counter neibour countries
   1      6       2    3    4    5    6    0
   2      7       1    3    6    7    8    9    0
   3      7       1    2    4    9   10   11    0
   4      7       1    3    5   11   12   13    0
   5      7       1    4    6   13   14   15    0
   6      7       1    2    5    7   15   16    0
   7      7       2    6    8   16   17   18    0
   8      6       2    7    9   18   19    0
   9      7       2    3    8   10   19   20    0
  10      6       3    9   11   20   21    0
  11      7       3    4   10   12   21   22    0
  12      6       4   11   13   22   23    0
  13      7       4    5   12   14   23   24    0
  14      6       5   13   15   24   25    0
  15      7       5    6   14   16   25   26    0
  16      6       6    7   15   17   26    0
```

```
step=  0 : 12341 23412 34123 4
step=  1 : 12343 23412 34123 4
step=  2 : 12343 43412 34123 4
step=  3 : 12343 43412 14123 4
step=  4 : 12343 43412 12123 4
step=  5 : 12343 43412 12121 4
step=  6 : 12343 43412 12121 2
! one solution for given initial states

step=  0 : 12312 31231 23123 1
step=  1 : 12342 31231 23123 1
step=  2 : 12344 31231 23123 1
step=  3 : 12344 41231 23123 1
step=  4 : 12342 41231 23123 1
step=  5 : 12342 43231 23123 1
step=  6 : 12342 43431 23123 1
step=  7 : 12342 43441 23123 1
step=  8 : 12342 43441 23143 1
step=  9 : 12342 43141 23143 1
! one solution for given initial states

step=  0 : 12121 21212 12121 2
step=  1 : 12321 21212 12121 2
step=  2 : 12323 21212 12121 2
step=  3 : 12323 41212 12121 2
step=  4 : 12323 41312 12121 2
step=  5 : 12323 41312 13121 2
! one solution for given initial states

step=  0 : 11111 11111 11111 1
step=  1 : 12111 11111 11111 1
step=  2 : 12121 11111 11111 1
step=  3 : 12123 11111 11111 1
step=  4 : 12123 41111 11111 1
step=  5 : 12323 41111 11111 1
step=  6 : 12323 43111 11111 1
step=  7 : 12323 43141 11111 1
step=  8 : 12323 43141 41111 1
step=  9 : 12323 43141 41411 1
step= 10 : 12323 43141 41412 1
! one solution for given initial states
```

FIG. 9.11

TABLE 9.1. Number of computation cycles for countries 1 to n in the map of Fig. 9.10 with initial states of four cases

Initial state	Number of countries n									
	30	31	32	33	34	35	36	37	38	39
(1234)*	10	11	12	12	12	13	14	22	46	58
(123)*	66	66	119	59	59	46	35	36	84	60
(12)*	17	17	20	18	18	18	18	83	24	44
(1)*	21	28	51	24	23	53	34	35	67	44

minism. So, it is difficult to predict the computation time. Also, it has some tendency to fall into an infinite loop of computation.

9.4 Conclusion

In this paper, we propose Part-Oriented Parallel Algorithms. Through five examples, we consider that asynchronous operations and nondeterministic executions are new categories implemented only by parallel programming, not by sequential programming.

However, to establish these categories in practice, it is necessary to devise a new style of design for parallel programs, such as, for example, part-oriented parallel algorithms, and to introduce a corresponding programming language. Object-oriented parallel programming is considered as a candidate for such a style, but in this paper we stay in the area of the procedure-oriented language familiar to conventional programmers.

In the future, these programs need to be run on real parallel computers.

References

1. Carriero N, Gelernter D (1989) How to write parallel programs: a guide to the perplexed. Comput Surv 21: 323–357
2. Watanabe K, Tsuji T (1986) Some types of parallel algorithms. Mem Fac Eng, Fukui Univ 34: 121–138
3. Watanabe K, Tsuji T (1988) Part-Oriented Parallel Algorithms (in Japanese). Mem Fac Eng, Fukui Univ 36: 9–24
4. Almasi GS, Gottlieb A (1989) Highly parallel computing. Benjamin/Cumming, pp 236–241
5. Chandy KM, Misra J (1988) Parallel program design—a foundation. Addison-Wesley, pp 98–115
6. Yamamoto T, Furukane U, Nogura K (1977) The Durand-Kerner and the Aberth Methods for Solving Algebraic Equations (in Japanese). J Inf Process 18: 566–571

10
ObjectTags: An Interactive Tool to Understand C Programs

Tsuyoshi Ohta[1], Atsuo Ohki[2], and Koichiro Ochimizu[1]

Summary: In this paper, we show an interactive tool named ObjectTags which frees a user from searching for declarations or definitions of identifiers separately appearing in the text of a program. ObjectTags allows a user to concentrate on understanding the behavior of the program because the user need not change his or her viewpoint to search for declarations or definitions of identifiers. ObjectTags works under a multi-window environment. Whenever a user has a question about the meaning of some identifier, he or she can create a QA window and remain it as long as necessary. This feature makes it easy for a user to switch viewpoints between C program codes and declaration or definition of identifiers, because the user does not need to search for them again.

ObjectTags is an interact cross reference system which can work on Sun and NEWS workstations under X-window system version 10 or 11. It can handle the full syntax of the C programming language.

Key words: C program — understanding — interactive cross reference system

10.1 Introduction

It is often the case that we need to understand a program written in the past, in order to modify it. In this case, the reader must simulate the action of the computer along the program code, remembering important data structures or calling sequences of procedures. It is necessary to:

1. Memorize data types and values of important data objects (i.e., variables, functions, etc.)
2. Understand any algorithm in the program, referring to the data objects memorized.

Generally speaking, the human being is forgetful, so renewing his or her memory by re-examining data types or values of variables or functions causes the interruption of the thought process.

---

[1] Department of Computer Science, Faculty of Engineering, Shizuoka University, Hamamatsu, 432 Japan
[2] Graduate School of Systems Management, University of Tsukuba, Tsukuba, 305 Japan

ObjectTags helps the user display the declaration or definition of identifiers in the QA window every time the user asks the meaning of an identifier, allowing the user to concentrate on understanding the behavior of the program.

Under the UNIX[3] environment, we can use a facility similar to ObjectTags to search for function definitions using the vi editor [1]. However, only one definition is available in this facility and we cannot use this facility with variables which are referred to more frequently than functions.

ObjectTags can answer the following types of question about the C [2] program:

1. How identifiers are declared or defined in program texts.
2. What data type the expression has. Especially, to what data type the pointer refers.

10.2 An Architecture of ObjectTags

Figure 10.1 illustrates an architecture of ObjectTags. Before using ObjectTags, the user must run an analysis program in advance, to create a prolog fact database which contains information about declarations or definitions of all identifiers. The analysis program is written in C language. We can use the question-answering facility of ObjectTags by issuing the GNU Emacs [3] command. When a user wishes to know about the data type of a variable, function, or expression, the user can specify it as a string and issue the query command. Then, ObjectTags opens a new window, called the QA window, and displays the answer. The answer consists of two types of message. One is the declaration or definition written in the program text. The other is an explanation in English. The latter is optional. If the user is not satisfied with the answer, ie., he/she has another question related to the answer,

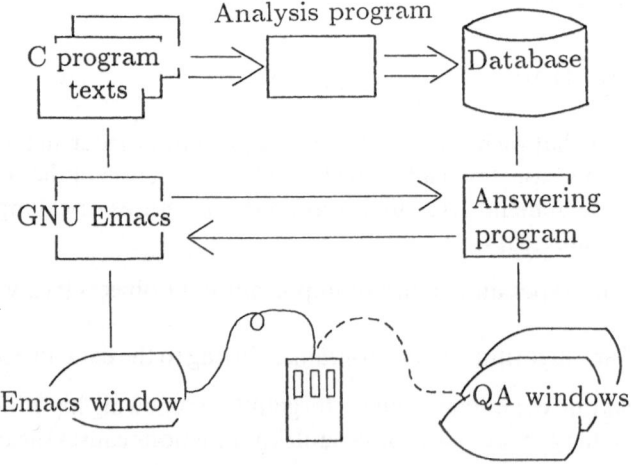

FIG. 10.1. An architecture of ObjectTags

---

[3] UNIX is a trademark of AT&T Bell Laboratories

ObjectTags allows the user to ask an additional question by specifying the string in the QA window. In this case, the answer is added to that QA window. The answering program is written in augmented C-prolog [4] which has the capability to handle the X-window system [5, 6] as described in the Appendix.

10.3 Organization of a Database

The database holds the information about declarations or definitions of all identifiers appearing in program texts. They are represented as Prolog facts of three-tuple:

(identifier, data type, position),

where position represents the location of declaration or definition of the identifier in the program text. The location is represented as a pair consisting of file name and byte offset from the top of the file

10.3.1 Representation of Data Type

We explain here the representation of various kinds of data type which are the second element of the three-tuple described.

10.3.1.1 Built-in Data Types

1. Type specifiers and storage class specifiers
   Type specifiers and storage class specifiers are represented as a list.

ex. [int], [static, char]

2. Pointer
   Pointers are represented as

pointer_to (data type),

where data type is a type to which the pointer refers.

ex. pointer_to ([static, int])

3. Array
   Arrays are represented as

array_of (number of elements, data type),

where number of elements is a list of tokens which represents the size of array. Data type shows an element type.

ex. array_of ([BUFSIZ, +, 1], [int])

4. Function
   Functions are represented as

function_returns (argument list, result data type).

ex. function_returns ([argc, argv], [void])

10.3.1.2 Structure and Union

Structures and unions are represented as follows in order to bind the identifier to the members of a structure.

struct_def_as(struct(identifier, position), structure members)

10.3.1.3 User-Defined Data Type

We can define a user-defined data type with typedef in C language. We represent it as follows, to bind a user-defined type name to its definition:

typedef_as(id(identifier, position), definition)

10.3.2 Variable Declarations and Function Definitions

Variable declarations and function definitions bind an identifier to its data type in the C program text. We represent this binding as follows:

id_decl_as(id(identifier, position), data type, initial value),

where initial value is a list of tokens which represent the initial value of variable.

In the case of function definition, the following fact is also created in a database to manage a scope of arguments of function.

func_range(identifier, file name, begin, end),

where begin and end indicate the beginning and end point of the function. They are byte offset from the top of file.

10.3.3 The Scope of Identifiers

The block is the basis for defining the scope of identifiers in C language. We should create facts about blocks to manage the scope of automatic variables which are only effective inside of the block. We represent all blocks with their identification number as follows:

block(file name, identification number, begin, end),

where begin and end indicate the beginning and end point of the block. They are byte offset from the top of the file.

10.3.4 Control Operations to the Preprocessor

The control operations to the preprocessor are not included in the specification of C language, but they give us important information when we understand C programs.

10.3.4.1 Include

In C programming, we usually create header files which have common declarations and definitions referred to from many program files. Because of this programming style in C, the search range of the declaration or definition of identifier should be extended to the header files.

When the analysis program meets this operation, it suspends the analysis of the current file and starts the analysis of the header file. When it finishes the analysis of the header file, the analysis program creates following fact and resumes the analysis which had been suspended.

include (current file name, position, header file name)

10.3.4.2 Define

The answering program must examine first whether the given identifier is defined as a macro. If the identifier is a macro name, the following fact is created:

pdefine (identifier, string),

where string is a macro definition of identifier.

10.3.4.3 Undef

When the analysis program meets this operation, it creates the following fact to specify that the macro definition of identifier is cancelled and is not effective after the position:

undef (identifier, position)

10.3.4.4 If, Ifdef, Ifndef, Else, Endif

These are the operations in order to support conditional compilation for distinguishing the system-dependent program codes in texts. When the analysis program meets these operations, it skips unnecessary program code and creates the following fact:

skip (file name, begin, end),

where begin and end indicate the beginning and end point of the skipped program code. They are byte offset from the top of the file.

10.4 Question and Answering Facility of ObjectTags

ObjectTags can answer a question issued by a user by retrieving the database defined in the previous section.

The answering part of ObjectTags works through four steps as follows:

1. Getting a question from the user as a string
2. Parsing a given string
3. Searching for identifiers from the database
4. Building up the answer

We describe each of these functions in more detail.

10.4.1 Getting a Question from the User as a String

Suppose the user reads a C program by using the GNU Emacs editor. If he or she wishes to know the data type of any data object in the text, he or she specifies the region of the data object by mouse. Next, he or she types the command or clicks the mouse to pass the string to the answering part of ObjectTags. The answering part of ObjectTags gets the string and interprets it as a question from the user.

10.4.2 Parsing a Given String

The next step is to parse the string and to make a parsing tree. There are two reasons to parse a string. One is to get identifiers in the string. Another is to decide the data type of root of parsing tree, if the string is an expression. This step is divided into two steps:

1. Separating a string into tokens
2. Making a parsing tree from the sequence of tokens

10.4.3 Searching Identifiers from the Database

All leaves of a parsing tree are identifiers. This step binds each leaf of the parsing tree to the declaration or definition of its identifier.

This step consists of three substeps:

1. To examine whether the identifier is a macro name using the facts pdefine and undef described in Sect. 10.3.
2. To examine whether the identifier is local, using the facts block and func_range..
3. To examine whether the identifier is global, using the fact include.

10.4.4 Building up the Answer

The answering part can decide the data type of the leaves in the given string so far. The answering part decides the data type of nodes in the parsing tree by reducing it according to the type conversion rules in C. Finally, the answering part creates a QA window on the workstation and writes the answer on it.

10.5 Example

We show an example in this section. An example program is the hoc program described in [7]. Figure 10.2 shows a typical screen layout when a user interacts with ObjectTags.

The upper window shows preparative activities for using ObjectTags. In this example, it shows there are six C program files and a Makefile in the current directory. By issuing the otags command, a user executes an analysis program. The file OTAGS is a database of these six programs. The first four facts are displayed.

The lower window is a GNU Emacs window in which the user read the code.c

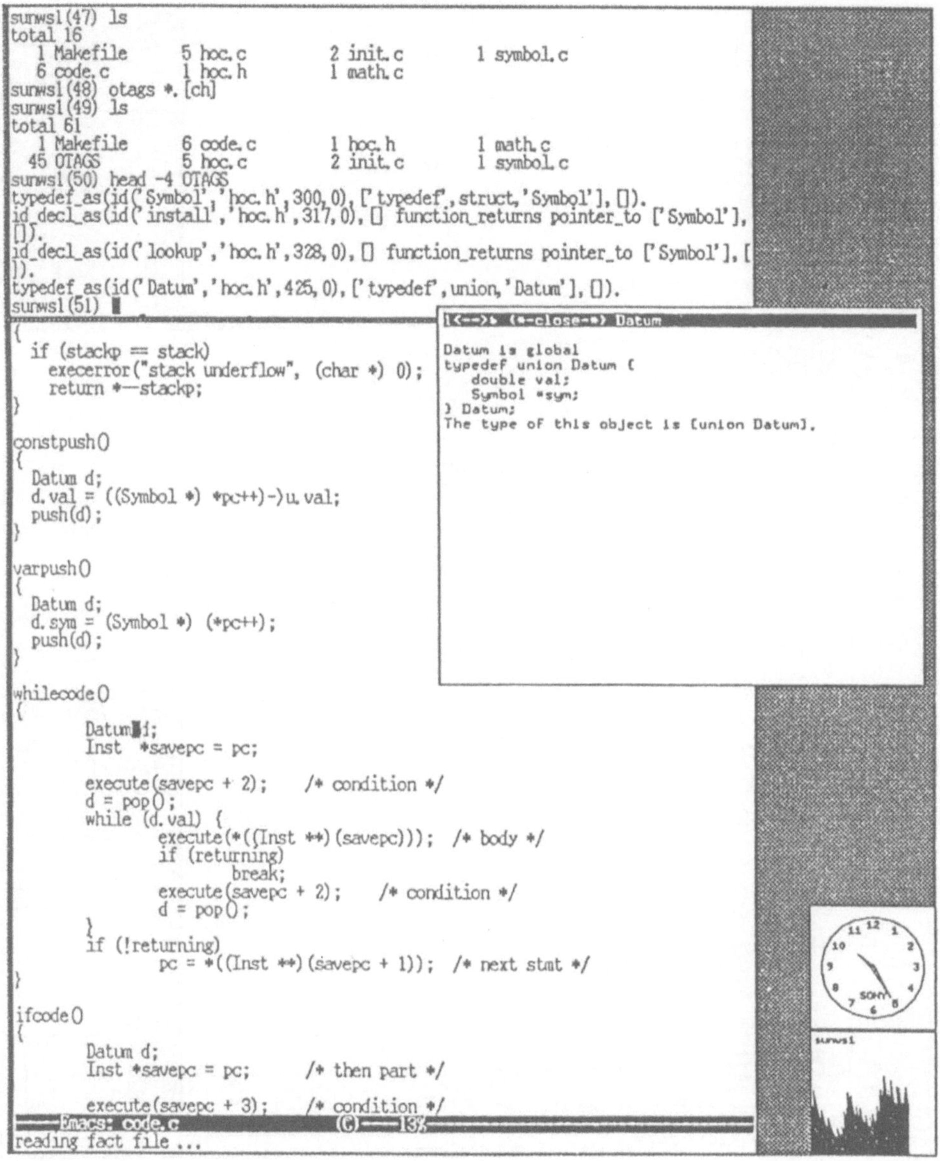

```
sunwsl(47) ls
total 16
   1 Makefile      5 hoc.c        2 init.c       1 symbol.c
   6 code.c        1 hoc.h        1 math.c
sunwsl(48) otags *.[ch]
sunwsl(49) ls
total 61
   1 Makefile      6 code.c       1 hoc.h        1 math.c
  45 OTAGS         5 hoc.c        2 init.c       1 symbol.c
sunwsl(50) head -4 OTAGS
typedef_as(id('Symbol','hoc.h',300,0),['typedef',struct,'Symbol'],[]).
id_decl_as(id('install','hoc.h',317,0),[] function_returns pointer_to ['Symbol'],
[]).
id_decl_as(id('lookup','hoc.h',328,0),[] function_returns pointer_to ['Symbol'],[
]).
typedef_as(id('Datum','hoc.h',425,0),['typedef',union,'Datum'],[]).
sunwsl(51) █
```
```
{                                          |X<-->% (%-close-%) Datum
   if (stackp == stack)                    |Datum is global
      execerror("stack underflow", (char *) 0);  |typedef union Datum {
   return *--stackp;                        |    double val;
}                                          |    Symbol *sym;
                                           |} Datum;
constpush()                                |The type of this object is [union Datum].
{
   Datum d;
   d.val = ((Symbol *) *pc++)-)u.val;
   push(d);
}

varpush()
{
   Datum d;
   d.sym = (Symbol *) (*pc++);
   push(d);
}

whilecode()
{
      Datum█d;
      Inst *savepc = pc;

      execute(savepc + 2);    /* condition */
      d = pop();
      while (d.val) {
             execute(*((Inst **) (savepc)));  /* body */
             if (returning)
                    break;
             execute(savepc + 2);    /* condition */
             d = pop();
      }
      if (!returning)
             pc = *((Inst **) (savepc + 1));  /* next stmt */
}

ifcode()
{
      Datum d;
      Inst *savepc = pc;    /* then part */

      execute(savepc + 3);    /* condition */
====Emacs: code.c                (C)----13%-------
reading fact file ...
```

FIG. 10.2. A typical screen layout

file. Suppose the user wishes to know the type definition of **Datum** at line 23; he/she specifies the beginning and end of the string on the window by using the mouse, and calls the answering part of ObjectTags by mouse (keyboard is also available). After a moment, a QA window appears on the middle right of the screen and shows the type definition of **Datum**. If the user is not satisfied with this answer, for example, he/she does not know the type definition of **Symbol**, then he/she can ask an

```
sunwsl(47) ls
total 16
    1 Makefile       5 hoc.c        2 init.c        1 symbol.c
    6 code.c         1 hoc.h        1 math.c
sunwsl(48) otags *.[ch]
sunwsl(49) ls
total 61
    1 Makefile       6 code.c       1 hoc.h         1 math.c
   45 OTAGS          5 hoc.c        2 init.c        1 symbol.c
sunwsl(50) head -4 OTAGS
typedef_as(id('Symbol','hoc.h',300,0), ['typedef',struct,'Symbol'], []).
id_decl_as(id('install','hoc.h',317,0), [] function_returns pointer_to ['Symbol'],
[]).
id_decl_as(id('lookup','hoc.h',328,0), [] function_returns pointer_to ['Symbol'], [
]).
typedef_as(id('Datum','hoc.h',425,0), ['typedef',union,'Datum'], []).
sunwsl(51) █
```

```
{
    if (stackp == stack)
        execerror("stack underflow", (char *) 0);
    return *--stackp;
}

constpush()
{
    Datum d;
    d.val = ((Symbol *) *pc++)-)u.val;
    push(d);
}

varpush()
{
    Datum d;
    d.sym = (Symbol *) (*pc++);
    push(d);
}

whilecode()
{
        Datum d;
        Inst *savepc = pc;

        execute(savepc + 2);    /* condition */
        d = pop();
        while (d.val) {
                execute(*((Inst **)(savepc)));   /* body */
                if (returning)
                        break;
                execute(savepc + 2);    /* condition */
                d = pop();
        }
        if (!returning)
                pc = *((Inst **)(savepc + 1));   /* next stmt */
}

ifcode()
{
        Datum d;
        Inst *savepc = pc;       /* then part */

        execute(savepc + 3);     /* condition */
```

```
[<-->]$ (*-close-*) Datum
Datum is global
typedef union Datum {
        double val;
        Symbol *sym;
} Datum;
The type of this object is [union Datum].

Symbol is global
typedef struct Symbol {
        char *name;
        short type;
        union {
                double val;
                double (*ptr)();
                int (*defn)();
                char *str;
        } u;
        struct Symbol *next;
} Symbol;
The type of this object is [struct Symbol].
```

```
=====Emacs: code.c           (C)===13%=====
reading fact file ...
```

FIG. 10.3. Answering an additional question

additional question by specifying the string on the QA window by mouse. Figure 10.3 shows a result of this activity. The answer to the query about **Symbol** is added to the QA window.

ObjectTags can provide a QA window for each question from the GNU Emacs window. Figure 10.4 shows an example of three QA windows which give the answers to three independent questions. In this example, they are questions about a type

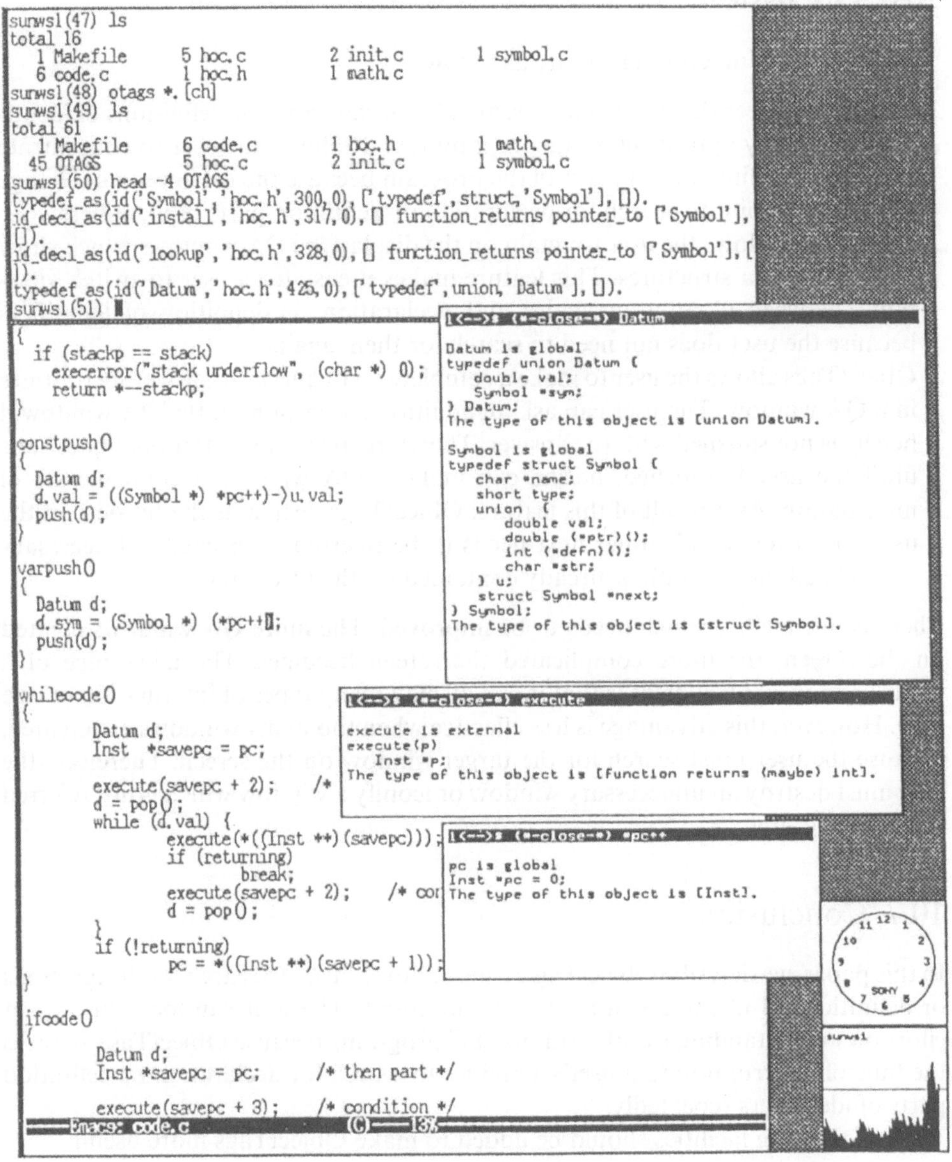

```
surwsl(47) ls
total 16
   1 Makefile        5 hoc.c        2 init.c        1 symbol.c
   6 code.c          1 hoc.h        1 math.c
surwsl(48) otags *.[ch]
surwsl(49) ls
total 61
   1 Makefile        6 code.c       1 hoc.h         1 math.c
  45 OTAGS           5 hoc.c        2 init.c        1 symbol.c
surwsl(50) head -4 OTAGS
typedef_as(id('Symbol','hoc.h',300,0),['typedef',struct,'Symbol'],[]).
id_decl_as(id('install','hoc.h',317,0),[] function_returns pointer_to ['Symbol'],
[]).
id_decl_as(id('lookup','hoc.h',328,0),[] function_returns pointer_to ['Symbol'],[
]).
typedef_as(id('Datum','hoc.h',425,0),['typedef',union,'Datum'],[]).
surwsl(51) █
```

```
                                        [(-->)* (*-close-*) Datum
{
  if (stackp == stack)                   Datum is global
     execerror("stack underflow", (char *) 0);   typedef union Datum {
     return *--stackp;                        double val;
}                                             Symbol *sym;
                                           } Datum;
                                           The type of this object is [union Datum].
constpush()
{                                          Symbol is global
                                           typedef struct Symbol {
  Datum d;                                     char *name;
  d.val = ((Symbol *) *pc++)->u.val;           short type;
  push(d);                                      union {
}                                                  double val;
                                                   double (*ptr)();
varpush()                                          int (*defn)();
{                                                  char *str;
                                               } u;
  Datum d;                                     struct Symbol *next;
  d.sym = (Symbol *) (*pc++█;             } Symbol;
  push(d);                                 The type of this object is [struct Symbol].
}

whilecode()
{                         [(-->)* (*-close-*) execute
  Datum d;               execute is external
  Inst *savepc = pc;     execute(p)
                             Inst *p;
  execute(savepc + 2);   /* The type of this object is [function returns (maybe) int].
  d = pop();
  while (d.val) {
          execute(*((Inst **) (savepc)));  [(-->)* (*-close-*) *pc++
          if (returning)
                break;                     pc is global
          execute(savepc + 2);   /* cor   Inst *pc = 0;
          d = pop();                        The type of this object is [Inst].
  }
  if (!returning)
        pc = *((Inst **) (savepc + 1));
}

ifcode()
{
  Datum d;
  Inst *savepc = pc;     /* then part */

  execute(savepc + 3);   /* condition */
```
Emacs: code.c   (C)──13%
```

FIG. 10.4. Three different types of QA windows

definition, a function name, and an expression. The answer to the query about the function name includes the definition of the type of arguments, while the answer to the question about the expression includes the declaration of identifiers appearing in the expression.

The results of question-answering routines can be retained on the screen for later use. If the user no longer needs the information in the QA window, he/she can destroy the QA window.
```

10.6 Discussion

The merits of using ObjectTags are as follows:

1. ObjectTags frees the user from searching for declarations or definitions of identifiers separately appearing in the program text. It allows the user to concentrate on understanding the behavior of the program because the user need not change his/her viewpoint to search for declaration or definition parts of identifiers.
2. ObjectTags allows the user to retain on the display the QA windows which show important data structures. This feature makes it easy for a user to switch viewpoint between C program codes and declaration or definition of identifiers because the user does not need to search for them again.
3. ObjectTags allows the user to make a complete set of question-answering routines in a QA window. The user can ask an additional question on the QA window if he/she is not satisfied with the answer. Therefore, by asking additional questions until the user is satisfied, he/she can make a QA window a complete set of information. As a result of this feature, ObjectTags decreases the burden on the user whenever the identifier next needs to be referred to, because all necessary and related information is already contained on the QA window.

There is one facility which needs to be improved. The more QA windows created on the screen, the more complicated the screen becomes. The advantage of a multi-window environment is that it can display many types of information at one time. However, this advantage is less effective when too many windows are created, because the user must search for the target window on the screen. Therefore, the user must destroy an unnecessary window or iconify a window which is not referred to for a long time.

10.7 Conclusion

In this paper, we describe ObjectTags, which allows a user to search for declarations or definitions of identifiers in reading C programs. The user can focus his or her effort on understanding the algorithms of C programs because ObjectTags reduces the time of interruption to a user's activities to search for declaration or definition parts of identifiers repeatedly.

The following facilities should be added to make ObjectTags more useful:

1. Answering questions about library routines.
   Our aim is to incorporate in ObjectTags a facility for examining online manuals under the UNIX environment. We often examine the function of a library routine or the meaning of its arguments to understand programs. In this situation, we can examine online manuals under the UNIX environment. However, we currently need a different operation from ObjectTags to examine online manuals using the man command. To avoid this different operation, we have almost completed the addition of a facility which can answer questions about library routines in the same manner.

2. Automatic retrieval of QA windows related to the question.
In the current ObjectTags, a user must specify each identifier desired. Therefore, the number of windows tends to increase. To solve this problem, we think that it is useful to add questions related to a given question automatically and display the answers on the same QA window. For example, when the user asks a question about a function name, ObjectTags automatically adds the questions about variables and functions appearing in the function, and displays all answers on one QA window. However, it is obvious that if we implement this mechanism blindly, we may introduce the complication of too much unnecessary information. Therefore, we may need some intelligent mechanism to avoid adding unnecessary questions.

3. Application to programming phase.
The Current ObjectTags focuses its function only on the understanding of C programs. It is more useful to extend this facility at the programming phase because a programmer often forgets his or her previously written program code. To support this, we must modify ObjectTags so that it can manage a database dynamically.

References

1. UNIX Programmer's Manual (1983) ctags, ex, vi. University of California
2. Kernighan BW, Ritchie DM (1978) The C programming language. Prentice-Hall
3. Stallman R (1986) GNU Emacs manual
4. Pereira F (1986) C-prolog user's manual
5. Gettys J, Newman R, Fera TD (1986) Xlib—C language X interface protocol version 10
6. Jones O (1989) Introduction to the X Window system. Prentice-Hall
7. Kernighan BW, Pile R (1984) The UNIX programming environment. Prentice-Hall

Appendix

This appendix shows the predicates and features added to C-prolog.

A.1 Window Stream

A window stream is an output stream and is identified by its name (literal atom). A window stream may be mapped to a window to be displayed. Like I/O streams, which an original C-prolog has, there is a current window stream which is defaulted to nill, denoted by '[ ]'.

stream_tell(S)
Opens the window stream named S, and makes it a current window stream. If S is already open, nothing is done except that it becomes a current window stream. Reopening a stream clears the previous contents of a window stream. Fails if a window stream cannot be created.

stream_tell_again(S)
Like stream_tell(S), makes a window stream named S, and it becomes a current window stream. The difference between stream_tell(S) and stream_tell_again(S) is that stream_tell_again(S) does not clear the contents of the stream.

stream_telling(S)
S is unified with the name of the current stream (including nill). Never fails.

stream_exists(S)
Succeeds if the window stream S exists.

stream_told
Closes the current window stream. After calling this, the current window stream is defaulted to nill.

The following predicates are for output to the current window stream. Their meaning may be clear.

stream_write(T)
stream_writeq(T)
stream_nl
stream_put(N)
stream_tab(N)

A.2 Window Management

create_window(W)
If W is a variable and is unbounded, creates a window, and W is unified with the window number (nonnegative integer). Fails if a window cannot be created. If W is bounded to an integer, succeeds when there exists a window whose window number is W.

destroy_window(W)
Destroys the window W. Never fails even if there exists no window specified by W.

map_window(W)
Maps a window W to the hardware display.

unmap-window(W)
Unmaps a window W from the hardware display.

map_stream_to_window(S, W)
Maps a window stream named S to a window W. The contents of the window stream are displayed to the window W and become visible to the user if W is mapped. If S is a variable and is unbounded, S is unified with the stream name currently mapped to the window W. Fails if a window W does not exist.

A.3 Mouse Usage

A mouse is used to create a window and to scroll contents of a window. For creating a window, the usage is the same as that of **XCreateTerm( )**.

Scrolling can be done by, first pointing to the appropriate character in the title line, and then pushing one of the three buttons. Or, more conveniently, while a mouse is in a window but not in the title line, push the left button to scroll down a half screen, or the right to scroll up.

A.4 Input with a Mouse

An input selected with a mouse can be read through the input stream user as follows:

mouse_input(ButtonNumber, Window, Stream, Input_string)

where **ButtonNumber** is the button used to select input, 0 for the right button, 1 for the middle, and 2 for the left. **Window** is the window number from which input comes. **Stream** is the window stream name currently mapped to the window.

Input can be selected with the mouse as follows:

1. Move the mouse to the head of the string you want to select.
2. While holding a shift key down, press a button (middle or right).
3. Move the mouse to the end of the string, and then release a button and a shift key. The left button selects a whole line.

11
Partial Order Transparency as a Tool to Reduce Interference in Monitoring Concurrent Systems

Jingde Cheng and Kazuo Ushijima[1]

Summary: In monitoring a concurrent system, since the behavior of the system is generally run-time dependent, there is an "uncertainty principle," i.e., any monitoring mechanism will interfere with the performance of the system and may even alter the behavior of the system. An important problem in monitoring a concurrent system concerns how to reduce the interference and alteration imposed on the behavior of the system by the action of monitoring. This paper proposes a new concept, named "partial order transparency," for monitoring concurrent systems. It is a minimum requirement for an execution monitor in order to reduce its interference to and alteration of the behavior of target systems. An execution monitor satisfying the requirement is transparent to a partial order with respect to occurrences of concurrent events during the execution of a target system. We select the programming language Ada as an object language for our discussion, and present an abstract model based on lattice theory for execution histories of concurrent Ada programs in terms of task interactions. The concept of partial order transparency is then formally presented based on this model.

Key words: monitoring — concurrency — program transformation — Ada

11.1 Introduction

Monitoring the behavior of a computing system (e.g., an executable specification, a program, or a group of programs on a distributed system) is a fundamental technique used in software development and maintenance, because it supports status reporting, tracing, testing, debugging, performance evaluation, tuning, and dynamic reconfiguration of the system. Thus, the monitoring plays a fundamental role in many software development and maintenance activities, and therefore an execution monitor is generally an indispensable component of a software development environment [1–5].

---
[1] Department of Computer Science and Communication Engineering, Kyushu University, Hakozaki, Fukuoka, 812, Japan

156

In monitoring a concurrent (centralized or distributed) system, since the behavior of the system is generally run-time dependent, there is an "uncertainty principle" [6, 7], i.e., any monitoring mechanism will interfere with the performance of the system and may even alter the behavior of the system. An important problem, called the *accurate monitoring problem*, in monitoring concurrent systems concerns how to reduce such interference and alteration. However, to our knowledge, no general solution has been proposed for this problem. In fact, since any run-time monitoring action has to interfere with the performance of a target system, it is impossible to completely eliminate the interference. Therefore, what we can do is to develop an execution monitor which interferes with the performance of a target system as little as possible and does not, if possible, alter the behavior of the system which we are interested in. To this end, we need an explicitly defined minimum requirement for an execution monitor with which we can measure the accuracy of behavior of a system monitored by the monitor. However, in order to reduce the interference and alteration imposed on the behavior of a target system by an execution monitor, what requirement should the monitor at least satisfy?

We consider that concurrent events occurring during an execution of a concurrent system are the most primitive entities in the behavior of the system, and that a temporal and/or causal order among the events is the most essential property of concurrency in the system. The temporal and/or causal order is generally a partial order. Thus, the events and the partial order are very important to allow programmers to observe and evaluate the behavior of their concurrent programs. Therefore, an execution monitor for concurrent systems should not and must not alter any of this behavior of target systems.

The programming language Ada was designed as a common language for programming large-scale and real-time software [8, 9]. In general, such software is concurrent. Testing and debugging concurrent Ada programs is an indispensable means for ensuring reliability of applications with Ada. Monitoring the behavior of a concurrent Ada program is necessary for testing and debugging the program. When we develop an execution monitor for concurrent Ada programs, we will, of course, be confronted with the accurate monitoring problem.

In order to solve the accurate monitoring problem, this paper proposes a new concept, named "*partial order transparency*," for monitoring concurrent systems. The concept is a minimum requirement for an execution monitor in order to reduce its interference with and alteration of the behavior of target systems. An execution monitor satisfying the requirement is transparent to a partial order with respect to occurrences of concurrent events in the execution of a target system. We selected Ada as an object language for our discussion, and present an abstract model based on lattice theory for execution histories of concurrent Ada programs in terms of task interactions. The concept of partial order transparency is then formally presented based on this model. We do not claim it is possible for an execution monitor to completely eliminate interference by the act of monitoring, but as we will show, we can certainly develop an interference-free execution monitor in the sense of partial order transparency.

In Sect. 11.2, we present some basic concepts of monitoring concurrent systems. In Sect. 11.3, we present the lattice model for execution histories of concurrent

Ada programs. In Sect. 11.4, we present the concept of partial order transparency. In Sect 11.5, we indicate why the partial order transparency is necessary for monitoring concurrent systems through a real example. Concluding remarks are given in Sect. 11.6.

11.2 Basic Concepts of Monitoring Concurrent Systems

Monitoring a program involves collection, recording, analysis, and display of information concerning the behavior of the program. In general, events occurring during the execution of a program are primitive objects for monitoring.

An event in a sequential program relates to either a control transfer, an access to a variable, or an I/O operation. On the other hand, an event in a concurrent program may not only relate to a local action inside a process but also relate to the creation and termination of a process or a communication and/or synchronization among processes. In the following discussion, we call an event a *sequential event* if it relates only to a local action inside a process, and call an event a *concurrent event* if it relates to an interaction between processes such as inter-process communication and/or synchronization.

A *target program* is the source text of a program to be monitored. A *target programming language* is the language used to write target programs. An *information extraction point* is a location in a target program where an event occurs during an execution of the program and has a semantic interpretation at target programming language level. A *sensor* is a section of code which is inserted within an information extraction point of a target program in order to collect the information concerning an event occurring at that point. A sensor may be in the form of a target programming language code or in the form of an object language code. The sensors in the former form are inserted within a target program, and the sensors in the latter form are inserted within the object program obtained by compiling a target program. A *subject program* is a program being monitored, i.e., the program obtained from a target program by inserting sensors. A *run-time monitor* is a program to communicate with the sensors of a subject program and to collect information concerning events occurring in the target program corresponding to the subject program. An *execution monitor* is a software system which inserts sensors into target programs, executes subject programs, and collects, records, analyzes, and displays information concerning the behavior of the target programs. An execution monitor is said to be *working with a source program transformation approach* if the sensors inserted by it have the form of a target programming language code; an execution monitor is said to be *working with an object program transformation approach* if the sensors inserted by it have the form of an object language code.

The information collection mechanism in monitoring may be *tracing* or *sampling*. In a tracing mechanism, the information collected by a sensor is passed to a run-time monitor every time a particular event occurs in a subject program. In a sampling mechanism, the information collected by a sensor is passed to a run-time monitor only when the monitor requests it.

In general, monitoring can be regarded as a sequential process in three steps as follows:

1. Preprocessing: an execution monitor generates the corresponding subject program for a target program.
2. Execution monitoring: the execution monitor executes the subject program and then collects and records information concerning the behavior of the target program.
3. Postprocessing: the execution monitor analyzes and displays the collected information.

11.3 Lattice Model for Execution Histories of Concurrent Ada Programs

In order to discuss the accurate monitoring problem formally, an abstract model for the behavior of target programs is indispensable. In constructing a formal model of a physical system, a good strategy is to define basic concepts in terms of such attributes as can be directly or indirectly observed and measured in the system. To model the tasking behavior of a concurrent Ada program, we define and use tasking events as primitive entities to be observed. Informally, a tasking event in a concurrent Ada program is an atomic tasking action whose occurrence can be detected at the Ada source code level. We regard the tasking behavior of a task as a tasking event stream. Thus, a state of a task which describes what that task is doing may be defined by two contiguous tasking events. By this modeling approach, we can concentrate our attention to the task interaction without regard to details inside tasks.

The primary mechanism for Ada inter-task communications is a rendezvous form [9]. It is assumed that tasks of all Ada programs considered in this paper communicate with each other using only a rendezvous form, even though Ada tasks may communicate with each other using shared variables. Thus, the tasking behavior of such an Ada program is determined by a given input and a sequence of synchronization and communication among tasks.

On the other hand, we make no assumption about the execution rates of concurrently executing tasks, except the finite progress assumption (i.e., rates of tasks are all positive) because we would like to understand the tasking behavior of a concurrent Ada program in terms of the interactions among its component tasks, without regard to the method by which those tasks are executed at certain rates.

The main program of an Ada program acts as if called by some environment task [9]. In the following discussion, such an environment task is named the *main task*. It is assumed that the main task has a virtual declarative part that includes declarations of the main program procedure and all library units needed by the main program.

Now, we decide what kinds of atomic tasking actions are detectable at the Ada source code level. According to the syntax and semantics of Ada tasking [9], the following 33 kinds of atomic tasking actions may occur in the lifetime of a task (i.e., the duration from the moment of its activation to the moment of its termination) and can be detected at Ada source code level. We specify each kind by a *tasking event name*, here defined as:

Elaboration-start, Elaboration-completion, Activation-start, Subtask-declaration-evaluation-start, Subtask-declaration-evaluation-completion, Activation-completion, Execution-start, Subtask-allocator-evaluation-start, Subtask-allocator-evaluation-completion, Simple-entry-call, Conditional entry-call, Timed-entry-call, Entry-call-cancellation, Acceptance, Simple-selection, Conditional-selection, Timed-selection, Termination-selection, Selection-cancellation, Rendezvous-start, Continuation, Abort, Aborted, Block-elaboration-start, Block-elaboration-completion, Block-execution-start, Block-execution-completion, Block-termination, Activation-exception, Execution-exception, Communication-exception, Completion, and *Termination.*

For the semantics of these atomic tasking actions, please refer to [9, 10]. Note that we define no tasking event name concerning a delay statement, except for delay alternatives in a select statement. This is because we regard actions according to the execution of a "pure" delay statement as actions inside a task.

Definition 3.1. A *tasking event e* is formally defined by an 8-tuple $e = (T, N, To, E, Me, B, Ma, t)$. In the 8-tuple, T is a unique identifier of a task where e occurs; N is the tasking event name of e; To is $\perp$ (denotes "undefined") or a unique identifier of a task, which is either created, called, or aborted by T; E is $\perp$ or a set of unique identifiers of entries to be used for communication of T with other tasks; $Me^{\cdot}$ is $\perp$ or a set of messages passed between T and the other task during their rendezvous; B is $\perp$ or a unique identifier of a subprogram called by T or a block statement executed by T; Ma is $\perp$ or a unique identifier of a master which directly creates T; t is the time the tasking event occurs (this time may be physical time in an interleaved implementation of Ada or virtual time [11] in a distributed implementation of Ada).

Definition 3.2. A *tasking event space*, denoted by **TES**(P, I), created by an execution of an Ada program P with a given input I, is a set of all tasking events occurring during the execution.

For any tasking event space **TES**(P, I), we may define a partial order on it according to the semantics of Ada tasking. This partial order can be regarded as a minimum constraint on the occurrence order of the tasking events during the execution of P with I. It is determined by I and the tasking semantics of P. For example, a task can only be activated after the start of execution of its master, and must terminate before the termination of its master, but different tasks depending on the master may start their executions, in particular their activations, in any order. Later, we define this partial order.

Definition 3.3. For any given **TES**(P, I), a binary relation **DE** $\in$ **TES**(P, I) $\times$ **TES**(P, I) is defined as follows. For any two elements $e_1 = (T_1, N_1, To_1, E_1, Me_1, B_1, Ma_1, t_1)$ and $e_2 = (T_2, N_2, To_2, E_2, Me_2, B_2, Ma_2, t_2)$ in the **TES**(P, I), $(e_1, e_2) \in$ **DS** if and only if e_2 occurs after the occurrence of e_1 and furthermore e_1 and e_2 satisfy either of the following conditions:

1. $T_2 = T_1$, and e_2 occurs immediately after the occurrence of e_1;
2. $T_2 \neq T_1$, and e_2 and e_1 achieve a synchronization between T_2 and T_1, such as synchronization about subtask declaration evaluation, task elaboration, task activation, rendezvous, task completion, and task termination.

If $(e_1, e_2) \in$ **DS**, then e_2 is called a *direct successor* of e_1.

A more formal definition of direct successor relation **DS** can be found in [4].

Now we explain some important properties of the tasking event spaces of Ada programs based on lattice theory [12, 13]. Because of the limitation of space, we omit all proofs.

Lemma 3.1. For any given **TES**(P, I), the transitive reflexive closure of **DS** on **TES**(P, I), called *tasking partial order* and denoted by $\leq_{TPO}$, is a partial order on **TES**(P, I), i.e., (**TES**(P, I), $\leq_{TPO}$) is a partially ordered set.

Lemma 3.2. For any given (**TES**(P, I), $\leq_{TPO}$), it has the least element (MAIN_TASK, Activation-start, $\perp$, $\perp$, $\perp$, $\perp$, $\perp$, t_A) where MAIN_TASK is the identifier of the main task of P, and t_A is the time the main task starts its activation; if (**TES**(P, I), $\leq_{TPO}$) is finite, then it has also the greatest element (MAIN_TASK, Termination, $\perp$, $\perp$, $\perp$, $\perp$, $\perp$, t_T) where t_T is the time the main task terminates.

Lemma 3.3. For any given (**TES**(P, I), $\leq_{TPO}$), its subset, all of whose elements have the same task identifier, is a chain.

Theorem 3.1. Any (**TES**(P, I), $\leq_{TPO}$) is a meet-semilattice; moreover, if (**TES**(P, I), $\leq_{TPO}$) is finite, then it is not only a lattice but also a complete lattice.

We call a lattice (**TES**(P, I), $\leq_{TPO}$) a *dynamic structure lattice* of Ada program P with input I. The dynamic structure lattices can be regarded as an abstract model for execution histories of Ada programs in terms of task interactions. We name this abstract model the "*lattice model*." It provides a basis for formally discussing the accurate monitoring problem of concurrent Ada programs.

Definition 3.4. Let $(L_1, \leq_1)$ and $(L_2, \leq_2)$ be two meet-semilattices. A mapping Ψ: $(L_1, \leq_1) \to (L_2, \leq_2)$ is called a *meet-homomorphism* if $\Psi(a \cap b) = \Psi(a) \cap \Psi(b)$ for any a, b in L_1 where $a \cap b$ denotes a greatest lower bound ("g.l.b." or "meet") of a and b. A meet-homomorphism is called a *meet-homomorphous one-to-one* if it is also a one-to-one. A meet-homomorphism is called a *meet-homomorphous onto* if it is also an onto. A meet-homomorphism is called a *meet-isomorphism* if it is both a meet-homomorphous one-to-one and a meet-homomorphous onto.

Definition 3.5. For any two dynamic structure lattices $(\mathbf{TES}(P,I)_1, \leqq_{TPO})$ and $(\mathbf{TES}(P,I)_2, \leqq_{TPO})$ if there exists a meet-isomorphism Ψ: $(\mathbf{TES}(P,I)_1, \leqq_{TPO}) \rightarrow (\mathbf{TES}(P,I)_2, \leqq_{TPO})$, which satisfies the following condition:

for any $(T_1, N_1, To_1, E_1, Me_1, B_1, Ma_1, t_1)$ in $\mathbf{TES}(P,I)_1$, if $\Psi((T_1, N_1, To_1, E_1, Me_1, B_1, Ma_1, t_1)) = (T_2, N_2, To_2, E_2, Me_2, B_2, Ma_2, t_2)$ then $T_1 = T_2$, $N_1 = N_2$, $To_1 = To_2$, $E_1 = E_2$, $Me_1 = Me_2$, $B_1 = B_2$, $Ma_1 = Ma_2$,

then we say $(\mathbf{TES}(P,I)_1, \leqq_{TPO})$ and $(\mathbf{TES}(P,I)_2, \leqq_{TPO})$ are *equivalent in dynamic structure* and denote this fact by $(\mathbf{TES}(P,I)_1, \leqq_{TPO}) \equiv (\mathbf{TES}(P,I)_2, \leqq_{TPO})$.

Lemma 3.4. For any concurrent Ada program P and any input I for it, the relation $\equiv$ on the set of dynamic structure lattices created by repeated executions of P with I is an equivalence relation. That is, for any $(\mathbf{TES}(P,I), \leqq_{TPO})$ in the set of dynamic structure lattices created by repeated executions of P with I, there exists an equivalence class of $(\mathbf{TES}(P,I), \leqq_{TPO})$, denoted by $[(\mathbf{TES}(P,I), \leqq_{TPO})]$, with respect to $\equiv$.

In the following discussion, when we use a notation $(\mathbf{TES}(P,I), \leqq_{TPO})$, we imply that it is some element of $[(\mathbf{TES}(P,I), \leqq_{TPO})]$.

11.4. Partial Order Transparency

When we monitor a concurrent Ada program, what we can observe is the behavior of a subject program of the program. It is not necessarily completely equivalent to the original behavior (i.e., without the act of monitoring) of the target program because of interference by the monitoring actions. It is clear that the accuracy of the program behavior assessed by monitoring depends on some transparency of the execution monitor to the monitored behavior of the target program. Due to the interference of monitoring actions, it is impossible to make an execution monitor completely transparent to the original behavior of the target program. However, it is possible to make an execution monitor transparent to a part of the original behavior of the target program. In other words, in order to monitor a target program accurately, the monitoring actions should not and must not alter any of those program behaviors we are interested in. According to various aims, we can define various transparencies for execution monitors. A weaker transparency is the "partial order transparency" we will now propose.

Here, we define formally the partial order transparency for an execution monitor for concurrent Ada programs. The basic idea of the concept is to make the monitor transparent to a partial order with respect to occurrences of tasking events during the execution of a target program. Our discussion is formally based on the lattice model for execution histories of concurrent Ada programs. The point is to discuss a correspondence between the execution history of a target program and that of subject program of the program, in terms of abstract algebraic structures of their dynamic structure lattices.

Definition 4.1. Let $(S_1, \leqq_1)$ and $(S_2, \leqq_2)$ be two partially ordered sets.

1. A mapping Ψ: $S_1 \to S_2$ is called an order homomorphism, an isotone, or an order-preserving mapping if it satisfies the condition: if $s_1 \leqq_1 s_2$ then $\Psi(s_1) \leqq_2 \Psi(s_2)$ for any s_1, s_2 in S_1 [12, 13].
2. A mapping Ψ: $S_1 \to S_2$ is called a *conservative homomorphism* or a *conservative mapping* if it satisfies the condition: if s_1 and s_2 are incomparable with respect to $\leqq_1$ then $\Psi(s_1)$ and $\Psi(s_2)$ are incomparable with respect to $\leqq_2$ for any s_1, s_2 in S_1.
3. A mapping Ψ: $S_1 \to S_2$ is called a *partial order homomorphism* or a *partial order preserving mapping* if and only if it is both an order homomorphism and a conservative homomorphism.

Definition 4.2. An execution monitor for concurrent Ada programs is said to be *partial order transparent* to target programs if it satisfies the following two conditions for any $(\mathbf{TES}(P, I), \leqq_{\mathrm{TPO}})$ of any target Ada program P with any given input I where $\Psi(P)$ is the subject program of P.

1. There exist a $(\mathbf{TES}(\Phi(P), I), \leqq_{\mathrm{TPO}})$ and a partial order homomorphism Ψ: $(\mathbf{TES}(P, I), \leqq_{\mathrm{TPO}}) \to (\mathbf{TES}(\Phi(P), I), \leqq_{\mathrm{TPO}})$.
2. For any $(T_1, N_1, To_1, E_1, Me_1, B_1, Ma_1, t_1)$ in $\mathbf{TES}(P, I), \leqq_{\mathrm{TPO}})$, if $\Psi((T_1, N_1, To_1, E_1, Me_1, B_1, Ma_1, t_1)) = (T_2, N_2, To_2, E_2, Me_2, B_2, Ma_2, t_2)$ then $T_1 = T_2$, $N_1 = N_2$, $To_1 = To_2$, $E_1 = E_2$, $Me_1 = Me_2$, $B_1 = B_2$, $Ma_1 = Ma_2$.

Note that the definition of partial order transparency requires that an execution monitor should preserve not only a temporal and/or causal order among concurrent events of a target program but also an incomparability among the concurrent events with respect to the temporal and/or causal order. This is an important and desirable property for an execution monitor because it provides a guarantee that all the possible behavior of a target program may be observed in monitoring.

If an execution monitor for concurrent Ada programs satisfies the partial order transparency, then it preserves the same tasking partial order $\leqq_{\mathrm{TPO}}$ in the behavior of the subject program of the program as that in the original behavior of the target program. As a result, any possible tasking partial order in the target program may occur in the subject program (Fig. 11.1a). If an execution monitor for concurrent Ada programs does not satisfy the partial order transparency, then it cannot preserve the same tasking partial order $\leqq_{\mathrm{TPO}}$ in the behavior of the subject program as that in the original behavior of the target program. As a result, only some of the possible tasking partial orders in the target program may occur in the subject program (Fig. 11.1b).

Here, we explain how to make an execution monitor, working with a source program transformation approach, satisfy the partial order transparency. Based on the lattice model, we define an equivalence between a target Ada program P and the transformed program $\Phi(P)$ with respect to abstract algebraic structures of their dynamic structure lattices. If the program transformation Φ guarantees that there is an isomorphism from every dynamic structure lattice of the original program P to a sublattice of the corresponding dynamic structure lattice of the trans-

set of all tasking partial   execution monitor   set of all tasking partial
orders in target program   orders in subject program

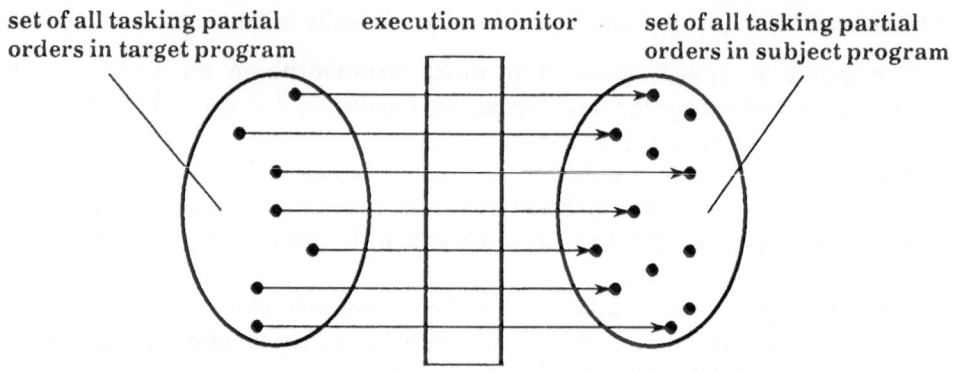

(a) execution monitor with partial order transparency

set of all tasking partial   execution monitor   set of all tasking partial
orders in target program   orders in subject program

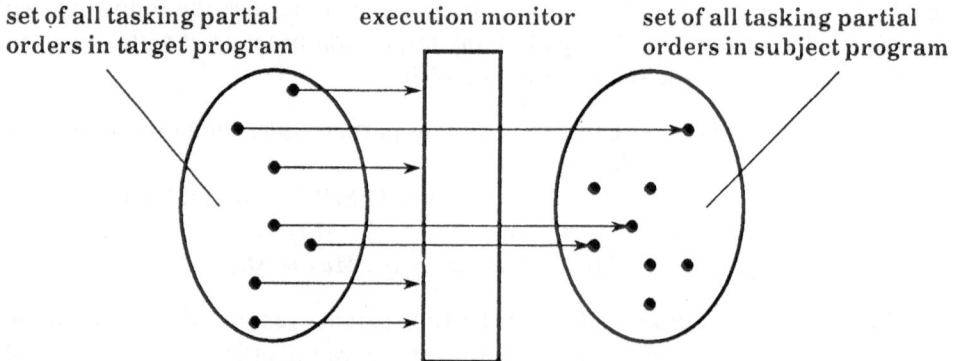

(b) execution monitor without partial order transparency

FIG. 11.1. Partial order transparency

formed program $\Phi(P)$, then the tasking partial order is completely preserved by the transformation. Thus, if the program transformation used in an execution monitor for concurrent Ada programs has that property, then the monitor is partial order transparent to target programs.

We regard an Ada-to-Ada program transformation as a partial mapping on a set of Ada programs, and specify it by a set of program transformation rules. Each program transformation rule is also a partial mapping on the set of Ada programs. We write Φ: $P(Ada) \to_R P(Ada)$ for an Ada-to-Ada program transformation, where $P(Ada)$ is a set of Ada programs and R is a set of Ada program transformation rules.

Lemma 4.1. Let Ψ: $(L_1, \leq_1)$ $(L_2, \leq_2)$ be a bijection where $(L_1, \leq_1)$ and $(L_2, \leq_2)$ are two meet-semilattices. Ψ is a partial order homomorphism if and only if it is a meet-isomorphism.

Definition 4.3. A program transformation Φ: $P(Ada) \to_R P(Ada)$ is called an *equivalent transformation for dynamic structures* if for any $(TES(P, I), \leq_{TPO})$ of any P in $P(Ada)$ with any given input I it satisfies the following three conditions:

1. There exist a $(\mathbf{TES}(\Phi(P), I), \leqq_{TPO})$ and a meet-homomorphism $\Psi\colon (\mathbf{TES}(P, I),$ $\leqq_{TPO}) \to (\mathbf{TES}(\Phi(P), I), \leqq_{TPO})$.
2. Ψ is a meet-isomorphism from $(\mathbf{TES}(P, I), \leqq_{TPO})$ to $(\Psi(\mathbf{TES}(P, I)), \leqq_{TPO})$.
3. For any $(T_1, N_1, To_1, E_1, Me_1, B_1, Ma_1, t_1)$ in $\mathbf{TES}(P, I), \leqq_{TPO})$, if $\Psi((T_1, N_1, To_1, E_1, Me_1, B_1, Ma_1, t_1)) = (T_2, N_2, To_2, E_2, Me_2, B_2, Ma_2, t_2)$ then $T_1 = T_2$, $N_1 = N_2$, $To_1 = To_2$, $E_1 = E_2$, $Me_1 = Me_2$, $B_1 = B_2$, $Ma_1 = Ma_2$.

An equivalent transformation for dynamic structures $\Phi\colon \mathbf{P}(\mathrm{Ada}) \to_R \mathbf{P}(\mathrm{Ada})$ preserves tasking events of the original program P and the tasking partial order $\leqq_{TPO}$ in the behavior of the transformed program $\Phi(P)$. Fig. 11.2 shows an isomorphism preserving the tasking partial order in a target program where dynamic structure lattices are shown by Hasse diagrams.

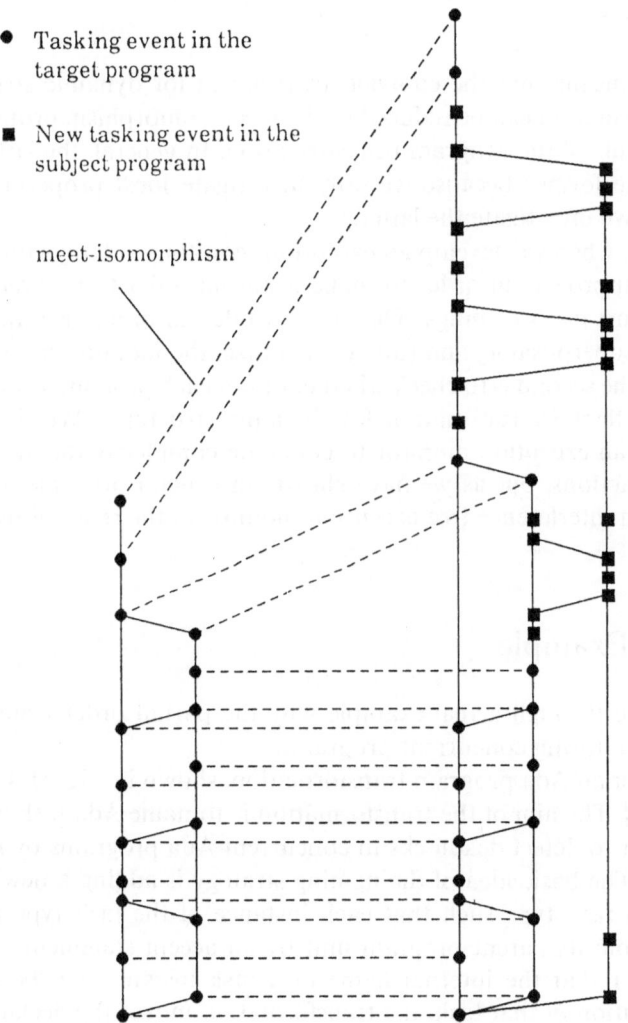

Lattice of the target program   Lattice of the subject program

FIG. 11.2. Preserving tasking partial order

Definition 4.4. Let Φ: $\mathbf{P}$(Ada) $\to_R \mathbf{P}$(Ada) be a program transformation. The program transformation rules in R are said to be *superposable* if they satisfy the following condition: for any P in the $\mathbf{P}$(Ada), there exists a sequence of indices $i_1, \ldots, i_n$ such that the equation $\Phi(P) = r_{i_n}(\ldots(r_{i_1}(P))\ldots)$ holds where $r_k \in R$, $k = i_1, \ldots, i_n$.

Lemma 4.2. If Ψ_1: $(L_1, \leqq_1) \to (L_2, \leqq_2)$ and Ψ_2: $(L_2, \leqq_2) \to (L_3, \leqq_3)$ are two meet-homomorphisms, then their composite $\Psi_2 \cdot \Psi_1$: $(L_1, \leqq_1) \to (L_3, \leqq_3)$ is also a meet-homomorphism.

Theorem 4.1. Let Φ: $\mathbf{P}$(Ada) $\to_R \mathbf{P}$(Ada) be a program transformation. If R satisfies the following conditions: (1) the program transformation rules in R are super-posable; and (2) any program transformation rule r in R is an equivalent trans-formation for dynamic structures; then Φ is an equivalent transformation for dynamic structures.

Theorem 4.1 means that the equivalence problem for dynamic structure of a program transformation can be reduced to the meet-isomorphism problem of each transformation rule of the program transformation. In general, the latter is easier to solve than the former because we only investigate local properties of target programs when we investigate the latter.

Consequently, when we develop an execution monitor working with a program transformation approach, in order to make it partial order transparent to target programs, we must do two things. The first is to design program transformation rules which are superposable, and satisfy, of course, the monitoring requirements of the monitor. The second is to check whether or not each program transformation rule is an equivalent transformation for dynamic structures. We do not claim it is possible for an execution monitor to eliminate completely the interference of the monitoring actions, but as we have shown, in general principle, we can certainly develop an interference-free execution monitor in the sense of partial order transparency.

11.5 A Real Example

Now, we indicate through a real example why the partial order transparency is necessary for monitoring concurrent programs.

Let us consider an Ada program transformation, shown in Fig. 11.3, which was proposed in [14]. The aim of the transformation is to name Ada task instances at run-time in order to detect deadlocks in concurrent Ada programs by monitoring their execution. The basic idea of the naming strategy is adding a new entry, say, SET-ID, to each task type such that each instance of the task type receives its internal name from its parent program unit by an accept statement of the entry SET-ID. In order that the internal name of a task instance can be referred to during the activation of that task, the transformation moves the declarations of a task body into an inner block.

However, this transformation seriously limits tasking behavior of the target

pattern : | *replacement* :

task type T **is** | **task type** T **is**
  {entry__declaration} | **entry** SET__ID (N : **in** INTEGER);
  {representation__clause} | {entry__declaration}
end; | {representation__clause}
  : | **end**;
task body T **is** | :
  [declarative__part] | **task body** T **is**
begin | ID : INTEGER;
  sequence__of__statements | **begin**
[exception | **accept** SET__ID (N : **in** INTEGER)
  exception__handler | **do** ID := N; **end**;
  {exception__handler}] | **declare**
end; | [declarative__part]
                                                 | **begin**
                                                 | sequence__of__statements
                                                 | [exception
                                                 | exception__handler
                                                 | {exception__handler}]
                                                 | **end**;
                                                 | **end**;

FIG. 11.3. Transformation of German's naming strategy

program, because all "original" task instances depending on a parent program unit can only start their activations in a total order in which the parent issues calls to those SET-ID entries, and consequently cannot concurrently start their activations according to the original semantics of the target programs. It is clear that this transformation is not an equivalent transformation for dynamic structures because it changes a partial order of task activations in the target programs into a total order of task activations in the transformed programs.

German [14] gave a proof that his method detects all deadlocks in Ada programs. The proof states: (1) "the addition of the monitor task and the changes in each of the original tasks do not alter the operation of the program on its original variables" and (2) "the monitor detects all deadlocks in a transformed program." Unfortunately, even if the words "all deadlocks" only denote the deadlocks defined in [14], we cannot say that the proof is correct because of the following two reasons.

First, any monitoring action will interfere with the performance of a target program and may even alter the behavior of the program. Therefore, there is no guarantee that monitoring actions do not alter the operation ordering of the program on its original variables. This is particularly true in the case of [14] because German's naming strategy has no partial order transparency. Thus, the first statement of the proof is incorrect in the sense of partial order transparency.

Second, a tasking deadlock in a concurrent Ada program, including the dead-locks defined in [14], may be time-dependent when the program includes some conditional entry call statements, timed entry call statements, or selective wait statements [15, 16]. Therefore, the first statement of the proof, whether it is correct or not, cannot be regarded as a sufficient criterion to evaluate the equivalence between a target program and a transformed program with respect to all potential deadlocks. In fact, since the program transformation in Fig. 11.3 changes a partial order with respect to the start of task activations into a total order, a transformed program is not equivalent to the target program with respect to all potential

```
package TASK__NAME__SERVER is
 type INTERNAL__ID__OF__TASK is private;
 function GET__TASK__ID return INTERNAL__ID__OF__TASK;
private
 type INTERNAL__ID__OF__TASK is new NATURAL;
end TASK__NAME__SERVER;

package body TASK__NAME__SERVER is
 task NAME__SERVER is
  entry GET__A__NEW__TASK__ID (ID : out INTERNAL__ID__OF__TASK);
 end NAME__SERVER;
 function GET__TASK__ID return INTERNAL__ID__OF__TASK is
  ID : INTERNAL__ID__OF__TASK;
 begin
  NAME__SERVER . GET__A__NEW__TASK__ID (ID);
  return ID;
 end GET__TASK__ID;
 task body NAME__SERVER is
  INTERNAL__ID__COUNTER : INTERNAL__ID__OF__TASK := 0;
 begin
  loop
   select
    accept GET__A__NEW__TASK__ID (
    ID : out INTERNAL__ID__OF__TASK) do
     INTERNAL__ID__COUNTER := INTERNAL__ID__COUNTER + 1;
     ID := INTERNAL__ID__COUNTER;
    end GET__A__NEW__TASK__ID;
   or
    terminate;
   end select;
  end loop;
 end NAME__SERVER;
end TASK__NAME__SERVER;
```

FIG. 11.4. Package TASK_NAME_SERVER

deadlocks in the sense of partial order transparency. There may arise a situation that some time-dependent deadlocks in a target program can never be observed in the program transformed by using that naming strategy. Thus, since there is no guarantee for an equivalence between a target program and a transformed program with respect to all potential deadlocks, the second statement of the proof is also incorrect in the sense of partial order transparency.

Now, let us discuss another program transformation, proposed in [17], with the same aim as German's transformation. The approach centers on introducing a task-name-server as a library package, named TASK_NAME_SERVER (Fig. 11.4), into the program library of an existing Ada programming support environment. Figure 11.5 shows the transformation of the naming strategy. Any target program refers to the task-name-server using a context clause. A local object, named TASK_ ID, to keep a task internal name, is introduced into the declarative part of every task body and initialized by invoking a function, named GET_TASK_ID, of the task-name-server. When a task instance is activated, the local object TASK_ID is elaborated at first. Thus, the task instance possesses its internal name which can be referred to during its activation.

This transformation does not impose a total order with respect to the start of task activations, such as German's transformation does, on the task instances to be named. All task instances of a transformed program are naturally (i.e., according to a run-time scheduler) activated and obtain their internal names. Named task instances can activate and execute in the same partial order as in that of the original target program. The transformation preserves all possible order with respect to the start of task activation in the behavior of the target program. We can prove that it is an equivalent transformation for dynamic structures.

From this real example, we can understand that partial order transparency is an essential requirement for monitoring concurrent programs. If an execution monitor for concurrent programs cannot preserve the same temporal and/or causal order among concurrent events of a target program in monitoring, then it will seriously limit the behavior of the target program in monitoring, and will lead to a situation in which some behavior of the target program can never be observed in monitoring.

11.6 Discussion

In order to solve the accurate monitoring problem of concurrent programs, we have presented an abstract model based on lattice theory for execution histories of concurrent Ada programs, and proposed the concept of partial order transparency based on the model. The partial order transparency can be regarded as a minimum requirement for an execution monitor in order to reduce its interference with and alteration of the behavior of target concurrent programs.

The partial order transparency proposed in this paper is only a conceptual requirement for execution monitors. How to define the partial order transparency for an execution monitor in terms of concurrent constructs of its target programming language, and how to prove that the monitor is partial order transparent to the behavior of target programs,depend on the definition of the target programming language.

```
pattern :                          |   replacement :
                                   |
procedure MAIN is                  |   with TASK__NAME__SERVER;
   :                               |   use TASK__NAME__SERVER;
   task body T is                  |   procedure MAIN is
    [declarative__part]            |      :
   begin                           |      task body T is
    sequence__of__statements       |       TASK__ID : INTERNAL__ID__OF__TASK
   [exception                      |       := GET__TASK__ID;
    exception__handler             |       [declarative part]
    {exception__handler}]          |      begin
   end;                            |       sequence__of__statements
   :                               |       [exception
end MAIN;                          |        exception__handler
                                   |        {exception__handler}]
                                   |       end T;
                                   |       :
                                   |   end MAIN;
```

FIG. 11.5. Transformation of our naming strategy

We have confirmed the effectiveness of the concept of partial order transparency in practice, by developing an event-driven execution monitor for concurrent Ada programs named "EDEN" [18, 19]. In comparison with other debuggers developed and/or proposed for concurrent Ada programs, EDEN is an interference-free execution monitor in the sense of partial order transparency. As a result, EDEN provides a guarantee for an equivalence with respect to the observability of time-dependent errors between a target program and the corresponding subject program.

References

1. Plattner B, Nievergelt J (1981) Monitoring program execution: a survey. IEEE Trans Comput 14 (11): 76–93
2. Joyce J, Lomow G, Slind K, Unger B (1987) Monitoring distributed systems. ACM Trans Computer Systems 5 (2): 121–150
3. Snodgrass R (1988) A relational approach to monitoring complex systems. ACM Trans Comput Sys 6 (2): 157–196
4. Cheng J (1988) Studies on monitoring concurrent programs. Doctoral dissertation, Department of Computer Science and Communication Engineering, Kyushu University, Japan
5. Ushijima K, Cheng J (1989) Monitoring concurrent systems: a survey. Proc IPSJ 1989 Symp CASE Environments, pp 125–132
6. LeBlanc RJ, Robbins AD (1985) Event-driven monitoring of distributed programs. Proc ICDCS 85, pp 515–522

7. LeDoux CH, Parker DS Jr (1985) Saving traces for Ada debugging. In: Barnes JGP, Fisher GA Jr (eds) Ada in use. Cambridge University Press, pp 97–108
8. United States Department of Defense (1980) "STONEMAN", requirements for Ada programming support environment
9. United States Department of Defense (1983) Reference manual for the Ada programming language (ANSI/MIL-STD-1815A)
10. Burns A, Lister AM, Wellings AJ (1987) A review of Ada tasking. Lecture Notes in Computer Science. Springer-Verlag, Vol. 262
11. Jefferson DR (1985) Virtual time. ACM Trans Program Lang Syst 7 (3): 404–425
12. Birkhoff G (1961) Lattice theory, Revised Edn. American Mathematical Society
13. Szász G (1963) Introduction to Lattice Theory. Academic
14. German SM (1984) Monitoring for deadlock and blocking in Ada tasking. IEEE Trans Software Eng SE-10 (6): 764–777
15. Cheng J, Araki K, Ushijima K (1988) Tasking communication deadlocks in concurrent Ada programs. ACM Ada Letters 8 (5) 61–70
16. Cheng J (to be published) A classification of tasking deadlocks. ACM Ada Letters 10
17. Cheng J, Ushijima K (1989) Naming Ada tasks at run-time. ACM Ada Letters 9 (2): 52–61
18. Cheng J, Ushijima K (1988) Detecting tasking communication deadlocks in concurrent Ada programs. Proc International Computer Science Conference '88, pp 138–145
19. Cheng J, Araki K, Ushijima K (1989) Development and practical applications of EDEN—an event-driven execution monitor for concurrent Ada programs (in Japanese). J Inf Process 30 (1) 12–24

12
Realtime Communication Processing System with Video Function in the Networking Environment

Takuto Harada[1] and *Yoshihiko Ebihara*[2]

Summary: With computers now numerous and widespread, the need to work jointly and in groups via networks has led to an interest in developing instantaneous and cooperative information processing. In this paper, we explain the system structure and the functions of the VTALK (Visual Talk) system, and note some subjects for further research.

VTALK supports realtime group work using multimedia information data such as images and character strings, and records these like video systems. VTALK supports two modes of recording: digest recording, that records the scene the user needs; and normal recording, that records the whole group work process. VTALK also supports three playback modes. The static playback mode plays back the last scene of the record, the digest playback mode plays the record partially, and the dynamic playback mode plays the entire record. Also, for playing back records that stand alone and for virtual playing of group work, VTALK supports a virtual communication function.

A prototype VTALK has been developed and has been successfully run on a 10 Mbps Ethernet.

Key words: video function — realtime communication — multimedia — group working

12.1 Introduction

With high performance computers and large memory capacities, computer resources and software for individual use are now of high quality. There are many computers, widely spread, and the resulting opportunities for joint work and group work via networks have led to an interest in developing instantaneous and cooperative information processing [1–4].

---
[1] Master's Program in Scientific Technology
[2] Institute of Information Sciences and Electronics, University of Tsukuba, Tsukuba, 305 Japan

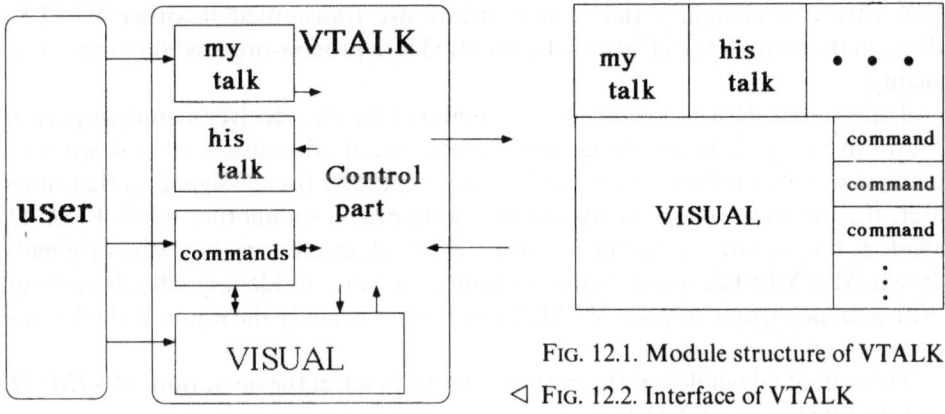

FIG. 12.1. Module structure of VTALK

◁ FIG. 12.2. Interface of VTALK

The group working software tools now available do not satisfy user demand. For example, some tools support realtime communication, but can handle only strings, not images. Another tool supports image processing, but it cannot support realtime communication with other people. When we are doing a sophisticated joint project on network workstations, there are many times that we encounter a problem such that we have to refer to past records. However, commercially based talk systems do not have time-lag information in their records, and it is not possible to play back the elapsed joint processing. So we cannot discuss the detailed contents and report to people fully and correctly.

In the network environment with UNIX workstations, VTALK can support strings and images in realtime, and makes it possible to communicate among many participants by using multimedia information, and to record data. We describe the system structure in Sect. 12.2, the main functions of VTALK in Sect. 12.3, the synchronization of VTALK in Sect 12.4, VTALK control architecture in Sect. 12.5, and subjects for further research in the future in Sect. 12.6.

12.2 System Structure

In this section we describe the system module structure and the man-machine interface. Figure 12.1 shows the module structure of VTALK, and Fig. 12.2 shows the man-machine interface.

A user can communicate with other users by writing strings on his *"my talk"* window, and drawing strings and figures on a common *"VISUAL"* window. *My talk* is a window that every user owns for him- or herself. *VISUAL* is a common window for every user. To discuss a subject actively without preventing users from thinking about it, VTALK permits users to write strings on their *my talk* windows. VTALK provides two ways of synchronization for the *VISUAL* window. In one, only one user can draw strings and figures on the *VISUAL* window at one time. In the other, every user can do this simultaneously. Also, each user can select the synchronization desired. We detail synchronization of the *VISUAL* window in Sect.

12.4. Strings and figures that a user draws are transmitted to other VTALKs through the control part. Data are transmitted by a process-process communication facility.

Transmitted data are received and analyzed by the receiver's control part as shown in Fig. 12.2. If the strings were written on another user's *my talk* window, they are written on the receiver's talk window that has been assigned to that other user. If there were strings or figures that were drawn on another user's *VISUAL* window, they are drawn on the receiver's *VISUAL* window as they were originally drawn. Also VTALK draws strings or figures in color, to identify who drew them. With a monochrome display, VTALK emphasizes brightly the frame of the *his talk* window.

The command window is the button window to select the operations of *VISUAL* and the functions of VTALK.

The control part of VTALK not only performs data reception but also analyzes other functions. We describe its module structure in detail and how to perform the functions, in Sect. 12.5.

12.3 Functions of VTALK

VTALK functions consist of drawing functions, video functions, and virtual communication functions.

12.3.1 Drawing Functions

Drawing functions are performed by *VISUAL*. Users work together as a group by using these functions. These include painting of basic figures such as lines and circles, figure-editing such as copying and erasing, making figures that are not supported by basic figures, and drawing graphics by handwriting.

Users can edit strings and figures on the *VISUAL* window, even if they did not draw them. With the making-figures function, users can draw any figures they need. These may be input through the *VISUAL* window and transmitted. Also, any figures which are printed on something can be input to the *VISUAL* window by scanner. Figures which are drawn with the making-figures function and input to the *VISUAL* window are held in common by all users who participate in this group work. So a user who did not make these figures can edit and show them on a display. Figures drawn by the making-figures function may be required for the next group session, so they are saved in a file.

12.3.2 Video Functions

Users can record and play back the group work with video functions. Video functions are performed by the control part, and consist of designation of the recording window, recording, playback, pause, stop, variable-speed forward search, and variable-speed backward search.

12.3.2.1 Designation of the Recording Window

In group work, information on windows is not always useful for all users. For example, when a user lectures on something on his talk window, the lecture is not useful for a user who knows the subject very well, but is for a user who does not. In the former case, the user need not record all of the windows. So a user can selectively specify the needed recording windows among the *my talk* window, *his talk* window, and *VISUAL* window.

12.3.2.2 Recording

Users can record the group work freely by themselves. Recording has no influence on any other user's activity, just like the recording of TV programs on a home video system. The file that is produced by the recording activity is called the recording file, and does not depend on the user or on the computer that produced it. We detail the recording file in Sect. 12.5.

When a user records the group work, there are generally two types of user demands. One is the complete recording of the group work. The other is partial recording that records the scene that the user needs. Therefore, VTALK supports two ways of recording: normal recording and digest recording.

The normal recording function records the designated window from the time the user presses the normal recording button until the stop button is pressed. With this function, a user can sequentially record group work that is on a window.

The digest recording function records the scene on the designated window while the digest recording button is pressed. With this function, the user can record only the scene he or she needs.

12.3.2.3 Playback

When a user wants to play back the recording file during group work, the contents of the recording file are transmitted to all users who participate in the group work. We show an example. Users A, B, C, and D are working as a group, and user D records the group work scenes with the normal recording function. For playing it back at the next group work session where all four users participate, user D plays it on his VTALK. As the recording file does not depend on the user and computer that made it, any VTALK with the recording file can play it. The VTALK that is playing the recording file gets data from the recording file and transmits them to other VTALKs through the control part (Fig. 12.3). In this situation, we can illustrate the VTALK that is playing the recording file as a TV station, the VTALK that is receiving it as a TV set, and the contents of it as a TV program. VTALK is independent of the devices or ports for receiving data from the local terminal, just as it is with data from remote terminals via the network. So, while playing the recording file, a user can use any function, just like working in a group in realtime. So the user can write strings on his *my talk* window and draw strings and figures on the *VISUAL* window. Also, as the module that performs the playback function does not depend on the module that performs the recording function (see Fig. 12.7 in Sect. 12.7), a

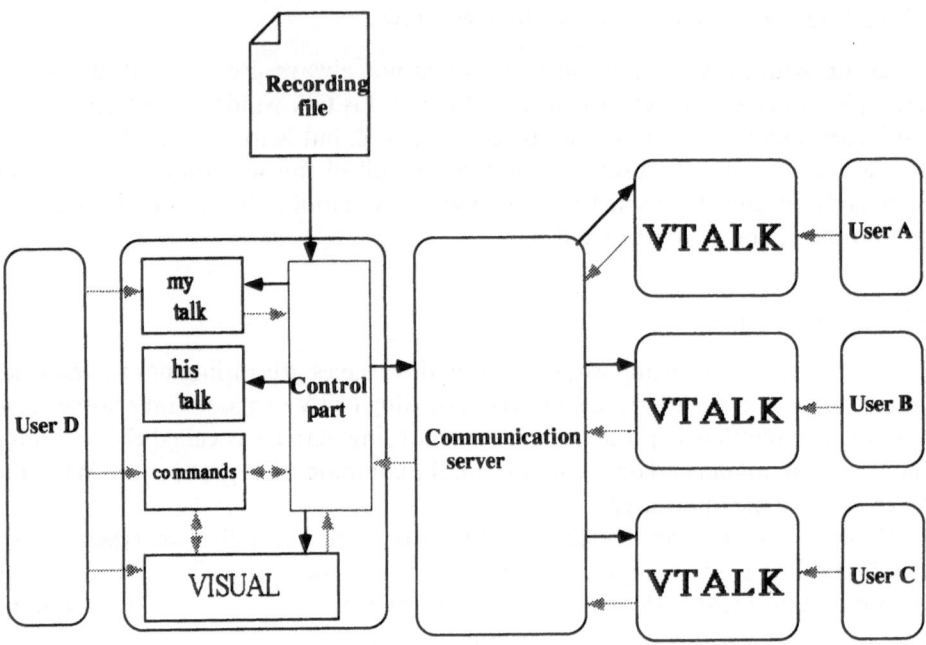

FIG. 12.3. Playback of the recording file

user may record the contents of the designated window while playing the recording file.

When a user plays the recording file, there may be a user whose previous record was in the recording file but who does not participate in this group work. In this case, VTALK makes the user's *his talk* window automatically write the record that is in the recording file, and then plays it. So he or she is called a virtual user (Fig. 12.4). After playing is finished, VTALK asks a user whether or not to remove the *his talk* window which VTALK made automatically.

Conversely, when a user plays the recording file, there may be a new user who did not participate in the last group work. But this makes no difference except that nothing is displayed on the opened window for the newcomer (Fig. 12.5).

We list the various cases in which a user plays the recording file in group working:

1. Users continue the group work from the last scene of the recording file without looking over its content.
2. Users continue the group work from the last scene of the recording file after looking over its content.
3. Users continue the group work from the last scene of the recording file after reaffirming its content.
4. Users only refer to the result of the group work.
5. Users look over the group working process.
6. Users want to know the group working process well.

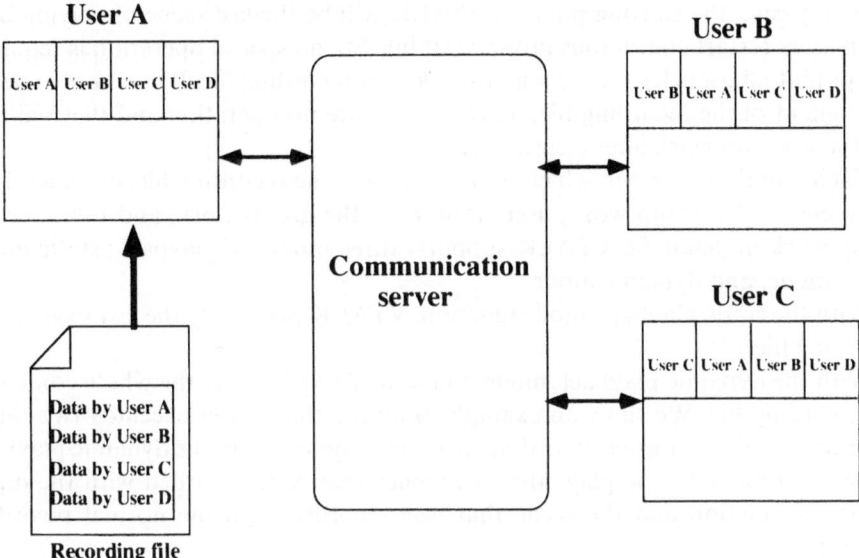

FIG. 12.4. Virtual user

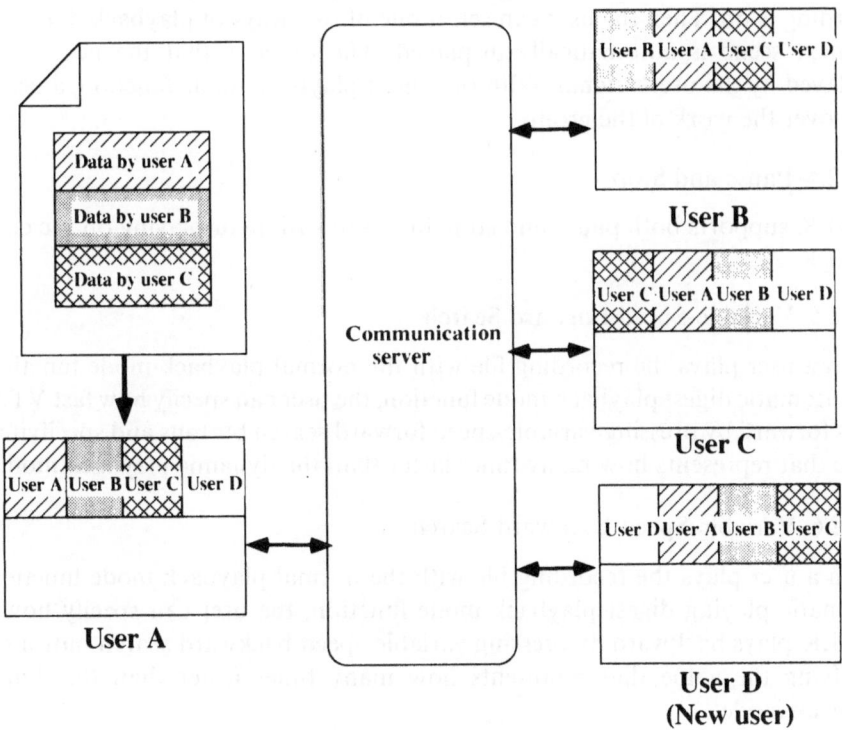

FIG. 12.5. Playback with new user

In any case, the starting point of VTALK will be the last scene of playing back when users restart continuous group working. So, no special operation is required, except that all users have to specify this file as a recording file. If users only refer to the content of the recording file, users will require no operation and they will just start new group work after clearing windows.

There are three cases in which users play back the recording file: users need the last scene of the group work, users look over the group work, and users see the group work in detail. So VTALK supports three modes of playback: static mode, digest mode, and dynamic mode.

With the static playback mode function, VTALK plays only the last scene of the recording file.

With the dynamic playback mode function, VTALK plays the whole content of the recording file. We show an example. Suppose that a user executed two digest recordings and one normal recording. If a user plays this with the dynamic playback mode function, VTALK plays the two scenes that were recorded with the digest recording function and the scene that was recorded with the normal recording function.

With the digest playback mode function, VTALK plays the scenes when the digest recording button is pressed, normal recording button is pressed, pause button is pressed while normal recording is on, or stop button is pressed while normal recording is on. Then the user can select one of two ways of playback. One is that the next scene is automatically displayed. The other is that the next scene is displayed by the user's signal. With the digest playback mode function, a user can look over the work of the group.

12.3.2.4 Pause and Stop

VTALK supports both pause and stop during recording or playing on the current VTALK.

12.3.2.5 Variable-Speed Forward Search

When a user plays the recording file with the normal playback mode function or the automatic digest playback mode function, the user can specify how fast VTALK plays forward by pressing variable-speed forward search buttons and specifying the value that represents how many times faster than the dynamic playback mode.

12.3.2.6 Variable-Speed Backward Search

When a user plays the recording file with the normal playback mode function or automatic playing digest playback mode function, the user can specify how fast VTALK plays backward by pressing variable-speed backward search buttons and specifying the value that represents how many times faster than the dynamic playback mode.

12.3.3 Virtual Communication Function

A user may play back a recording file personally to confirm the group work. For this case, VTALK supports the virtual communication function. The virtual com-

Fig. 12.6. Virtual communication function

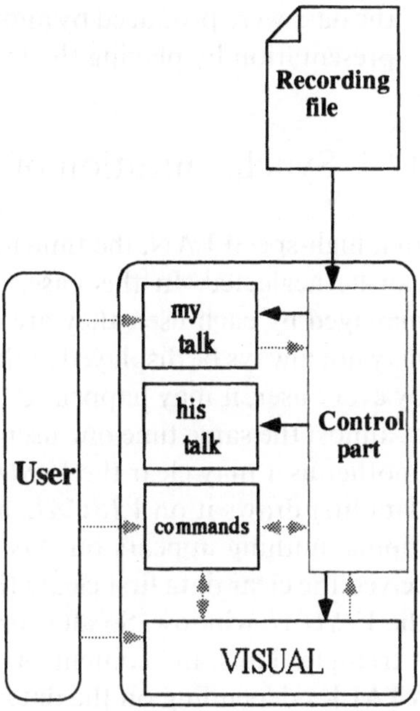

munication function is the function by means of which the user can use VTALK without communicating with others. With this communication function, a user can play back a recording file personally (Fig. 12.6). Playback of a recording file with the virtual communication function looks like playback of a videotape.

Using the virtual communication function, we can offer the following environment:

1. Reaffirmation of group working and edit of a recording file.

The difference between VTALK with the virtual communication function and the normal VTALK is whether it communicates with the communication server. So, while VTALK is playing a recording file with the virtual communication function, the user can write strings on his *my talk* window, and draw strings and figures on the *VISUAL* window, just like group work in realtime. With this function, the user can modify the result of the group work, and work on it personally.

2. Indirect conversation

If a user sends a recording file to a user who did not participate in the group work, the receiving user can play it back. The user is given the environment just as if he or she participated in the group work. Then the second user will be able to add strings on the *my talk* window, draw strings and figures on the *VISUAL* window on recording, and send back the recording file. Thus, they will be able to communicate indirectly at any time.

3. Dynamic presentation

A recording file is input data to draw strings and figures on VTALK. So, any user can also play back data that are based on the recording file format, even if the data were produced by another editor. In this way, a user can make a dynamic presentation by playing the recording file that was made by another editor.

12.4 Synchronization of VISUAL Window

In a high-speed LAN, the time for transmitting data from one VTALK to another can be neglected. In this case, as the *my talk* window and *his talk* window are managed by each user, they are consistent with all VTALKs—though the strings may not always be displayed at the same time. But as the *VISUAL* window is shared by every user, it may happen to be inconsistent with some VTALKs. For example, at almost the same time one user may draw a triangle on the *VISUAL* window and another user may clear the *VISUAL* window. A VTALK that received the triangle data first draws it on *VISUAL*, and then clears *VISUAL*. So, after processing two inputs, nothing appears on this *VISUAL* window. But another VTALK that received the clear data first clears the *VISUAL* window, and then draws a triangle on the *VISUAL* window. So after processing two inputs, this *VISUAL* window shows a triangle. Thus, the content of *VISUAL* window may be inconsistent among all VTALKs depending on the data received time.

VTALK supports two types of synchronization, synchronization such that the content of the *VISUAL* window is always the same among all VTALKs, and synchronization such that the content of the *VISUAL* window is not always the same at every moment among all VTALKs but does not remain inconsistent.

12.4.1 Exclusively Controlled Synchronization

There may be a group whose users do not want *VISUAL* windows to be inconsistent at any moment. For this kind of group work, VTALK supports synchronization such that the content of the *VISUAL* window is always the same among all VTALKs. In this synchronization, VTALK permits only one user at a given time to draw strings and figures on the *VISUAL* window. This synchronization has the fault that users can not do group work actively because only one person can draw strings and figures on the *VISUAL* window at one time.

How does VTALK give a user the right to draw strings and figures on the *VISUAL* window? There are many ways to achieve access-right control:

1. Users elect a chairman, who decides to give a user this right.
2. A user who has this right designates a user who can draw strings and figures on the *VISUAL* window in the next turn, and then gives the right to that person.
3. VTALK makes a virtual ring of users, and passes the right through it. This is the same as the token-passing control that is one of the network access control methods.
4. Users who want to draw strings and figures on the *VISUAL* window present a right permission demand. Then, VTALK passes the right to demanding users in turn. Each demand is a reservation of the access right.

In Cases 2–4, VTALK should limit the time that a user owns the right so that it is not monopolized by a single user. In Case 1, a user may not be given his or her fair share of the right, but it is given to users who demand it, and a chairman can direct the group work. In Case 2, users may not be given their fair share of the right, but all users in the group are in the same position. In Case 3, a user can be given a fair share of the right, but the right may also be given to a user who does not need it.

In Case 4, a user can be given a fair share of the right, but the following problem may happen. For example, user A draws strings and figures on the *VISUAL* window, and user D who disagrees with user A presents a right permission demand. At that time, user B and user C have already presented right permission demands, and user B and user C draw strings and figures that have no relation to the strings and figures of user A. In this situation, if user D draws strings and figures against user A's, in spite of the group work having taken another direction, user A will want to reply by drawing strings and figures. If users repeat this action, users cannot advance the group work.

VTALK supports Method 1, because it is the most popular in group work.

12.4.2 The Alternative Mode of Synchronization

(Synchronization such that the content is not always the same, but does not remain inconsistent.)

There may be a group whose user do not mind temporary inconsistencies in any *VISUAL* window. For this kind of group work, VTALK supports a synchronization such that the content of the *VISUAL* window is not always the same among all VTALKs, but at any moment when no-one is drawing strings or figures on the *VISUAL* window, the content of *VISUAL* windows is set the same on all VTALKs. In this synchronization VTALK permits every user to draw strings and figures freely on the *VISUAL* window, and the users can work actively as a group.

12.5 Control Part

The control part of VTALK communicates with the communication server, controls the synchronization of the *VISUAL* window, performs the video function and virtual communication function, and manages the figures drawn by the making-figure function. The control part consists of three parts: communication part, recording part, and playback part (Fig. 12.7).

12.5.1 Communication Part

During a group work session, the communication part talks with the communication server. The data that is sent from the *my talk* module and *VISUAL* module are put in the form of Fig. 12.8, and transmitted to the communication server. A communication packet contains user ID (identification), relative time from start of VTALK, command, and data. The user ID tells VTALK which user made this packet, that is, which user drew strings or figures on a *my talk* window or *VISUAL* window. The relative time from start of VTALK is used to maintain the consistency

FIG. 12.7. Control part

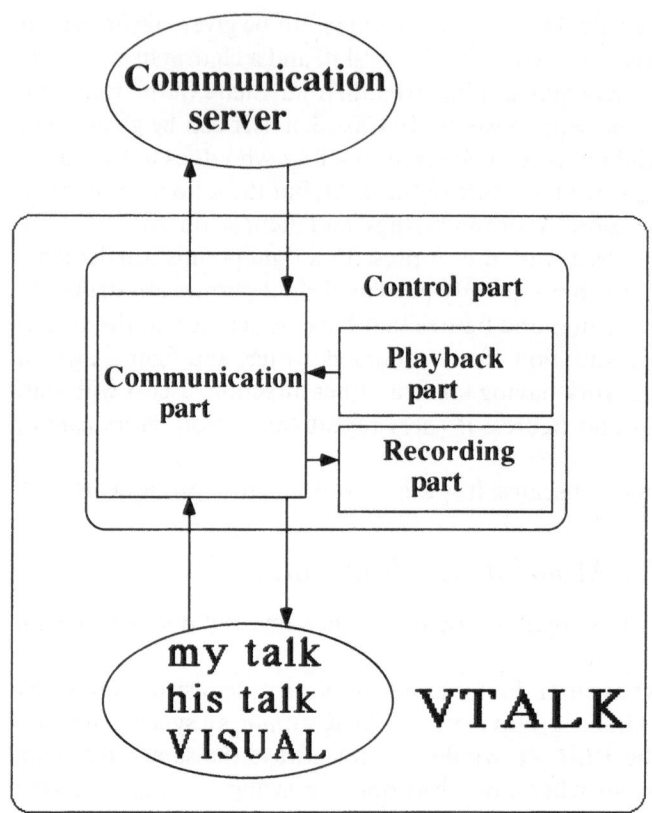

<table>
<tr><td>Start
flag</td><td>User ID</td><td>Relative time from
start of VTALK</td><td>command</td><td>Data</td><td>Stop
flag</td></tr>
</table>

FIG. 12.8. Data structure of communication packet

of synchronization in the *VISUAL* window, digest playback, variable-speed forward search, and variable-speed backward search. Command shows the operation done by the user. Data are strings or figures required in order to draw on VTALK. The data sent from the communication server are analyzed, and are sent to the module on which the strings or figures are displayed.

When VTALK plays back a recording file during group work, the communication part sends data from the playback part to the *my talk* module, *his talk* module, *VISUAL* module, and communication server, in addition to the normal management of the data from the *my talk* module, *VISUAL* module, and communication server.

When VTALK plays back a recording file with the virtual communication function, the communication part merely sends data from the playback part to the *my talk* module, *his talk* module, and *VISUAL* module, not to the communication server.

When the user records the group work with the normal recording function, the communication part sends data for the designated window to the recording part. The communication part also manages figures that the user (or other users) made with the making-figure function. Also, it manages an ID assignment table whenever a user selects a figure by a figure ID. Each figure is uniquely assigned a figure ID at the communication part. The first time, a new figure is transmitted to all participating VTALKs. Once an ID has been assigned among the VTALKs, all VTALKs use this assigned ID to transfer the same figure beginning with the second time, in order to effectively save transmission time for the large volume of figure data.

The communication part also controls the synchronization of the *VISUAL* window. In the synchronization such that the content is always the same, the communication part manages the right to draw strings and figures on the *VISUAL* window, and gives it to another VTALK. In the synchronization where the content is not always the same but does not remain inconsistent, the communication part controls the synchronization of the *VISUAL* window by the relative time from the start of VTALK in the communication packet.

12.5.2 Recording Part

The recording part performs the recording function. A recording file form is decided by the recording function that the user selects. When a user presses the digest recording button, the recording part stores the data needed to restore VTALK, user ID, etc., and the screen data, in a recording file. When a user presses the normal recording button, the recording part does a digest recording first, and then records the data that is sent from the communication part. Then, when the user presses the stop button, the recording part does a digest recording again. When the pause button is pressed on normal recording, the recording part does a digest recording. Figure 12.9 shows the format of a recording file.

12.5.3 Playback Part

The playback part performs the playback function, variable-speed forward search, and variable-speed backward search.

With the static playback mode function, the playback part sends the last screen data recorded by digest recording to the communication part.

With the digest playback mode function, the playback part sends the screen data that were recorded by digest recording to the communication part, by turns. When a user selects the playback such that the next scene is automatically displayed, the playback part sends data to the communication part at the regular interval that the user designates. When a user selects the playback such that the next scene is

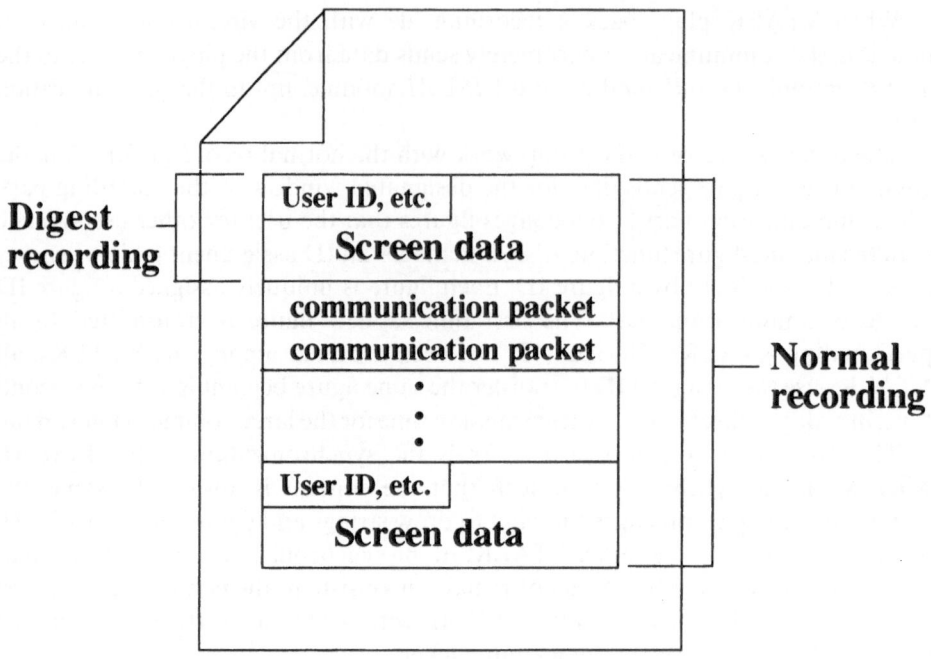

FIG. 12.9. Recording file

displayed by the user's signal, the playback part sends data to the communication part according to the user's signal.

With the dynamic playback mode function, the playback part sends to the communication part the screen data that were recorded by digest recording first, and then data of communication packets generated according to the relative time from the start of VTALK. The playback part performs variable-speed forward search and variable-speed backward search by operating "relative time from start of VTALK" in Fig. 12.8.

12.6 Discussion

We have described the main features of the functions and the structure of VTALK that support realtime image communication and video functions. A prototype VTALK has currently been developed on the UNIX X11.R4 window system. The VTALK has been installed on workstations connected to a 10 Mbps Ethernet at the University of Tsukuba. The prototype VTALK has demonstrated experimentally that it works efficiently and successfully, although the Ethernet itself is a short-distance network. Figure 12.10 shows an example of interactive processing on a display terminal.

Enhancing features of VTALK are summarized as the following:

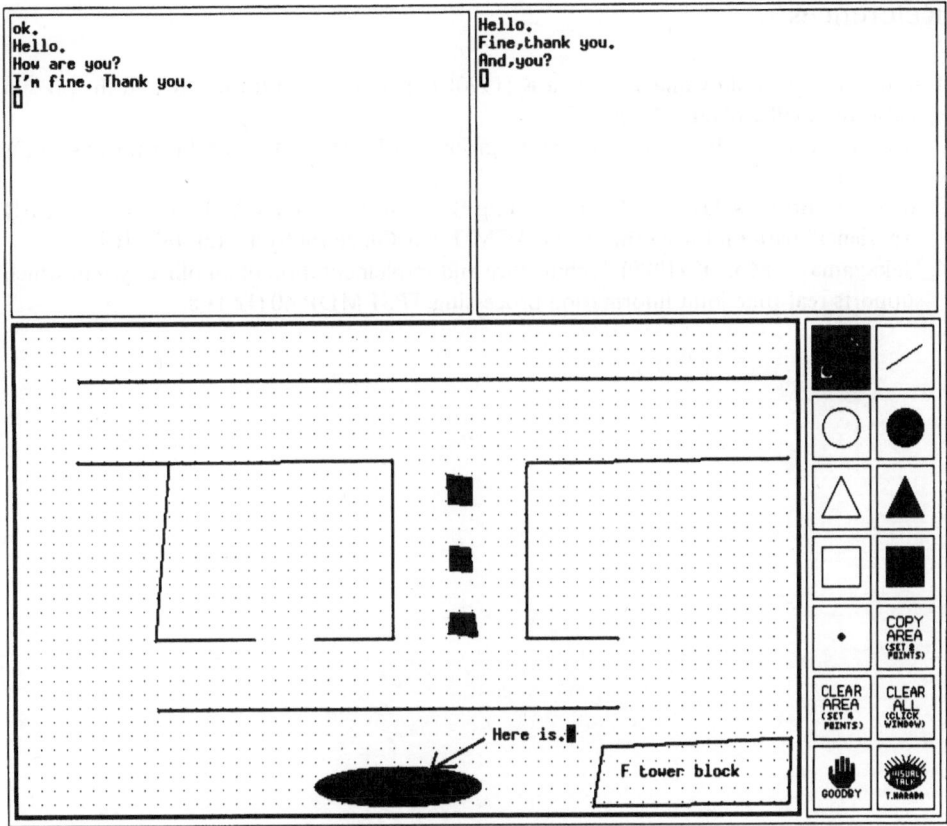

FIG. 12.10. An example of VTALK

- VTALK can easily refer to the past content of group work and can handle an instantaneous and cooperative type of multimedia information processing, such as meetings and conferences. We believe that VTALK is helpful for making breakthroughs to new ideas by helping people in different places to work together.
- For developing user applications, VTALK will serve effectively as a visual network editor without programless processing.

The following aspects of VTALK are subjects for further experimental research:

- Responsiveness of VTALK for long-distance networks.
- Addition of other multimedia information like voice data into VTALK.
- Comparison study of the performance of the various synchronization methods of Sect. 12.4.

Acknowledgment. This paper has been greatly improved by the insight and comments of Professor James W. Higgins of the University of Tsukuba.

References

1. Matsushita Y, Yokoyama T, Okada K (1990) The necessity of teamware and the present status of it. IPSJ MDP 44 (2): 1–7
2. Grief I, Sarin S (1987) Data sharing in group work. ACM Trans Office Inf Syst 5 (2): 187–211
3. Stefik M, Bobrow DG, Foste G, Lanning S, Tatar D (1987) WYSIWIG revised: early experiences with multiuser interfaces. ACM Trans Office Inf Syst 5 (2): 147–167
4. Nakayama Y, Mori K (1989) Architecture and implementation of an office system which supports real-time joint information processing. IPSJ MDP 40 (1): 1–8

13
A User-Friendly Software Environment for Designing and Verifying Communication Protocols

Norio Shiratori, Hiroaki Yamamoto, and Kaoru Takahashi[1]

Summary: This paper presents a user-friendly software environment for protocol design, consisting of EXPA, NESDEL, NESDEL-to-EXPA transformation, and EXPA-to-NESDEL transformation, where EXPA is a protocol verification method based on extended reachability analysis and NESDEL is a protocol specification language. The aim of this system is to provide a user-friendly interface by providing the two transformations as well as by extending the existing reachability analysis, so that the productivity of protocol development can be enhanced. We first give a protocol verification method, EXPA, which is an extension of the existing reachability analysis. In EXPA, the concept of "backward perturbation" is introduced to improve the verification capability, so that the user interface of EXPA is superior to that of the existing verification methods based on reachability analysis. In general, the intelligibility of a specification language expression is much superior to that of a verification expression based on reachability analysis. For this reason, we give a procedure for directly reflecting the results of verification on a specification language, into an expression for verification. Our user-friendly system has been developed on a Toshiba AS3000 workstation.

Key words: protocol — specification — verification — user interface — finite state machine — reachability analysis

13.1 Introduction

Communication protocols are components of vital importance in a modern computer communications system. Many communication protocols can be modeled as two communicating finite-state machines which exchange messages over two one-directional FIFO (first in, first out) channels [1, 2]. For several years there have been numerous works on developing the communicating finite-state machine approach to protocol specification [1–5], analysis [6–16], and synthesis [17–19].

---

[1] Research Institute of Electrical Communication, Tohoku University, Aoba-ku, Sendai, 980 Japan

Also, software environments for designing and verifying communication protocols have been proposed to improve the productivity of protocol and communication software development [20–24]. With the communicating finite machine model, it is most convenient and efficient for a human designer to design protocols graphically and also to verify them by looking at graphical representations of reachability graphs. For this reason, several graphical tools for protocol design and reachability analysis have been developed [8, 20, 21, 24].

In general, the intelligibility of a specification language expression such as SDL [4] is much superior to that of a verification expression based on a reachability analysis. Therefore, it is very convenient and efficient for a human designer to verify (or "debug") protocols by looking at a specification language expression instead of looking at a reachability analysis expression. By considering this problem, we were motivated to develop a software environment which helps a designer to design a protocol easily. The purpose of this work is to construct a user-friendly software environment for designing and verifying communication protocols in order to advance the productivity of protocol development. In our software environment, the following two functions are introduced and integrated for improving the user interface:

1. Extension of existing reachability analysis
2. Provision of two transformation algorithms between specification language expression and reachability analysis expression

With respect to the first enhancement, we give a protocol verification method, EXPA, which is an extension of the existing reachability analysis. In EXPA, the concept of "backward perturbation" is introduced to improve the verification capability, so that the user interface of EXPA is superior to that of the existing verification methods based on reachability analysis. For example, EXPA can automatically detect the origins which lead to protocol errors, as well as occurrences of protocol errors such as deadlock. So far, in the case of existing reachability analysis, a human designer has had to find the origins of protocol errors by analyzing the reachability graph by him- or herself. Therefore, EXPA can provide a user-friendly environment to a human designer.

Concerning the second major improvement, in general, the intelligibility of a specification language expression is much superior to that of a verification expression based on reachability analysis. Therefore, we give a procedure for directly reflecting the results of verification on a specification language expression, as well as a transformation procedure from a specification language expression into an expression for verification.

This paper is structured as follows. In the next section, we outline our system, which consists of a verification algorithm, a protocol specification language, and two types of transformation algorithm. Then, in Sect. 13.3, we give the protocol verification algorithm EXPA based on reachability analysis. The reachability analysis [6–8] is known as one of the practically useful methods based on the finite-state machine approach. This reachability analysis is significantly improved and generalized in EXPA by introducing the concept of backward perturbation. In Sect. 13.4, we present NESDEL [24] (NEtwork protocol Specification and DEscription Language) as a protocol specification language. In Sect. 13.5, the two transformation procedures, NESDEL-to-EXPA transformation and EXPA-to-NESDEL transformation, are given to enhance the user interface. Some supporting tools are given in Sect. 13.6.

13.2 Outline of a User-Friendly Software Environment for Designing and Verifying Communication Protocols

Our user-friendly software environment consists of EXPA, NESDEL, a NESDEL-to-EXPA transformation, and an EXPA-to-NESDEL transformation (Fig. 13.1). Here, EXPA is a protocol verification method based on reachability analysis, and NESDEL is a protocol specification language. Details of these components in the system are given in later sections. The system works as follows. A user enters the system with protocols described in NESDEL. Then, the system transforms the NESDEL expressions into EXPA expressions for verification, by using the NESDEL-to-EXPA transformation rules. The resultant EXPA expressions are inputs to EXPA. Next, the system lets EXPA work, and then reflects the results of verification on the NESDEL expressions, by using the EXPA-to-NESDEL transformation rules.

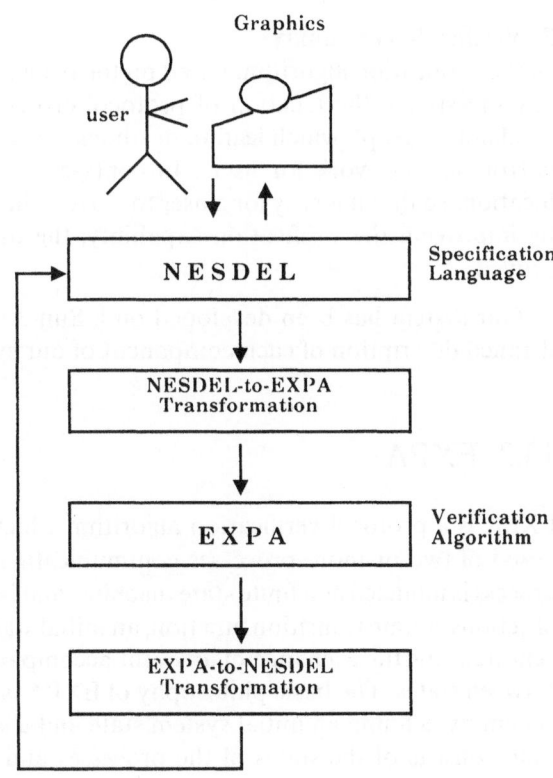

FIG. 13.1. A user-friendly software environment for protocol development

The attractive points of our system in terms of the user interface are discussed in the following.

1. Intelligibility

In the protocol verification methods based on reachability analysis, a user first describes a protocol by using some specification language such as state transition diagram, SDL [3], ESTELLE [5], etc. Then it is transformed into the expression for verification and is verified. After verifying a protocol, the results are given by the expression depending on the reachability analysis. Hence, the user must analyze the transitions in a reachability graph corresponding to the results of verification, by him- or herself. From the intelligibility point of view, this expression is inferior to the initial one, which was in a specification language. For better intelligibility, it is imperative that the results of verification, as well as inputs to the verification system, are given in some specification language. In our system, shown in Fig. 13.1, this function is provided by the EXPA-to-NESDEL transformation. Let us suppose that a protocol described in NESDEL is given to a verification method as an input. In our system, the NESDEL-to-EXPA transformation procedure transforms NESDEL expressions into EXPA expressions and then carries out verification. The results of verification are transformed into corresponding NESDEL expressions by the EXPA-to-NESDEL transformation procedure. Therefore, the user can see the verification results on the NESDEL expressions described by him or her. Therefore, the user interface can be greatly improved, since the intelligibility of NESDEL expressions is much superior to that of EXPA expressions.

2. Verification capability

In the verification algorithm based on the reachability analysis, a user must personally investigate the location of protocol errors, i.e.,the error transition arcs in a reachability graph which lead to deadlocks, unspecified receptions, and so on. This is troublesome work for users. In contrast, EXPA can automatically detect the locations so that it is easy for a user to correct the errors of protocols. Consequently, by improving the verification capability, the user-friendliness is significantly improved.

Our system has been developed on a Sun-3 workstation. We also give a more detailed description of each component of our system in the rest of this paper.

13.3 EXPA

EXPA is a protocol verification algorithm which can be applied to systems composed of two or more processes communicating with each other. In EXPA, each process is modeled as a finite state machine, and is represented by a set of states, a set of actions, a state transition function, an initial state, and a set of final states. Here, an action means the exchange of an event accompanying the execution of a transition between states. The basic philosophy of EXPA is to examine all possible states of a system by defining an initial system state and a set of final system states. A system state consists of the states of the processes and the states of the communication

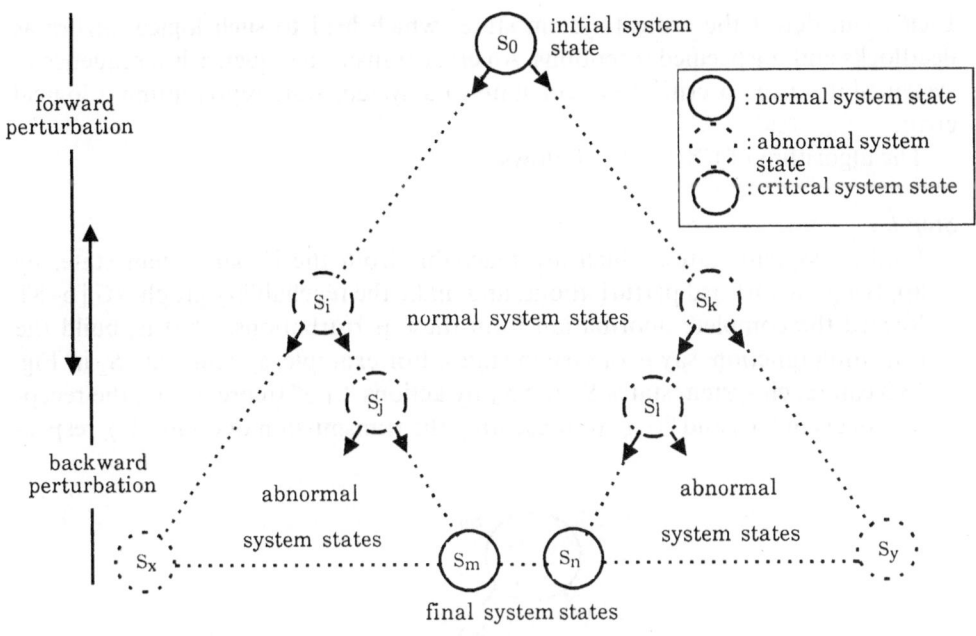

FIG. 13.2. Classification of system states

channels between the processes. The verification algorithm based on the reachability analysis detects the occurrence of protocol errors, such as deadlock, and produces a reachability graph. By using this reachability graph, a designer starts from an initial system state and traces the whole reachability graph, so that he or she will be able to detect design errors which lead to protocol errors. EXPA is a generalization of the reachability analysis theory and it can detect the locations of critical system states (defined later) which cause logical errors, as well as occurrences (system states) of logical errors such as deadlock. The main idea in the EXPA algorithm is to give a backward perturbation as well as a forward perturbation. A backward perturbation is a reachability analysis which starts from a final system state. By the backward perturbation, all the system states can be classified into two groups, a set of *normal system states* and a set of *abnormal system states* (Fig. 13.2). A normal system state is a system state which is reachable from an initial system state and has access to a final system state. An abnormal system state is a system state which is reachable from an initial system state and does not have access to a final system state. A normal system state which has immediate access to an abnormal system state is called a *critical system state*. As a result of the backward perturbation, EXPA can detect the following logical errors automatically, and notify the designer: (a) state deadlocks, (b) unspecified receptions, (c) loops, (d) buffer overflow (channel overflow), (e) critical system states, and (f) error transition sequences. A critical system state indicates a system state which leads to logical errors in the protocol; for example, a transition from the critical system state to an abnormal system state is a design error. If this transition occurs, the system state cannot reach the set of final system states. By performing backward perturbation,

EXPA can detect the critical system states which lead to such logical errors as deadlocks and unspecified receptions. An error transition sequence is a sequence of system states from a critical system state to a system state representing a logical error.

The algorithm of EXPA is as follows.

Step 1

Find all system states, which are reachable from the initial system state, by applying the forward perturbations, and make the reachability graph *RG* [6–8]. Record the complete information from these perturbations. That is, build the transition function, say δ, of system states. For example, system state S_2 in Fig. 13.3 can reach system states S_3 and S_4 by actions " + 3" (representing the reception of event "3") and " − 1" (representing the transmission of event "1"), respec-

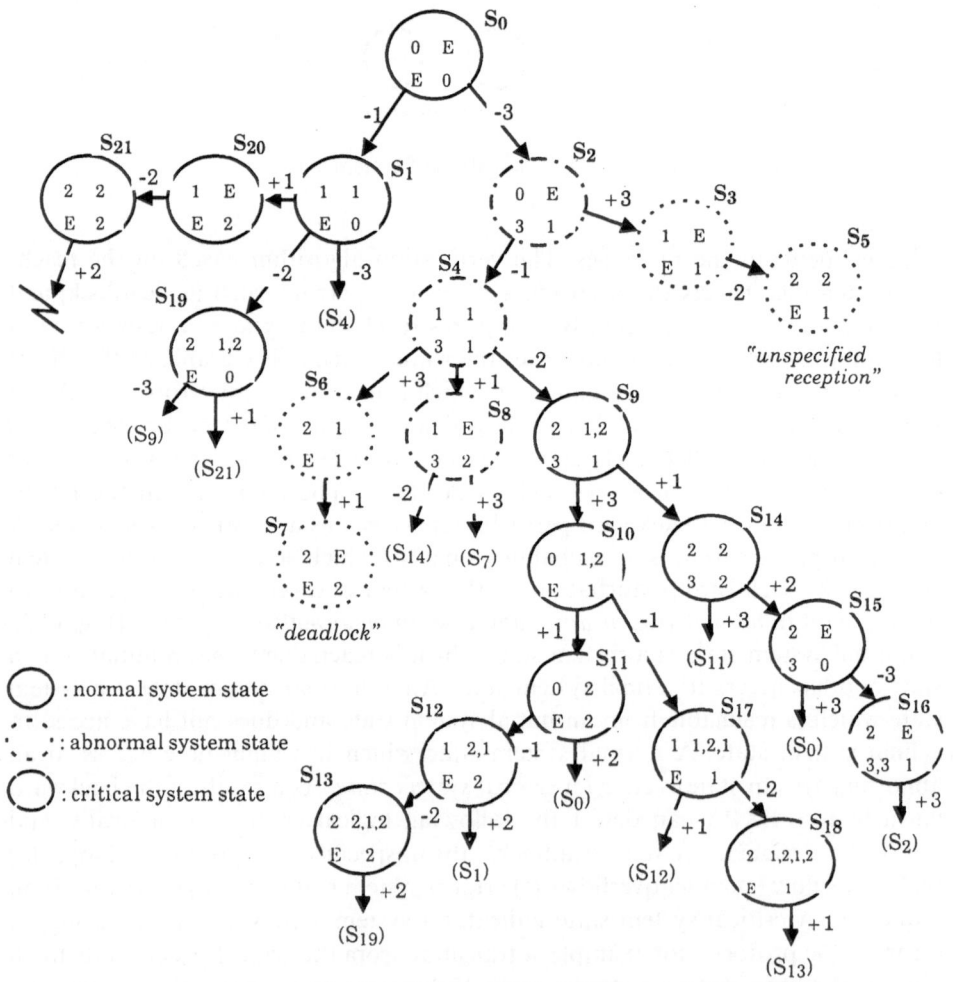

FIG. 13.3. Reachability graph corresponding to Fig. 13.4

tively. So, we get $\delta(S_2, +3) = S_3$ and $\delta(S_2, -1) = S_4$. These pieces of information are used to give the backward perturbation in Steps 2 and 3.

Step 2

For all system states found in Step 1, obtain the inverse function, say δ^{-1}, of state transition, by using the information from the forward perturbations recorded in Step 1. Given a system state and an action, the function δ^{-1} gives the set of system states which have access to the system state by the action. For example, system state S_7 in Fig. 13.3 can be reached from system state S_6 by action "$+1$". So, we get $\delta^{-1}(S_7, +1) = \{S_6\}$.

Step 3

Perform the backward perturbation, which is a perturbation starting from the final system states, by using δ^{-1} given in Step 2, and classify the system states into normal system states and abnormal system states.

Step 4

Find the critical system states and then make the error transition sequences, and report them. Detect loops in the sets of the normal system states and the abnormal system states, and report them. For example, in Fig. 13.3, system state S_2 is a critical system state since it is a normal system state which has immediate access to abnormal system state S_3.

(end of the algorithm)

Next, we give a simple example of the execution of EXPA. In this example, we consider a system consisting of two processes, represented in Fig 13.4. In Fig. 13.4, a circle indicates the state of a process. A directed arc and its label represent the

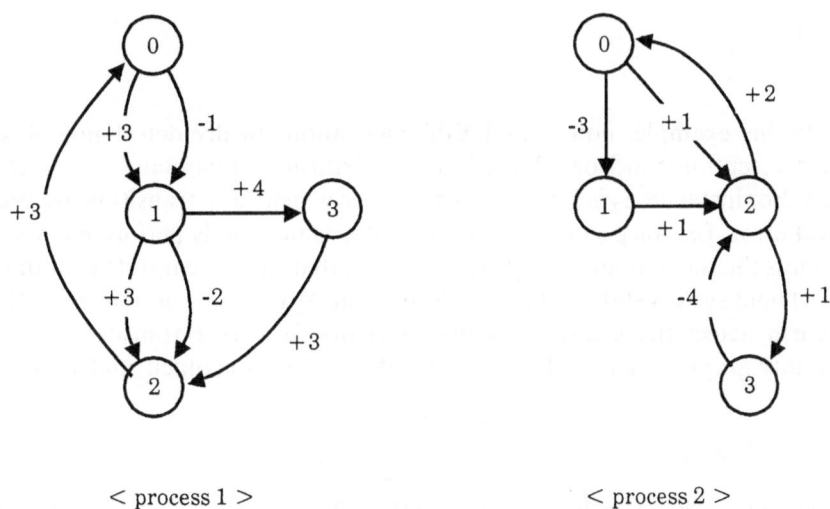

< process 1 >   < process 2 >

FIG. 13.4. Finite state graph representation of processes

transition between two process states and the action which causes the transition, respectively. The protocol illustrated in Fig. 13.4, is given to EXPA as an input, and then the information concerning the logical errors is obtained from EXPA as an output. For example, the reachability graph generated by the execution of EXPA is shown in Fig. 13.3. We represent a system state in the form of a matrix, as shown in Fig. 13.3. In the matrix form, the top-left element represents the state of process 1, and the bottom-right element represents the state of process 2. The top-right element represents the state of the half-duplex FIFO (first in, first out) channel from process 1 to process 2. Similarly, the bottom-left element represents the state of the half-duplex FIFO channel from process 2 to process 1. The special symbol E is used for denoting the state of the empty channel. In this example, we assume that the initial system state and the final system state are both S_0, that the capacities of the two channels are both 5, and that all events are exchanged perfectly. Then, we obtain the following results:

1. Normal system states

$S_0, S_1, S_2, S_4, S_8, S_9, S_{10}, S_{11}, S_{12}, S_{13}, S_{14}, S_{15}, S_{16}, S_{17}, S_{18}, S_{19}, S_{20}, S_{21}$

2. Abnormal system states

S_3, S_5, S_6, S_7

3. Critical system states

S_2, S_4, S_8

4. Error sequences

① $S_2 \to S_3 \to S_5$,   ② $S_4 \to S_6 \to S_7$,   ③ $S_8 \to S_7$

5. Unspecified reception

S_5

6. Deadlock

S_7

From this example, note that EXPA can automatically detect not only unspecified receptions·and deadlock, but also critical system states and error sequences. For instance, S_2 is a critical system state which has a transition arc causing a logical error, i.e., unspecified reception. If this transition is performed, a system state enters the set of abnormal system states, so that the system state cannot reach the set of final system states. That is, this arc from S_2 to S_3 is a design error. Hence, EXPA can detect the locations of design errors, i.e., error transition arcs in a reachability graph, which lead to unspecified reception, deadlock, and so on.

13.4 NESDEL

The protocol specification language NESDEL [24] corresponding to SDL [3] has been designed so that it possesses the following desirable characteristics: (a) easy to use and understand, and (b) no ambiguity (strictness of description). For the purpose

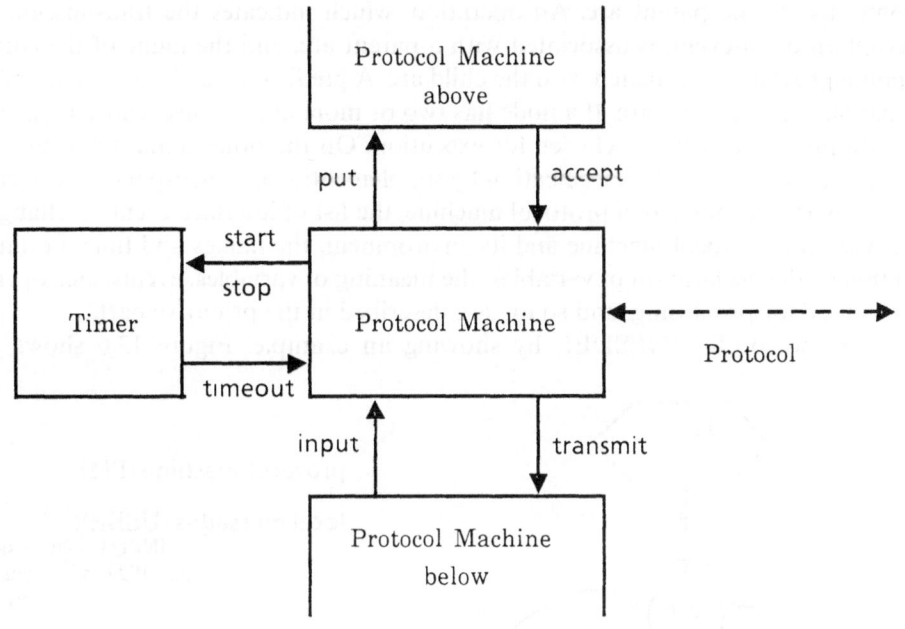

FIG. 13.5. Environment of a protocol machine

of (a), NESDEL uses a graphical representation. Such graphical representation is good for human understanding, especially in the case of large and complex specifications. For the purpose of (b), NESDEL has introduced a program-like representation. A NESDEL specification is written using both representation forms. NESDEL describes a protocol specification in terms of the protocol machine expressing the behavior of the protocol. Here, a protocol machine is modeled by using a finite state machine, augmented by the addition of variables and procedures. Fig. 13.5 shows the model of the environment of a protocol machine.

A NESDEL specification consists of two parts: a *directed graph* part and a *primitive* part. The directed graph part expresses the control flow of the protocol. It corresponds to an ordinary state transition diagram. The primitive part defines symbols such as variables, messages, and operations used in the graph part. A basic SDL specification [3] contains ambiguous descriptions as it permits the use of a natural language expression. (In order to augment basic SDL vis-à-vis strictness of description and introduction of structuring concept and procedures, etc., some recommendations have been made [4]). To avoid ambiguity, primitive expressions are introduced in the NESDEL specification. A primitive expression is a kind of high-level programming language expression. The notable features of NESDEL are better intelligibility and avoidance of ambiguity in protocol specifications, by using directed graph expressions and primitive expressions at the same time.

In NESDEL, a directed graph part is described by using four kinds of nodes, arcs, and arc labels. A node may be expressed hierarchically, that is, it may be expressed by using another NESDEL expression. An arc, which indicates a transition between two nodes, is represented using a *parent* arc (thick arc) and a *child* arc (thin arc) connected to the parent arc. An operation, which indicates the transmission or reception of an event, is associated with a parent arc, and the name of the corresponding event is associated with the child arc. A predicate may be associated with a parent arc or a child arc. If a node has two or more arcs, an arc whose predicate is interpreted as "true" is chosen for execution. On the other hand, the primitive part gives the details of a specification by supplementing its corresponding directed graph part. The name of a protocol machine, the list of interface events exchanged between the protocol machine and its environment, the names and timeout limits of timers, the declaration of variables, the meaning of variables, events, etc., operations used for processing, and so on, are described in the primitive part.

Now, we outline NESDEL by showing an example. Figure 13.6 shows an

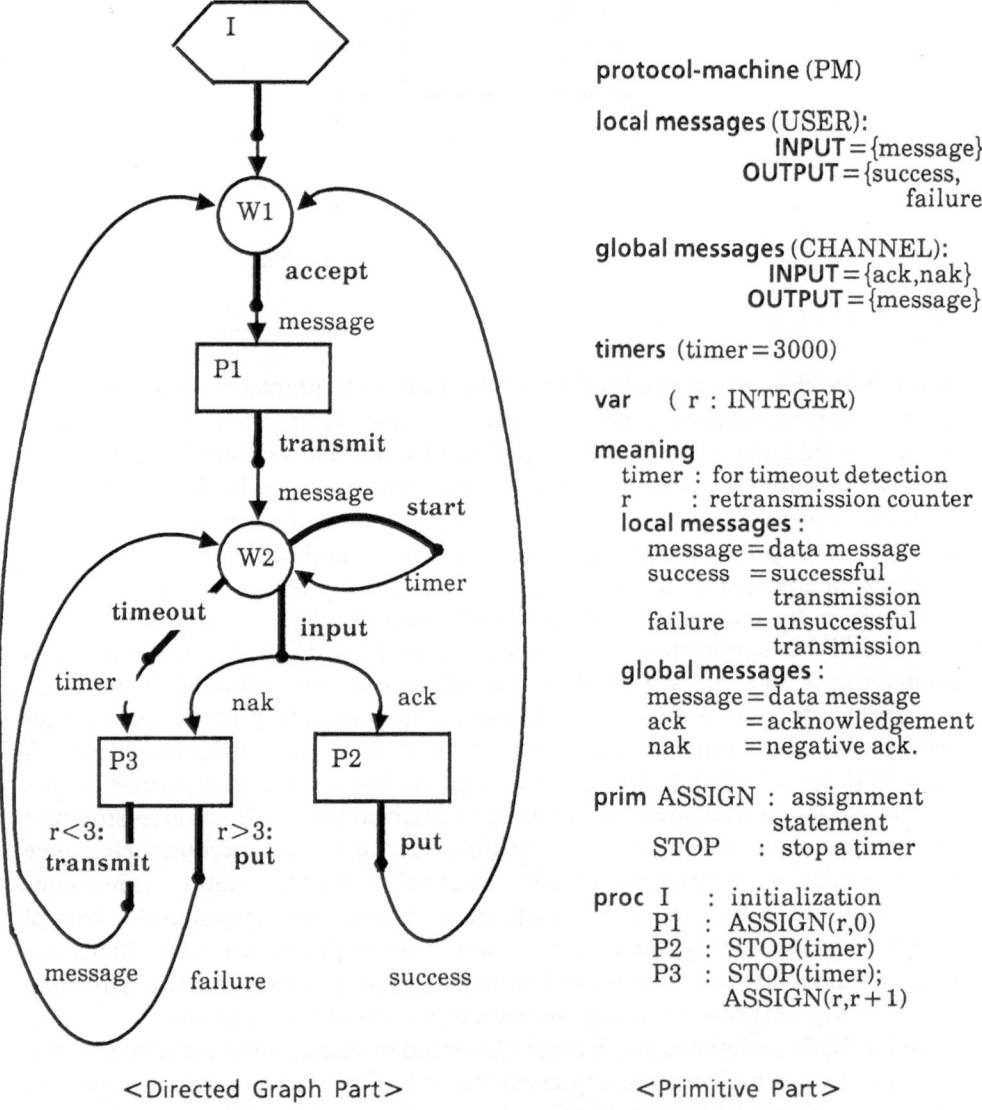

<Directed Graph Part>   <Primitive Part>

FIG. 13.6. An example of specification by NESDEL

example of a NESDEL specification. It represents the behavior of a protocol machine (which works with the environment shown in Fig 13.5) implementing the following simple protocol:

⟨**protocol**⟩
1. The user (i.e., the layer above) requests the protocol machine to transmit a message.
2. The protocol machine transmits this message to the peer protocol machine, through the layer below. At this time, a timer is activated for retransmission.
3. If the protocol machine receives an acknowledgment from the peer protocol machine, through the layer below, then the message "success" is returned to the user. If a negative acknowledgment is received or the retransmission timer goes off, then the message is retransmitted. This retransmission is permitted up to three times. In the case of four consecutive occurrences of timeout or reception of negative acknowledgment, the protocol machine returns the message "failure" to the user, without retransmitting the message.
4. Repeats Steps 1–3.

In Fig. 13.6, the transition arc from node W_1 to node P_1 and its arc labels "accept" and "message" in the upper part of the directed graph, for instance, mean that when the protocol machine is in node W_1 called *W-node*, the protocol machine receives the message "message" from 'the protocol machine above' and then moves on to node P_1, called *P-node*, for processing. (In NESDEL, a W-node is used to indicate that the protocol machine waits for the occurrence of an interface event). The processing of node P_1 is described in the procedure definition section, identified with key word "proc," in the primitive part. In this example, node P_1 performs "ASSIGN$(r, 0)$", i.e., assignment of the value zero to the integer variable "r". In node W_2 the arc labeled with "start" and "timer" indicates that when entering this node, timer timer is activated once. In this node, when a timeout happens, the transition to node P_3 occurs. On the other hand, when an acknowledgment or negative acknowledgment is received, the transition to node P_2 or transition to node P_3 occurs, respectively. The transition arc from node P_3 to node W_2 and its arc labels indicates that, after the processing of node P_3, if the value of the variable r is less than or equal to three, then this transition can take place and message message is transmitted to 'the protocol machine below' during this transition. The interface events exchanged between the protocol machine and 'the protocol machine above' are listed in the local message definition section, labeled with key word "local messages," in the primitive part. Similarly, the interface events exchanged between the protocol machine and 'the protocol machine below' are listed in the global message definition section, labeled with key word "global messages." The meaning of the interface events, variables, etc., is described as comments in the meaning description section, labeled with keyword "meaning."

As seen in this example, the specifier can freely define and use operations to be used in the description of P-nodes. In NESDEL, such an operation is called a *protocol-dependent primitive* and is defined in the protocol-dependent primitive definition section, labeled with key word "prim," in the primitive part. On the other hand, operations (see Fig. 13.5) such as "accept," "put," "input," "transmit," "start," "stop," and "timeout" are called *common primitives*, in the sense that they can be commonly used for any protocol, and can be used as labels of arcs in the directed graph part. The common primitives "accept" and "input" are used to indicate the reception of an interface event from 'the protocol machine above' and 'the protocol machine below', respectively. "put" and "transmit" are used to indicate the transmission of an interface event to 'the protocol machine above' and 'the protocol machine below', respectively. The activation and suspension of a timer, and the occurrence of a timeout are indicated by using the common primitives "start," "stop," and "timeout," respectively.

NESDEL has proved very useful in specifying existing protocols, e.g., X.25 protocol and HDLC.

13.5 Transformations Between the Languages

In this section, we describe the algorithms for performing the transformations between the languages mentioned in the previous sections. We provide two transformation algorithms, for transforming (1) NESDEL expressions into EXPA expressions, and (2) EXPA expressions into NESDEL expressions. Transformation algorithm (1) is used for verifying protocols specified in NESDEL. Transformation algorithm (2) is used for making the results of the protocol verification performed in EXPA expressions, which are the output of transformation algorithm (1), reflect on the original NESDEL expressions corresponding to the EXPA expressions.

13.5.1 Transformation from NESDEL into EXPA

There exist some differences between NESDEL expressions and EXPA expressions. Thus, a NESDEL expression has to be transformed into the corresponding EXPA expression to validate a protocol specified in NESDEL. Traditional validation methods based on the reachability analysis including EXPA require finite state transition graphs without predicates and variables, in order to represent protocol specifications to be validated, as inputs to these methods. However, as described in Sect. 13.4, a NESDEL expression is based on a finite state transition graph with predicates and variables. Therefore, transformations of NESDEL expressions into EXPA expressions become difficult, so that, until now, the user has had to do this transformation using heuristics. To overcome this difficulty, we have introduced predicates and variables into EXPA expressions, and have augmented the original EXPA described in Sect. 13.3. Thus, the current version of EXPA can accept expressions with predicates and variables as its inputs, and the choice of a possible transition is determined depending on not only the transmission or reception of an event but also the evaluation of a predicate accompanying the transition. By this augmentation, we have succeeded in building an algorithm for the NESDEL-to-EXPA transformation.

Algorithm
Let $G = (V, E)$ be a NESDEL expression. This algorithm takes G as an input and makes EXPA expression $G' = (V', E')$ as an output.

Step 1. Initial setting.

  $V' \leftarrow V$ and $E' \leftarrow \Phi$ (empty set)

  Comment: As seen in an example of specification of NESDEL (Fig. 13.6), nodes of NESDEL expressions may have associated processes. Retain information on variables and processes effecting the evaluation of the predicates.

Step 2. Processing of each edge in E.

  Choose an edge e from E and then do the following according to the label of e:

  2.1 If the label is "[P, transmit, message]" then it is changed into "[P, negative integer]," and $E' \leftarrow E' \cup \{e\}$. Go to Step 3.

  2.2 If the label is "[P, input, message]" then it is changed into "[P, positive integer]" and $E' \leftarrow E' \cup \{e\}$. Go to Step 3.

  Comment: P is a predicate and "message" represents any message used in NESDEL such as nak, ack, message, and so on. Furthermore, if messages are the same,then they are changed into the same integer; however, the sign of integer depends on whether an operation of the label is "transmit" or "input."

  2.3 If the label is concerned with a timer such as "start," "stop," or "timeout" then go to Step 3 (i.e., this edge is ignored).

  2.4 If the label is concerned with a process of a higher layer such as "put" and "accept" then it is removed from e and $E' \leftarrow E' \cup \{e\}$. Go to Step 3.

Step 3. If $E = \Phi$ then halt, otherwise go to Step 2.

  Comment: In this stage, a table concerned with a correspondence between NESDEL expressions and EXPA expressions is made, to use in EXPA-to-NESDEL transformation, described in the next section.

                                                              (End of algorithm)

For example, the graph in Fig. 13.7 is obtained by applying the NESDEL-to-EXPA transformation to the NESDEL expression given in Fig. 13.6.

We note that differences between G and G' are only in edges and their labels. The labels of processes concerning communication with other processes are retained (2.1 and 2.2 in Step 2) and the labels of processes concerning communication with processes of higher layers are removed (2.4 in Step 2). Edges with labels related to timers are removed (2.3 in Step 2). In short, G' differs from G in terms of a communication with a process of higher layer and a timer. Since logical errors such as deadlocks, unspecified receptions, and overflow are independent of communication with processes of higher layers and timers, this transformation algorithm does not affect these logical errors . That is, if there exists a deadlock (unspecified reception, overflow) on a NESDEL expression, then there exists a deadlock (unspecified reception, overflow) on the corresponding EXPA expression, and vice versa. Therefore the following proposition holds.

Proposition 1

Suppose there are n processes which communicate with each other. Let G_i be a NESDEL expression of process i and G_i' be an output of the NESDEL-to-EXPA

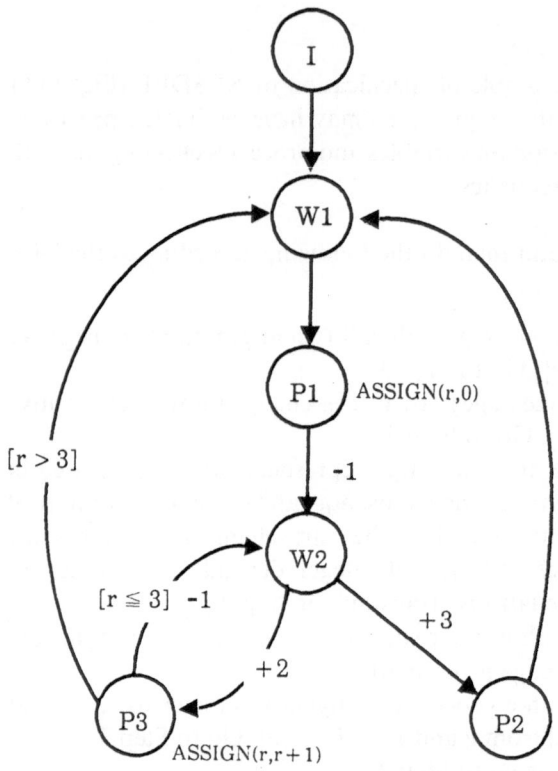

Fig. 13.7. An example of a NESDEL-to-EXPA transformation

transformation algorithm for input G_i. Now, suppose that logical errors of the protocols are restricted to deadlocks, unspecified receptions, and channel overflow. Then there exists a logical error on $G_1, \ldots, G_n$ if and only if there exists a logical error on $G'_1, \ldots, G'_n$.

13.5.2 Transformation from EXPA into NESDEL

EXPA generates a reachability graph of system states and informs users of any logical errors. But it is not easy for users to understand an EXPA expression or a reachability graph, which is inferior to a NESDEL expression in intelligibility. Therefore, in order to improve the intelligibility, we would like to obtain the logical errors in the form of a specification language, viz. a NESDEL expression.

In the following, we present an EXPA-to-NESDEL transformation algorithm. This algorithm consists of two stages, the decomposition stage and the transformation stage. In the decomposition stage, system states and sequences of system states are decomposed into states of each process which are components of a system state. In the transformation stage, outputs of the decomposition stage are transformed into NESDEL expressions. Since a NESDEL expression has been given as input to the NESDEL-to-EXPA transformation, it is easy to design the transformation stage using the information on transformation from the NESDEL expression into the EXPA expression. Let N be the number of processes in a communications system. Then the algorithm is given as follows:

Algorithm

(I) *Decomposition stage*
This stage consists of two decomposition steps.
    1. *Decomposition of system states*
    Given a system state S in the reachability graph as input, find corresponding states of each process on the EXPA expression.
    2. *Decomposition of sequences of system states.*
    Given a sequence S of system states in the reachability graph as input, let S be $S_1 \rightarrow \cdots \rightarrow S_k$, where each S_j $(1 \leq j \leq k)$ is a system state. A_i $(1 \leq i \leq N)$ is a variable and takes a sequence of states concerned with process i as its value.
        (1) Let q^i be a state corresponding to process i in system state S_1. Then, for all i $(1 \leq i \leq N)$, $A_i \leftarrow q^i$.
        (2) Repeat $j = 1$ to $(k - 1)$
        If $S_j \rightarrow S_{j+1}$ is caused by a transition of process i, $A_i \leftarrow A_i \circ (q',j)$, where q' is a state corresponding to process i in S_{j+1} and '$\circ$' means a concatenation of string.
      Comment: If A_i is a $q \circ (q_1,j_1) \circ (q_2,j_2) \circ \cdots \circ (q_m,j_m)$, this sequence means that transition $S_{j_1} \rightarrow S_{j_1+1}$ has been caused by a state transition $q \rightarrow q_1$ of process i. Similarly $S_{j_2} \rightarrow S_{j_2+1}$ has been caused by $q_1 \rightarrow q_2$ of process i, and so on.

(II) *Transformation stage*
This stage takes the output of the decomposition stage as input. The information of the NESDEL-to-EXPA transformation given in the preceding subsection consists of the correspondence between nodes (states), edges (state transitions), and actions of expressions in NESDEL and EXPA. We call this information NESDEL–EXPA information. By using this information, the algorithm of this stage is constructed as follows:
    Let an input to this stage be $A_i = q \circ (q_1,j_1) \circ (q_2,j_2) \circ \cdots \circ (q_m,j_m)$ and an output from this stage be B_i.
Step 1. Initial setting.
        Find a state, corresponding to q, of process i on the NESDEL expression by using the NESDEL–EXPA information, and set it to B_i.
Step 2. For $J = j_1, j_2, \ldots, j_m$, do the following:
        Find a state, corresponding to a state q_J, of process i on the NESDEL expression by using the NESDEL–EXPA information and $B_i \leftarrow B_i \circ (u, J)$, where u is a state corresponding to q_J.

For all i $(1 \leq i \leq N)$, Steps 1 and 2 are performed.

(End of algorithm)

The EXPA-to-NESDEL transformation algorithm has been constructed by using NESDEL–EXPA information. NESDEL–EXPA information contains de-

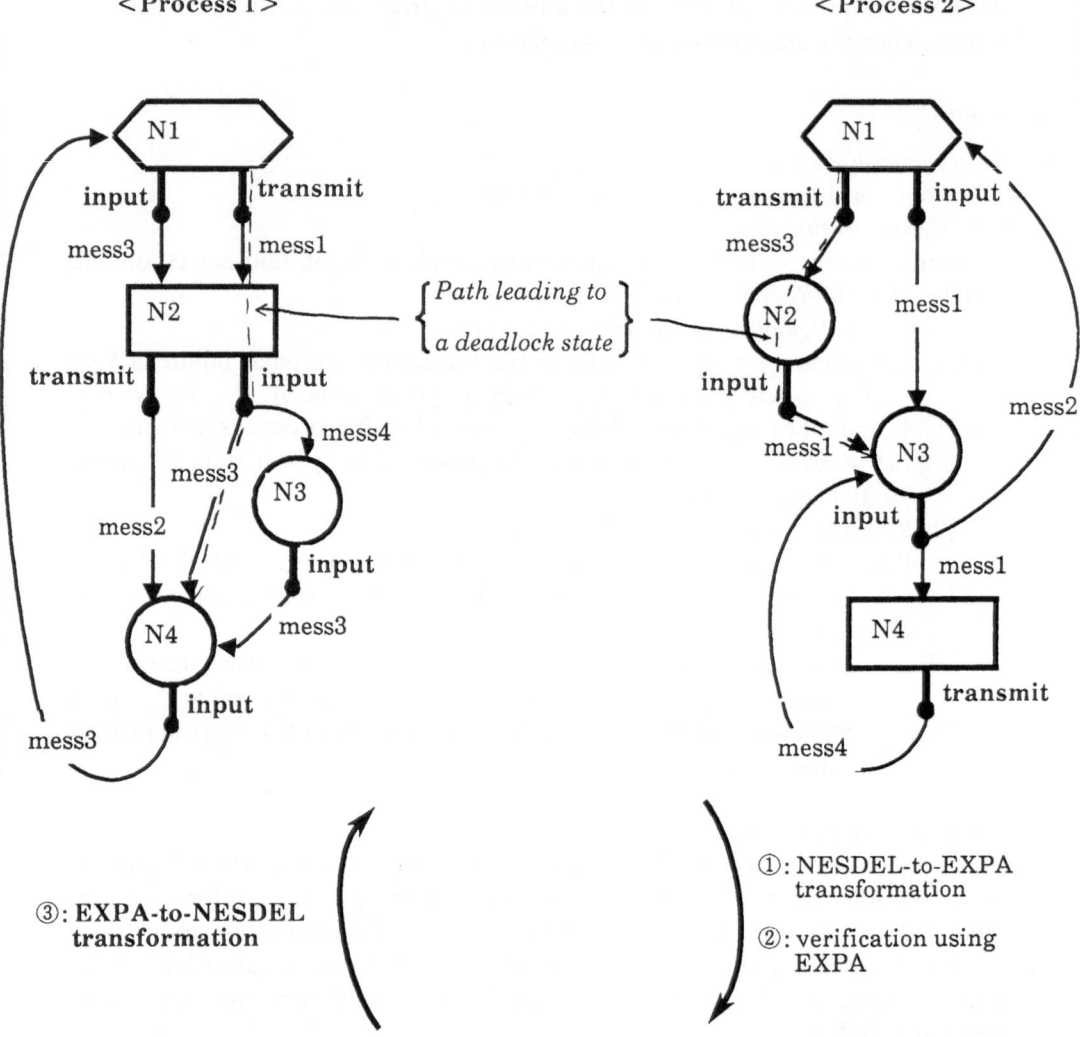

<Process 1>   <Process 2>

Reachability graph

FIG. 13.8. An example of an EXPA-to-NESDEL transformation. *mess*, message

tailed information on the correspondence between NESDEL expressions and
EXPA expressions, and can be stored as a file after performing the NESDEL-to-
EXPA transformation. Hence, for the EXPA-to-NESDEL transformation algo-
rithm, the following proposition holds.

Proposition 2
The EXPA-to-NESDEL transformation algorithm transforms a system state consisting of processes and channels into a state of each process expressed in NESDEL.

Also, a sequence of system states is transformed into a sequence of states of each process.

Figure 13.8 shows an example of this transformation. In this figure, i.e., NESDEL expression, state N_4 of process 1 and state N_3 of process 2 correspond to the "deadlock" state in the reachability graph, as shown in Fig. 13.3. Also, paths leading to a deadlock state are indicated in each NESDEL expression.

13.6 Supporting Tools

We have been developing a number of software tools used for supporting the aforementioned languages and the transformations between those languages. In this section, these tools are introduced.

13.6.1 The Knowledge-Based NESDEL Editor

As stated in Sect. 13.4, a NESDEL specification comprises a primitive part and a directed graph part. Therefore, its editor should provide not merely the capability of editing text but also the capability of editing graphs. Moreover, it is important to present the users with an appropriate *working environment* to edit protocol specifications. Also, the provision of a verification function plays an important role in checking specifications. The editor has three functions: (1) edit, (2) verification, and (3) intelligent *help*. The provision of a user-friendly interface should be a requirement, so that this editor can present the users with an appropriate working environment. For this purpose, we are now studying the development of a knowledge-based user interface. In this user interface, a user of the editor is modeled, by using the history of the user-editor communication which reflects the user's thinking process. By integrating such knowledge, i.e., a "user model," into the editor, we construct a user-friendly interface.

A real example, produced by this editor, is illustrated in Fig. 13.9. It is a hard-copy of the display on the TOSHIBA AS3000 color bitmap display. We have completed the implementation of the major portions (i.e., the editing function) of the editor.

13.6.2 The NESDEL-to-EXPA Translator, the EXPA Executor, and the EXPA-to-NESDEL Translator

We have been developing three tools, which are closely related to each other, for verifying protocols written in NESDEL. They are: (1) the NESDEL-to-EXPA translator, which is used for the transformation of NESDEL expressions into EXPA expressions; (2) the EXPA executor, by which the EXPA expressions given as the results of the NESDEL-to-EXPA translation are verified using the EXPA verification algorithm; and (3) the EXPA-to-NESDEL translator, which is used for making the results of the verification performed by the EXPA executor reflect on the original NESDEL expressions corresponding to the EXPA expressions.

We have completed the implementation of the NESDEL-to-EXPA translator, the EXPA executor, and the EXPA-to-NESDEL translator. A real example, produced by these three tools, is demonstrated in Figs. 13.10 and 13.11. It is a hard-copy

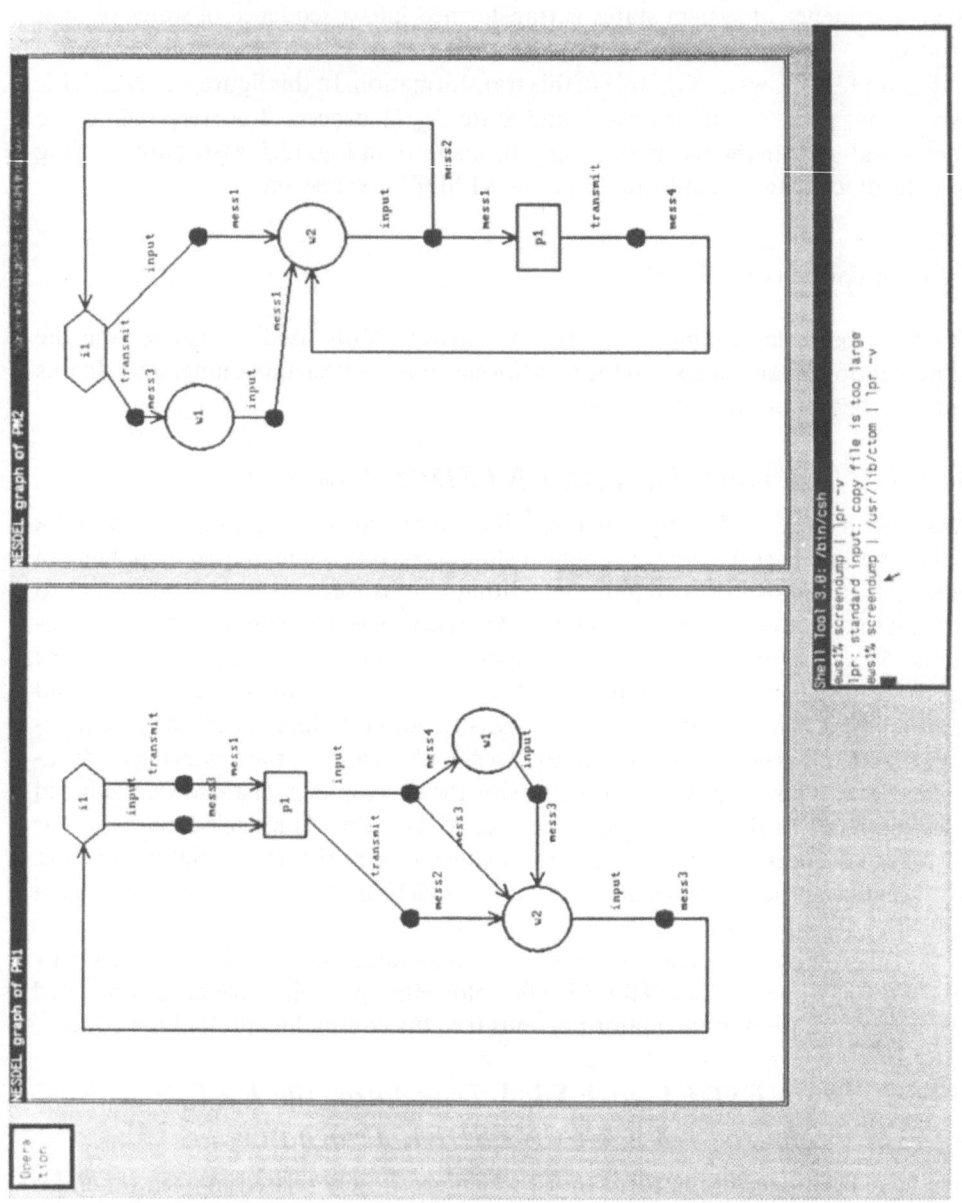

Fig. 13.9. A real example produced by the NESDEL editor

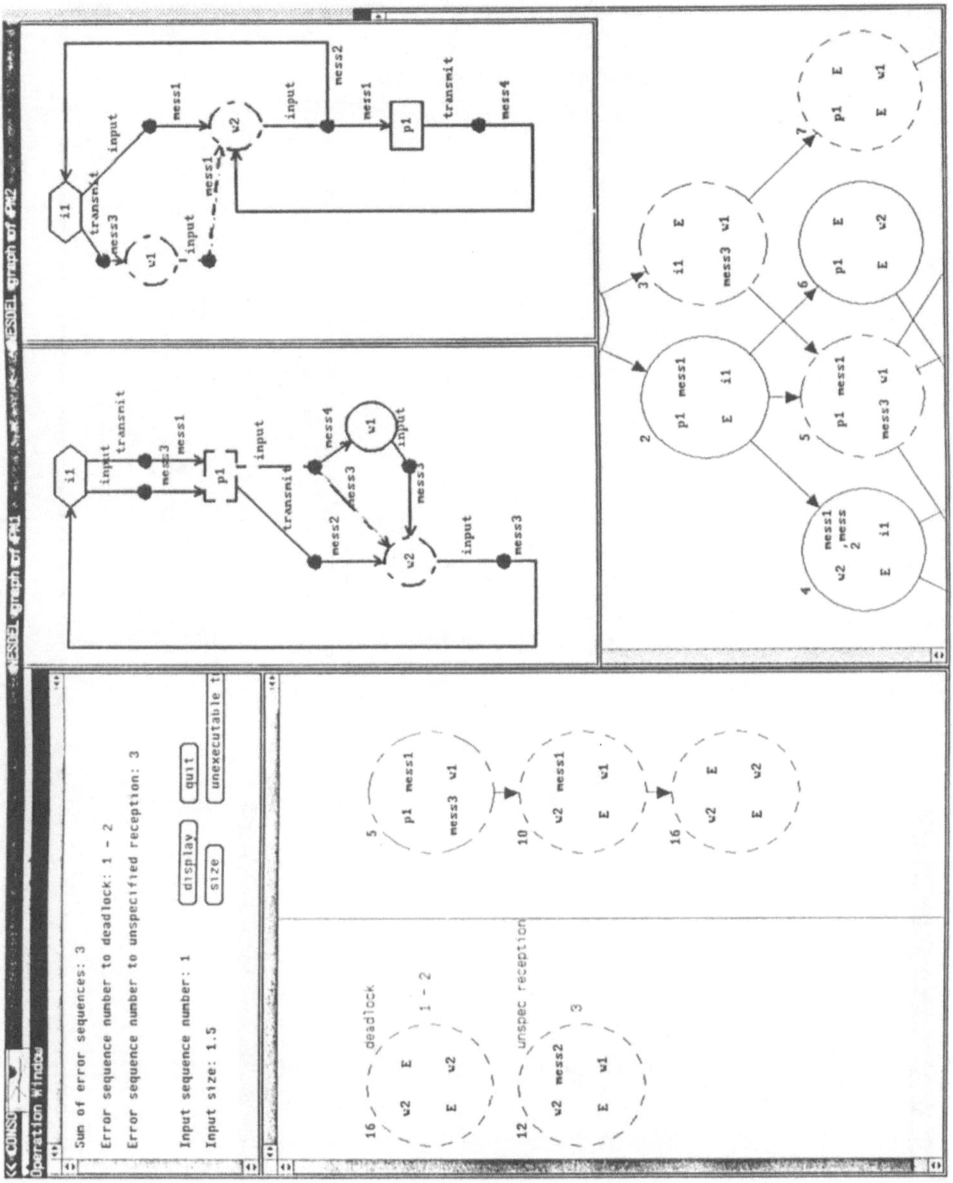

FIG. 13.10. A real example produced by the verification tools(1)

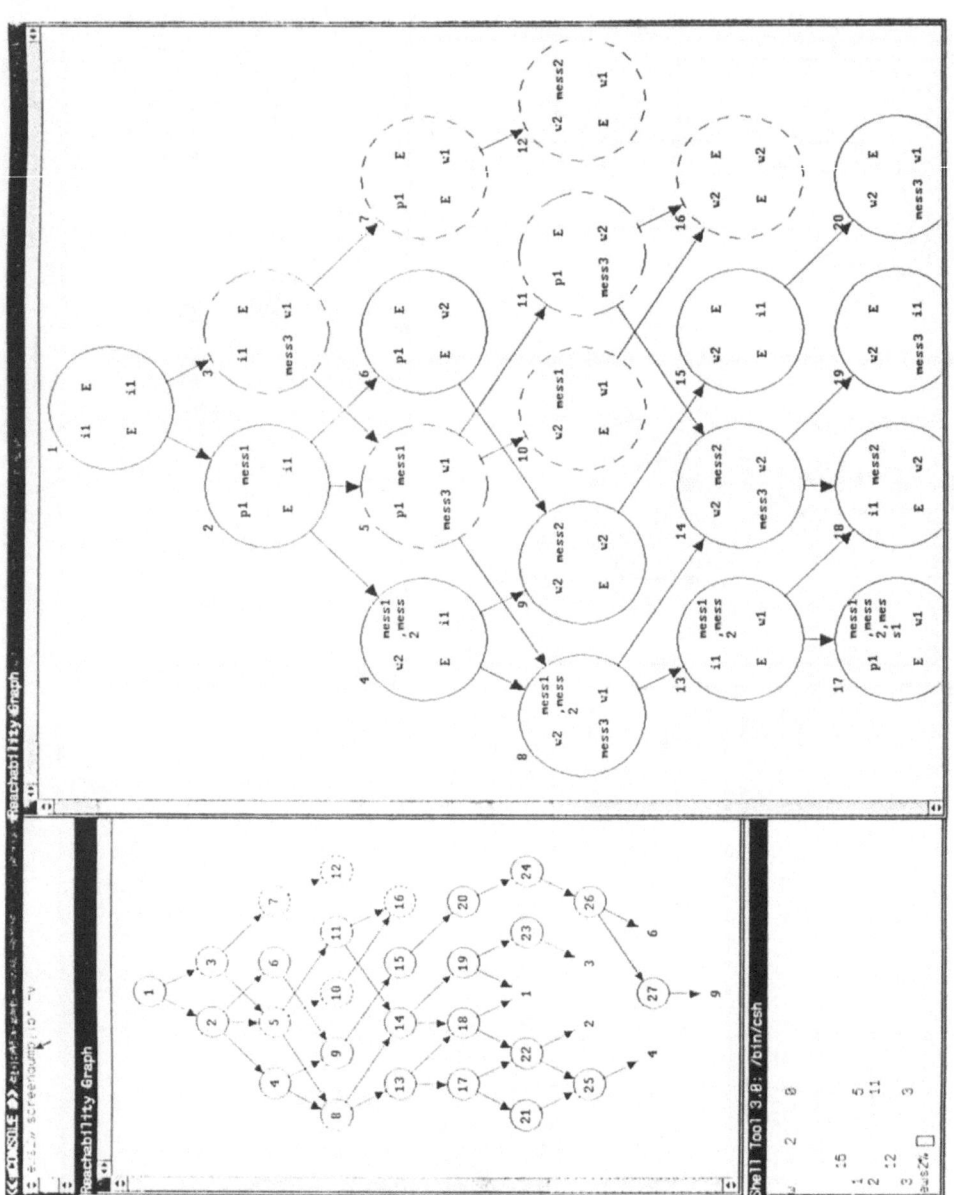

FIG. 13.11. A real example produced by the verification tools(2)

of the display on the TOSHIBA AS3000 color bitmap display. In Fig. 13.10, the right upper part represents the results of validation of a NESDEL expression, and the right lower part shows the results of validation of an EXPA expression. Also, the left lower part shows protocol errors, i.e., deadlock and unspecified reception, and the path from a critical state to a deadlock state.

13.7 Conclusion

In this paper, we have described a software environment for designing and verifying communication protocols. In this software environment, we have provided the specification language NESDEL, the verification algorithm EXPA, and two transformation algorithms, i.e., NESDEL-to-EXPA and EXPA-to-NESDEL, in order to improve the user interface.

Given a protocol specification in NESDEL by using the knowledge-based NESDEL editor, its verification can be mechanically performed with the assistance of the protocol verification system. We have found our software environment to be useful for specifying and verifying a variety of communication protocols. The unified graphical interface and the tools, i.e., NESDEL, EXPA, and two transformation algorithms, make it easy to use. Consequently, it is expected that the development cost of protocols will be reduced.

References

1. Danthine A (1980) Protocol representation with finite-state models. IEEE Trans Commun COM-28 (4): 632–642
2. Bochmann GV, Cerny E, Gagne M, Jard C, Leveille A, Lacaille C, Maksud M, Raghunathan KS, Sarikaya B. (1982) Experience with formal specifications using an extended state transition model. IEEE Trans Commun COM-30 (12): 2506–2513
3. Rockstrom A, Saracco R (1982) SDL-CCITT specification and description language. IEEE Trans Commun COM-30 (6): 1310–1317
4. CCITT (1984) Functional specification and description language (SDL). CCITT Recommendations Z.100–Z.104
5. ISO (1987) ESTELLE—A formal description technique based on an extended state transition model. ISO/DIS 9074
6. Rubin J, West CH (1982) An improved protocol validation technique. Comput Networks 6: 65–73
7. West CH (1978) General technique for communication protocol validation. IBM J Res Dev 22 (4): 393–404
8. Zafiropulo P, West CH, Rudin H, Cowan DD, Brand D (1980) Towards analyzing and synthesizing protocols. IEEE Trans Commun COM-28 (4): 651–660
9. West CH, Zafiropulo P (1978) Automated validation of a communications protocol: the CCITT X.21 recommendations. IBM J Res Dev 22: 60–71
10. Lam SS, Shankar AU (1984) Protocol verification via projections. IEEE Trans Software Eng SE-10 (4): 325–342
11. Blumer TP, Sidhu DP (1986) Mechanical verification and automatic implementation of communication protocols. IEEE Trans Software Eng SE-12 (8): 827–843

12. Yu Y-T, Gouda G (1982) Deadlock detection for a class of communicating finite state machines. IEEE Trans Commun COM-30 (12): 2514–2518
13. Schultz GD, Rose DB, West CH, Gray JP (1980) Executable description and validation of SNA. IEEE Trans Commun COM-28 (4): 661–677
14. Gouda MG, Yu Y-T (1984) Protocol validation by maximal progress state exploration. IEEE Trans Commun COM-32 (1): 94–97
15. Sidhu DP, Blumer TP (1986) Verification of NBS Class 4 transport protocol. IEEE Trans Commun COM-34 (8): 781–789
16. Brand D, Zafiropuro P (1983) On communicating finite-state machine. J ACM 30 (2): 323–342
17. Bochmann GV, Sunshine C (1980) Use of formal methods in communication protocol design. IEEE Trans Commun COM-28: 624–631
18. Gouda MG, Yu Y (1984) Synthesis of communicating finite-state machines with guaranteed progress. IEEE Trans Commun COM-32 (7): 779–788
19. Zhang Y-X, Takahashi K, Shiratori N, Noguchi S (1988) An interactive protocol synthesis algorithm using a global state transition graph. IEEE Trans Software Eng 14 (3): 394–404
20. Aggarwal S, Barbara D, Meth KZ (1988) A software environment for the specification and analysis of problems of coordination and concurrency. IEEE Trans Software Eng 14 (3): 280–290
21. Chow C-H, Lam SS (1988) PROSPEC: An interactive programming environment for designing and verifying communication protocols. IEEE Trans Software Eng 14 (3): 327–338
22. Billington J, Wheeler GR, Wilbur-Ham MC (1988) PROTEAN: A high-level Petri net tool for the specification and verification of communication protocols. IEEE Trans Software Eng 14 (3): 301–316
23. Shiratori N, Gohara J, Noguchi S (1982) A new design language for communication protocols and a systematic design method of communication systems. Proc 6th Int Conf Software Engineering, pp 403–412
24. Shiratori N, Takahashi K, Noguchi S (1986) IDESS/85: Intelligent support system for protocol and communication software development. Proc 8th Int Conf Computer Communication, pp 543–548

14
MOA—
A Model of a Computer Environment and Its Interface for Supporting Highly Intelligent Human Work

Hiroyuki Tominaga[1] and Naoyuki Nide[2]

Summary: A model for describing cooperative work which requires high intelligence is introduced. The supporting system and its interface within a uniform framework is described. For this model, the amalgamation of a hypertext system and an inference system is adopted. This paper provides a realistic example of the use of the model in the medical field, and gives a description of system behavior in this model. A formal description of the model is also presented.

Key words: hypertext — inference system — computer environment—intelligent human work

14.1 Introduction

There are two well-known issues concerning interactive information systems which are intended to support highly intelligent human work: one is how to enhance the user-friendliness of the interface, and the other is to work out ingenious ways to allow human interventions to the machine. One of the recently noted innovations in the use of computers in the office is the development of the so-called hypertext system, another very flexible tool [1]. On the other hand, research in artificial intelligence has given us greater expectations of the power of inference engines, for which careful consideration and selection of applications can enhance the capability and usefulness of the system. More precisely, it is essential to work out and elaborate the mechanism of interactive communication by which the machine should interact with the human—how the human should help the machine, or should be helped by the machine, in order to gain a better result out of automatic deduction. This paper proposes a model of man-machine cooperation to perform highly intelligent work, which involves a highly sophisticated interface, such as the hypertext system, and automatic deduction. We present an example in the field of medical care, as a suitable application domain.

---

[1] Research Institution for Mathematical Sciences, and
[2] Educational Center for Information Processing, Kyoto University, Kyoto, 606 Japan

Conventionally, most of the efforts in automatic deduction, such as in the domain of medicine, were intended to replace all human reasoning by a computer system, and therefore required complicated rules, a large knowledge base, and consequently, intolerably long execution times before a result, if any, could be attained. For instance, in medical diagnosis, it is not fruitful to try to let the machine determine the name of the illness of a new patient solely by inputting large amounts of data obtained from the results of the examinations and tests. It would, at most, output an unsatisfactory trivial answer. Rather, the machine should simply provide the knowledge on which the deductions are based, and leave the final judgement to the doctor in order to have practically plausible results.

On the other hand, when the part of the knowledge base relevant for the diagnosis is located by the doctor, he or she will have to perform a judgement which requires more refined and detailed data or knowledge than that in his or her own random access brain memory. Therefore, a doctor will often have to consult a medical encyclopedia before understanding a problem and reaching a concrete solution. In such cases, a machine should have a more positive role than simply showing the relevant part of the texts of handbooks; namely, a direct contribution to the solution of problems using deductive mechanisms. For instance, in order to determine the type of virus from many factors obtained from testing, the doctor does not have the whole table in mind which gives all possible combinations of the factors needed to determine the type of virus. Such a problem domain, which is limited and concrete, can give a suitable role to the machine, whereas wide and vague domains cannot.

The objective of the work presented here is to work out a more effective scheme or model of interaction and cooperation between man and machine to perform work. In other words, we assume an expert in a specific field is the user of the machine, and try to figure out an environment which will provide that expert useful support and a flexible and practically usable interface. In order to achieve such goals, the machine should always see to it that the user is aware of what can be done by the machine in real time. The machine should be able to illustrate the changing state of the task, and understand the real-time user's need and intention, both of which require deductive processes by the machine. Such an environment will be realized by the ingenious amalgamation of a hypertext system and an inference system.

In the first section, we analyze intellectual tasks with a machine in the field of medicine. In the second, we present a model of the man-machine interaction. In the third section, we illustrate the behavior of the model in a simple medical diagnosis and treatment. The fourth section gives a formal description of the model, and the final section gives the conclusion and discusses future work.

14.2 Analysis of Man-Machine Interaction for Intelligent Work

14.2.1 Analysis of Medical Diagnosis

Here, we consider highly intelligent work such as performing a series of tasks by generating, inputting, and/or retrieving dynamic data about some specific object, which involves deductive and inferential processes as well as looking into static knowledge bases such as documents and an encyclopedia. For the case of medical care, the knowledge base consists of the medical encyclopedia and handbooks of medicine which contain technical knowledge for diagnosis, treatment, and so on. On the other hand, the dynamic data consist of the information on the target object "specific patient," and this is written down in charts.

Three aspects in the following list characterize such highly intelligent work. In medical care, the correspondence between the activities mentioned and these three aspects is obvious.

– Knowledge management
  Access to the general knowledge base
– Data maintenance
  Management and use of the dynamic data structures of a specific object
– Solving problems
  Generation of information regarding the object by inference

Furthermore, in the case of medical care, we analyze the progress of intelligent work (Fig. 14.1). The top half of the figure expresses a process locating a partial knowledge system about a specific object from the whole system, based upon a human's heuristic judgement. In the process, information obtained from tests or doctor's questions is written down on the chart on demand. On the other hand, the bottom half of the figure expresses a process solving concrete problems using the

FIG. 14.1. The progress of medical care

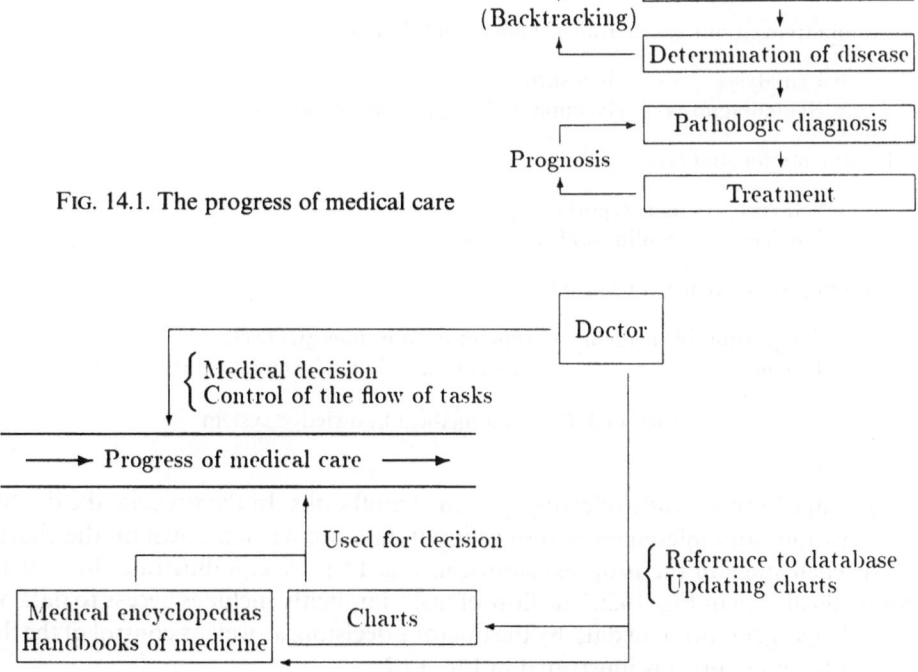

FIG. 14.2. The data flow and control of medical care

- Content of medical encyclopedia and handbooks of medicine

  o Disease   ··· outline, pathologic diagnosis, treatments, supplement any items
  o Examination··· purpose, method, judgement
  o Medicine   ··· elements, usage, effects, side effects

- Hierarchies of classification of diseases

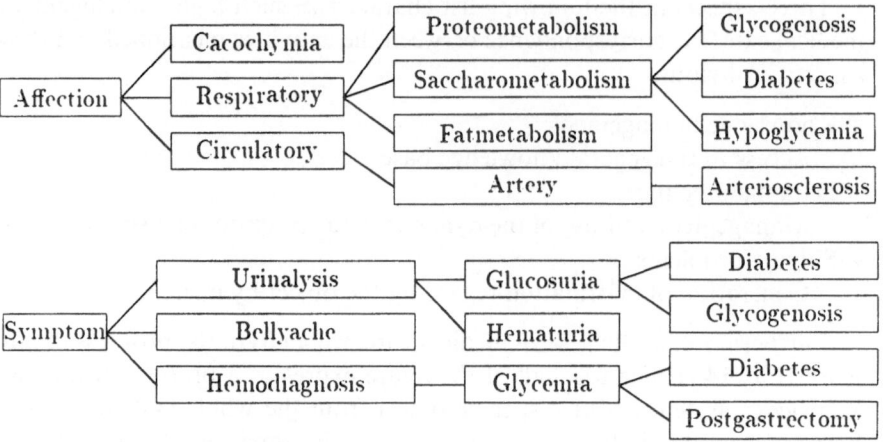

- Pathologic diagnosis for diabetes

  o Type   ··· IDDM (insulin-dependent diabetes mellitus), NIDDM (non insulin-
                   dependent diabetes mellitus)
  o Progress   ··· subclinical, boundary, incipient, middle, last
  o Complications··· arteriosclerosis, neuropathy

- Examination about saccharometabolism and diabetes

  o Urinalysis   ··· glucosuria
  o Hemodiagnosis··· glycemia, GTT (glucose tolerant test)

- Treatments for diabetes

  o Self-care ··· diet, ergotherapy
  o Medicine ··· insulin, oral medicine

- Attention with treatment of diabetes

  o Adaptation of medicine··· type of insulin, allergy check
  o Prognosis   ··· prevention of hypoglycemia, calorie control

FIG. 14.3. Part of a medical knowledge system

knowledge located while referring to some handbooks. In the process, the doctor's observations and inferences as well as input data are written down on the chart.

At each stage in the progress shown in Fig. 14.1, we can illustrate three phases for medical care in Fig. 14.2. The flow of tasks implicitly includes access to data and knowledge, generation of data by the doctor's decision, as well as control of the flow itself. Overall control is illustrated in Fig. 14.2.

The doctor intervenes at various points during the flow of tasks, based on his or

---

p345   disease/cacochymia/saccharometabolism

【Diabetes Mellitus】

● Outline
   Diabetes is ···.

● Diagnosis
   The point of diagnosis of diabetes is ···. In the case of ···. the
   patient will not have diabetes, and see "Glycogenosis". If ···. then
   the patient will have incipient diabetes.

   　　o Questions
   　　　　· Subjective signs — ···.
   　　　　· Habits　　　　— ···.

   　　o Examinations
   　　　　· Glycemia　 — ···.
   　　　　· Glucosuria — ···.
   　　　　· GTT　　　　— ···.

● Treatments
   It is important ··· for the treatment. If ···. then therapy-1 is
   efficient. If ···.

   　　　　　· Diet　　　　　　— Control of calories makes ···.
   　　　　　· Ergotherapy — ···.
   　　　　　· Insulin　　　　— ···.
   　　　　　· Oral medicine— ···.

   　　o Therapy-1
   　　　　　···.

   　　o Therapy-2
   　　　　　···.

● Type
   The type of diabetes ···. If ···. then IDDM ···.

   　　o IDDM
   　　　　　···.

   　　o NIDDM
   　　　　　···.

● Complications
   The complicated diseases ···. If blood ···. see "Arteriosclerosis"
   <p85>. If exercise ···. see "Neuropathy" <p146>.

FIG. 14.4. Format of article on diabetes in a medical encyclopedia. *GTT*, glucose tolerant
test; (*N*)*IDDM*, (non)insulin-dependent diabetes mellitus. (Modified from [2])

her judgements. A doctor occasionally consults an encyclopedia of medical care and medicine, and as well, considers the data on the state of the patient, and updates the data of the patient as necessary.

14.2.2 What Kind of Data and Knowledge Do We Work with?

Here, we present part of the hierarchy of knowledge to be used in medicine, and show in what data structures it is stored (Fig. 14.3). We choose diabetes as a typical example. Note that "hierarchies of classification of diseases" is used as a set of indexes for searching disease. ("Affection" or "symptom" is one entry in a varied reference index).

The knowedge concerning diabetes in a medical encyclopedia appears in the data

---

Diabetes   Name : (   )   [first] · [revisit]

• Basic data

    o Age (   ) years old
    o Sex [male] · [female]
    o Pregnancy [yes]( ) months · [no]

• Subjective signs

    [hydrodipsia] · [polyuria] · [lassitude] · (   )

• Habits

    o Drinking [yes]{[everyday] · [often]} · [no]
    o Smoking [yes]{( ) pieces} · [no]
    o Eating [fat] · [irregular] · [unbalance] · (   )

• Anamnesis

    [hypertension] · [apoplectic] · [cirrhosis] · (   )

• Examinations

    o Glycemia (   )mg/dl
    o GTT (   )mg/dl
    o Glucosuria (   )mg/dl

• Observations

• Treatment history

FIG. 14.5. An example of the chart of a diabetic patient

structures in Fig. 14.4. Note that there are two kinds of knowledge: one is an explanation about a certain matter, another is a method of judging (such as "If ..., then ... "). In addition, we include the title, the indexes (such as disease/cacochymia/saccharometabolism), and the reference information (such as "If ..., then see '...' ⟨p 123⟩") in Fig. 14.4 are included in the information on diabetes.

Finally, the chart of a patient which contains the dynamic information and is manipulated by the relevant doctors looks normal (Fig. 14.5).

14.3 A Model of Highly Intelligent Work with Collaboration with Computers

14.3.1 An Interactive Supporting System for Highly Intelligent Work

In this section, we present a scheme, *MOA*, which models interactive behavior between man and machine for achieving highly intelligent work. We call the supporting system in this model *moa* (in lower case letters). *MOA* assumes that its users are experts in a particular field of knowledge. Therefore, the system is intended to help the user and promote the quality and efficiency of the user's work.

Three aspects mentioned in the previous section are supported in the model:

1. Support for knowledge management
   – Distributed knowledge database
2. Support for data management
   – Dynamic data structure and flexible user-interface
3. Support for solving problems
   – Suitable inference engine

In addition, to provide necessary and sufficient support at each stage of the progress shown in Fig. 14.1, a distributed inference system is suitable. Also, a hypertext system is a sufficient tool for management of such a knowledge database (discussed later, in detail). Therefore, we adopted the approach of the ingenious amalgamation of an extended hypertext system and an inference system (Fig. 14.6) in the model. In this model, hypertexts deal with knowledge for use as well as knowledge for reading.

Each hypertext corresponds to a module in the distributed inference system. As a result, an intelligent browser of hypertexts can be controlled by the output data

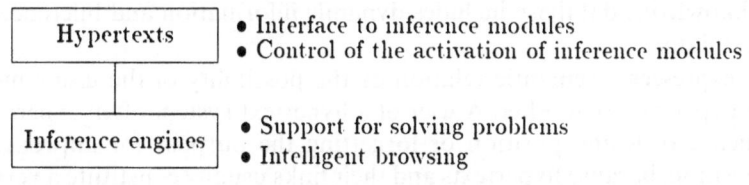

FIG. 14.6. The amalgamation of a hypertext system and an inference system

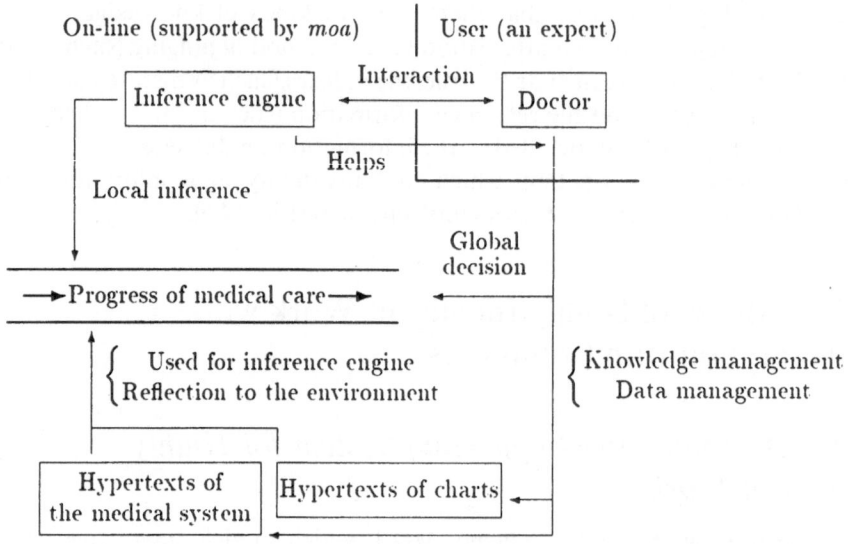

FIG. 14.7. The flow of data and control for the field of medicine in the *MOA* model

from inference engines. On the other hand, hypertexts can serve as I/O interfaces to inference modules or control the activation of them.

We do not specify any concrete mechanism for the inference engines in this paper. Rather, we only include the interface into *MOA*. The engines should be suitably specified according to a particular application.

For instance, the following is the flow of data and control for the field of medicine, in *MOA*. In Fig. 14.7, note that the inference engine in *moa* is mainly used for local decisions according to a user's request, and global decisions to control the flow of the tasks are left to the user. Also, by means of hypertexts, regarded as the knowledge database and medical charts in the system, the environment for such intelligent work is established.

14.3.2 The Extended Hypertext System in MOA

We consider an extension of a hypertext system as the user-interface of a supporting system, which *MOA* describes.

A hypertext system basically consists of hypertexts and links between them, to enable a flexible approach for a database system rather than a straight approach. Each hypertext corresponds to a unit of the distributed knowledge database. In *MOA*, a knowledge database includes dynamic information and inference rules as well as text data.

A link expresses a semantic relation or the possibility of the user's movement from one hypertext to another. A user of a hypertext system often experiences the inconvenience of losing position or forgetting the purpose for approaching the current position, because hypertexts and their links usually constitute a very flexible network.

To solve this problem, many hypertext systems have hierarchies into themselves, which represent "is-a" or "element-of" relations between distributed knowledge systems. In *MOA*, among the hypertexts, a hierarchical relation termed a "part-of" relation is introduced. Knowledge about a certain field is represented by a tree of hypertext, rather than a single one. Hence, a substructure of knowledge corresponds to a subtree. As concerns text data, the hierarchical relation is regarded as a section-subsection relation. In the case of the inference system, the relation is regarded as a module-submodule or predicate-term relation.

We sometimes have to express some links corresponding to miscellaneous relations between bodies of knowledge other than the hierarchical relation. In *MOA* we can use such a link between two hypertexts. A link also represents the possibility of moving one hypertext to another. On the other hand, the hierarchical relation is not used to express the possibility of moving between hypertexts. It simply shows the position of each body of knowledge in the whole knowledge system. Therefore, if the relation is visualized, the sketch must be a hypertext and embedded sub-hypertext (Fig. 14.9).

Another way to revise a hypertext system is to provide some kinds of links corresponding to various relations. Also, the management of many links has to be considered.

In *MOA*, a kind of link corresponding to the "element-of" relation (which is distinguished from another kind of link corresponding to an exceptional relation) is introduced, to be used in searching for information.

In fact, among many sub-hypertexts in a certain hypertext, we provide an index which manages a set of them, and make links from the index to its elements. An index of a set of indexes can also be provided. Then, a classification of sub-hypertexts, which is used for searching but does not represent this structure, is established (just like the index "A" in a dictionary manages words whose initial letter is "a"). Note that this link represents a relation between brother nodes of a hierarchical tree. In addition, *MOA* allows different classifications in the same hypertext.

Furthermore, to provide a flexible hypertext system, dynamic creation of hypertexts and changes of linking will have to be allowed.

14.3.3 The System Organization

We describe the system organization and a virtual screen, a user-interface object, based upon the extended hypertext system, using a medical example.

In *moa*, data and knowledge are decomposed into primitive parts called objects. An object consists of a name as its title, the text to present the relevant piece of knowledge, the data and rules which are used by the inference engines, and auxiliary control data. Among the objects, a hierarchical relation is introduced. An object is identified by its location in the hierarchy and its name (or the same name can be used by more than one object in different locations in the hierarchy). For instance, the following tree (Fig. 14.8) shows the constitution of a hierarchy concerning the medical system.

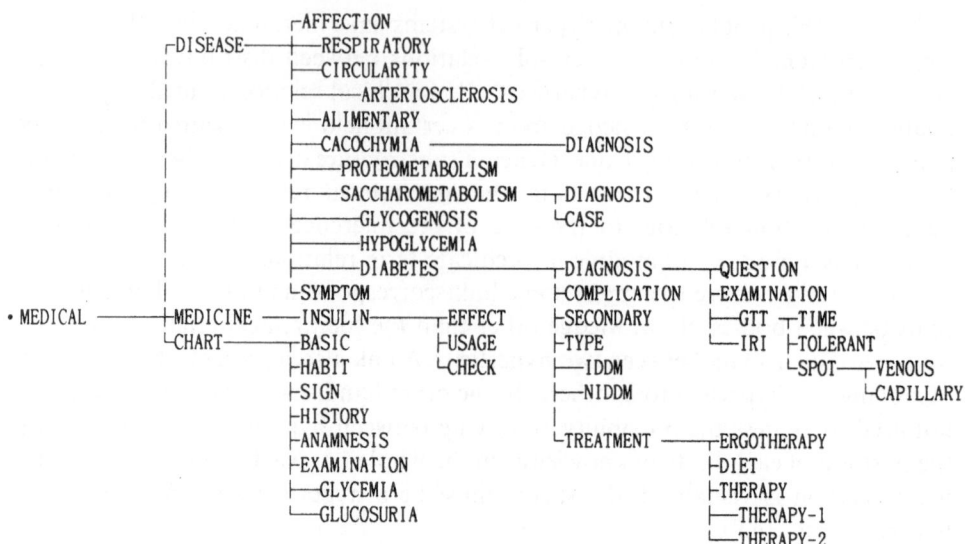

Fig. 14.8. The hierarchy of hypertexts in *moa*

In addition, each object has two kinds of links: one represents an "element-of" relation between brothers; the other represents some exceptional relations.

For instance, the subobjects in "DISEASE" make hierarchies of classifications of diseases (see Fig. 14.3). In Fig. 14.8 we suppose more "element-of" links and exceptional links for explanation. (In Fig. 14.8, among the brothers in each object, the depth of indent shows the level of the classification.)

To model the user-interface in *MOA*, we use a virtual screen which images the real system output on a display terminal. The following two figures (Figs. 14.9 and 14.10) are typical examples of virtual screens. A visualization of such relations is mentioned in [3]. The outermost thick frames only show the ranges of the screens. Inside them, many objects are displayed as rectangles which are called items in the form of hypertext. Each item corresponds to an object in the system, and has a label which reflects the position of the corresponding object in the hierarchy. Note that the label contains more information, mentioned after some symbol such as "/", ":", "⇒" (for example, "⇒" shows that the link represents an exceptional relation).

An item which is opened in the screen is called a card, and an item which is closed is called an icon. A card whose frame is a solid line expresses a real hypertext; its text and its lower items are shown inside it. A card whose frame is a broken line acts only as an index; it is regarded as a set of items and its elements (or possibly subsets) are shown inside it.

In *MOA*, a series of texts is displayed by hierarchical arrangement of their corresponding hypertexts on the virtual screen. Therefore, we can achieve such flexible control that a knowledge subsystem which a person wants to tap is located (just like setting the user's viewpoint of the knowledge), and only the suitable text is displayed. A card is text which is displayed for the user, and an icon corresponds

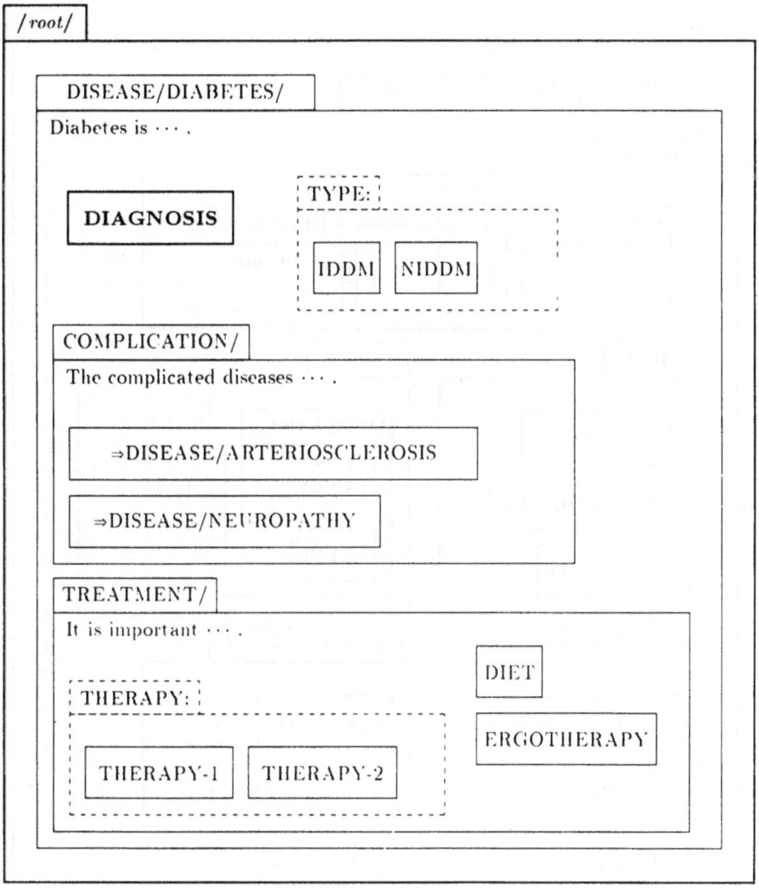

FIG. 14.9. Display image of hypertext in *moa*

to text which is closed at the time to hide the information, that is, an icon is regarded as a candidate which the user may select in the near future.

Note that an icon inside a broken-lined card and an icon whose label has the symbol "⇒" show the destination of the user's movement.

In addition, from the human point of view, each card is a unit phase in the global flow of the intelligent work, which can be controlled by browsing through the cards.

Items on the screen show the user various kinds of working environment, such as the current view of the user, the status of inference, the reason why the user referred to a card, the history of retrieval, and so on. For example, the item whose frame is a thick line has an attribute "marked," which shows that the item is selected or activated by the user. Also, the top-level card inside the root item corresponds to the current phase. Nishio and Yamada describe another approach to express this working environment [4].

The user's operations and the system behavior are described in Sect. 14.4, in which we also mention the way to control the inference system by hypertexts, and information retrieval in hypertexts.

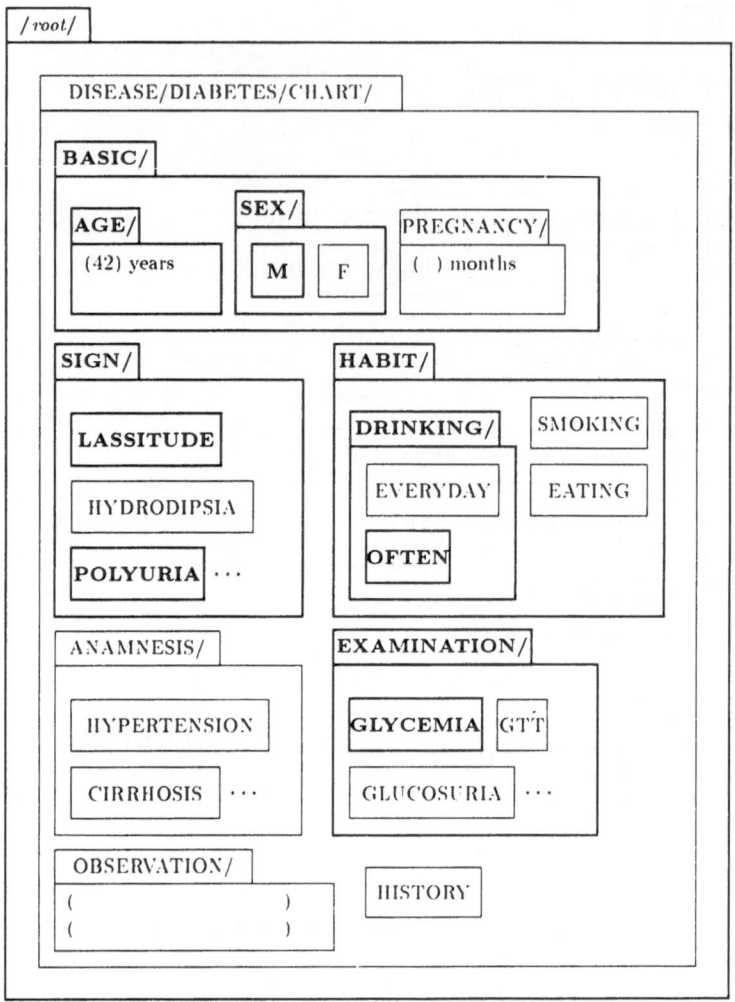

FIG. 14.10. Constitution of chart in *moa*

14.4 The Behavior of the System

We use an example of a medical diagnosis system in order to demonstrate how a typical *moa* system works [5]. In the example *moa* deals with a patient with diabetes. For simplicity and clarity, there are several instances which are not realistic in actual medical practice.

14.4.1 To Diagnose an Illness

When seeing a patient for the first time, a doctor tries to deduce the nature of the illness from questions about symptoms and illness history, subjective signs, anamnesis, and applying basic examinations such as urinalysis, blood pressure,

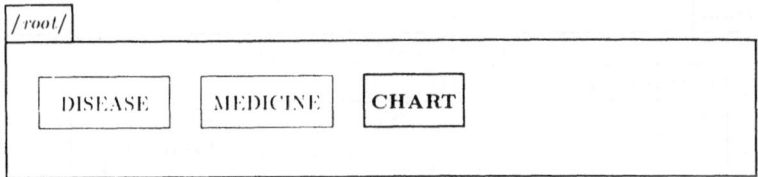

Fɪɢ. 14.11. The initial window in *moa*

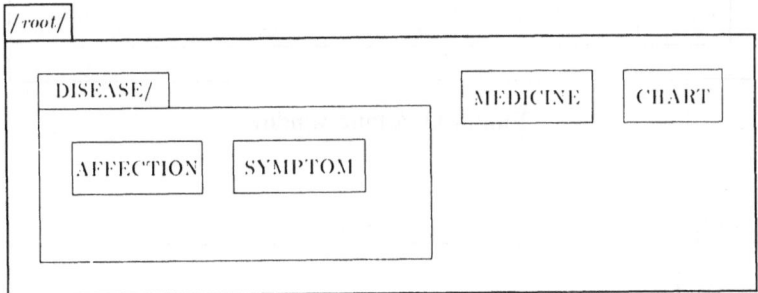

Fɪɢ. 14.12. A second window

body temperature, and pulse. In this stage, *moa* helps the doctor by providing a hypertext to illustrate the relevant knowledge, and also a chart which keeps the results of various examinations. In addition, the display can indicate to the doctor how far his or her work with *moa* has progressed, and also indicate what has been done to that point.

When first invoked, *moa* brings up a window such as in Fig. 14.11, where the window can be regarded as the root of the hierarchy of relevant knowledge of medical care.

We describe inputting some data into the *moa* system as follows: the user specifies one of the displayed items, scans the possible operations with respect to the specified item, for example, by a menu table, then chooses an operation. In addition, *moa* allows the user to input numerics, such as values of examinations, by a keyboard.

Now, the doctor opens the "CHART" to input the results of the questioning and the basic examinations (see the chart of Fig. 14.10 in the previous section). Then, suppose the doctor suspects the patient has a type of saccharometabolism and wants to determine the disease.

When the doctor opens the icon "DISEASE," two icons "AFFECTION" and "SYMPTOM" as indexes of diseases are displayed inside "DISEASE" (Fig. 14.12). To mark "DIABETES" as a current field, the frame of the card changes to thick lines, which shows that the phase of determination starts, while the icons "MEDICINE" and "CHART" disappear from the screen.

Here, the method for information retrieval is described. When the user opens (or unfolds) the item corresponding to an index, some of the "element-of" linked objects are displayed as candidate items inside the broken-lined item. The user selects an item, and then the selected object is displayed at a suitable position on the screen

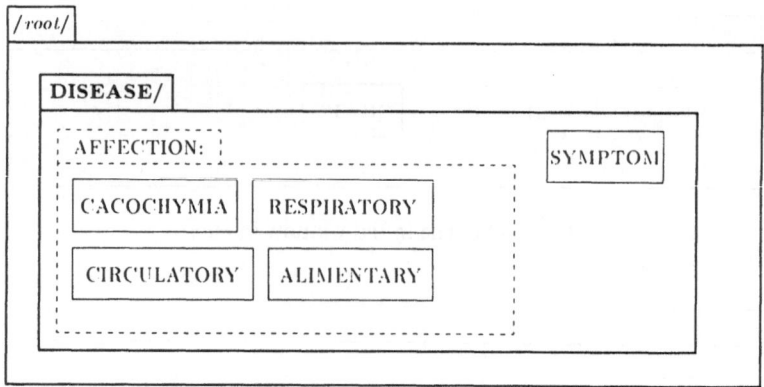

FIG. 14.13. A third window

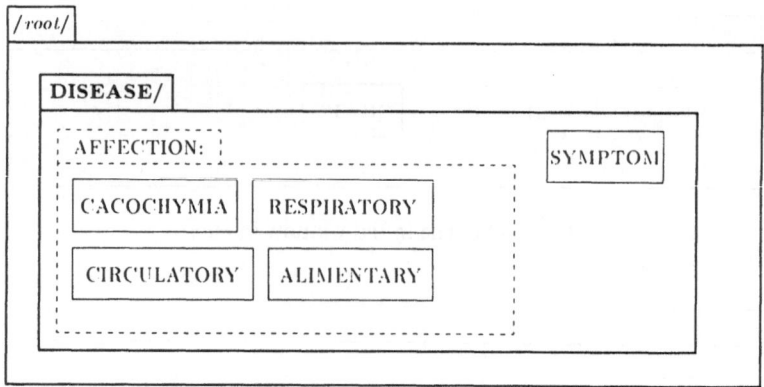

FIG. 14.14. The window when "SACCHAROMETABOLISM" has been selected

according to the object hierarchy, while the index item is closed. It seems to move from the index item to the selected item.

The user unfolds "AFFECTION" (Fig. 14.13) and then selects "CACOCHYMIA"

Then, the user unfolds "CACOCHYMIA," and selects a subset "SACCHARO-METABOLISM." To help his or her own diagnosis, the doctor opens "SACCHARO-METABOLISM" as a card and refers to its text (Fig. 14.14). Note that the same object can be used as index or hypertext on demand.

If the doctor has enough conviction that the patient has diabetes from this process so far, he or she unfolds "SACCHAROMETABOLISM" (Fig. 14.15) and selects an element "DIABETES."

In the event of a mistake, the doctor can go back and search another possibility, referring to the history, or by intelligent browsing. At any time, *moa* provides some candidates and the doctor makes final decisions.

After deciding that the patient has diabetes, the doctor marks "DIABETES" (Fig. 14.16), and opens it, and then "DIABETES" becomes the current field (Fig. 14.17).

In this way, searching for the necessary object is performed by using a hierarchy, a classification, and text information, while the control facility of the system is

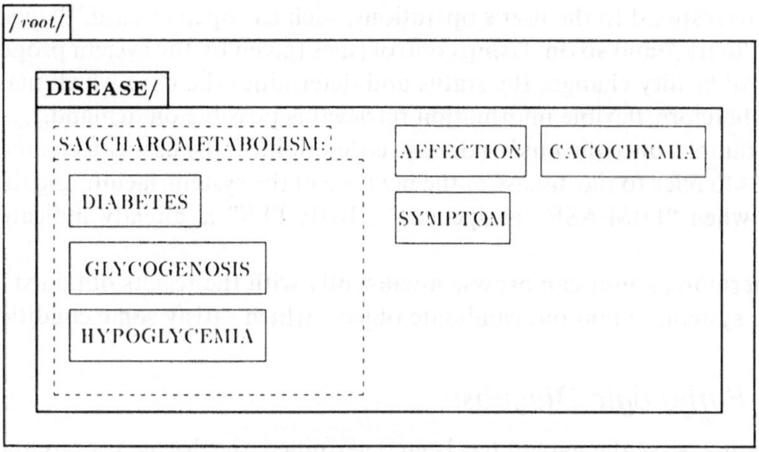

FIG. 14.15. The window after "SACCHAROMETABOLISM" has been unfolded

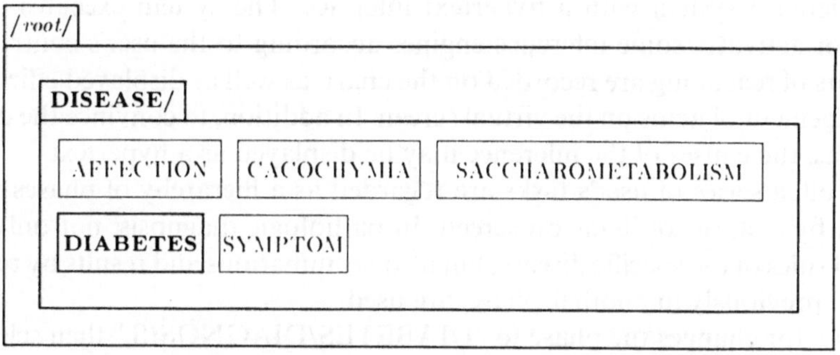

FIG. 14.16. The window after "DIABETES" has been marked

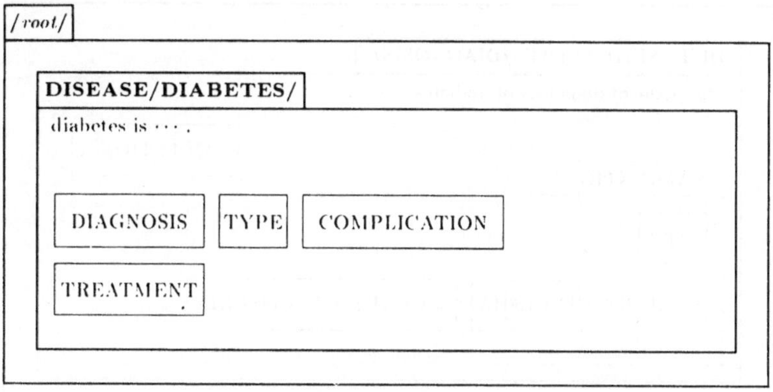

FIG. 14.17. The window after "DIABETES" has been opened

running to respond to the user's operations, such as "open as card," "open as set," "select," "mark," and so on. Using control rules (given by the system programmer), the control facility changes the status and determines the data which manage the screen. Therefore, flexible information retrieval is possible on demand.

For example, once the kind of disease is determined, the user can change the link of indexes to refer to the disease at the next use of the system, facilitating the search. That is, when "DISEASE" is opened, "DIABETES" is already indicated as an element.

Furthermore, a user can browse intelligently with the results obtained from the inference system, to find out candidate objects which satisfy some conditions.

14.4.2 Pathologic Diagnosis

After the disease of the patient has been determined, the doctor tries to understand more precisely the condition of the patient, so-called pathologic diagnosis, by further questioning or examination. Pathologic diagnosis consists of, for example, progress of disease, type, or possibility of complications. In this process, *moa* is a system which not only shows texts giving information on the disease but also acts as an inference system with a hypertext interface. The system executes an input routine or activates some inference engines according to the user's control. Then, the results of reasoning are recorded on the chart, as well as displayed efficiently by an arrangement of items on the virtual screen. In addition, to convince the doctor of the results, the causes of the inference may be displayed as a hypertext.

After all, a series of user's tasks are regarded as a hierarchy of phases which is reflected by a status of items on screen. In pathologic diagnosis, not only proper data and rules of the specific disease, but also examinations and results by reasoning obtained previously in another phase, are used.

The doctor changes the phase to "DIABETES/DIAGNOSIS," then selects suitable items in "EXAMINATION," which stands for a set of examinations for diabetes (Fig. 14.18).

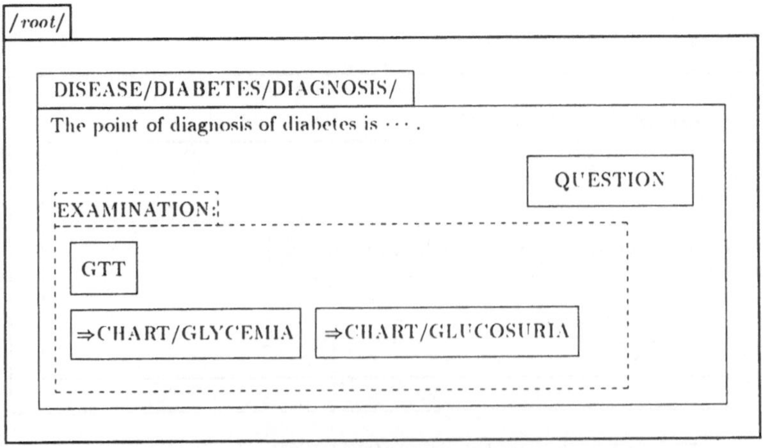

FIG. 14.18. The window after "EXAMINATION" has been selected

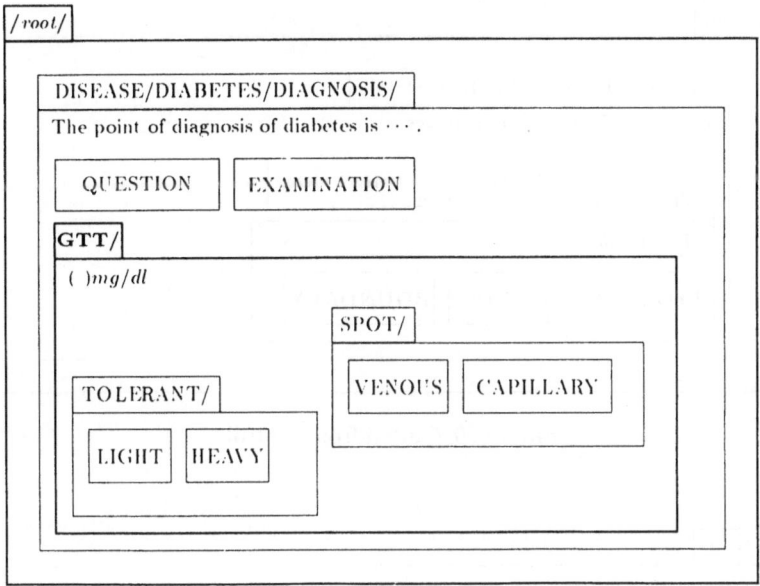

FIG. 14.19. The window after "GTT" has been activated. *GTT*, glucose tolerant test

The doctor opens and activates "GTT" (Fig. 14.19). The object "GTT" controls the GTT inference module; its user-interface, and the activation for its inference rules. Next, the input routine of GTT starts. The input data of GTT consist of the actual value and some auxiliary parameters to make the examination precise, such as "TIME," "TOLERANT," and "SPOT." "SPOT" and "TOLERANT," which are primitives of inputting, are regarded as predicates, and their subobjects, such as "LIGHT" and "VENOUS," are regarded as terms.

There are two different ways of terminating input. One is the case when the user must choose just one candidate from the ones which the system shows (see "TOLERANT" and "SPOT" in Fig. 14.19). In this case, the system can automatically judge the termination of input. Another is the case when the user can select more than one, or can input arbitrary data. In these cases, the user has to indicate the termination of input (see "CHART/SIGN" in Fig. 14.10).

When the inputting of data on GTT is completed, the object "GTT" sends some internal data to its inference module and calls the inference engine. Then, some results are obtained by inference and they are returned to the object as internal data. The control facility displays the items corresponding to the results as the output of the system (see "BOUNDARY" in Fig. 14.20).

After closing the card "GTT," only the results of the GTT module remain on the screen, such as "GTT/BOUNDARY" in Fig. 14.21, and the others disappear. Then, using the data according to the results in "GLYCEMIA" and "GLUCOSURIA," which have been obtained before, as well as the results from the submodule "GTT," the inference engine associated with the object "DIABETES/DIAGNOSIS" infers the conclusion, such as "INCIPIENT" in Fig. 14.21. Moreover, for example, the external icon "⇒DISEASE/DIABETES/IDDM"shows both the suspicion of IDDM and the possibility of movement.

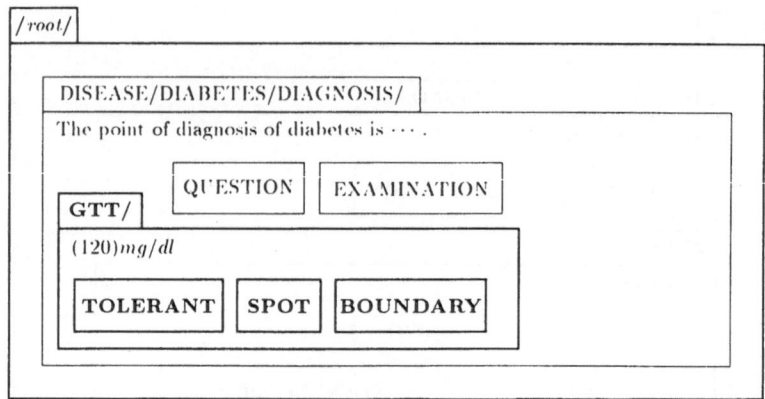

FIG. 14.20. Output from control

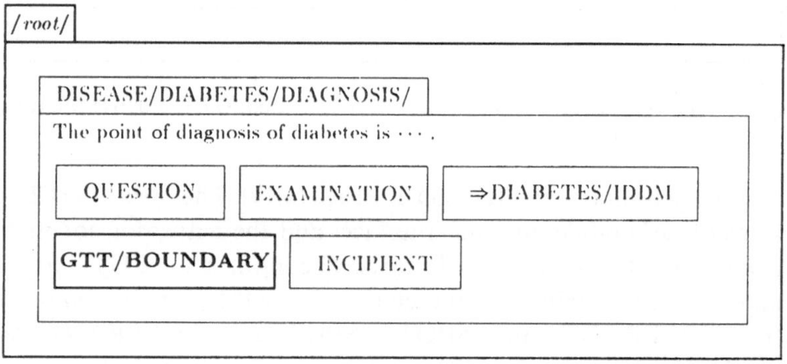

FIG. 14.21. An inference ("INCIPIENT") and an external icon ("⇒DIABETES/IDDM")

Note that the inference is performed by only the inference engine of "DIABETES/ DIAGNOSIS," while only the results of the other inference modules are used. If the necessary results of the others have not yet been given, the system only indicates the link to the appropriate object as an external icon to help the user's decision.

14.4.3 Treatment

According to the patient's condition, some possibilities for treatment are listed. After checking some factors such as the patient's constitution and the adaptation of medicine, the doctor starts the actual treatment, then necessary examinations as prognosis is performed again, and pathologic diagnosis is repeated until the patient recovers. The system assists the doctor to decide on a treatment by referring to the handbooks of medicine as well as to information on the specific disease. It also records the doctor's observations.

Now, the user changes the current field to "DIABETES/TREATMENT" (Fig. 14.22).

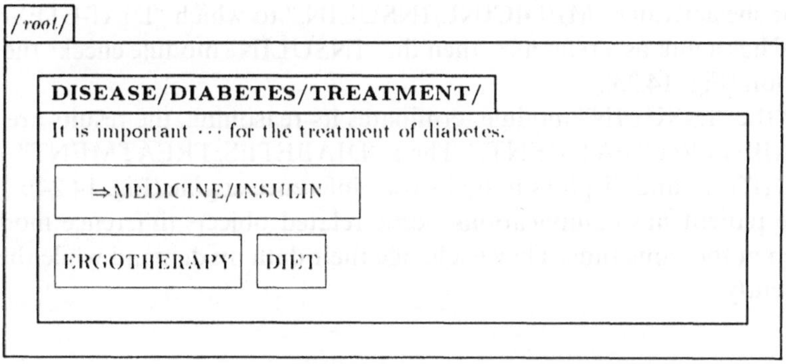

FIG. 14.22. "DIABETES/TREATMENT" window

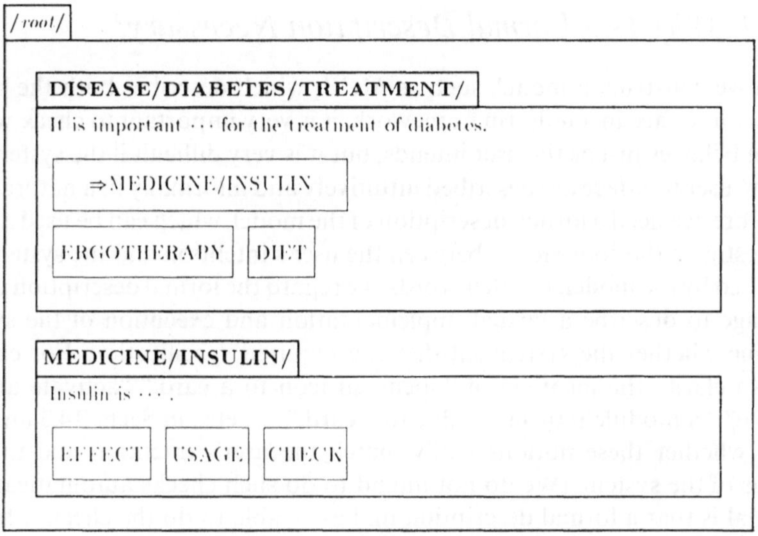

FIG. 14.23. "INSULIN" module

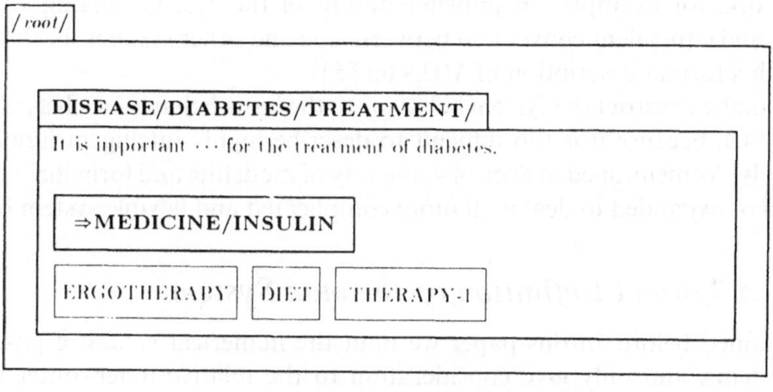

FIG. 14.24. An inference ("THERAPY-1")

He or she activates "MEDICINE/INSULIN," to which "DIABETES/TREAT-MENT" has a link as a reference, then the "INSULIN" module checks the patient's adaptation (Fig. 14.23).

After the "INSULIN" module terminates its reasoning, the results are returned to "DIABETES/TREATMENT." Then "DIABETES/TREATMENT" finds out "THERAPY-1" and displays it, by its own inference engine (Fig. 14.24).

If the patient has complications, some related objects (inference modules) are activated at the same time. They exchange their data on demand while they reason concurrently.

14.5 Toward a Formal Description of *MOA*

14.5.1 *Why Is a Formal Description Necessary?*

When we construct a model, such as *MOA*, which describes both the system and the user interface in a uniform framework, it is very important to check whether the system behaves just as the user intends, but it is very difficult if the system behavior and the user interface are described intuitively and informally in a natural language. Therefore, we need a formal description of the model, which can be used as a method to investigate the consistency between the user's intention and the system behavior described by the model. In other words, we regard the formal description as a pseudo language to describe a virtual implementation and execution of the system, and examine whether the system satisfies the required specification. For example, we have to clarify the meaning of "opens an icon to a card," "activate an inference module," "a module returns a value to a card," ..., etc., in Sects. 14.3 and 14.4, and check whether these notions really match the user's intention and the expected actions of the system. (We do not intend to do such checks automatically; what is essential is that a formal description makes us able to do the checks.) In addition, we can point out any inconsistency in the specification; these tend to go unnoticed if we use a natural language.

Furthermore, a formal description can be a powerful tool to discuss a variety of future work; for example, an implementation of the system, linking with other systems, and equivalent conversion between *moa* and other systems. In this section, we sketch a formal description of *MOA* (cf [6]).

Note that we restrict the system behavior to the basic behavior such as illustrated in Sect. 14.4, because it is too difficult to describe highly intelligent human work completely. As mentioned in Sect 14.4, the way of modeling and formalizing must be modified or expanded to deal with more complicated and flexible system behavior.

14.5.2 *A Formal Definition of the moa System*

As mentioned before, in this paper we omit the numerical values of positions or sizes of items, and only give consideration to the relative inner–outer relations between cards and icons on the display.

The aim of the definition given here is not to describe directly the human manipulations explained in Sect. 14.4, but to give the framework for them. Writing actual human manipulations is just like combining some kind of primitives given by the definition in this section (which is also similar to programming). Besides, the inference engines are treated as black boxes which are actually linked to the system as a kind of library function; this definition only gives the mechanism of linking of the inference engines, but not actual ones.

Hence, the *moa* system defined here is, as a whole, separated into two large parts: one is composed of the internal information and mechanisms which access or modify them, and the other is the control facility of the display.

moa-system ::=
  ⟨*control-facility, screen manager*⟩
control-facility ::=
  ⟨*internal-status, control-rules*⟩
internal-status ::=
  ⟨*screen-info, internal-data*⟩

Screen-info consists of all information needed to determine the screen, and *internal-data* consists of other information. When *screen-info* is given, the screen is uniquely determined by the map from *screen-info* to the real screen, which is a part of *screen-manager*, described afterward.

screen-info ::=
  ⟨node-tree,

  a 4-tuple of
  - *name* ... symbol
  - *text* ... currently (possibly empty) string
  - *attribute* (used when a node is displayed as a card)
  - *icon_map* ... a subset of node × *attribute*
      (pairs of icon and its attribute)
  for each node,

  a subset of nodes
      (which means the set of visible nodes as cards)
  ⟩

Note: *name, text, attribute*, and *icon-map* can be regarded as maps from the set of nodes.

Here *attribute*, the third member of the 4-tuple, is a set of information to determine how to display a card, giving details such as "*thick_line*," "*broken_line*," and so on. When a node is displayed on the screen as a card, its attribute is determined by *attribute* of the corresponding 4-tuple.

Icon-map of a node keeps the information on which nodes should be shown as icons inside the node if the node itself is seen as a card. Note, however, that though the node is not currently seen on the screen, it still has an *icon-map* set (possibly empty, of course). *Attribute* in *icon_map* provides attributes of icons as well as cards. How the virtual screen is determined will be described later.

internal-data ::=
⟨for each node
  • data except *screen-info*
⟩

Intuitively speaking, it includes, for example, a pair of variables local to a node, plus their value assignment, many possible kinds of link from each node, etc. Here, a link is represented as a set of nodes which do not have to be children of the node from which the link is stretched.

Currently, *internal-data* is accessible from every node. Information hiding must be done by a programmer.

Links can also be used to decide *icon_map*. If a link, or a union or an intersection of many links, is set to *icon_map* of a 4-tuple corresponding to a node with a suitable *attribute*, and the node becomes visible as a card on the screen, then the icons displayed inside the card are determined according to the link(s). In such a way, the difference from the human view between "open as a set," "select," etc., can be expressed by the information in *attribute*.

screen-manager ::=
⟨a map from *screen-info* to real screen,
  a map from real user-manipulation to *operation*
⟩

The "real user-manipulation" means a definite manipulation, for example, "put the mouse-cursor onto a certain item on the screen, and then select a point on a pull-down menu." However, note that this formalism does not include such "definite manipulations." The system knows "the user said to me that he (or she) wants to open a particular icon as a card," but does not know whether "he/she said so by selecting a pull-down menu" or "by pressing the SHIFT key and clicking the right button of the mouse." It knows only information which is independent of the way of instruction.

Mapping from *screen-info* to the real screen is given as follows. It is able to be replaced by another mapping, but we establish it here. The details will be described later using some examples with figures.

Every node which is an element of "a subset of node," the third member of *screen-info*, is seen on the screen as a card. A descendant node is seen inside of an ancestor node.

Inside each node, nodes corresponding to its *icon_map* are seen as icons. In addition, a *text* is displayed, and cards and icons are decorated depending on *attribute*.

To every node seen as a card or an icon, a label is added which reflects the position of it in the node-tree, using the *name* corresponding to it.

operation ::=
  functor(node, node...)

Functor corresponds to an actual system action. For example, if N, M are nodes, then *open*(N), *link*(N, M) are *operations* (*open*, *link* are *functors*).

control-rules ::=
    a map from *operation* to *status-updating-procedure*
    status-updating-procedure ::=
        a procedure to update *internal-status*
          (inference engines are called from it as black boxes)

A *status-updating-procedure* is defined as, for example, "add a node *N* to the set of nodes which are seen as a card." Conditional branching is possible in procedure definition. On finding the value of conditional expressions, *interval-data*, already introduced, can be used and inference engines can be called. This is the way of linking inference engines in this formalism.

Note that this definition does not tell which node-trees are static or dynamic. For example, we have restricted the node-tree to be static until Sect. 14.4 for simplification, but this restriction is not necessary here. It is preferable to remove the restriction, because it makes it easy to introduce dynamic creation, deletion, or movement of nodes in the future, by considering modification of node-trees by *status-updating-procedures*.

14.5.3 An Intuitional Correspondence with an Actual System

In this section, we give an intuitional correspondence between previous definitions and the elements or actions of an actual system, using simple examples.

Let there be a node-tree:

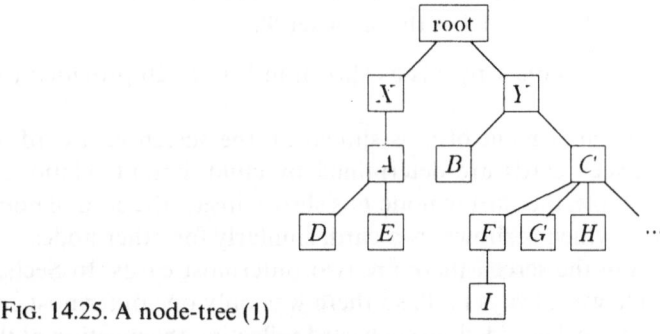

FIG. 14.25. A node-tree (1)

where *root*, *X*, *Y*, ... are nodes. We give a *screen-info* such as:

Name of each node
    $name(root) = root$ $name(X) = x$ $name(Y) = y$
    $name(A) = a$ $name(D) = d$ $name(C) = c$
    $name(F) = f$ $name(G) = g$ $name(I) = name(E) = i$
    Other nodes also have *names*, but they are omitted here

Here, *root*, *x*, *y*, ... are symbols. Different nodes may have the same *name*. An analogy of class–instance relations can be expressed if we give a restriction that nodes of the same *name* have to have the same *text*, "internal-status," etc.

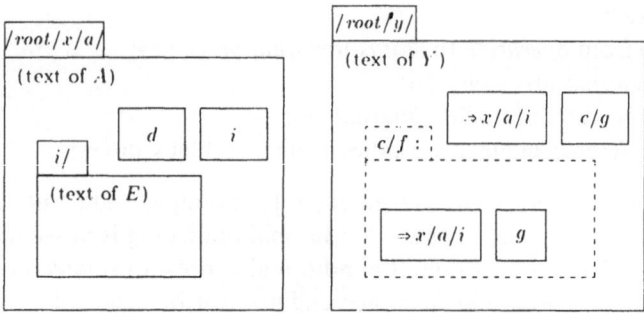

FIG. 14.26. Display image (1)

Attribute of each node
   "*Broken_line*" for F, "*solid_line*" for others

Icon-map
   $icon\_map(A) = \{\langle D, solid\_line\rangle, \langle E, solid\_line\rangle\}$
   $icon\_map(Y) = \{\langle G, solid\_line\rangle, \langle E, solid\_line\rangle\}$
   $icon\_map(F) = \{\langle G, solid\_line\rangle, \langle E, solid\_line\rangle\}$
   $icon\_map(G) = \{\langle I, solid\_line\rangle\}$
   $icon\_map(E) = \phi.$
   $icon\_map(\ )$ is defined also on other nodes, but is omitted here

A set of nodes (the third element of *screen-info*)
   $\{A, E, Y, F\}$ Let this be a set Ψ.

The whole screen is as shown in Fig. 14.26 provided that text of F is empty by chance.

Each element of Ψ is shown on the screen as a card. Inside–outside relations between cards are determined by child–parent relations between nodes. In this example, the card of node F is shown inside the card of node Y, the nearest ancestor of F which is shown as a card; similarly for other nodes.

On the screen there are two outermost cards. In Sects. 14.3 and 14.4, the root node was always in Ψ, so there was only one outermost card.

A label is added on each card reflecting the position of the node in the node-tree. The outermost card's label is the list of *names* of nodes from the root to the node of the card, called full-path. A card which is just inside of another card has a label of relative path from the outside card. In both cases, '/' or ':' is added behind the label, according to whether the card's attribute is *solid_line* or *broken_line*. This is a convention to keep the correspondence with Sects. 14.3 and 14.4.

For example, the card of node A has the label "/root/x/a" (just like a UNIX pathname). On the other hand, the card of node F has the label "c/f:". Note that a relative path does not have "/" on the head.

From now on, if there is not any possibility of confusion, we call the "card of node X" the "card X." Similarly, we call the "icon of node X" the "icon X."

Inside each card, icons are displayed depending on *icon_map*; for example, since *icon_map(A)* = {⟨*D*, *solid_line*⟩, ⟨*E*, *solid_line*⟩}, the icons *D* and *E* are displayed inside the card *A*, with the attribute "*solid_line*". To make it simple to formalize, in this case *E* is shown as an icon, no matter whether *E* is shown as a card or not. This is different from Sects. 14.3 and 14.4, but it is not an essential difference.

On the other hand, *icon_map(G)* = {⟨*I*, *solid_line*⟩}, but *G* is not visible as a card. Therefore the node *I* is not shown as an icon. Note that icons of a card *X* do not have to be children nodes of *X*; see *icon_map(Y)*, etc., of the example given.

We can think of some method to decide labels of icons, but let us choose one such that labels of icons in a card *X* are determined depending on whether *X*'s attribute is *solid_line* or *broken_line*.

If an icon exists inside a card whose attribute is *solid_line*, its label is generally full-path of the icon. Here, we assume that "/*r*/" can be abbreviated to "⇒". For example, the icon *E* inside the card *Y*, which has the *solid_line* attribute, has the label "⇒*x/a/i*", which is the abbreviation of the full-path of the node *E* ("/*r/x/a/i*"). As an exception, if the icon is a descendant of the card, it has a label of relative path from the card to it. For example, the icon *D* inside the card *A* has the label "*d*," which is the relative path from *A* to *D*.

On the other hand, if an icon is inside a card which has *broken_line*, its label is a relative path from the parent of the card to it, under the condition that it is the card's brother node (or brother's descendant). Otherwise it is the same as the previous case. For example, the icon *G* inside the card *F* has the label "*g*," the relative path from *C* (the parent of *F*) to *G*, because *G* is a brother node of *F*. However, the icon *E* inside the same card has the label "⇒*x/a/i*", because it is not a brother of *F*. (We do not define the case in which a card's attribute is neither *solid_line* nor *broken_line* here, because it is not necessary.)

The reason why we adopt such a complicated way to decide labels of icons is

TABLE 14.1. A table of correspondence in terms

Section 14.3	This section (14.5)
Object	Node (of tree)
Item	Card, icon
Name	Medium notion between *name* (of node) and label (of card or icon)
Control data	*Attribute* (in *screen-info*)
Supplemental information	Total information including parent-child relation of nodes and set of visible nodes, etc.
Rules (of inference module)	To be described later
Data	*Internal-status*
Difference between opening an object as a set and opening one as a card	*Attribute* of a card; difference between methods to decide labels of icons
External icon and internal icon	No special differences except whether its label has '⇒' or not (semantic difference between them is represented in definition of *operation*; described later)

that we want to clarify the correspondence with Sects. 14.3 and 14.4. It is the same in the case of determining labels of cards. From the theoretical point of view, a simpler way of determining labels would be preferable. However, we have to make sure that our definition can really deal with the examples we have shown.

On every card, the corresponding node's *text* is displayed. In addition, each card or icon has attributes on the screen, such as "*broken_line*" or "*thick_line*," according to *attribute* in *screen-info*.

As mentioned before, this is not the only possible mapping from *screen-info* to the real screen, but we establish this mapping here. A completely different-looking system can be constructed if we adopt another mapping.

There is the following correspondence (Table 14.1) between the notions of Sect. 14.3 and this section:

14.5.4 A Representation of an Operation

Let us consider the example of opening the icon G (in the example of Fig. 14.25) in the card Y.

The screen manager knows that "the user did a manipulation to open G," and issues an *operation* '*open*(G).' The *status-updating-procedure* corresponding to it is represented by the following assignment statement. (Here we take no notice of grammar; it is sufficient to define the change of *internal-status* strictly.)

$$the\_set\_of\_visible\_nodes := the\_set\_of\_visible\_nodes \cup \{G\}$$

After applying this *status-updating-procedure*, *internal-status* will be changed as:

Ψ becomes A, E, Y, F, G
(no other changes)

Since *screen-info* has been changed, the new screen is as follows (Fig. 14.27):

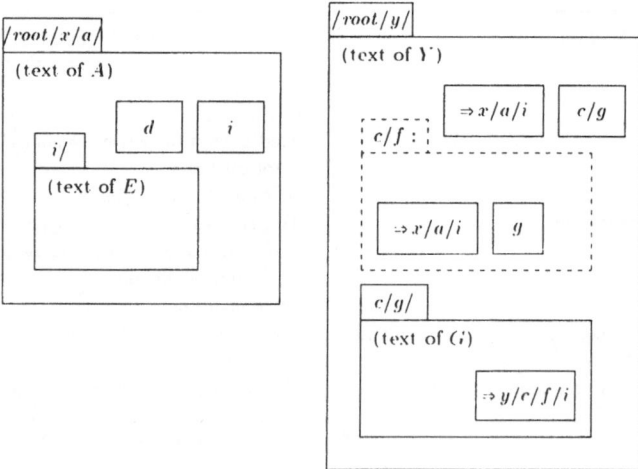

FIG. 14.27. Display image (2)

From the human viewpoint, it looks like the card G has opened at the appropriate position. Since $icon\_map(G)$ is $\{\langle I, solid\_line \rangle\}$, the icon I is displayed in the card G.

It is also possible to change $icon\_map(G)$ and then open the card G continuously by a single user-manipulation. For example, let $link1$ and $link2$ be maps from icon to set of icons, and let them be part of *internal-data*. By preparing the following two *status-updating-procedures*, we represent two 'open's of different meanings:

1. For an icon X,
      set $icon\_map(X)$ to $link1(X)$ and then add $\{X\}$ to *the_set_of_visible_nodes*

2. For an icon X,
      set $icon\_map(X)$ to $link2(X)$ and then add $\{X\}$ to *the_set_of_visible_nodes*

Note that the end-users do not have to program these procedures; if they are necessary, it is sufficient to program them into the system from the start.

From the human point of view, it may seem to be more natural to have such procedures as basic manipulations, but such an approach tends to make their meanings vague. So this formalism regards them as a kind of macro definition, rather than introducing them as primitives, which make it easier to define their strict semantics by decomposing them to more primitive changes ("assignment statement," for example).

14.5.5 Programming of Manipulations

In this section, we explain the principle of manipulation programming by a system programmer (rather than an end-user) of *moa*. The main significance of this is to formalize the mechanism to reflect the user's intentions to the system. It is impossible to prepare all the manipulations for the system from the start, but preparing only necessary and minimal ones makes the system stiff. So it must be possible to add user-manipulations by programming on demand.

In addition, linking with inference engines is also done in this mechanism in the form of calling library functions.

As in the previous sections, we provide neither a definite method nor a language for it. We sometimes use a λ-style pseudo language, but it does not mean that the system actually uses such a language; it is only for explanation.

Programming of manipulations can be split into the following three steps:

1. Programming a *status-updating-procedure* (inference libraries can be used as black boxes)
2. Defining an *operation* which causes the procedure (i.e., changes *control-rules* map)
3. Defining a manipulation which issues the *operation* (i.e., changes the second element of *screen-manager*)

From now on we assume that a *status-updating-procedure* can take nodes as arguments which are passed from the corresponding *operation*. In fact, such an example has already appeared; the *operation* "open" passes a node as argument to the corresponding procedure, which can now be rewritten into the following form:

$$\lambda n(the\_set\_of\_visible\_nodes := the\_set\_of\_visible\_nodes \cup \{n\})$$

14.5.5.1 A Simple Procedural Example

Let us take the example of defining a manipulation "open a specified icon Y inside a card X and erase all icons inside X at once."

- Definition of *status-updating-procedure*

$$\lambda mn(icon\_map(m) := \phi; \quad \psi := \psi \cup \{n\})$$

- Definition of *operation*

  An *operation select*(X, Y) causes the procedure above, with two nodes X, Y as arguments.

- Definition of manipulation

  When an icon Y is inside a card X, and a user gives an order "open Y and delete icons in X" to the system by some means, then the system issues the *operation select*(X, Y).

After defining these, a new manipulation is added to the system. When a user does this manipulation to an icon B inside a card A, an *operation select*(A, B) is issued according to the second element of *screen-manager*. Then *internal-status* is changed as follows: B is added to the set Ψ as an element, an *icon_map*(A) becomes ϕ. According to the new *internal-status* and the first element of *screen-manager*, the screen is updated. On the new screen, B is visible as a card and there are no icons inside A. From the human viewpoint, this acts like "selecting B from a set A" in Sect. 14.4.

In some cases, a single manipulation can issue an *operation* with two arguments. For example, in the case of the *operation select*(A, B), the system knows two nodes A and B, but the user has done only a "single" manipulation. In this case, we can also write a procedure including a conditional branching, depending on whether A is an ancestor of B. This fact provides us a typical way of expressing a difference between external icons and internal ones. Of course, in some cases *select*(A, B) may be issued by a series of some manipulations.

As we have seen, an arbitrary manipulation can be defined if we can write what change we expect. We can write changes of *internal-status* or the real screen as a *status-updating-procedure*.

At present, *MOA* does not have a mechanism to localize rules to a card; this is currently simulated by conditional-branching. The following example shows a way to localize some rules to a card A.

$$\lambda n(if \ n = A \ then\ldots; else\ldots)$$

14.5.5.2 An Example Showing Linking of an Inference Engine

A system can realize a variety of flexible user-manipulations by calling various kinds of library functions in *status-updating-procedures*. In this section we explain an example in which we call a library of an inference engine and another library like a kind of system call. From now on, we consider that *status-updating-procedures* can return values.

Let there be a node-tree:

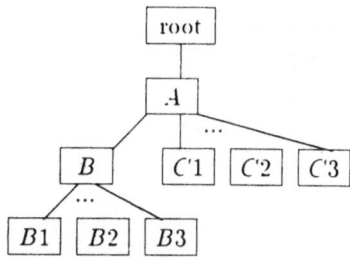

FIG. 14.28. A node-tree (2)

and assume that an icon B is inside a card A. The outline of the manipulation flow is as follows: a user opens B as a card (this means the activation of inference, to the user) and inputs the required data. The system automatically judges the end of inputting, then closes the card B and starts inference. Depending on the outcome of the inference, the system displays one of $C1$–$C3$ as an icon inside A.

To make it simple, we assume that inputting data is done by clicking just one of the icons $B1$–$B3$, i.e., selecting one candidate from three. Under this assumption we can decide the end of inputting by simply deciding whether at least one of those icons has been clicked.

To illustrate a concrete image, we explain the user manipulations in the style of a pull-down menu.

– User-manipulation 1

  Put the mouse cursor on the icon B inside the card A, and then select "start" from the pull-down menu

– The *operation* issued by user-manipulation 1

  start_inference(A, B)

– The *status-updating-procedure* caused by the *operation* "*start_inference*"

  $\lambda mn($
   icon_map$(n) := \{B1, B2, B3\}$;
    /* Here the set $\{B1, B2, B3\}$ is assumed to be static */
   $\Psi := \Psi \cup \{n\}$;

   while (the undermentioned *status-updating-procedure* named χ with
    an argument n returns true)

   begin
    read just one user-manipulation and
     issue the corresponding *operation*; ...(1)

   end;

   $\Psi := \Psi - \{n\}$;

call an inference engine with suitable arguments and
    assign the returned value to the node m's *internal-data*;...(2)

case (the value returned above) **of**
    1: *icon_map*$(m) = C1$;
    2: *icon_map*$(m) = C2$;
    3: *icon_map*$(m) = C3$;
end;
)

– A user-manipulation 2

Click the icon $B1$ inside the card B

– The *operation* issued by the user-manipulation 2

mark$(B, B1)$

– The *status-updating-procedure* caused by the *operation* "*mark*"

λmn(change an element $\langle n, X \rangle$ of *icon_map*(m) to $\langle n, thick\_line \rangle$)
    here X is an arbitrary *attribute*

– The *status-updating-procedure* χ

$\lambda m($
    if no icons in *icon_map*(m) have the *attribute* "*thick_line*"
    then
        return false;
    else
        return true;
)

In this example, the 1st *status-updating-procedure* calls another procedure χ, an inference engine as a library function(1), and a system call library(2).

User-manipulation 1 issues the first *operation*, which causes the first procedure with two arguments A, B. Firstly, B is opened on the screen as a card, inside which the three icons $B1$, $B2$, and $B3$ appear.

The next "*while*" loop checks the end of inputting. It calls the procedure χ with an argument B which returns true if at least one of the icons $B1$, $B2$, or $B3$ has the *attribute* "*thick_line*". If not, the system executes a library (a *moa* system has to provide it as a standard library) which calls its own user-interface, that is, its user-manipulation interpreter. It is just like executing "*system*(*gets*(*buf*))" in the C language.

Here, if the user clicks one of $B1$–$B3$ inside B, then the procedure "*mark*" makes its *attribute* "*thick_line*". From the human point of view, it is just a marking of an icon. At this time, the condition of the "*while*" loop returns true, so the system quits the loop. In other words, the system automatically judges the end of inputting and starts inference (after closing the card B).

Of course it is also possible to keep the information about the selection not by *search-info* but by *internal-data*. In this case the selection is not visible on screen, but the system knows it.

Depending on the value returned from the library of an inference engine, just one of $C1$–$C3$ appears in the card A. In this way the system displays the outcome of inference on the screen.

14.5.5.3 An Example Showing Inputting of Numerics

To handle numerical input, from now on we consider that *status-updating-procedures* can also take numerics as arguments. For example, it is possible to write a procedure which takes a node and a numeric as arguments and assigns the numeric to a suitable variable in the node's *internal-data*. (If there are only few possible values, it is also possible by defining some procedures with a node argument and no numeric arguments.)

Let us take the following example:

– A user-manipulation

First, click the text part of a card A. Then, a special window for numeric input appears, so input a number n.

– The *operation* issued by this manipulation

$set\_value(A, n)$

– The *status-updating-procedure* caused by "*set_value*"

$\lambda mx($
  a particular variable in m's *internal-data* := x;
  the *text* of m := " $\times \times$ *mg/dl in GTT*"
$)$

Here " $\times \times$ " is a string converted from the numeric x

Let us assume the *text* of A is "( )*mg/dl in GTT*" and a user inputs 120 into the numeric input window. (Again this window is not included in the formalization.)

The procedure (with two arguments whose values are A, 120) assigns 120 to a variable in A's *internal-data* and changes A's *text* to "*120mg/dl in GTT*". From the human point of view it is just like inserting numerical data into a blank of the *text*.

14.6 Conclusion and Future Work

We have proposed a model called *MOA* for describing a support system for intelligent human work and the interface for that system.

We gave a brief analysis of intelligent work in the medical field, then discussed the required specifications for the support system and its framework including information interchanges between the components of the system. Note that inference engines do not carry out their inference processes, but only offer possible choices from which the user, who is assumed to be an expert in a specific field, selects necessary information. In other words, it is important to provide a flexible user-interface using hypertext, rather than to search for perfect information [7, 8].

On the other hand, we gave a constructive representation of dynamic knowledge and inference rules based on hypertext, in which knowledge and rules are decomposed and localized to hierarchical and flexibly linked subcomponents. Each component is shown on screen as a card which also corresponds to a phase, a stage of routine work from the human viewpoint. Moving from one card to another is naturally regarded as flow control.

In addition, we proposed a unified system in which each card of hypertexts acts as an inference module, and an inference engine acts as an intelligent browser for searching information. The formal description of the model was also given.

From two standpoints, we list some future work toward practical applications to a medical information system.

First, we point out the importance of further investigation on the inference mechanism [9, 10]. For example, we may need to introduce tense logic into inference mechanisms, because medical treatments are highly dynamic real-time operations. A doctor has to deal with patients with dynamically changing status of disease, so is is important that the doctor should be able to access both the patients' current status and their past status easily. A possible approach to making such access efficient, we propose, is a version of tense logic which has the notion of time hierarchy, such as phases, subphases, and events. In such a logic, it is possible to write, for example, "the status of a patient at the second check-up on the last consultation," in which the doctor's view of the flow of the medical treatment is naturally reflected.

As another example, we mention the possibility of introducing a logic by which it is possible to perform an inference to a certain extent from insufficient data. This feature is useful when, as in MOA, the system lists some candidates using insufficient data, and the user selects necessary information. We are thinking of adopting the default logic. In addition, we may have to deal with approximate data. Fuzzy logic seems to be a good candidate to use in such cases.

Next, it will be necessary to enrich the user interface. One possible way is to introduce multi hypermedia [11]. This enables the system to treat various on-line objects, for instance, X-ray photographs, CT scanner displays, or electrocardiograms. Of course, these objects have to be placed in a hierarchy, and be linked flexibly, while the system has the information-hiding capabilities. It is also important to consider direct input/output (I/O) to such objects. Currently, MOA does not treat multiple media directly, but takes them into consideration by treating them uniformly as objects which have internal data and attributes.

Another important theme is to consider the requirements for implementation as a multi-user system. For example, in a large hospital the system has to keep many patients' data. To protect their privacy, system security will be very important.

Acknowledgments. Thanks to Prof. R. Nakajima at Kyoto University for useful advice and great cooperation while translating, and to T. Suzuki and K. Masuda for fruitful discussions. Also, thanks to T. Tsutsui, J. Arai, and S. Yorita for lending literature willingly.

References

1. Conklin J (1989) Hypertext: An introduction and survey. IEEE Trans Comput 20: 17–41
2. Kameyama M, Kameda H, Takaku H, Able O (eds) (1988) Today's diagnosis, 2nd edn. Igaku-shoin, Tokyo, p 1014–1022
3. Harel D (1988) On visual formalism. J ACM 31(5): 514–530
4. Nishio N, Yamada H (1987) Computer-assisting environment for idea processing. Document Processing and a Human Interface 15(2): 1–8
5. Arai M, Horiden S (1987) Expert systems for diagnosis. Inf Process 28(2): 177–186
6. Anzai, Y, Kondo T (1986) Object-oriented production-embedded knowledge representation language OPHELIA and its applications. Comput Software 3(3): 43–60
7. Ueno H (1987) Expert systems. Inf Process 28(2): 147–157
8. Mizoguchi R, Kakusho O (1987) The recent trends of expert system research. Inf Process 28(2): 207–217
9. Nitta K (1987) Knowledge representation and inference mechanism of expert systems. Inf Process 28(2): 158–166
10. Watanabe M (1987) Knowledge acquisition for expert systems. Inf Process 28(2): 167–176
11. Takeuchi A, Kumagai H, Wake T (1988) Knowledge Media Station (1)–(6), overview. Proc 37th Japan Information Processing Society National Conference: 1246–1257

References

[illegible reference list]

GROUP B

15
An Object-Oriented Native-Language Support for the Andrew Toolkit

Kazuhiro Kitagawa, Hirohisa Ogawa, Akira Yamaguchi, and Nobuo Saito[1]

Summary: The development of a generic, highly flexible, and extensible native-language support facility has becomes necessary for computer users. We have designed and developed a native-language support interface for the Andrew Toolkit, incorporating an object-oriented programming approach, and developed applications to run on it. We have designed a uniform data model which can handle any native language. Using the object-oriented programming language's code-sharing facility, we share the program code as much as possible based on its data model. We incorporate the MVC (Model View Controller) model of Smalltalk to support native-language processing. Each native language has its own data model and view. This mechanism provides advantages when extending an existing program. Incorporating this design, a program which supports the dynamic loading of objects on the Andrew Toolkit becomes able to support native-language processing without any modification.

In this paper, we will describe the design of the native-language support and data model, and discuss the advantages of our idea, through the experimental development of a native-language processing application, and the extension of an existing program.

Key words: Native-language support — object-oriented approach — the Andrew Toolkit — compound document manipulation

15.1 Introduction

The library of procedures for a text manipulation system often becomes large and rich in functionality. In the case of multilingual text processing, these procedures become much more complex, especially if they form one giant set of modules that can manipulate all the languages. It is difficult for a programmer to extend a text-processing system that does not incorporate data abstraction. Extensibility usually requires access to and manipulation of internal data. If the implementation

---

[1] Department of Mathematics, Keio University, Kohoku, Yokohama, 223 Japan

language does not provide a data encapsulation facility, allowing this access is dangerous. For example, each Latin language has a different quotation mark. Each library should have access to these data, and if libraries share data for quotation marks, we must take care that these data hold the correct data value. But if these data cannot be shared, access to the data is straightforward.

For multilingual text processing internal data should not be shared by each of the languages. However, it is possible to share some functions, such as line breaking, or pagination functions, among several language-processing modules. By specifying different parameters, we can change the action of a procedure without changing the procedure itself. To support the effective development of multilingual text-processing systems, the implementation language needs to provide code sharing.

Also, another problem is that a multilingual system becomes bigger and bigger. Assume that there is a multilingual document manipulation system using static linking. If a user processes only English text, the linked libraries which process the other languages are never used.

An object-oriented approach offers a solution to these problems. The Class mechanism for object-oriented language provides data protection, code sharing through inheritance, and provides flexibility through dynamic loading at run time.

Our aim is to develop a portable interactive multilingual text manipulation system, running under a general window system, and to make an existing application program manipulate a native language without any modifications. To achieve our objectives, we decided to use a window-independent toolkit which supports dynamic loading. There are several window programming toolkits that are running under the existing window system. From our review of these window toolkits, the Andrew Toolkit was judged to be the most portable, powerful, and advanced toolkit. The Andrew Toolkit [1, 2], developed by the Information Technology Center of Carnegie Mellon University, is a window toolkit for multimedia applications and is distributed as contribution software in X11. Also, the Andrew Toolkit includes a class compiler that supports object-oriented programming. For this reason, we decided to develop a multilingual system running under the Andrew Toolkit.

The Andrew Toolkit is a window-independent user-interface toolkit to develop multimedia applications, and the implementation takes an object-oriented approach, incorporating the MVC (Model View Controller) model of Smalltalk-80 [3], supporting high-level functionality. This toolkit supports the development of window applications that integrate various objects, such as text, graphics, and images, as well as editors that allow users to edit different kinds of objects, including text, equations, graphs, and tables, through a single program.

The Andrew Toolkit is written in the Andrew Class System (Class) [4]. Class language is an object-oriented programming system providing single level inheritance. Class is implemented as a preprocessor of the C compiler. In standard Unix, the linkage editor must run before a program is invoked. In contrast, the Andrew Class system supports dynamic loading of objects. This means that an object is loaded after the program is started. Dynamic loading is useful for the multimedia editors which load arbitrary objects.

The important objects in the Andrew Toolkit are *dataobject* and *view*. A dataobject is a basic data model for information to be displayed and maintains data for various objects. A view maintains information about how a dataobject is to be displayed, and is responsible for interaction among users and computer. The separation of dataobject and view results in a great advantage. It is very easy to build an application program where there are multiple views from one set of data. To manipulate a multimedia document, the Andrew Toolkit provides a text object which supports a structured document.

The idea of the work described in this paper was to design a native-language support interface. The libraries of procedures were developed as a part of the Andrew Toolkit object. Here, we will show how inheritance and data encapsulation could be used for multilingual text manipulation, and how a hierarchy of these primitives can compose a complex multilingual text-processing system which provides high flexibility and extensibility. As a result of incorporating this design, existing programs which provide dynamic loading of objects become able to process any native language without modification of the source program.

15.2 An Overview of Class Hierarchy

Important aspects of the Andrew class organization and class hierarchy for multilingual manipulation are shown in Fig. 15.1. Classes starting with letter *i* provide native-language support primitives; *i* stands for *internationalized*.

The following are the most important derived classes used in multilingual text manipulation:

- *iview*: drawing and event handling
- *igraphics*: actual screen handling
- *idataobject*: maintaining various data objects including multilingual text
- *isimpletext*: maintaining multilingual character data

Iview (Internationalized View) maintains all of the information on the event

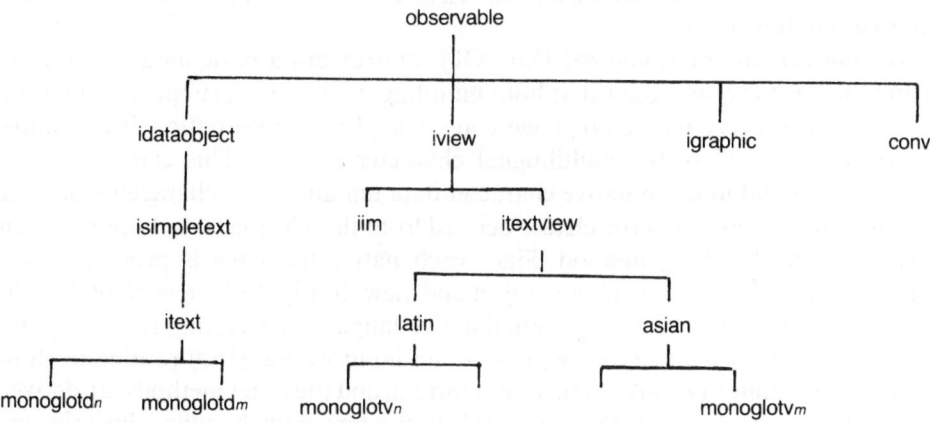

FIG. 15.1. Class organization for native-language processing

handling, such as key bindings that specify an editing operation, and key map information, and it also calls code conversion methods, and provides a drawing screen. *Iview* calls *igraphics* (Internationalized Graphics) methods as macro methods to draw the screen. Actual screen drawing is supported in this class.

Itextview (Internationalized Textview) is a class derived from *iview* and supports a multilingual view. The hierarchy of derived classes from *iview* is guided by the desire to share codes as much as possible without compromising the logical relationship. *itextview* is a basic polyglot class and defines basic internal data and methods used in each subclass. The following are the classes for the multilingual text view currently developed:

- *latin*: super class for Latin languages
- *asian*: super class for Asian languages, such as languages which have a large number of characters

The *manoglotv$_n$* is an actual view class to draw each language. There is a view for each native language. Most of the methods inherited from the super class are not overloaded. Views for less familiar languages for us, such as Arabic or Russian, are not supported at present; these are still under development.

The *latin* and *asian* classes provide general methods and define internal data which are shared by each derived class. These classes are designed with the aim of providing code sharing for the programmer, not to divert attention to the screen drawing. So, a programmer need not override the inherited screen-drawing methods. For instance, a *latin* class provides a line-drawing method. A programmer can use this method without any modification. Changing an instance value, a programmer and user can manage this procedure. This means that they only need to prepare instance functions and some special functions. Hence, each of the monoglot views provides only keymaps, menu items, messages, language translation functions (like ASCII to Japanese), and instantiation procedures. Also, each of these has its own data object, as will be shown.

Igraphics is responsible for actual screen drawing, and the aim of this class is to hide the underlying window-drawing model. Methods provided in this class are used in *iview*. *Classes* derived from this class call window libraries on which the Andrew Toolkit runs.

Idataobject (Internationalized Data Object) provides a basic data structure to maintain various object data that hold multilingual text data, supporting uniform data access to every native language code. *Isimpletext* (Internationalized Simple Text) maintains all of the multilingual character streams. This class only provides general and uniform native character data handling, like character insertion, deletion, and so on. All of the classes derived from this class need not prepare their own character-handling method. Since each native language is processed as a different object, it has its own data object and view. In Fig. 15.1, *monoglotd$_n$* has the corresponding view *monoglotd$_m$*. Actual native-language processing is done by this pair. This class, *monoglotd$_n$*, only provides an input/output (I/O) routine to show the language name in Andrew data object format, and the other methods are derived from its super class, *itext*. Since general native text data handling libraries are provided in the super classes, a programmer who wants to process another native language, only needs to prepare read and write routines in a subclass of *itext*. Of course, to support a data object for Arabic, a programmer need prepare only I/O and initialize routines.

Iim (Internationalized Interaction Manager) is responsible for communication between a user and the view. The aim of this class is to hide the underlying window system. All the inputs are processed in this class, and then *iim* sends them to the appropriate class derived from *iview*. When a user wants to input a non ASCII character from an ASCII keyboard, *iim* posts the key code input from the keyboard to the monoglot *iview* class. Then, the $monoglot_v$ class calls conversion functions from ASCII to a target language which is provided with *conv* subclasses, and if necessary, the $monoglot_v$ class posts their data to *iim* to change key mapping, menu items, and so on. Finally, the converted data are sent to the appropriate $monoglot_d$.

15.3 Basic Data Structure for Multi Byte Text Data

The Andrew Toolkit cannot handle the 2-byte code as data object and text object. Basically, the Andrew Toolkit maintains a data object as a single-byte character stream. Adaptation of a data object to the 2-byte code is necessary. In this section, we show the basic data structure of native-language support for the data object.

We provide *idataobject*, which supports multilingual text handling in data objects. *Idataobject* defines the basic data structure which holds any 1-byte or 2-byte character code. This data structure is defined as a *longword* in *idataobject*. Classes derived from *idataobject* can hold any multilingual text data. The data structure of this longword is shown in Fig. 15.2.

When the text has single byte data, data is stored in the *Character Code0* entry, and the language identifier is set into *Character Table0*. In this case, no other entry of longword is used. When the text has 2-byte data, high byte data is stored in *Character Code1*, low byte data is stored in *Character Code0*, and the language identifier is set into *Character Table1*. In this case, *Character Table0* is never used. The text data maintained include ISO 8859 and ISO 2022.

To hold the longword stream, we prepare two classes, *isimpletext* (Internationalized Simple Text) and *itext* (Internationalized Text), to access multilingual text data objects. *Isimpletext* maintains multilingual text data as a simple longword stream, and the *isimpletext* class defines basic native-language data access primitives, such as insertion, deletion, etc. We prepare these methods for all of the derived classes from this. Since this class provides primitives for access to the native-language data objects, a programmer can share these methods in any native language.

Character Table 1	Identify high byte
Character Table 0	Identify low byte
Character Code 1	High byte code
Character Code 0	Low byte code

FIG. 15.2. Data structure of *longword*

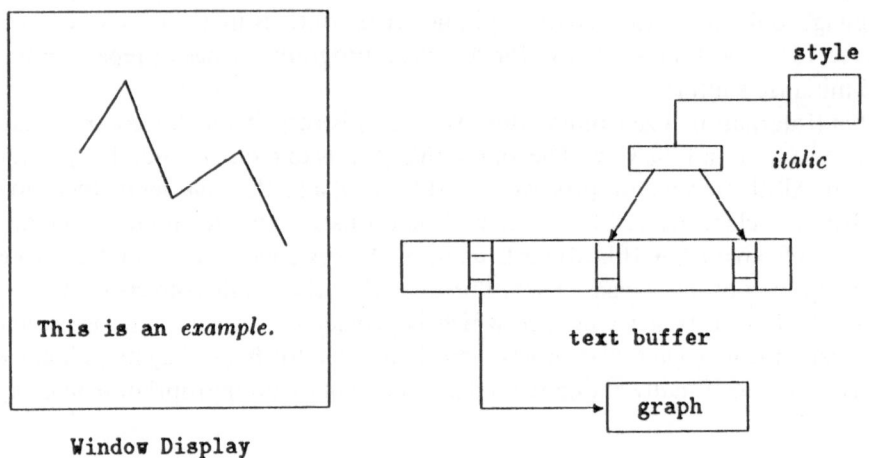

FIG. 15.3. Example: *Itext* holds text and table data

Itext is a subclass of *isimpletext* that supports structured document data manipulation, and can hold various objects including tables, equations, images, figures, and so on. Figure 15.3 illustrates the feature that *itext* holds text data, including italic text and table data. *Itext* holds the style sheet as a different table for the longword stream. The style sheet table points inside of the longword stream which specifies attributes of the stream (e.g., fonts, indentation, etc.).

When *itext* finds data which cannot be maintained as a simple longword stream, *itext* marks this longword which specifies that this longword has a different object. A marked longword holds 377 in octal value in each entry. Information about this mark is maintained in another internal table that points to the different object.

When reading from file and saving to file, I/O methods provided in *idataobject* translate a longword stream into/from ISO 8859 and ISO 2022. If *itext* has a marked longword, these I/O libraries save the data as a different object.

Real data object handling methods are provided for subclasses of *itext*. Since these classes provide basic native-language access methods and structured documents, a programmer need prepare only I/O (read and write) routines, not access primitives (e.g., insertion, deletion, etc.) in this class.

15.4 Drawing and Input for Multilingual Text

As mentioned before, the other main part of this system consists of the interaction manager and view. In the MVC model, the interaction manager is the controller and a view is a view. Each window application has its own interaction manager, and *iim* maintains all of the events from keyboard and mouse. The aim of this interaction manager is to hide the underlying window system from an application program.

The *iview* class specifies a generic structure for a minimum set of drawing methods and event-handling tables for screen update, notifying resize of window, and key binding tables that define window operations. The class uses *igraphic* methods to draw a screen. The aim of the *igraphic* class is to hide the underlying window system from an application program. *Igraphic* defines all of the screen-drawing methods, and these methods are used in *iview*. *Iim* and *igraphic* are two classes which make this toolkit more portable.

Itextview specifies the generic structure for drawing multilingual text. Classes derived from *itextview* maintain additional information according to their individual language attributes. All of the native-language screen-drawing classes are derived from this class. To reduce programming work, we provide a class intermediate between *itextview* and the real native-language view class. In the current version, we provide two classes, *latin* and *asian*. The *latin* class provides basic, general data and functions for the Latin languages, whereas the *asian* class provides these mechanisms for the Asian languages which have a large number of characters based on Chinese characters (kanji). Since, English, French, and German can share functions and data prepared for these languages, but these shared items cannot be used by Japanese, for instance, we designed this view class organization. For example, the class for English, which is derived from the *latin* class, maintains only information concerned with English. If necessary, a subclass of this *itextview* and an intermediate class provide translation facilities from ASCII to a target language (e.g., ASCII to kanji characters). Hence, classes derived from *itextview* provide translation from ASCII to another language facility. Details of this model are shown in the latter sections.

15.4.1 View Tree

One window consists of several views. The views in a window make a tree, called a *view tree*. An example of a view tree is shown in Fig. 15.4. In this figure, *astextview*

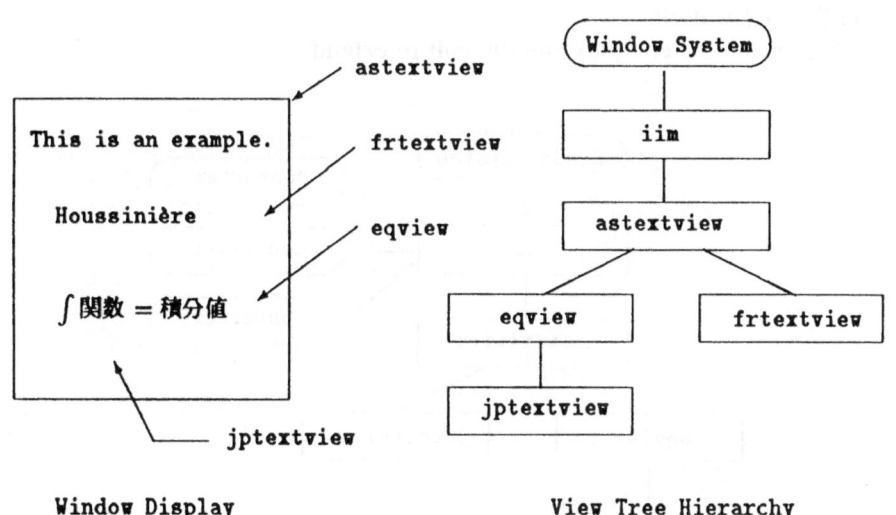

Window Display   **View Tree Hierarchy**

FIG. 15.4. An example of a view tree

is a view for the ASCII-based world, *frtextview* is for the French, and *jptextview* is for the Japanese. Also, *eqview* can load multiple objects at run time. In this figure, the equation editor loads Japanese text data in it. The interaction manager exists at the top of the view tree. *Iview* is always a child of *iim*. In this example, *itextview* maintains the whole window drawing and this window has a couple of children of *itextview*.

The *iim* is a component of the Andrew Toolkit that handles input events from the keyboard and mouse. Each window has its own interaction manager. The interaction manager receives all events for the window from the underlying window system, and it passes each event down to its focused child view without any processing. Only a focused view can receive an event from *iim*. Then this view changes the screen and notifies the status to its parent.

View is responsible for drawing the screen and event handling. When *view* receives an event, *view* looks up the keymap defined in it, and the corresponding method is invoked.

Hence, the interaction manager provides general event processing, but it does not define special event handling for its child view. *View* class defines these event-processing routines.

15.4.2 Model for Multilingual Text Drawing and Input

To input multilingual text, some conversion method from ASCII strings into destination strings may be needed. To support this facility, two design models are considered. One is that *iim* supports conversion facilities, and the other is that each *iview* has its own conversion mechanism. These design models are shown in Figs. 15.5 and 15.6.

Characteristics of the former model, shown in Fig. 15.5 are:

– Simplifies the view tree.
– Simplifies *iview* itself.
– *Iim* becomes more complex and difficult to extend.

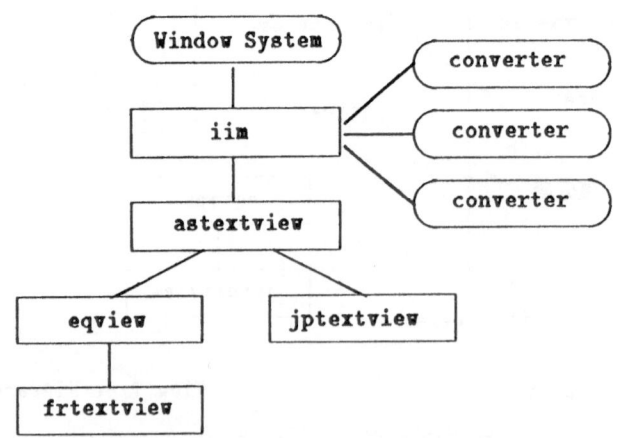

FIG. 15.5. View tree for multilingual text (1)

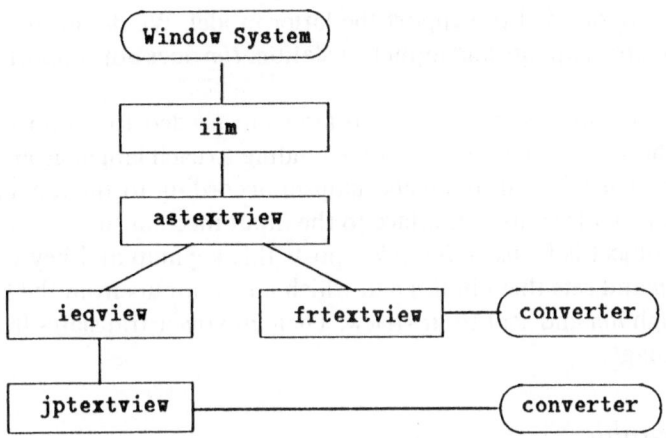

FIG. 15.6. View tree for multilingual text (2)

– *Iim* has to provide a new communication protocol between *iim* and each converter.
– A user must specify which language the user wants to input.

This model is the usual method used for non-object oriented multilingual text editing.

Iim maintains event-handling tables and data for language conversion. A user who wishes to input non-ASCII data must specify which language he or she wants to input, explicitly. In this case, *iim* becomes much more complex, to support all of the conversion facilities. If we add a new conversion mechanism, we have to change *iim* itself. This makes *iim* difficult to extend. Nevertheless, each view is still simple.

The second model is shown in Fig. 15.6. In this model, each *iview* has its own translation facility. *Iim* does nothing except send inputs to *iview*. The following are the characteristics of this model:

– Simplifies *iim* structure.
– Internal data for translation are protected from other language translation functions.
– Provides much more flexibility.
– Easy to extend.

The aim of the *iim* is to hide the underlying window system. Also, methods for event handling are provided in *iview*. In case of Fig. 15.5, *iim* provides particular event-processing methods for conversion. All the event-handling methods should be provided in *view*. When we add the new conversion facility onto *iim*, a programmer must access internal data that maintains all the data for conversion. This is very dangerous. These data should be protected between each conversion module.

The latter model will provide more flexibility and extensibility. Providing a different view, it is easy to provide another conversion for the same language without the extension of *iim*. Since each view has a conversion method, internal data for the string translations are protected from other views. Also, the conversion facility is automatically selected by focusing on to *iview*.

Therefore, we decided to support the latter model. We designed *itextview* supporting both screen update and input translation. *Iim* does not support a translation facility.

Furthermore, various translation libraries are needed to support multilingual text input. There are several *iviews* corresponding to each language and conversion method. Each *iview* has an input mechanism according to the language which it handles, and provides a user interface to the input mechanism.

When an object is focused, *itextview* posts this keymap and key binding information to *iim* and sets them in it. Data which a user inputs from the keyboard are passed through *iim* and sent to *itextview*. Then, *itextview* translates from ASCII to a target language.

15.4.3 Igraphic

The *igraphic* class provides screen-drawing functions in a window-independent manner. These methods are called from *iview* as a macro drawing method. This *igraphic* class hides the output model of the underlying window system.

We made simple extensions to *igraphic* to handle longword characters as an argument of this method.

15.5 Experimentation

We have developed libraries for native-language support and a complete program for a native-language support editor called *iez*, shown in Fig. 15.7. In addition, we developed a write routine which can translate from an internal Andrew data object

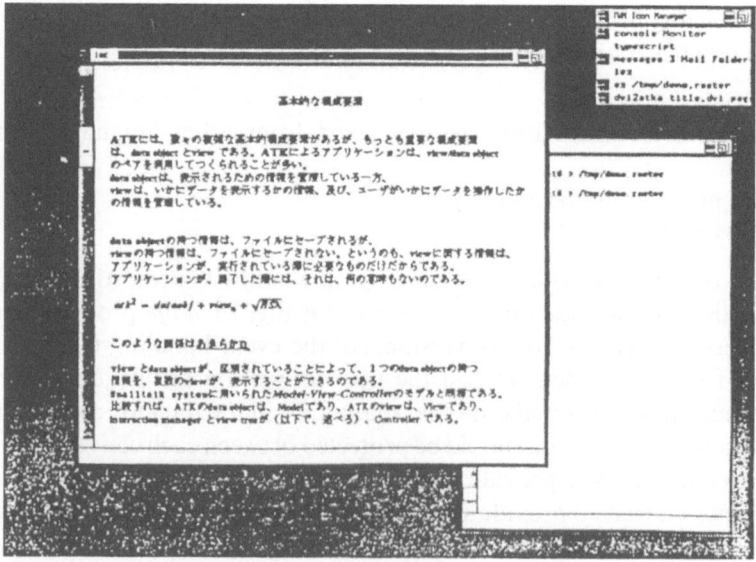

FIG. 15.7. Iez: native-language support editor

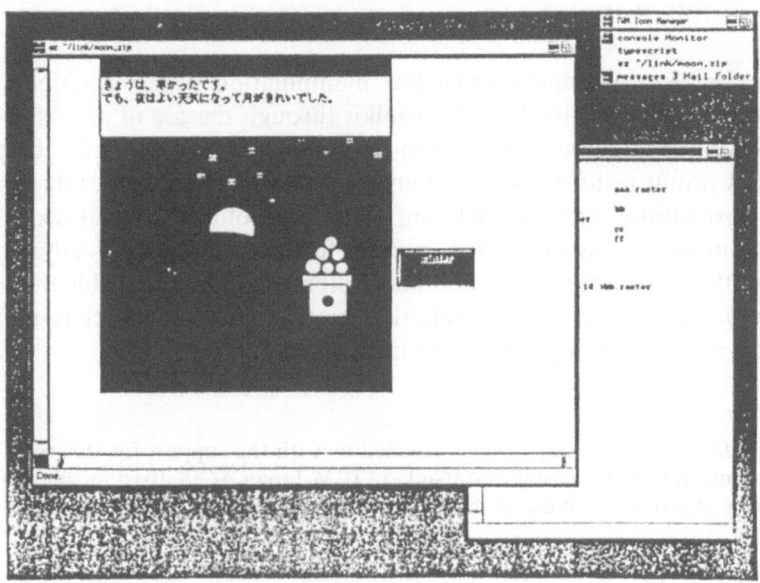

Fig. 15.8. Drawing editor which loads Japanese object

to T$_E$X data format. These libraries are provided as class methods. Raster image, line drawings are converted to PostScript, and these data are embedded in a T$_E$X dvi code. Thus, our system works as a T$_E$X frontend processor too.

In the Andrew Toolkit environment, this design method provides much greater benefit to the extension of existing non-native language support tools to provide native-language processing. Using this method, these tools (e.g., raster editor, drawing editor, and equation editor) become able to support a native language without any modification of the programs written in the Andrew Toolkit. To provide native-language support, these programs should be recompiled, because super classes are changed. Figure 15.8 shows an example of this screen. This window shows a drawing editor, called *zip*. Originally, this editor could not handle the native language. Since primitives are changed as defined in some upper classes of the class tree, we recompiled this zip object. The zip object now supports dynamic loading of objects, so we can load Japanese text with this command, as in Fig. 15.8.

In general, the object-oriented design method provides much benefit, when compared with our experience of the development of Japanese T$_E$X. In the case of the extension of T$_E$X, we monitored the extent of damage caused from operations performed on Japanese and English functions. Furthermore, WEB [5], which describes a document and a program in the same text, attempts to provide good document and modular structures, but the implementation language lacks data encapsulation. This could not be extended easily to suit Japanese text formatting and processing. In Pascal, which is the implementation language of T$_E$X, the data of a main procedure are global variables; there are also a lot of global variables. These aspects required attention, whereas during the development of the object-oriented multilingual system, attention to them was not necessary.

15.6 Conclusion

We have developed a multilingual text manipulation system running under the Andrew Toolkit and extending this toolkit through the use of an object-oriented approach. The inheritance mechanism provides both power and flexibility for the package, without restoring a large number of existing functions. Objects support data encapsulation, useful for defining abstraction of multilingual text manipulation. This makes it easy to develop complex functions. Dynamic loading of objects simplifies the text manipulation and makes libraries more extensible than do existing procedural languages. As a result, the object-oriented approach to multilingual document manipulation produces significant benefits.

Acknowledgments. IBM Japan has provided us with the support for this research work. Special thanks go to Ms. Toshiko Matsuda of IBM Japan ACIS division, who has contributed greatly to our work. We also thank the ITC research members for their comments via e-mail.

References

1. Palay AJ, Hansen WJ, Kazar ML, Sherman MS, Wadlow MG, Neuendorffer TP, Stern Z, Bader M, Peters T (1988) The Andrew Toolkit: An overview. In: Proc USENIX Technical Conference, February 1988
2. Borenstein NS (1990) Multimedia application development with the Andrew Toolkit. Prentice Hall, Englewood Cliffs
3. Goldberg A, Robson D (1983) Smalltalk-80: the language and its implementation. Addison-Wesley, Massachusetts
4. Palay AJ (1989) The Andrew class system (manual). Information Technology Center, Mellon University Press, Carnegie
5. Knuth DE (1983) The WEB system of structured documentation (technical report). Stanford University Press

GROUP C

16
The GALAXY Distributed Operating System

*Mamoru Maekawa, Kentaro Shimizu, Xiaohua Jia, Pradeep Sinha,
Kyu Sung Park, Hyo Ashihara, Naoki Utsunomiya,
Hirohiko Nakano, and Singo Yamashita*[1]

Summary: The GALAXY distributed operating system aims at true network transparency both for the local-area networks and for the wide-area networks. The basic mechanism to accomplish this is the three-level object-naming scheme which has many features for reliability, efficiency, and flexibility. Based on this naming scheme, a network-wide virtual address space called the uniform address space is constructed. It facilitates smooth load and information sharing. The mechanisms for unified data sharing and synchronization for this global address space are provided. The provision of static and dynamic data replications is useful for improving both reliability and performance. The process structure of GALAXY is efficient and flexible enough to realize a fine grain of concurrency in single/multi-processor systems. Global process management based on process migration is indispensable for the network-transparent distributed processing. In GALAXY, an object-based environment is implemented on its process-based system architecture. The object group is a key mechanism in an object-based environment to realize hierarchical, integrated object processing and management.

In this paper, we first discuss the design goals and requirements of GALAXY, and then describe the main concepts and mechanisms for achieving these requirements.

Key words: distributed operating system — network transparent naming — light weight processes — data replication — object groups

16.1 Introduction

In recent years, distributed processing on a large number of high-performance computers connected by a network has become a major computation environment. Such a style of distributed processing has many advantages—performance, reliability, easy information sharing, modularity, availability, scalability, etc., which are well known and widely acclaimed. However, it tends to suffer from difficulties of

---

[1] Department of Information Science, Faculty of Science, Bunkyo-Ku, University of Tokyo, 113 Japan

consistency control and administration, due to the distributed nature of the systems. One of the most important requirements for operating systems is to hide the physical distribution of hardware and software resources as much as possible, while providing a view of the logically centralized system to users. The GALAXY distributed operating system is designed to realize such transparent distributed processing on a network of node computers with single/multi processors.

It is known that a distributed system is most successful when its structure resembles and directly reflects the structure of the real-world user community or applications. This is understandable because a network is an infrastructure for human activities. With this in mind, we have designed GALAXY so that it appears to be a collection of autonomous objects which communicate with each other. On the other hand, we believe that a single-level address space is most convenient at the programming level. Although there exist a number of computational models, almost all current computers are based on the model that consists of multiple processors with a shared memory. This model is presently most common and the realization of many programming paradigms based on this simple model are widely understood. For these reasons, we also adopted network-wide single-level address space in GALAXY.

Existing distributed operating systems vary from those which merely provide interconnection of autonomous systems, to those which provide a network-transparent environment by integrating distributed resources. The distributed systems that are designed to support a heterogeneous environment based on a wide-area network [1, 2] tend to provide the restricted form of distributed processing, such as network communication and file systems. In this case, the security and reliability are especially important issues of the system design. On the other hand, many existing distributed operating systems [3, 4] aim at network transparency for systems based on high-performance workstations connected by a high-speed local-area network. Although it would be possible to extend such a system to wide-area networks, this kind of approach degrades efficiency and cannot provide satisfactory solutions for security and reliability issues.

The GALAXY distributed operating system aims at true network transparency, both for the local-area networks and for the wide-area networks. The basic mechanism to accomplish this is the three-level object-naming scheme which has many features for reliability, efficiency, and flexibility. Based on this naming scheme, a network-wide virtual address space called the uniform address space was constructed. It facilitates smooth load and information sharing. The mechanisms for unified data sharing and synchronization for this global address space are provided. The provision of static and dynamic data replications is useful for improving both reliability and performance. The process structure of GALAXY is efficient and flexible enough to realize a fine grain of concurrency in single/multi-processor systems. Global process management based on process migration is indispensable for the network-transparent distributed processing. In GALAXY, an object-based environment is implemented on its process-based system architecture. The object group is a key mechanism in an object-based environment to realize hierarchical, integrated object processing and management.

In this paper, we first discuss the design goals and requirements of GALAXY, and then describe the main concepts and mechanisms for achieving these requirements.

·Performance	·Network-transparency	·Global naming
·Reliability	·Location independency	·Replication
·Availability	·Fault transparency	·Partition
	·Performance stability	
·Scalability	·Concurrency transparency	·Migration
·Flexibility	·Replication transparency	·Virtualization
	·Migration transparency	
·Usability	·Scaling transparency	·Synchronization
	·Programming-level transparency	·Communication
	·Autonomy	·Resource management
·Smooth sharing		
	·Efficiency in local operations	·Caching
	·UNIX compatibility	·Error recovery
	·Open structure	·Layered structure
		·Encapsulation

FIG. 16.1. Design goals and requirements

16.2 Goals and Requirements

Figure 16.1 lists the design goals and requirements of GALAXY. The most important concept to achieve the main goals is network transparency. The principal transparencies are discussed here:

Location independency
Location independency is the most important and extensive among the transparency requirements. There are two factors in location independency:

1. An object at any node can be accessed without the knowledge of its physical location (location independency of request-receiving objects).
2. An object at any node can issue an access request without the knowledge of its own physical location (location independency of request-issuing objects).

In the address-space space view, an address space may be scattered over a number of nodes; each portion of the address space is mapped to an object which may reside at any node. In GALAXY, any executor can access any portion of the address space.

Fault transparency
Various types of failures of hardware or software components should be masked from users and application programs. Data replication and hardware switching are important mechanisms for fault transparency. The reliability techniques such as atomic transactions are also important.

Performance stability
Performance stability means that a system is reconfigured to improve the performance of individual jobs as well as the performance of the total system as loads

vary. This is accomplished by executor migration; data migration, replication, and partition.

Concurrency transparency

Several users and application programs can operate concurrently on shared data without interference between them. Proper concurrency control mechanisms should be used to maintain consistency of the shared data. Although some fine locking mechanisms are already known, problem-oriented mechanisms are very effective for achieving good performace.

Replication transparency

This enables users or application programs to access multiple instances of files or other data objects without the knowledge of the objects being replicated and/or partitioned.

Migration transparency

Movement (migration) of any type of object does not affect the operation of users or application programs. The system should maintain the transient state for the object migration.

Scaling transparency

This means that the change of the system scale does not lead to a change in the system structure, or to the application programs. The system which has no centralized component that can become a bottleneck has better potential to be scaled up in size.

Programming-level transparency

These transparency requirements must be achieved at the programming level as well as at the end-user level. Network-wide virtual memory is a key mechanism to achieve this. The shared-memory semantics realized on the network-wide virtual memory allows a programming model to be compatible with the conventional centralized systems; any program that runs on a single machine should be able to run on multiple distributed machines without any modification of the program.

Besides these transparency requirements, the following requirements should be satisfied to make our distributed computational environment truly useful and convenient:

Autonomy

Each node or subset of nodes in the system must also function when standing alone. At least, each node computer should be provided with appropriate software to enable it to perform the minimum local operation.

Efficiency in local operations

Access to local objects should be as efficient as in nondistributed systems. This is important because most operations in distributed systems are local operations.

UNIX compatibility
The system must be compatible with the UNIX operating system, at least at the source-code level.

Support of heterogeneous systems
The system must support different types of machines and networks. A high degree of transparency must be supported across the various machines.

The rest or this paper describes new concepts and mechanisms or GALAXY, which are designed for achieving these goals and requirements.

16.3 Object Naming and Locating

Naming and locating are very frequently used operations, and they play an important role in the design of any operating system. Especially in the case of distributed operating systems, where a large number of objects are distributed all over the system, the need to assign global names to all the objects makes naming a more important issue. Object locating is an important function of naming mechanisms. Because the naming mechanism supports references to objects, it directly influences both the ease with which users refer to objects, and the efficiency of locating objects.

16.3.1 Three-Level Naming Scheme

Figure 16.2 shows the three-level naming scheme of GALAXY [5, 6]. An *external name* is a human-oriented, character-string name. One or more external names can

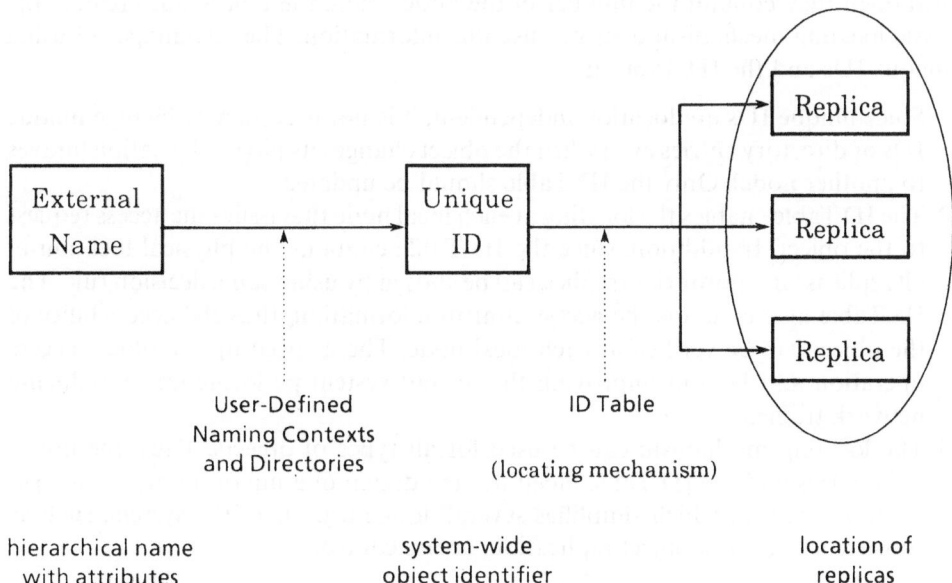

FIG. 16.2. The three-level naming scheme of GALAXY

be given to an object. An external name is completely independent of the physical location and structure of the object that it identifies. The scope, structure, and resolution mechanism or external names are defined by a *naming context*. There are multiple, user-, and system-defined naming contexts in the system. A naming context is also a GALAXY object, and its name is registered in another naming context. Although the structure of external names can be defined by users, there exists a system-defined global naming context which constructs a tree-structured name space. The reason why the tree-structured naming is used as the basic naming structure is that tree-structured naming is used widely and has proved to be sufficient for discriminating correlated objects from others and managing them as a hierarchical group. The data structure used for the name resolution is directories. A directory maintains the mapping of external names to unique identifiers (IDs).

A *unique ID* is a system-wide unique identifier which is assigned to each object. Unique IDs are used by the system and user programs to reference objects. There exist objects which are assigned unique IDs but have no external names. Typical examples of such objects are system objects and temporary objects, for which external names are not necessary. In GALAXY, one object may have multiple replicas. A unique ID identifies a logical entity of an object; all the replicas of an object are given the same unique ID. The physical location of replicas, namely a list of nodes where the replicas exist, is obtained from the unique ID by the *locating mechanism*. The data structure used for the locating mechanism is a system-wide management table called *ID table*. Unique IDs and all the information necessary to access objects are maintained in the ID Table. Each entry corresponding to a unique ID is called an IDTE.

In GALAXY, unique IDs arc also location independent and the object location must be obtained from unique IDs which construct a system-wide, flat name space. Although they contain the number of the node where the object was created, the basic locating mechanism does not use this information. The advantages of using unique IDs and the ID Table are:

1. Since unique IDs are location independent, it is not necessary to change unique IDs or directory entries even when the object changes its physical location (moves to another node). Only the ID Table should be updated.
2. The ID Table enables the locating at each local node that issues the access request to the object. In addition, since the ID Table contains the physical location of all replicas, an appropriate replica can be chosen by using some decision rule. The ID Table also contains the access control information; thus the accessibility of the object can be verified at each local node. These speed up the object access operation and help in improving the overall system performance by reducing network traffic.
3. The locating mechanism can be used for all types of objects. Thus, the use of unique IDs and the ID Table facilitates the design of a uniform object management mechanism which simplifies several design aspects of the system, such as consistency control, object replication, access control, etc.

In GALAXY, any type of object is managed by a special module dedicated to the type. We call such a module by the general term *object manager*. For example, process objects are managed by a process manager, file objects are managed by a file manager, and so on. For the basic type of objects, the object manager resides in each node. Each object manager manages a subset of the objects on the node, and they cooperatively manage all the objects of the type. When an operation invocation message is issued, the corresponding object manager is invoked. Locating objects is divided into two steps:

1. Get the number of the node where the replica exists.
2. Get the physical address (device numbers, disk blocks, etc.) which is local to each node.

Step 1 is executed by the *ID Manager* which manages the ID Table. In Step 2, each object manager performs the locating operation by using local information maintained by it. In an actual object access operation, Step I can be preceded by Step 2 for the sake of efficiency. That is, an object manager first searches the objects that it manages. If the object is not found, then the object manager invokes the ID Manager to get the entry of the ID Table and ascertain the nodes where the replicas of the object exist. The object manager selects an appropriate replica and forwards the request to an object manager on that node; this object manager performs the same locating operation.

16.3.2 External Names

16.3.2.1 Network-Transparent Name Resolution

In many conventional operating systems, an object name is directly mapped to its physical location. In GALAXY, an external name is first translated to a unique ID, which in turn is used for the locating of its replicas. In tree-structured names, each directory hierarchy is implemented as a directory object, which consists of a pair of a component name and the corresponding unique ID. This unique ID may identify the next level of directory object. The traversal of the directory tree can be done recursively until a leaf (i.e., a non-directory object name) is reached. Since directories are also objects, they can be replicated and migrated just like any other type of object. Thus, the mechanism of name resolution itself is implemented in a network-transparent manner. Another feature of GALAXY's name resolution is that the unit of the name resolution is taken as a single object, instead of a subtree as in many conventional distributed file systems. This enhances the mobility of an object because the migration of an object can be performed completely independently any other objects.

The basic name resolution algorithm for tree-structured names is remote pathname expansion, which is used by many conventional operating systems. In this algorithm, the pathname is expanded at each node that stores a pathname component. However, this algorithm requires the directory accesses for successive component name resolution, and is also inefficient for direct directory access operations such as wild card expansion or listing a directory. In order to overcome these problems, GALAXY uses name caches, as described in Sect. 16.3.2.2. In addition, GALAXY provides the mechanism to define a structure-free name resolution algorithm such as hash-based resolution for each naming context.

16.3.2.2 Name Caches

A name cache is used at each node for caching of necessary directory entries. A name cache of each node consists of those directories and directory entries that correspond to the component names of the pathname of an object that was recently used to access the object from the node. It has the same structure as that of the hierarchical directory, except that it has the following characteristics:

1. The directories in a name cache normally contain a small number of entries as compared to their corresponding regular directories, because only the entries required at a node are cached.
2. The name caches always reside in memory.

In addition to the (component name, unique ID) pair, each entry of the name cache directory has the following fields:

- *Life of the entry*—when a new entry is created in a name cache directory, the value of this field is initialized to a constant value L. Whenever a name cache entry is accessed, its life is reinitialized to L. If the life expires, then that entry is called a dead entry.
- *Next directory's memory location pointer*—this field points to the memory address of another directory in the name cache when it is also cached.

New cache entries are created in the name cache at the time of locating an object whose one or more pathname components are not available in the name cache. Dead entries are replaced with new entries while searching for space for new entries. If there are no dead entries to be replaced, new space is allocated for the name cache for new entries. Since only necessary entries are placed in the name cache of a particular node, we assume that the space cost for the name cache is not so high. Note that a complete miss (not even one component of the pathname is found in the local name cache) will never happen because the root directory's unique ID is cached in the name cache of all the nodes.

Since the name cache contains unique IDs instead of the physical location, a name cache entry becomes stale only in the following two cases:

1. An object has been deleted but its name mapping is still present in a name cache [type 1].
2. A component name of a directory has been deleted or renamed, but the old component name is still present in a name cache [type 2].

Note that a name cache entry does not become stale when an objects location changes due to the migration of the object. Various methods of updating or invalidating a state cache entry can be conceived such as strict consistency, periodic invalidation, on-use consistency, and gradual invalidation. GALAXY employs a mixed approach. For an update of type 1, we use the method of on-use consistency control; stale cache entries are detected and deleted at the time of use. This is because for an update of type 1, stale cache entries will never cause a name to be mapped to the wrong object. Our mechanism first extracts the corresponding unique ID from the name cache, and searches the ID Table of the node for the unique ID. If this unique ID is not found, the desired object has been deleted and its cache entry is stale. For on-use invalidation, there is no need for an object manager to maintain a list of names of the objects being managed by it. For an update of type 2, the method of gradual invalidation is basically used for maintaining name cache consistency. In this method, the update message is gradually propagated from the node on which an update took place to the nodes where corresponding stale cache entries are located. In GALAXY, instead of sending the update message to all the nodes, it is gradually propagated only to the nodes present in the copy list entry of the corresponding IDTE. This helps in narrowing down the scope of a multicast to a great extent. Due to the use of the gradual invalidation method, temporary inconsistency of the name cache entries exists during the time required to propagate the message from the node where the update took place to the node where the stale name cache entry is located. But the temporary inconsistency of the name cache entries does not cause any serious problem to the users, although in some cases it degrades the efficiency of detecting and informing the users about the correct status of object names within the system.

16.3.2.3 Reliability Parameters

In order to improve the reliability of the object-locating mechanism, a set of reliability parameters have been defined in GALAXY, the users are given the flexibility to choose and specify through these parameters the degrees of reliability desired for the (node, pathname) pairs for the various objects and object names being used by a particular user from a specified node. These parameters are based on the various possibilities of the locations of the directories or their replicas which correspond to the pathname components of the desired object. The parameters are:

- *Subpath reliability*—for a (node, pathname) pair, the subpath reliability of the object-locating operation is the presence of the necessary directories on the client node (specified node) for tracing the components of the pathname up to the subpath right at the client node, without communicating with any other node. The longer the subpath which can be traced right at the client node, the better is the reliability of object-locating operation for that (node, pathname) pair. A special case of subpath reliability is *complete-path reliability*, all the directories necessary for tracing the given pathname are located on the client node. With subpath reliability of this degree, the object-locating operation does not depend upon any other node, since the complete pathname can be expanded at the local node of the client.

  m-stage reliability—an object-locating operation is said to be *m*-stage reliable when *m* hops are required during pathname expansion for locating the desired object. In our method of pathname expansion, a *hop* is defined as the passing of the remaining pathname components from one node to another node which has the next component's directory when the remaining components of the pathname cannot be further resolved on the present node. *m*-stage reliability of the object-locating operation for a given pathname basically depends upon the number of directories, corresponding to the contiguous components of a given pathname, that are replicated on the same node. The larger the number of such contiguous directories on a single node, the larger portion of the pathname can be resolved on a single node.

– *k-path reliability*—An object-locating operation is said to be *k*-path reliable when there are at least *k* possible paths between any two contiguous directories corresponding to the components of the given pathname starting from its root directory to the last directory of the given pathname. Note that the term *path* here means the logical object-locating path (path of the pathname from one directory to another) and not the physical path of the network. Obviously, this reliability factor comes into picture only when $m > 0$ for *m*-stage reliability or when subpath reliability is less than complete-path reliability. The larger the value of *k* for a given pathname, the more reliable the object-locating operation for that pathname will be, against network failures. The value of *k* will depend upon the degree of replication and locations of the directories concerned.

Using these three parameters, a user in GALAXY can specify the reliability requirements for locating certain objects from certain nodes. Depending upon the users' specifications, the system automatically replicates the necessary directories at the proper nodes. If the user does not specify any reliability requirement for the objects being used by that user, the system does not make any special attempt to improve the reliability of the object-locating operation of these objects for the user. The detailed design is given in [7].

16.3.2.4 Multiple Naming Contexts

There are two approaches to the realization of global naming in conventional distributed systems. These are:

1. Using a separate name space for each node
2. Using a single global name space for all nodes

Many recent distributed file systems such as NFS and RFS use the first approach, along with a method called remote mount. In these systems, each node in the network has its own file system in which remote file systems are locally mounted. This approach allows for each node to register only necessary names, but it lacks the absolute naming facility; the same object can have different names when viewed from other nodes. Many recent distributed operating systems [8–10] use the second approach, which can realize a completely location-independent naming. However, this approach has the following problems:

1. Names become too long for assigning unique names to individual objects. This is inconvenient, especially for users.
2. Typically, the name space has a tree structure and its name resolution proceeds by following a path through the name tree, starting at its root or the current directory. Thus, the cost of resolving names is dictated, to a large extent, by the depth of the name tree. This cost may be too high for some names in a single global name tree.

To overcome these problems, GALAXY takes another approach:

a. A user or an application program can define their own naming context.
b. There is a single global name tree and any portion of it can be mounted to the user's naming context.
c. Each naming context may be global and is completely independent of the physical location; node boundaries are transparent to users and application programs.

Thus, a user can define the logical scope of names; thereby, the user's name space becomes smaller than that of other approaches without degrading network transparency.

16.3.2.5 Descriptive Naming

Tree-structured names cannot easily represent various relations among objects. In order to incorporate the advantages of tree-structured names and to overcome their disadvantages, GALAXY uses the tree-structured names as the basis and provides the facility for attaching naming attributes to the links between two names. The attributes are represented as labels attached to the links. This facilitates denoting general semantic relations among objects. The system primitives for attribute-based naming are similar to Lisp functions which manipulate property lists.

16.3.3 Unique IDs

16.3.3.1 Basic Locating Mechanism

There are several types of object-locating mechanisms that have been proposed and used by conventional distributed systems.

The simplest mechanism is that based on broadcasting, in which the access request for the desired object is broadcasted to all other nodes if it is not found in the local node, and the node currently having the desired object then replies back to the accessing node. This mechanism cannot be used in a large system because the amount of network traffic generated for each request is proportional to the number of nodes in the system.

The second method is a centralized naming server. Only a particular node (center node) has the locating information, namely the entire ID Table in our case. However, this method is prohibitive because every access request to a remote node requires an inquiry to the center node, and because it becomes impossible to access an object if the center node crashes.

The third and another extreme approach is that every node has a full copy of the ID Table. This is also not realistic, especially in a large system, because a large space cost is incurred in each node to store the entire ID Table. In addition, it is not easy to keep consistency among the copies.

The chaining method, which is used by DEMOS/MP [11] for locating migratable processes, could also be used as the general object-locating mechanism. In this method, chains are maintained to keep track of the present location of a particular object. When an object is migrated from one node to another, a pointer is maintained at the source node to point to the destination node. When an access request for a particular object is generated, the creating node is first accessed and then the chain is traversed until the current object location is reached. The disadvantages of this method are: (1) the object-locating cost is directly proportional to the length of the chain; (2) it is difficult, or even impossible, to access an object if an intermediate node in the chain crashes, and (3) the cost for maintaining the chains is large and they complicate the system management.

Unlike any of these approaches, GALAXY basically allows the locating of any object by using the information stored in the local node and this information is always correct. To achieve this with low cost, each node has the minimum required copy which consists of the following unique IDs:

1. Unique IDs that are contained in the directories or in the name cache of the node. These unique IDs are necessary because when an external name is resolved to a unique ID, that unique ID must be available in the node, otherwise further operations for locating that object cannot be carried out.
2. Unique IDs that are used by the process running on the node. When a name cache is enabled, these unique IDs should be in the name cache.

In order to ensure the presence of these unique IDs in the node's ID Table, each entry of the ID Table (IDTE) has two kinds of reference counts according to the two categories of unique IDs.

16.3.3.2 Highly Concurrent ID-Table Consistency Management

Since an IDTE can have multiple replicas, it is important to maintain consistency among these replicas. Many approaches for concurrency control, such as global locking, transaction processing, and timestamp ordering, have been developed to maintain the consistency of replicated data objects, but they are not particularly suitable for ID Table management.

The consistency control mechanism of the replicated IDTEs takes advantage of the special structure and use of the ID Table; that is, the ID Table consists of structured entries (IDTEs), which are accessed independently. Each IDTE is a collection of fields, and an update of each field can be done incrementally and also independently; an update can be done by a sequence of insertion and deletion operations to each field.

The following primitives are provided for the IDTE management:

– ReadIDTE(*ID*, *field*)
  Return the contents of *DIR(ID).field*, which denotes the *field* in the IDTE for the specified *ID*.
– InsertItem(*ID*, *field*, *item*)
  Insert *item* in *DIR(ID).field*.
– Delete Item (*ID*, *field*, *item*)
  Delete *item* from *DIR (ID).field*.

Two update operations, *InsertItem* and *DeleteItem*, are commutative operations; that is, the final result produced by a sequence of these update operations does not depend on the order in which the operations are executed. Only in the case that two update operations are performed on the same item in the same field of the same IDTE, the execution order of the two update operations should be serialized.

This property makes it possible to design an update mechanism on replicated IDTEs with high concurrency and efficiency.

Read and update operations are directly done to the local replica of the ID Table. The system executes an update operation issued by a local user on the local replica and returns the control to the user immediately. The update operation is propagated later to other nodes holding a replica, with no need of synchronization. In order to allow updates to an IDTE even during an insertion of a new replica of the IDTE, we define the node which makes a new replica of an IDTE at another node to be the parent of the newly created replica. The node in which the parent resides has to keep on informing other replicas of the IDTE until all the other replicas come to know the newly created replica.

The access consistency is checked when the location information in an IDTE is used to locate the corresponding object. The algorithm guarantees the final consistent state of replicas of an IDTE when the update requests are executed at all nodes in the system and no new update is issued.

Compared with other concurrency and consistency control mechanisms which guarantee strict consistency among replicas of data, our approach has the following characteristics:

1. Neither global locking nor timestamp ordering is required.
2. Updating operations can be issued and executed with no need for synchronization of each other.
3. Accesses to directories are allowed even during an insertion of a new object replica or an IDTE replica, as well as during a deletion or an object replica or an IDTE replica.

The mechanism of GALAXY can survive both node failure and network failure. The correctness and applicability or the algorithm are discussed in [12].

16.3.3.3 Generation of Unique IDs

In order to guarantee the uniqueness of each unique ID, it consists of two fields: the *time stamp (TS)* field and the *node number (NN)* field. Each field consists of 8 bytes. The TS field contains the time stamp assigned to the unique ID by the node that has created the object. The NN field contains the number of the node where the unique ID is created.

The value of the TS field is created in the following way in order to guarantee the uniqueness of TS, even if the node operates as a stand-alone node, and even if it crashes and is restarted:

1. The value of the hardware timer is set to variable T.
2. The node's logical time which is stored in a particular location on the disk is set to variable S. For a diskless workstation, this location is allocated in the disk of a file server.
3. The logical time S is obtained by:

$$S = \max\{T, S\} + R$$

where R must be much larger than the interval time of storing S on the disk.

It may be observed that even if the unit of time for incrementing the TS field is 1 μs, the time period represented by the TS field is 2^{64} μs (3×10^5 years). Obviously, this time period is dominant over the lifetime of the system. Similarly, the NN field is long enough to assign unique numbers to all the nodes.

Since unique IDs consist of many bytes, it might degrade efficiency that both users and system programs always use system-wide unique IDs when accessing objects. For this reason, we define an eight-byte (two-word) short-format ID to make the local operation efficient. This short-format ID is effective in each local node. Short-format IDs are generated by using real-time time stamp. A short-format ID has a *remote bit* at the most-significant bit (MSB) of the higher word. The ID whose remote bit is zero indicates that the object is created in the local node and has not been migrated, and its (long) unique ID is obtained by concatenating the node number to the short-format ID. The ID whose remote bit is set indicates that the object has been migrated from a remote node, and its unique ID is given by translating the short-format ID with the table lookup. Each node maintains a table whose entry consists of a unique ID and the corresponding short-format ID. This table is only used for the latter case. The time stamp or a short-format ID represents the time the ID is generated. When a remote bit is zero, this time is equal to the time that the object is created.

16.4 Computation Model

16.4.1 Variable-Weight Processes

Concurrent computing is employed in various levels of computing systems. The operating system is traditionally the most important level providing concurrent computing facilities. As it is expected that concurrent computing is being diversified and is increasing in importance, the facilities provided by current operating systems are found to be no longer adequate. At least the following two factors are required to be solved for the enhancement of the present concurrent computing facilities:

1. Kernels or operating systems themselves to become too large, forming one mono- lithic structure. They must allow concurrent operations within themselves to provide higher modularity and faster response times.
2. Concurrent processing languages and concurrent processing applications require more efficient and flexible parallel computing capabilities.

Current solutions for these requirements are lightweight processes and coroutines. The common definition of the former is that a lightweight process is a process that shares an address space with other processes. They allow lightweight concurrency on single/multiple processor systems. However, they still have the following defici- encies:

a. The number of processes is limited to a small number.
b. Process creation and deletion require a fairly large overhead.
c. Process switching may cause a large overhead.

d. They are not adequate to support the fine grain of parallel processing required by various applications.
e. An application program cannot control scheduling and other aspects of processes.
f. It is difficult to distribute lightweight processes over different nodes of a distributed system.

Another solution, the coroutine, has long been used to provide pseudo-parallelism within and under the control of an application program. The number of coroutines can be fairly large, and their switching and space cost can be minimized because they are under the direct control of their application program. Coroutines, however, suffer the following deficiencies:

a. They do not provide true parallelism even if the system is equipped with sufficient processors.
b. A wait by one of the coroutines causes all coroutines to stop, because they run as a single process as far as the operating system is concerned.
c. Communications among coroutines are not as rich as communications among processes.
d. There is no mechanism to protect coroutines from each other, should such a need arise.
e. Coroutines cannot be distributed over different nodes of a distributed system.
f. Operating systems are not aware of and do not support coroutines.

As such, neither lightweight processes nor coroutines can provide adequate solutions for the needs of current and future parallel computing. Furthermore, at present, concurrent processing capabilities provided by operating systems, distributed systems, and language systems, are all isolated and are not under a uniform interface. This makes it difficult to write programs that contain various types of processes and interactions among them.

Ideally, operating systems should provide a variety of processes whose properties vary so as to meet a variety of needs of application programs, including operating systems themselves. For this purpose, we propose the notion of *variable-weight processes*. Variable-weight processes are a set of processes whose weight varies. *Weight* is defined as an amount of resources owned and accessed by a process. The amount of the resources is measured in two dimensions: space and time. From another perspective, weight is measured by absolute weight and relative weight. Absolute weight is evaluated by the absolute amount of resources. The relative weight is defined between a pair of processes. Variable-weight processes allow a program to use a suitable set of processes with different weights. Furthermore, a generic interface can be provided for suitable weights of processes to be chosen at loading time or even at run time

16.4.2 Executor/Domain Model

The process model of any operating system should meet the following requirements:

a. Allow flexible and efficient information sharing

b. Allow efficient process management, including context switching and process creation/deletion.

c. Allow user-defined scheduling so that users can tune the use of resources to their needs.

Conventional process models tend to emphasize (b), and often neglect or make light of requirements (a) and (c). GALAXY meets all three requirements by introducing the *executor/domain model.*

An executor is an active entity that either owns or has access rights to domains. A domain is a unit of information that is identifiable by name, and locatable. The set of domains either owned or accessed by an executor is called the executing domain of the executor. The set of domains common to two executors are those that are shared by these executors; this set is called the executing domain of the executor. Since the executing domain is arbitrarily defined for each executor, the shared domains can be very flexibly defined for a group of executors.

An executor itself is described by a data structure called an executor descriptor, which is also maintained in some domain. This descriptor allows for a very detailed description, such as which registers are used for the executor, where the stack is allocated, and so on. If desired, a user may elect to use a bare central processing unit (CPU) as the executor. Alternatively, a user may choose a fully equipped process, that is, a process that owns its address space and all other resources. This flexibility enables the minimization of overheads involved in process management operations such as context switching or process creation and deletion. Since executor descriptors themselves are maintained in a domain, it is quite straightforward to change the characteristics of executors.

Scheduling of executors is primarily a job of the kernel of the operating system, but in some cases, it is desirable to enable a user to write his or her own scheduler. GALAXY allows this in the light-weight process level. For the kernel-supported lightweight processes, most scheduling is performed by the user-supplied scheduler. The kernel supports only those operations that catch an interrupt signal, execution mode switching, and access control.

16.4.3 Microprocesses

16.4.3.1 Basic Ideas

There are two approaches taken in conventional operating systems to implement lightweight processes or threads: in-kernel implementation and out-of-kernel implementation.

In the in-kernel implementation, the kernel performs scheduling; therefore, parallelism and preemption are given by the kernel scheduler. A serious disadvantage of this approach is potential cost. A trap or system call is necessary to cross the user process/kernel protection boundary when the operations mentioned are executed. In addition, the kernel must maintain the management data in its virtual address space.

Coroutine packages are widely used as an out-of-kernel implementation of lightweight processes. Their advantages and disadvantages were discussed before. It requires extra cost to make a coroutine preemptive. For example, SunOS 4.0 and some other extensions of UNIX use coroutines as lightweight processes, and implement their preemptive capability by using the set-timer facility of the UNIX operating system. This approach degrades the efficiency because it requires system calls to generate the timer interrupts for switching coroutines. It is also very difficult to implement truly asynchronous event handling completely at the library level. SunOS 4.0 provides the asynchronous read facility by using the SIGIO signal, but it has a limitation that only one lightweight process can actually use a nonblocking read facility at a time, since signals cannot be delivered to individual lightweight processes.

GALAXY takes a hybrid approach for implementing lightweight activities. We call this implementation for lightweight activities *microprocesses*. Unlike conventional lightweight processes and coroutines, microprocesses have **all** of the following features:

1. Microprocesses are preemptive.
2. Multiple system calls can be issued within microprocesses.
3. A page fault or other traps caused by one microprocess should not stop the other microprocesses.
4. Microprocesses are migratable.
5. Microprocesses can run in parallel on multiprocessors.
6. Microprocesses can be used for real-time processing.
7. A user can control the scheduling of microprocesses in a flexible manner.
8. The above facilities are realized with low cost and are executed efficiently.

Although microprocesses are implemented as the user-level representation of an executor in our model, the mechanism itself can be integrated into kernel-supported thread/process mechanisms in conventional operating systems.

16.4.3.2 Mechanisms

Microprocesses are basically user-level activities in the following senses:

1. Their scheduling is directly controlled by a user program.
2. Their creation and deletion are processed at the user-program level.
3. Communication among microprocesses is processed at the user-program level.
4. The run-time contexts of microprocesses are maintained in the user program area (i.e., out of the kernel).

These properties of microprocesses enhance the flexibility and reduce the weight of activities. In addition, the kernel provides the following facilities to support microprocesses:

1. Efficient timer handling for supporting microprocess-level context switching and timeouts; microprocesses can be switched by the clock interrupts, and each microprocess can specify the timeout. This is necessary for realizing preemption and real-time processing efficiently at the microprocess level.
2. Reliable event handling for supporting microprocess-level exception handling and synchronization. This is necessary to allow each microprocess to issue a system call and handle the page fault and other kinds of traps.

As for the first facility, GALAXY supports lightweight system calls called *quick system calls* so that a user can manipulate the timer facility efficiently. Quick system calls differ from other kinds of system calls in the following respects: (a) they never cause an error during the execution in the kernel, and (b) their execution is never interrupted by other processes.

These reduce the overhead of executing a system call dramatically, because error handling and dispatcher invocation when returning from a system call are not required. In addition, to reduce the number of system calls, the kernel automatically sets the next time of the context switch for microprocesses every time the timer expires.

As for the second facility, the kernel only provides the facility to identify events for each microprocess. Each executor holds a list of the event structures, each of which corresponds to an asynchronous event affecting the executor. An event number in the event structure is used for identifying events. As a typical example, a microprocess identifier is used as an event number for each occurrence of blocking operation issued by a microprocess. The event number is given as a parameter of the event handler function so that it can notify the occurrence of the event to a microprocess.

16.4.3.3 Implementation of Servers

There are several methods to implement servers. The simplest method is to implement a server such as:

```
while (TRUE) {
  ReceiveAny (&pid, msg);
  do_it( );
}
```

In this method, the response time may be long if it takes much time to perform the requested service. One solution of this problem is to create a process for each service.

```
while (TRUE) {
  ReceiveAny (&pid, msg);
  if (Fork( )) {
    do_it( );
    /* NOT REACHED */
  }
}
```

This method is used for implementing various daemon processes in UNIX. The problem of this method is that it takes too much overhead for creating/deleting processes and it can require a large memory space because ForkProcess copies the address space of a parent process to create the child process.

A method that has been used in recent operating systems is to implement such a structure by using lightweight processes. In GALAXY, the most "lightweight" method can be used to implement a server by using microprocesses, or coroutines if not preemptive. In this case, each microprocess executes the request service. This method is useful when the operation includes block-type operations. In GALAXY, the most "lightweight" method has the following structure:

```
/* declare the interrupt handler */
   CatchEvent(E_IPC, handler);
/* coroutine i */
   ...
   If (AsyncSend(pid, msg, eventno) != OK)
      coroutine_sched(eventno);
   ...
/* coroutine scheduler */
coroutine_sched(eventno)
int   eventno;
{
   «store the coroutine environment specified by eventno»
   if («no coroutines are executable (coroutine run queue is empty)»)
      ReceiveAny(ID, msg);
   «switch to the next executable coroutine»
}
/* interrupt handler */
handler(eventno)
int   eventno;
{
   «enqueue the coroutine eventno into the coroutine run queue»
}
```

The coroutine scheduler is also invoked when a coroutine completes its work.

16.5 Global Process Management

Global process management is indispensable to network-transparent distributed processing. This is implemented by the mechanism of *process migration.*

16.5.1 Process Migration

Process migration involves the movement and reallocation of processes dynamically among the nodes in a distributed system to improve system performance. With the rapid increase of the communication speed of networks and the processing speed of processors, the total overhead incurred in process migration has been reduced considerably. Process migration has a wide range of objectives and is desirable in a distributed system for the following reasons:

1. Reducing average response time of processes
2. Higher maximum throughput
3. Higher throughput
4. Speed-up of individual jobs

5. Efficient usage of hardware and software resources
6. Reducing the number of replicas of objects
7. Improving system reliability
8. Improving system availability
9. Improving system security

Process migration involves two steps: the selection of a process and a destination node, and the actual transfer of the selected process to the destination node. The first is known as the problem of process migration policy, and the latter is taken care of by the process migration mechanism.

16.5.2 Policies of Process Migration

The problem of process migration policies is especially important for the objectives of reducing the average response time and increasing the (maximum) throughput. Load balancing is an important technique to achieve these objectives. Static load balancing is to balance the stationary load of each node by using the job arrival rate and the service rate. It is possible to obtain the mathematical solution or imagine the total system behavior under particular conditions. On the other hand, actual systems change their state dynamically. Dynamic load balancing based on each stage of system behavior is required for better load balancing.

Our analysis [13] shows that dynamic load balancing gives rise to a significant reduction in the response time even after stationary load balancing is achieved. The upper limit of performance with stationary load balancing is given by the performance of the model in which each node has its own queue, and the length of each queue is balanced. (We assume that each node has the same service rate.) On the other hand, the upper limit of performance with dynamic load balancing is given by the performance of the model in which there is a single queue in the system, and all the processes are put in this queue. We also reveal that very precise load information is a key for this significant performance improvement, by using the Markov chain model where each state is defined by the number of processes in each node.

16.5.3 Mechanism of Process Migration

Migration of a process involves the transfer of the following types of information from source node to destination node:

1. State of the process which consists of the contents of registers, scheduling information, input/output (I/O) states (request queues, data buffers, etc.), access control information, etc.
2. Address space of the process

Out of the two items, the cost of migrating a process is dominated by the time taken to transfer its address space. Hence, an efficient mechanism for transferring the address space is necessary. The existing distributed operating systems that support process migration use one of the following three methods used for the transfer of address space during process migration:

1. *Freezing*—in this method, the execution of a process is stopped while its address space is being migrated. This method is used by DEMOS/MP [11] and LOCUS [9]. The problem of this method is that a process may be stopped for a long time for the transfer of its whole address space.
2. *Pretransfer*—in this method, the address space is copied from the source node to the destination node while the process is still running on the source node. This method is used by V System [14]. Although the pretransfer reduces the time during which a process is stopped, it may increase the total time for migration, since pages that repeatedly become dirty during the pretransfer may have to be transferred several times.
3. *Transfer-on-Reference*—in this method, the address space is copied after the process begins execution on the destination node. When a page is referenced by the process, it is copied from the source node. This method is used by Accent [15]. Although this method also reduces the time during which a process is stopped, it may result in a large communication overhead if most of the pages need to be transferred one-by-one on a demand basis.

GALAXY takes an intermediate approach in that the switching of execution is done in the middle of the address space transmission. It is based on the following principles:

1. Those pages that have a very high probability of being referenced in the near future are not pretransferred because they may be immediately accessed and modified. These pages are identified by the concept of a working set. They are transferred with the process' state; during this time, the process is frozen.
2. Those pages that have a reasonably high probability of being referenced in the · future are pretransferred. The pretransfer operation is done only for one round for pages resident in memory. Some pages that become dirty during the pre-transfer operation are transferred with the process' state.
3. Other pages are post-transferred. That is, the remaining pages are transferred after the process has started its execution on the destination node. The pages of the migrated process which were not pretransferred are gradually post-transferred or transferred on demand, namely, when the reference of the page causes a fault on the destination node.

Note that post-transfer is different from transfer-on-reference, and is basically done to avoid the problem of residual dependencies on the source node. Post-transfer of pages with a low probability of access is also better than pretransfer of all pages, in that the execution of the migrated process can be started immediately. Moreover, post-transfer decreases the possibility of redundant transfer of pages.

GALAXY also provides an effective mechanism to minimize the cost of transferring the address space. It first checks whether the destination node has the same executable image; if so, it omits the transfer. This check is easy because every object has a system-wide unique ID and the process' address space is backed by any kinds of storage objects in GALAXY. Such a mechanism is also used for implementing the migration of lightweight processes in which coprocesses share the address space.

Another important issue in process migration is the management of the transient state. In GALAXY, there are two major situations:

1. Process migration takes place during the execution of kernel calls.
2. A message is sent to a process being migrated; before it receives the message it is migrated to the destination node.

A simple method to avoid the first situation is to inhibit process migration during the processing of kernel calls. As for the second, the problem is solved by the object-locating mechanism based on unique IDs. This problem is treated as a more general object-locating problem: an object migrates from node A to another node B after a process in node N issues an access request and before node A accepts it. One solution for this problem is that taken by V System: node A returns a negative reply to node N, which indicates that a message reaching node A late is not delivered. This solution degrades the transparency and can cause a situation in which the same sequence of operations is repeated until the object is finally located, if the process migrates successively during short intervals. To avoid such a situation, a link is maintained from node A to node B, so node N's request is directly forwarded from node A to node B. The purpose of using links in our method for keeping track of an object's location is different from that of the chaining mechanism used in DEMOS/MP as discussed before. This chaining information is deleted, when all the IDTEs are updated and this is notified to node A. Note also that, unlike DEMOS/MP, the failure of a node having information about the link will not affect the accessibility of any object except those on the failed node.

16.6 Uniform Address Space

For high-level users, GALAXY appears to be a collection of autonomous objects which communicate with each other by message passing. The common naming, locating, and access mechanism to every type of object at every node in the network gives the transparent uniform object space view.

On the other hand, "processors with a shared memory" is the presently most common and familiar computation model for programmers. Information access by load/store instruction instead of I/O operation or message passing is efficient and easier to program, as in shared memory among processes and memory-mapped files.

Therefore, GALAXY also provides a view of a contiguous information (address) space, called the uniform address space view [16], which is realized by the mechanism of network-wide virtual memory. This view is also network-transparent to user programs.

All objects in the system, each or which has its private address space, form a system-wide uniform address space. The address is defined by a pair (UniqueID, address in an object).

The uniform address space is manipulated by some operations described below. Each process takes in some portion of the uniform address space to its process' address space by these operations. After that, any portion of any object can be directly accessed by normal memory access instructions. The process itself is also an object. Its address space can be viewed as a subspace of the uniform address space. In usual single level storage, a process' address space and storages belong to different levels. Although shared memory-mapped files can be used as shared memory, this brings some restrictions. In GALAXY, both the process' address space and storage objects (extension of files and virtual memory objects) can be manipulated equivalently.

16.6.1 Basic Primitives

GALAXY provides a uniform address space and copy/unify mechanism which can not only integrate the object space view and address space view, but also provide information-sharing mechanisms between portions of the uniform address space.

Unification is the operation which makes two areas in the uniform address space logically identical for a load/store operation on the address space. For example, shared memory and memory-mapped files are simulated by unifying process-to-process and file-to-process, respectively. It provides a more flexible, efficient, and unified interface.

The following list is a rough sketch or basic primitives for storage management which provide a uniform interface to storage objects and processes:

- Copy(*SrcObject, SrcAddress, DstObject, DstAddress, Npages, options*)
  The data contained at the position *SrcAddress* in the object *SrcObject* are copied to the position *DstAddress* in the object *DstObject*. The amount of data to be copied is specified by *NPages* in page. The Copy primitive is implemented by copy-on-write for the copy within a local node, and by copy-on-reference for the copy across the node boundaries.
- Unify(*SrcObject, SrcAddress, DstObject, DstAddress, Npages, options*)
  The area specified by *SrcAddress* and *SrcObject* is unified to the area specified by *DstAddress* and *DstObject*. After the unification, they have the same contents, and the data written to one area can be accessed from the other. An object (or part of it) can be unified to many objects. For implementation reasons, the unification cannot be recursive, although it can be nested. Therefore, the unification yields a tree-structured relation among objects. The unification is implemented by physical sharing within a local node. It can also simulate a network-wide shared memory with remote nodes.
- Split(*Object* 1, *Address* 1, *Object* 2, NPages, *options*)
  Two objects *Object* 1 and *Object* 2 which have already been unified are split. The source area may be a part of an object; in this case the source is specified by the position *Address* 1 in *Object* 1 and the length specified by *NPages*.

Primitives for synchronization are also provided.

16.7 Data Replication

16.7.1 Static Replicas and Dynamic Replicas

Data replication has been implemented in recent operating systems. The purposes of replicating data are summarized as follows:

1. To enhance reliability and availability (fault tolerance)
2. To increase performance and parallelism—replication dynamically changes. The number and location or replicas are dynamically determined.

For the purposes of reliability and availability, the number and location of replicas may be statically determined. However, in order to improve the system performance, it is necessary that data allocation is done dynamically and automatically by the system. In addition, it should be noted that replicating a whole set of data can be needless or even harmful, due to the locality of data access. GALAXY provides a new replication mechanism which allows the creation of a dynamic partial replica of a file, which we call a *dynamic replica* [17]. A dynamic replica initially contains no data and is created page by page on an on-demand basis.

16.7.2 Automatic Dynamic Replication

It is desirable that file allocation is done dynamically and automatically by the system itself. Unfortunately, when multiple copies of files are allowed, deciding on an optimal file allocation is computationally difficult. Still, caching or temporal replication of remote files in local memory spaces can be very useful for improving performance.

We consider a mechanism called *Dynamic Replica (DR)*, which is a partial copy of a file dynamically generated at a node requesting file accesses. A *DR* initially contains no data and is created page by page on an on-demand basis.

As this implies, a remote file access causes a requested page to be fetched to the primary storage of the requesting node, and then an actual access is made, no matter whether *DR* exists or not, unlike a remote query to a database. Like a cache, the fetched page remains at the node, which is available for later accesses. Unlike a cache, a *DR* is a global object of the system which exists beyond the lifetime of a process, and can be shared among processes and nodes.

The whole *DR* itself, as well as each page in the *DR*, is dynamically created on demand. The condition to create a *DR* of an object is obtained from the rate of read and write access to the object, the distance from the original (static) replica of the object, and the rate of access to the DR when it is created. Each node can decide whether to create a *DR* or not, independently and autonomically. *DR*s appear and disappear in nodes with their size being increased and decreased dynamically according to the alteration of access.

Although this demand-replicating algorithm does not guarantee a global optimum, it is simple and efficient. More importantly, decisions are made locally, disregarding other replicas or the global structure.

16.7.3 Consistency of Replicated Data

When the system holds multiple replicas of data, the system should maintain their consistency. A simple way is a write-all, read-any policy which is effective when the rate of reading is much higher than that of writing. Weighted voting is a more generalized policy to guarantee that the latest version of the object is always accessed.

Another method to keep consistency of *DR*s when the pages in static replicas are updated is simply invalidating the corresponding pages in the *DR*, instead of updating them. The invalidated pages are fetched again with the new value from a static replica when they are accessed. When a *DR* is updated, static replicas are updated and other *DR*s are invalidated through the static replicas. So, *DR*s do not have to know other *DR*s.

Consistency with concurrent access, such as transaction-oriented concurrency control and instruction-level coherency control, is a different problem from this replica control. The cache validation problem should be considered also in shared remote access to nonreplicated objects. Although global two-phase locking is a reliable method, if the constraints on concurrency can be relaxed, performance can be improved.

16.8 Object-Based Environment and Object Groups

16.8.1 Object Model in GALAXY

GALAXY provides a multi-user, object-based interface on the process-based operating system structure. In this environment, hardware/software system components such as files, devices, processes, etc., are defined as objects. Conceptually, at the user level, objects can be viewed as active entities which are instances of abstract data types and act upon each other by means of invoking actions associated with individual entities; an action is invoked by sending an explicit message to another object.

In our object model, there are two kinds of objects: *primitive objects* and *user-defined objects (UDOs)*. A user can define new types of active objects as UDOs. A UDO consists of one or more component objects and an activating process. A component object is either a primitive object or a UDO. The activating process has control of component objects and executes the requested operations. The appearance of activity of objects at the user level is an illusion created by the efforts of activating processes.

A UDO is managed by a manager that is defined for the object type by users, but its locating is executed by the system-defined UDO manager. The UDO manager accepts the object-to-object communication primitives, and invokes the ID manager to get the IDTE which contains the type of the object. If the destination object is a primitive object, the request to perform the operation is issued to an appropriate system-defined object manager. If the destination object is a UDO, the UDO manager locates the node at which the object manager for the object resides. Unlike in primitive objects, the IDTE of UDOs contains the ID of the object manager.

16.8.2 Object Groups

It is often useful to be able to view some set of correlated objects as a logical entity and perform operations on this entity. Such a group of objects can be constructed based on various relations among objects. GALAXY provides the mechanism of object grouping called *object groups* [18], which realizes integrated object processing and management in a distributed environment, providing a consistent and uniform interface independent of any physical aspects of objects. Object groups are implemented on an object-based environment of GALAXY. However, we believe that the mechanism of object groups can also be applied to many other object-based or object-oriented distributed/nondistributed systems.

16.8.2.1 Basic Functions and Applications

Group communication
Group communication is one of the most important functions of object groups. There are two primitives for group communication:

1. SendGroup(*GroupID, Message, Method*)
   Send *Message* to members of the object group specified by *GroupID*. *Method* specifies the communication method for the send operation. It can specify a *k*-reliable, buffered/unbuffered, and synchronous/asynchronous group communication method. We define a group operation to be *k*-reliable if at least *k* members of the group are guaranteed to have had the operation performed on them.
2. ReceiveGroup(*GroupID, MessageList, Filter, Method*)
   Receive any number of messages stored in *MessageList* from members of the object group specified by *GroupID*. *Method* specifies the communication method for the receive operation. *Filter* is a function provided to examine each incoming message, keeping only those that meet certain predefined conditions.

The function of group communication is applied to active objects such as processes. All-reliable and synchronous communication is useful for controlling a group of objects. One can suspend, resume, or terminate all the active objects that run in parallel. 1-reliable or *k*-reliable operations are especially useful for implementing servers. 0-reliable, asynchronous operations are used to broadcast a message that is not so important to member objects; the message broadcast by this operation is lost if not received immediately by a receiving object.

Group access control
An object group may have an access control list associated with it, just like non-group objects. Access control is applicable to a group of both active objects and passive objects.

Group resource management
Object groups provide the mechanisms for allocating resources to and managing resources among the member objects of a group. They are also used as a unit of migration, replication, etc.

Generic group operations
Generic group operations include creation and deletion of a group; union, intersection, and set-difference of any two groups; and join and remove of members. These operations can be specified by generic primitives that can be applied to any

type of object. This simplifies both the code that uses the grouping facilities, and the system interface.

Group hierarchies
Every object may belong to one or more object groups. Group hierarchies are defined based on the inclusive relations among groups. They are useful for implementing hierarchical servers and hierarchical resource management.

16.8.2.2 Implementation in GALAXY

An object group is also an object of GALAXY and has a unique ID. The locating of an object group can be processed by the locating mechanism just as for any other type of object. The IDTE of an object group has the group bit on, which indicates an object group of the type specified in the IDTE. The group bit allows the system to distinguish efficiently between an object group and a non-group object.

The data maintained for object groups comprise: (1) a list of its members, (2) information about group hierarchies, (3) message buffer, and (4) resource utilization information, etc.

A *group manager* manages the object groups by using this information; it executes group operations, collects the information about resource utilization, and maintains the membership and hierarchy of object groups. The membership information (group ID, member object ID) pair is maintained by each object manager to make it possible to obtain the unique IDs of groups to which the member objects belong.

Object groups have many interesting issues such as ordered groups, programming interface, replication of object groups, optimization for hardware multicasting, lightweight implementation for system use, and so on.

16.9 Organization of the GALAXY Distributed Operating System

One of the most important issues in designing the structure of a distributing operating system is the size of a replicated kernel in each network node, all of which cooperate to provide network-transparent facilities. In a large kernel approach, services are provided more efficiently than in the case where they are offered outside the kernel. However, this approach reduces the overall flexibility and configurability of the resulting operating system. This approach is taken by LOCUS [9], Sprite [4], and so. Another approach is a small kernel approach, in which the majority of services are executed by separate servers. They are usually implemented as processes and can be programmed separately. A small kernel provides the process scheduling, interprocess communication, and other basic sets of primitive operations. One extreme of this approach is that all the servers outside the kernel are designed to be location independent. This approach accomplishes the maximum flexibility, but it degrades efficiency. In V System [3], each node has replicas of local servers as well as distributed kernels. For the sake of efficiency, the local servers are implemented as procedures in the kernel program, but they can be invoked by a

User Level	User Programs	·Applications ·Command Interpreter ·Utilities ·Libraries
	User Management	·User Agent ·User Management
	Object Group	·Group Manager
	Object-Oriented Interface	·Class Manager ·UDO Manager
	External Name	·Name Server
	Servers	·Object Servers
Network Level	Network-Wide Object Management	·Data-Flow Manager (II) ·File Manager (II) ·Process Manager (II)
	Network-Wide Address Space	·Storage Manager (II)
	Resource Management	·Resource Manager
Local Virtual Level	Data-Flow Management	·Data-Flow Manager
	Object Management	·File Manager ·Process Manager ·Storage Manager
	ID Management	·ID Manager
	Network Management	·Network Manager
Physical Level	Page I/O	·Pager
	Secondary Space Management	·Secondary Space Manager
	Device Management	·Device Drivers
Non-Process Level	Nucleus	·Process Handler ·Message Handler ·Main Memory Handler
	Kernel	·Process Scheduler ·Interrupt Handler

FIG. 16.3. System organization of GALAXY

user-process using the standard interprocess communication facility. In addition, the kernel provides a uniform interface to the facility for interprocess communication, both in a local node and across node boundaries. The higher-level servers are implemented by location-independent processes.

Our approach is similar to that of V System, but its design is more structured. Figure 16.3 shows the organization of GALAXY. There are four levels: Non-process level, Physical level, Network level, and User level, each of which consists of several further layers.

The Non-process level consists of the Kernel layer and the Nucleus layer. The kernel catches, interrupts, saves and restores registers, and performs the low-level process scheduling. The Nucleus modules execute basic interprocess communication, process handling, and memory management. They are implemented as procedures in the kernel.

The Physical level consists of the Device Management layer, the Secondary Space Management layer, and the Page I/O layer. The Device Management layer is composed of device drivers. The Secondary Space Management layer implements file structures on various types of storage devices. Several modules in this level are implemented by lightweight processes that share the same address space. The programs in the Non-process level and the Physical level run in privileged mode.

The Local Virtual level performs the local object management. The ID Manager of this level realizes the location-independent access to various types of objects. The Network level performs the network-wide object management. Network-wide virtual memory, object migration, object replication, etc., are realized in this level. Most modules in these two levels are implemented as processes that have separate address spaces.

The User level provides services such as object naming, user management, implementation of the object-based environment, etc. The modules in this level are implemented as distributed servers; they can be located at any node and their programs are location independent. Other modules under this level are implemented as local servers, but a user can invoke both categories of modules by using the same interprocess communication facility.

16.10 Conclusions

We have described the main features of the GALAXY distributed operating system. Figure 16.4 illustrates the relations among these and other features not described in this paper, such as data-flow management, key/lock access control, and several basic mechanisms for network communication, storage management, input/output, etc. All of these features are very important to achieve true network transparency in a large distributed system.

GALAXY is now under development in the Department of Information Science at the University of Tokyo, under the support of IBM Japan Ltd. The implementation of the prototype is now complete; it includes the process migration, network communication, lightweight processes, etc. We are currently conducting experiments to measure the performance of each system component.

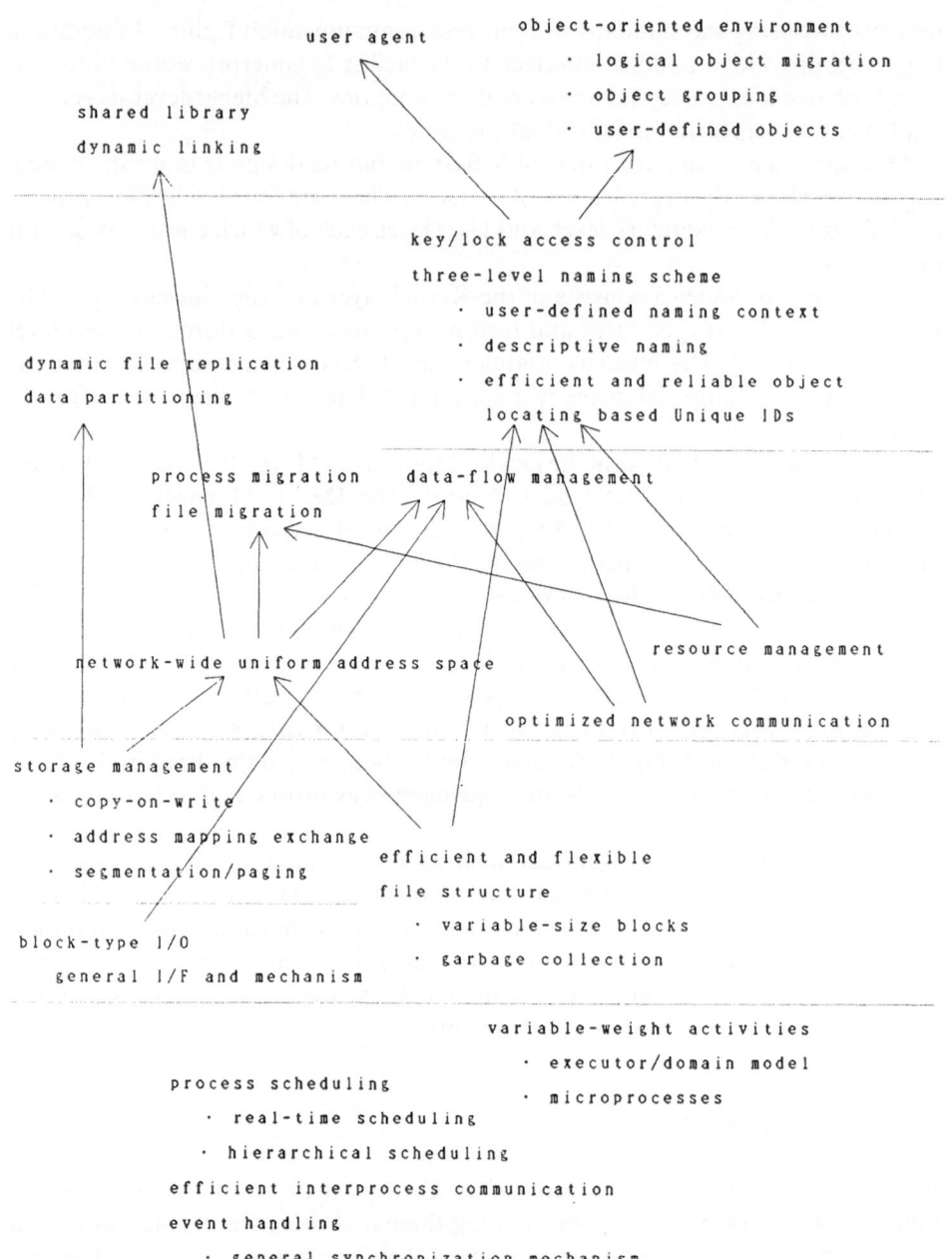

FIG. 16.4. Relations among the features of GALAXY. *I/O*, input-output; *IDs*, identification

References

1. Spector AZ, Kazar ML (1989) Uniting file systems. UNIX Review 7 (3): 61–71
2. Anderson DP, Ferarri D (1988) The DASH project: an overview. Technical Report, University of California, Berkeley
3. Cheriton DR (1988) The V distributed system. Commun ACM 31 (3): 314–333
4. Ousterhout JK, Chevenson A, Douglis F, Nelson M, Welch (1988) The Sprite network operating system. IEEE Trans Comput 21 (2): 23–36
5. Shimizu K, Maekawa M, Ashihara H (1989) Names and name resolution in distributed operating systems (in Japanese). Comput Software 6 (3): 19–34
6. Sinha P, Shimizu K, Maekawa M, Utsunomiya N (to be published) Network-transparent object naming and locating. J Inf Process
7. Sinha P, Shimizu K, Utsunomiya N, Maekawa M (to be published) A highly reliable and efficient object locating mechanism in GALAXY distributed operating system. IEEE Trans. Parallel Distributed Comput
8. Leach PJ, Levine PH, Douros BP, Hamilton JA, Nelson DL, Stumpf BL (1983) The architecture of an integrated local network. IEEE J Selected Areas Communication SAC-1 (5): 842–857
9. Popek GJ, Walker BJ (1985) The LOCUS distributed operating system architecture. Computer Systems Series, MIT Press
10. Keeffe D, Tomlinson GM, Wand IC, Wellings AJ (1985) PULSE: an Ada-based distributed operating system. Academic
11. Powell ML, Miller BP (1983) Process migration in DEMOS/MP. In: Proc 9th ACM SIGOPS Symp Operating Systems Principles, pp 110–119
12. Jia X, Nakano H, Shimizu K, Maekawa M (1990) Highly concurrent directory management in distributed systems. In: Proc 10th Int Conf Distributed Computing Systems, pp 416–423
13. Park K-S, Ashihara H, Shimizu K, Maekawa M (1990) Process migration policies in distributed operating systems (in Japanese) Trans Inf Process 31 (7):
14. Theimer MM, Lantz KA, Cheriton DR (1985) Preemptable remote execution facilities for the V-System. In: Proc 10th ACM Symp Operating Systems Principles, pp 2–12
15. Zayas ER (1987) Attacking the process migration bottleneck. In: Proc 11th ACM Symp Operating Systems Principles, pp 13–22
16. Ashihara H (1989) Data sharing in distributed systems. Master's thesis, Department of Information Science, University of Tokyo
17. Ashihara H, Shimizu K, Maekawa M, Hamano J (1987) File access improvements in distributed systems by on-demand replication of files. Technical Report, 87-26, Department of Information Science, University of Tokyo
18. Shimizu K, Maekawa M, Hamano J (1988) Hierarchical object groups in distributed operating systems. In: Proc 8th Int Conf Distributed Computing Systems, pp 18–24

17
A Multimedia Workstation, *Yougao*

Satoshi Abe, Koji Nakamura, Mamoru Maekawa, Yasuro Kawata, Kiyoshi Suzuki, Tateki Sano, Yu Gu, Kentaro Shimizu, Takashi Kato[1]

Summary: This paper describes the design and the implementation of the *Yougao* multimedia workstation. *Yougao* is designed to be object-oriented. It models the virtual work space using objects called "views" and "scenes." Using views and scenes which manage spaces hierarchically, surrealistic modeling is possible. *Yougao* has full-color high resolution graphic ability and a hi-fi sound board. High level graphic abilities such as arbitrary degrees of transparency, an abstract color model, and anti-aliasing are supported at the system level. Text is handled with a text manager which has sophisticated formatting abilities. All graphic and text objects can be transformed in various ways. Media representation is completely independent of the device, and all media can be integrated using a media interface description language called *R*.

Yougao also has a graphic-oriented human interface to manipulate objects located in the virtual space. The application is realized by defining new objects in the work space. The kinds of media that *Yougao* can handle are text, graphic, image, music, voice, animation, and video. *Yougao* is based on a distributed environment, and it allows the transfer of still images and video through networks, and these objects can be simultaneously displayed with other objects.

Key words: multimedia processing — human interface — media integration — view-scene model

17.1 Introduction

The human interface is one of the major areas that need to be revolutionized to make computers truly easy to use and useful. Based on this recognition, various developments have been made to improve human interfaces. One important development is an integration of various kinds of information representations and manipulations, known as *multimedia processing* [1, 2].

---

[1] Department of Information Science, University of Tokyo, Bunkyo-ku, Tokyo, 113 Japan

The *Yougao* multimedia workstation is an effort to advance the technology of multimedia processing. *Yougao* is divided into three major layers:

1. Media-handling layer: this layer provides basic functions to represent, manipulate, and transfer various kinds of information such as text, graphics, image, sound, and animation, which are called *media.*
2. Integration layer: this layer provides a uniform interface to integrate the basic functions provided in the media handling layer. This is given as a language, called the *R* language. The roles of the *R* language are threefold:
   a. to provide a means to manipulate various media,
   b. to provide a model of media information, and
   c. to provide a human-interface development environment.
3. Manipulation layer: this layer is a visual interface to the integration layer. This is useful because the *R* language is a textual language.

We first describe a model of media integration, the *view-scene model,* in Section 17.2; this model is the basis of multimedia processing in *Yougao.* Section 17.3 then describes the media handling layer. A separate description is given for each kind of medium. Section 17.4 is a short description of the manipulation layer. A description of the *R* language is not included due to the limitation of space. It is basically an object-oriented language with strong enhancements for media representation and handling. The manipulation layer itself is written in the *R* language. The *R* language will be reported elsewhere. Section 17.5 discusses issues in implementation. Section 17.6 concludes the paper.

17.2 View-Scene Model

17.2.1 Views and Scenes

Yougao provides a powerful means to lay out objects in a space. Users walk about in a virtual space, and place various kinds of objects freely in the space. They can scatter objects or they can put them in order. The virtual work space can be designed at will. Suppose the virtual work space is a study room. It is furnished with a desk, a table near the window, and a bookshelf on the wall. Out from the window, a pounding sea can be seen. Near the window lies a plant pot, vividly shining under the light from the lamp on the ceiling. On the wide work desk are some folders lying in an unorganized manner. Various sorts of documents necessary for work are in these folders. A drawing is hung on the wall, and next to it a clock is ticking the time. The wall of the opposite side can be a screen for video ...

Each media object itself too can have a certain spatial structure [3, 4]. For example, a desk is made up of a wide board on the top, a drawer, and usually four legs. A telephone has a handset and an operation panel; the operation panel has various switches on it. A clock consists of a clock face, an hour hand, a minute hand, and a second hand. A book is composed of pages. On each page, texts, figures, and photos are printed. A figure is a combination of a drawing and a caption, both of which are placed in a space.

As has been illustrated, the arrangement and allocation of objects in a space are a key concept in the multimedia environment.

Traditionally, most systems support only down to the level of windows, and icons, i.e., the level of the user's virtual work space. The arrangement of a user's real work space, such as the layout of figures in a document, or the arrangement of components in computer-aided design (CAD), is handled by the specific application programs. *Yougao* handles virtual and real work space in an integrated manner. The concept of views and scenes is introduced for this purpose. A view represents an object which is placed in a space, and a scene represents the space in which objects are placed.

A scene can be "mapped" onto a view, by which the structure of views and scenes is constructed. This structure can be dynamically changed. Figure 17.1 shows an example of the view-scene structure.

A screen is a physical display device such as a video screen. *Yougao* supports a multi-screen environment, i.e., a *Yougao* system can have more than one screen. For example, view1 is hanging under screen1. This means that view1 is displayed in screen1. Figure 17.2 (see p. 310) is a photo of screen1. Under view1 is hung scene1. Scene1 is usually called the root scene. Under scene1 are hung view11, view12, view13, etc. These are all objects placed in scene1.

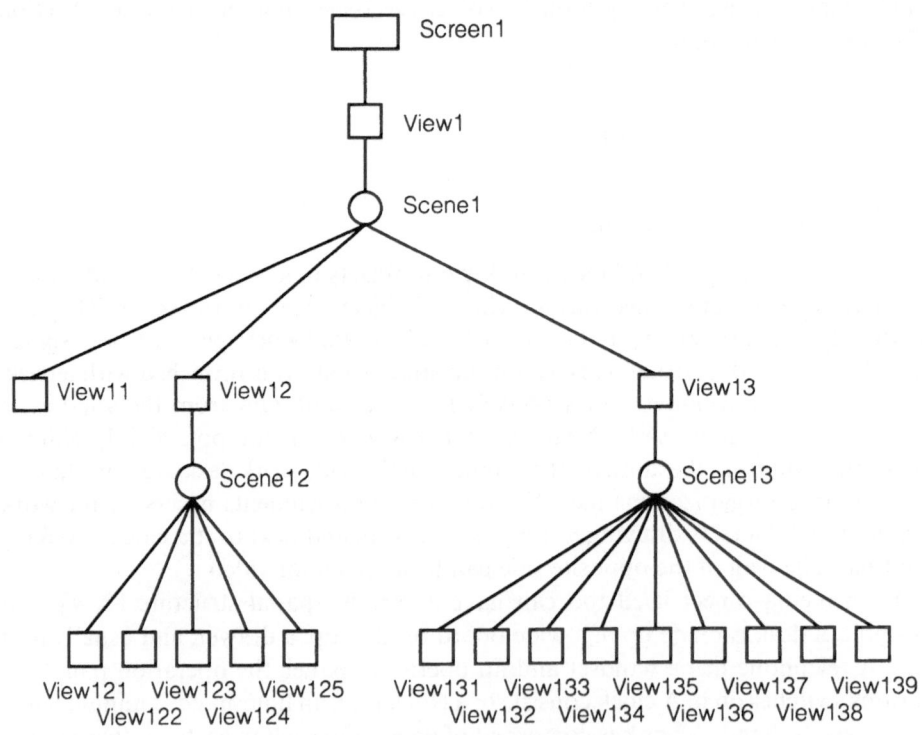

FIG. 17.1. View-scene structure

17.2.2 Views

In the view-scene structure, some views are leaves, and others are nodes. Among node views are: scene views, under which is hung a scene; filter views, under which is hung a view; and rendering views, under which is hung a model.

17.2.2.1 Leaf Views

A leaf view is the one at which the view-scene structure ends; an example is view11 in Fig. 17.1. Such a view has shape, color, transparency, etc., and therefore is "drawable." Views of this kind appear frequently. Examples of views of this kind are: decorations in a virtual work space, simple icons, and book leaves inserted between pages of a book. These leaf views decorate the screen.

17.2.2.2 Scene Views

A scene view is a view onto which a scene is mapped, such as view1 and view12 in Fig. 17.1. A scene view itself has shape, color, and transparency. The shape is the clipping boundary of the view under the scene; the color specifies the background color of the view; and the transparency is the transparency of the scene as a whole. The most understandable example of scene views is documents as stated before. For example, paper of a document can be defined as a scene view. The shape, color, and pattern of the scene view are those of the paper. Sentences, photos, pictures, etc. are arranged on the paper. This is represented by the view-scene structure in which the scene sentences, photos, pictures, etc., are arranged, is hung under the paper object, i.e. is "mapped" onto it.

Of course, the scene view is not always used to represent practical objects such as documents, but also used to map other virtual spaces onto. For example, a crystal ball through which a different scene can be seen, can also be modeled.

17.2.2.3 Rendering Views

A rendering view is a view which generates images out of a model. Interesting applications of rendering views would be: making scores out of a music description and plotting the graph of a wave out of signal data. View121 is a view which produces a pie chart out of a table (Fig. 17.3). Rendering views can be also used for media conversion to figures or images. For example, voice signals can be recognized and converted to characters by a rendering view; rendering of a three-dimensional (3D) graphics model is one application of rendering views in its literal sense. One characteristic of rendering views is that a rendering view references other objects, i.e., models. The reason why rendering views are thus distinguished from others will be explained later.

17.2.2.4 Filter Views

Sometimes it is necessary to display a view which already has shape after modifying it with various effects. In such cases, filter views are utilized. Why are they called "filter" views? It is because they do not affect the view-scene structure. The view

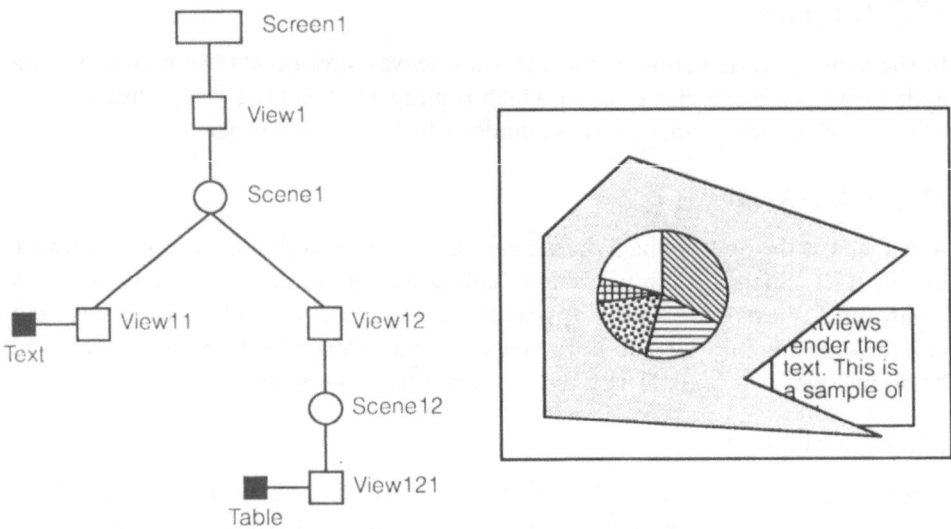

FIG. 17.3. Rendering views

under a filter view is transformed and displayed according to the function of the filter view. The functions of filter views are: geometric transformation, such as projective transformation; alteration of color attributes of pixels, such as hue, brightness, transparency, etc.; and spatial transformation, such as blurring, smoothing, and edge enhancing.

Filter views are attachable/detachable; without changing the original image, various kinds of filters can be attached and detached. Effective filters and frequently used ones are put into the library for easy utilization. The image itself and variable parameters for displaying it are thus clearly separated, which facilitates the building of more abstract systems.

Fig. 17.4 illustrates filter views.

17.2.3 Multiple Views

A model may be referenced by more than one view at the same time. These views are called multiple views. Multiple views allow more flexible view-scene structures.

Suppose there is a shape model of a 3D object. Four rendering views reference this model. These four rendering views produce pictures of an object seen from above, from the front, from the right, and from the right upper front. If the model of the object is altered, then this alteration is transferred to all these views and the four pictures are redrawn at the same time.

Another application is as follows: the model is a spreadsheet, and a pretty printed table and a bar graph reference it. If a value in the spreadsheet is changed, both the table and the graph are redrawn accordingly (Fig. 17.5).

Still another application would be editing of structured documents. The model of a structured document is referenced by two views. One view is an editing window

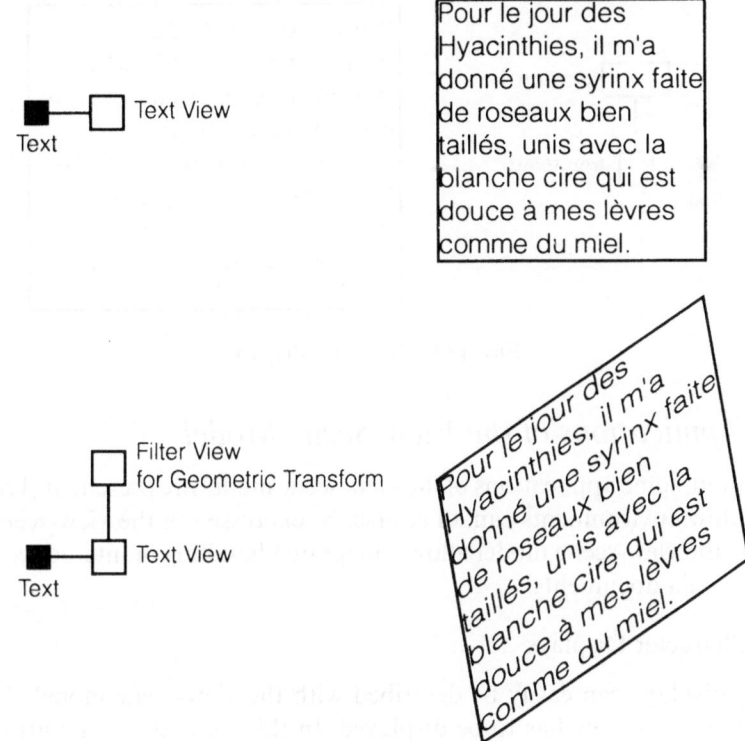

FIG. 17.4. Filter view

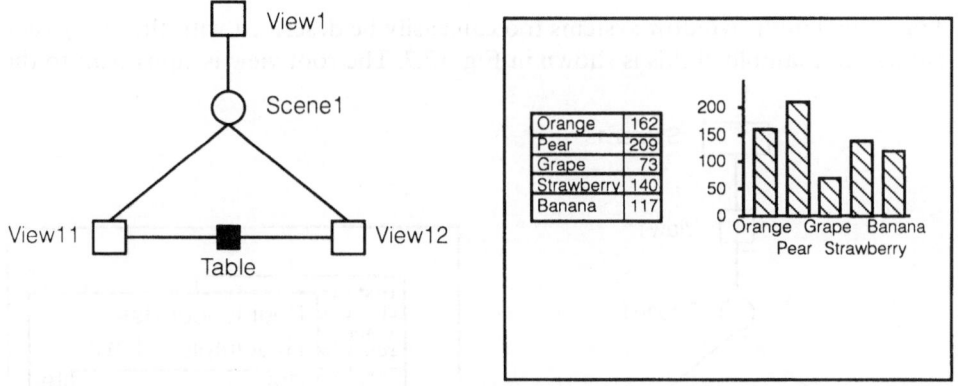

FIG. 17.5. Multiple views

of the description of the document in a language specifically designed for this purpose, and another view is a window to show the resulting output in the what-you-see-is-what-you-get (WYSIWYG) style. If the structure of the document is altered in the editing window, the change is reflected in the WYSIWYG window at the same. This will be a document layout system in which the structure can be edited while the final output is shown at the same time.

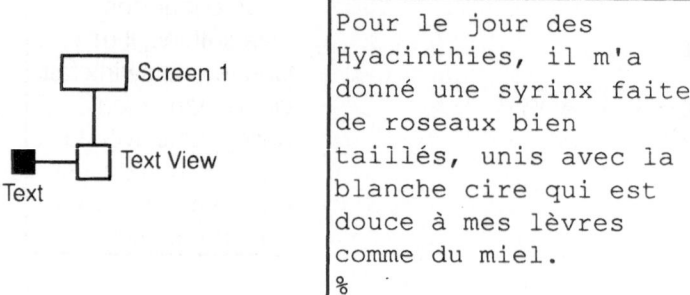

FIG. 17.6. Character display

17.2.4 Applications of the View-Scene Model

In this section, some applications of the view-scene model are presented. Traditional multi-window environments can, of course, be expressed in the view-scene model. Moreover, the view-scene model allows integrated handling of interactive graphics and multimedia documents.

17.2.4.1 Character Displays

Character displays can easily be described with the view-scene model. As in Fig. 17.6, only the root view has to be displayed. In this case, no spatial arrangement with scenes or with the view-scene structure is necessary at all.

17.2.4.2 Traditional Multi-Window Systems

Traditional multi-window systems too can easily be described with the view-scene model. An example of this is shown in Fig. 17.7. The root view is equivalent to the

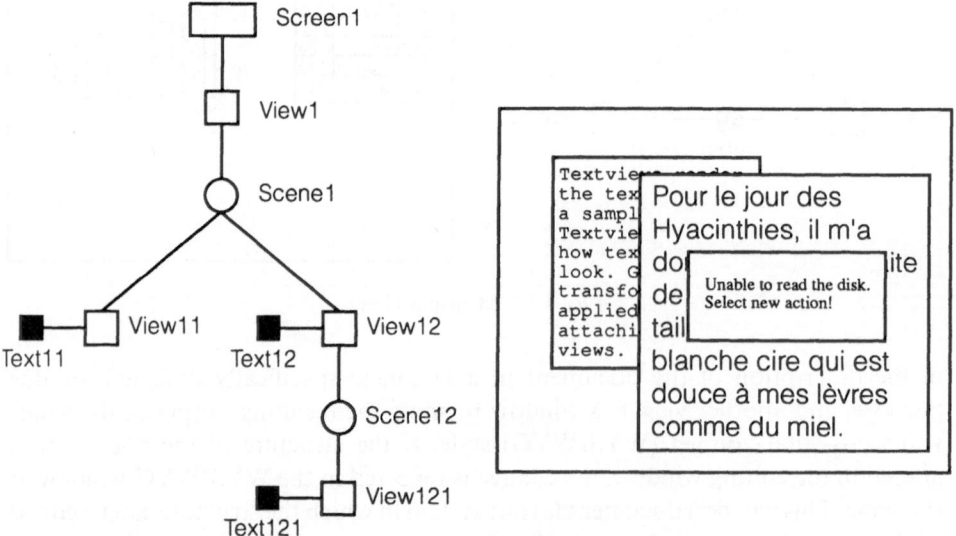

FIG. 17.7. Traditional multi-window system

"desk top" or the "work space" in the traditional window system. Onto this view is mapped the root scene. Each window in the desk top is defined as a view placed in the root scene. The shape of a view is arbitrary; it does not have to be a rectangle.

In some window systems, windows can have a structure. This structure can be represented by the most primitive view-scene structure of mapping of a scene to a view. For example, view12 in Fig. 17.7 is a scene view and hangs view121 underneath it. View12 corresponds to a parent window, and view121 corresponds to a child window.

17.2.4.3 Grouping

Grouping of elements plays an important role in modeling of complicated graphics objects, as in CAD. Grouping also can be expressed with the view-scene model. Fig. 17.8 shows an example.

Grouping is handling a set of objects as a unit. Multi-level grouping is pretty common. A group is similar to a window as to the structure, but they look different. A window has a fixed shape and is explicitly displayed so; a group has no fixed shape and is not displayed.

View11 in Fig. 17.8 has a quadrangular shape. Its children windows view131 and view132 are clipped according to the shape of the parent window view11. In contrast, view12 is not displayed and does not clip its children.

How is the shape of a scene view described? It is described as a completely transparent, and infinitely big, board. This allows the structuring of views without the scene view's existence being noticed.

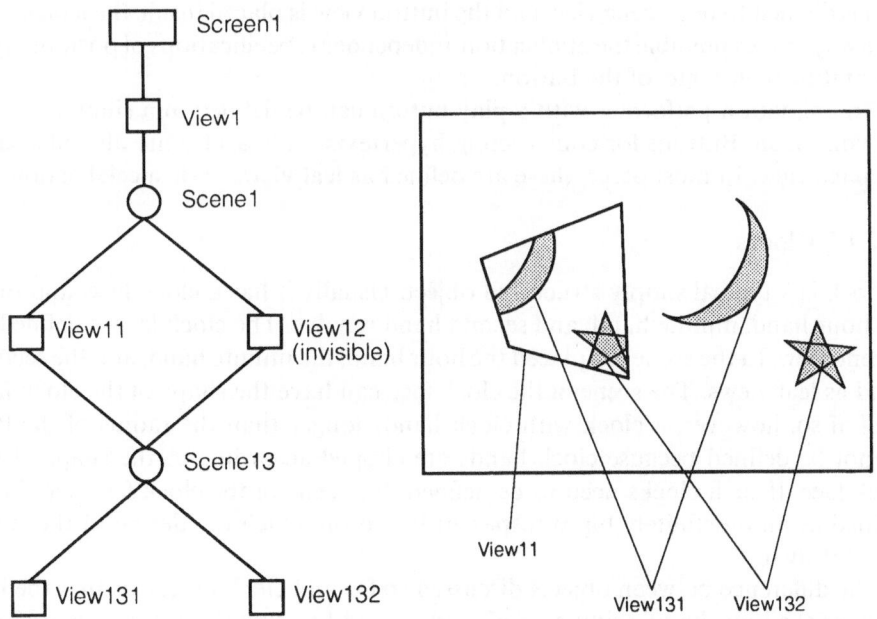

FIG. 17.8. Grouping

17.2.4.4 Multimedia Documents

A multimedia document is a collection of characters, images, figures, photos, voices, animations, icons, etc. Arrangement of these components can be represented in the view-scene model.

In the first place, a page is defined as a scene view. If more than one page exists, which is an ordinary case, the same number of scene views are defined. Only the page which is now displayed needs to be mapped to the view which represents the page. If a view of a page is defined and the scenes to be mapped onto it are switched, the pages of the document can be turned over one by one. Each view of sentences, figures, etc. is placed in the scene which is mapped to the page view.

Data of voices and music are invisible as they are, and therefore cannot be included in the view-scene structure. If they cannot be seen on the screen as well, their handling will be difficult; thus, they are symbolized by visible objects such as icons. Icons can be regarded as rendering views which reference music objects. They can be placed anywhere in multimedia documents, just as figures can.

There are various possible styles for telling *Yougao* to play the music data. In the simplest style, the music icon itself has a play button, and music is played by clicking on the button. To attach a button to a music icon, the designer has two choices, depending on whether he or she regards the icon and the button as two different objects or not. If they are considered a unit, the icon has to be able to know that the mouse button was clicked on it; then it has to know the local coordinates of the clicking point to see in which part the mouse button was clicked; and if the mouse cursor was on the button of the icon when the mouse button was clicked, it will play the music.

The other choice, i.e., defining the icon and the button as different objects may introduce a little more complexity, but it is better for modularization of objects. The icon is defined to be a scene view and the button view is placed inside the icon scene. This way makes possible the application-independent specifications of position, size, orientation, color, etc. of the button.

An animation performer with a play button can be defined in a similar way to the voice icon. Buttons for constructing hypertexts, sliders, etc., are also placed in the page view. In most cases, these are defined as leaf views with special actions.

17.2.4.5 Clocks

A clock is a typical simply structured object. Usually it has a clock face, and on it the hour hand, minute hand, and second hand revolve. The clock face is defined as a scene view. In the scene are placed the hour hand, the minute hand, and the second hand as leaf views. The scene of the clock face can have the shape of the clock face itself; if so, however, a clock with clock hands longer than the radius of the face cannot be defined because clock hands are clipped according to the shape of the clock face. If such clocks need to be defined, the scene of the clock face should be defined as an indefinitely big transparent board on which the design of the clock face is drawn.

The difference between objects discussed so far and clock objects is that the leaf views of the hour hand, minute hand, and second hand work on their own. Views can move freely in a scene. Various constraints can be enforced on the moves of views: mechanical constraints, constraints because of an electromagnetic field or gravity field, or semantic constraints. All the clock hands are attached to an axis in the case of a clock, and this is an example of mechanical constraints. Such constraints are in the hands of the programmer who specifies actions of each view, and they are not expressed in the view-scene structure.

If a clock is regarded as an object which has depth, i.e., a three-dimensional object, the same strategy is taken. The clock face is defined to be a scene view, but this view is indefinitely big and is filled with transparent substance. Inside the scene revolve the clock hands.

17.2.4.6 Video Monitors

A video monitor is an object to display motion pictures on. Usually it is composed of a screen and an operation panel. The video monitor as a whole is defined as a scene view. The operation panel is also defined as a scene view and various kinds of switches and sliders are placed in it. Each switch or slider is then defined to be a leaf view with its specific actions.

17.2.5 Virtual Space

A three-dimensional work space mentioned earlier can be expressed in the view-scene model. The room itself is a scene view, and inside it various furniture is placed as child views.

As for the user, it would be natural to define a user as a view because the person is in the scene, just as the views of the clock and the desk in the room are, and moves around. In the view-scene structure, however, how a scene is shown is specified by the parent view of the scene. Thus, from within a scene, the scene cannot be seen.

To solve this problem, another view is introduced. This view is a virtual camera whose position, angle, and scope are specified, and is called the "camera view." The parent view of the scene is linked to the camera view so that the scene is rendered according to the view field of the camera view. Then, if the camera view moves, the way the scene is shown is changed; thus, the user is represented by the camera view. Such a one-to-one link between a camera view and a scene view is called a view point link.

View point links can be dynamically connected and disconnected. The scene view can have more than one camera view. If a camera view represents "myself" and another represents "another person," then "myself" can see "another person," just as "myself" can see other objects in the scene.

A camera view has an arbitrary shape. It can be transparent and therefore invisible.

17.2.6 Structural Operations in the View-Scene Model

A view-scene structure can be dynamically changed. Some operations are presented here.

17.2.6.1 Transformation

Views can be transformed in two ways. One way to transform a view is to apply a filter view on top of it in the view-scene structure. The other way is to make use of a "transformation matrix." Most views have a 3 * 3 (in two-dimensional transformation) or 4 * 4 (in three-dimensional transformation) matrix called a transformation matrix. A transformation matrix specifies the type of projective transformation

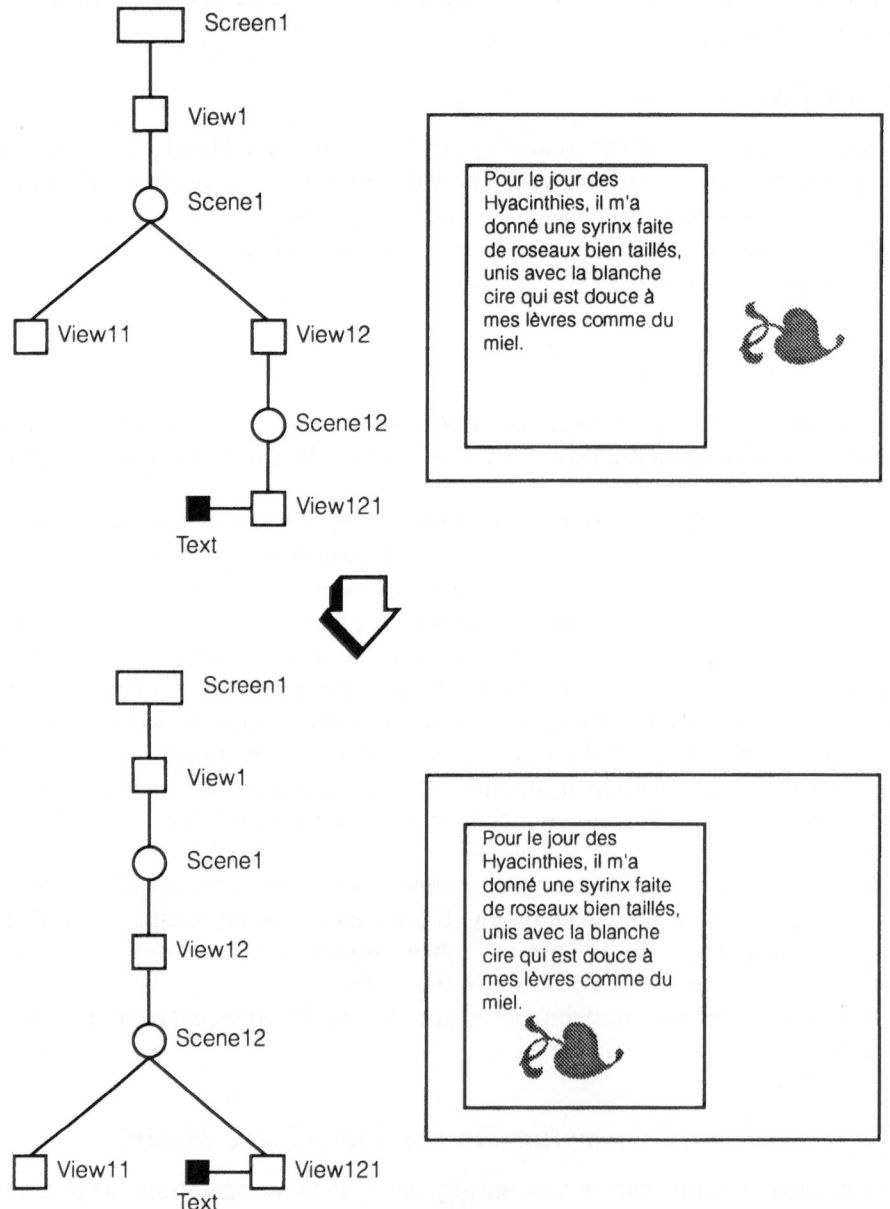

FIG. 17.9. Posting

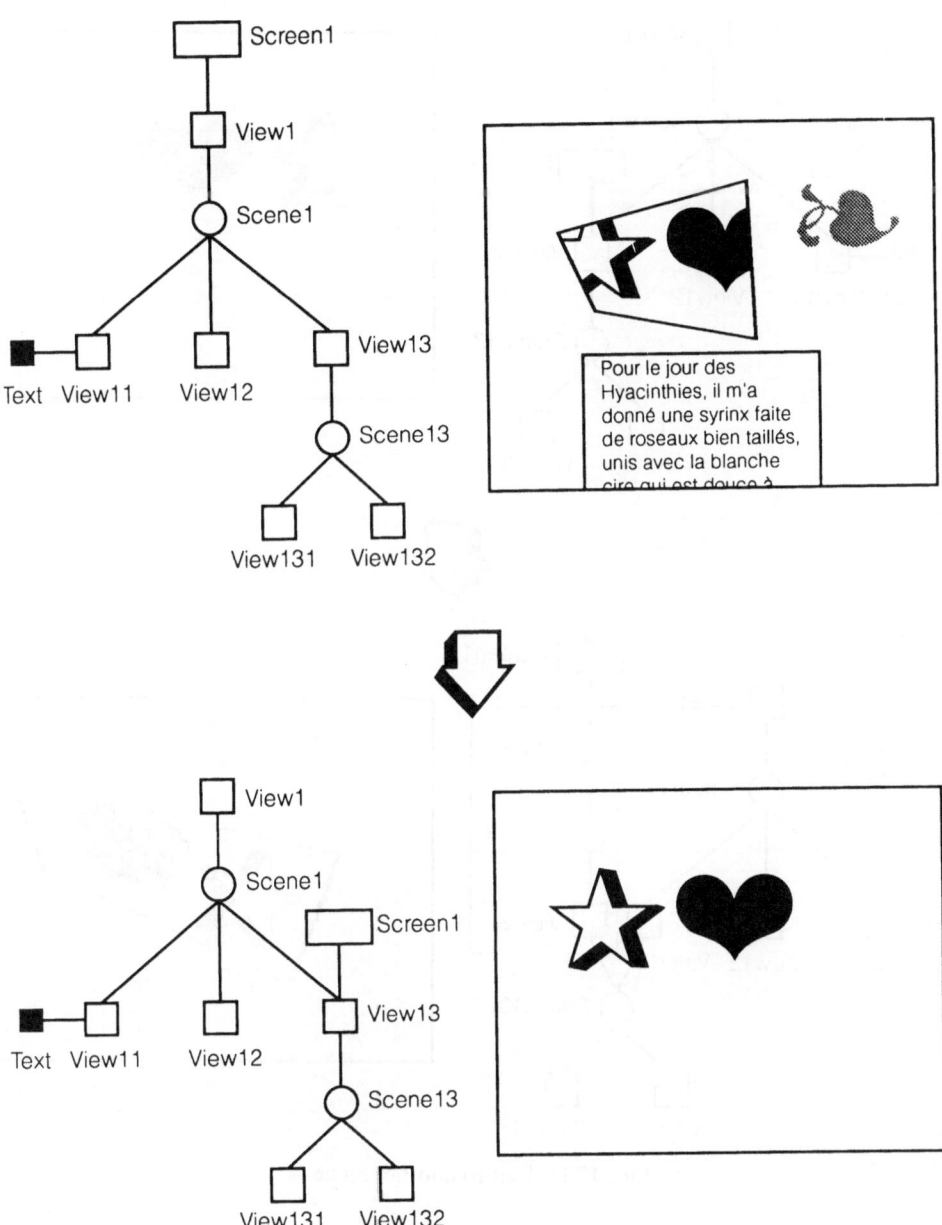

FIG. 17.10. Entry

which is applied on the shape of the view. A view can be scaled, rotated, slanted, skewed, and distorted only by changing its own transformation matrix. In such cases, filter views are not necessary.

17.2.6.2 Duplication

A view can be duplicated in three ways: static duplication, multiple views, and dynamic duplication or *cloning*.

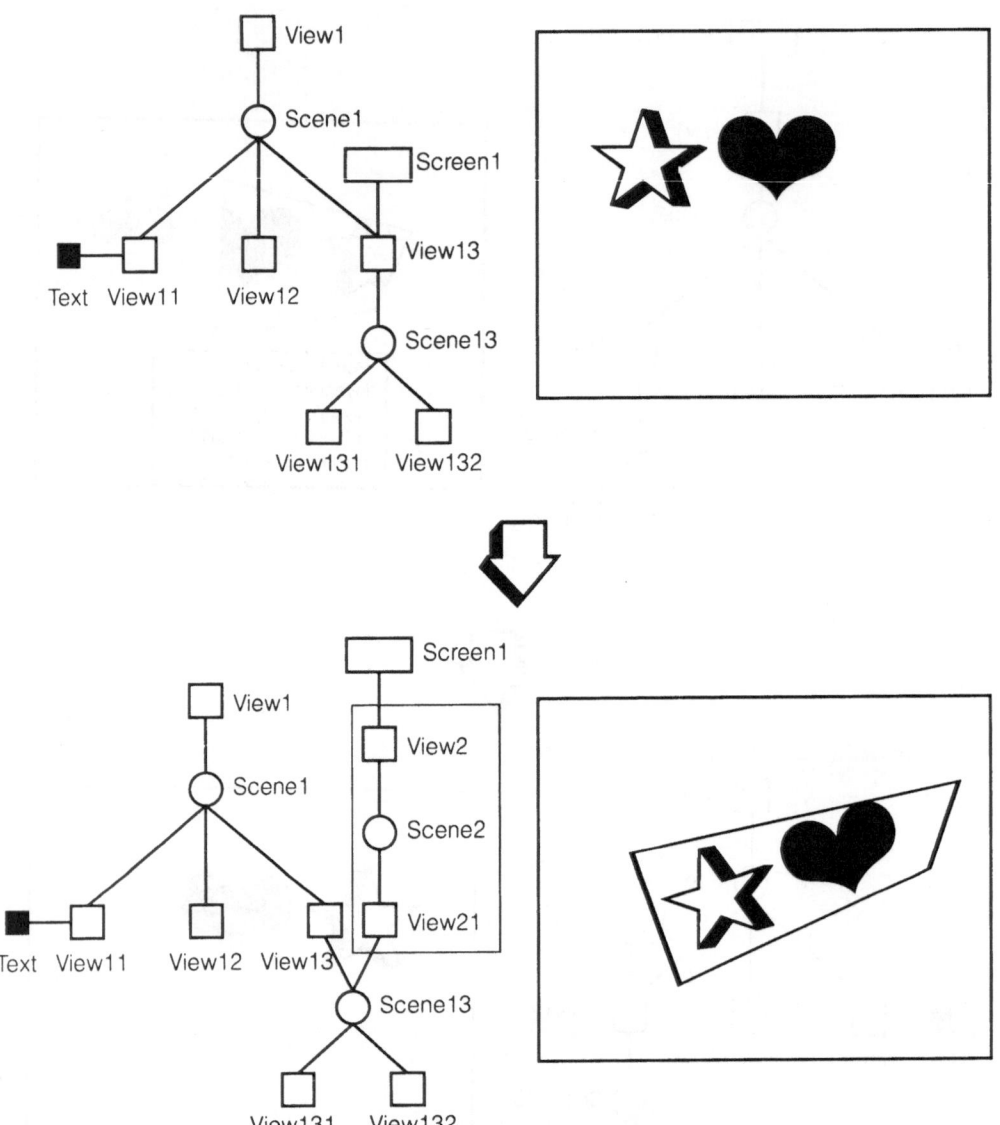

FIG. 17.11. Exit to another scene

Firstly, a view can be statically copied to another totally different object. Each of the original and the duplicate has its own state and the states of the two are the same at the time of duplication. The state of one is not affected by that of the other. Thus, after the duplication, they act as completely different objects, and in the course of time, they may come to have different shapes as well as view points or transformation matrices.

Secondly, multiple views are possible. This is realized by defining another view referring to the same model. The original view and the new one may have different definitions, such as the way to render the model; they are different views, but they refer to the same object. Examples of this kind of duplication are two rendering views referring to the same three dimensional models, one of which renders the model in the wire-frame while the other does ray-tracing. Transformation of one view has no effect on another view. When the model is modified through a view, the change is reflected on all the views referring to the same model.

The third way is *cloning*. A clone is a dynamic copy of an object; they share instance variables. They are treated as two different entities. Changes to one view affect the other view immediately.

17.2.6.3 Posting

Posting is one of the most basic operations of the view-scene structure. It is to move a view on one level to another level in the structure. Suppose a letter and a picture are in the same scene. In order to paste the picture to the letter, the picture must change its level; it has to move into the scene which the letter defines. This "paste" operation is a typical example of posting. If the picture is to be taken off the letter, it can be done also by posting. In this case, the picture moves to the higher level.

Posting is often combined with duplication. Fig. 17.9 shows an example.

17.2.6.4 Entry and Exit

Users can enter a lower scene. This is achieved by moving the screen (Fig. 17.10) to the lower level. The view to which the screen n sticks is called "screen n's current view." Similarly, the scene hanging to screen n's current view is called "screen n's current scene."

There are two ways to exit from the scene. One is to simply change the screen's level, which is the opposite operation of the entry operation. The other is to add a new view-scene-view structure on the top of the current scene and then to move the screen to the new top-view (Fig. 17.11).

17.3 Media Handling

17.3.1 Two-Dimensional Graphics

17.3.1.1 Graphic Objects

Two basic graphic representations are supported in *Yougao*: shape representation and image representation. Users have the choice of the stencil-paint model, path model, and graph model for composing shapes. Composite shapes are converted to a collection of primitive two dimensional shapes such as rectangles or circles. The shape representation including primitives is device-independent. When a renderer actually draws the shape in the frame memory, this shape representation is no longer device-independent.

The image representation is an array of sampled pixels. An image itself can be clipped to have an arbitrary shape using a transparency specification as a mask. The image representation also has device-independency. Image renderers apply interpolation and anti-aliasing in order to get fine pictures. They always refer to the original image even when they transform the image extremely.

17.3.1.2 Color Model

Yougao supports full-color graphics. Unlike other traditional systems, it can deal with several color models such as hue saturation value (HSV), hue value chroma (HVC), and National TV Standards Committee (YIQ), besides the red, green, and blue (RGB) model. Most graphics systems have three planes for red, green, and blue values; however, *Yougao* has a number of planes (the number of planes depends on implementation) called "abstract planes." Pictures are drawn in the abstract planes. The color values in the abstract planes are interpreted in the final stage when they are written in the physical frame memory by a color converter. The color converter converts the abstract values to physical values appropriate for the specific hardware (normally RGB values).

Abstract planes also allow the use of another parameter for brightness. Normally, a pixel value written in the frame memory represents the relative voltage of the Cathode-ray tube (CRT). Human eyes are, however, known to perceive brightness in the log scale. *Yougao* allows the use of log-scaled brightness.

Color is also device-independent. In reality, however, 8-bit deep color values are frequently used by convention and because of the ease of use.

17.3.1.3 Transparency

Another characteristic of *Yougao*'s graphics is that graphical elements can have an arbitrary degree of transparency. This is realized by the "alpha value" which shows how opaque the pixel should be. The alpha value is defined as follows:

$$Ip = Ib + \text{alpha}(If - Ib), \qquad 0 \leqq \text{alpha} \leqq 1$$

where Ib, If, and Ip represent the intensity of the background, the foreground, and the output, respectively. Notice that normally the pixel intensity is not linear to the pixel value to be written in the frame memory.

Thus, objects can be overlapped with anti-aliasing so images can be synthesized more naturally. Figure 17.12 shows how to define each pixel color. The concept of half-transparency can be expanded to define operations between the image to be overlaid and the image to be underlaid.

For example, a magnifier can be defined as a simple graphic object. Whenever a magnifier is placed in the screen, the underlaid screen image is magnified. No operations are required to the underlaid objects. It is interesting because of the simplicity of the magnifier; it is defined as a static object.

17.3.2 Texts

In *Yougao*, texts are not considered as simple sequences of characters; texts may have a structure. For example, chapters, sections, or floating blocks can be expressed in this structure. The structure may also include formatting information, such as

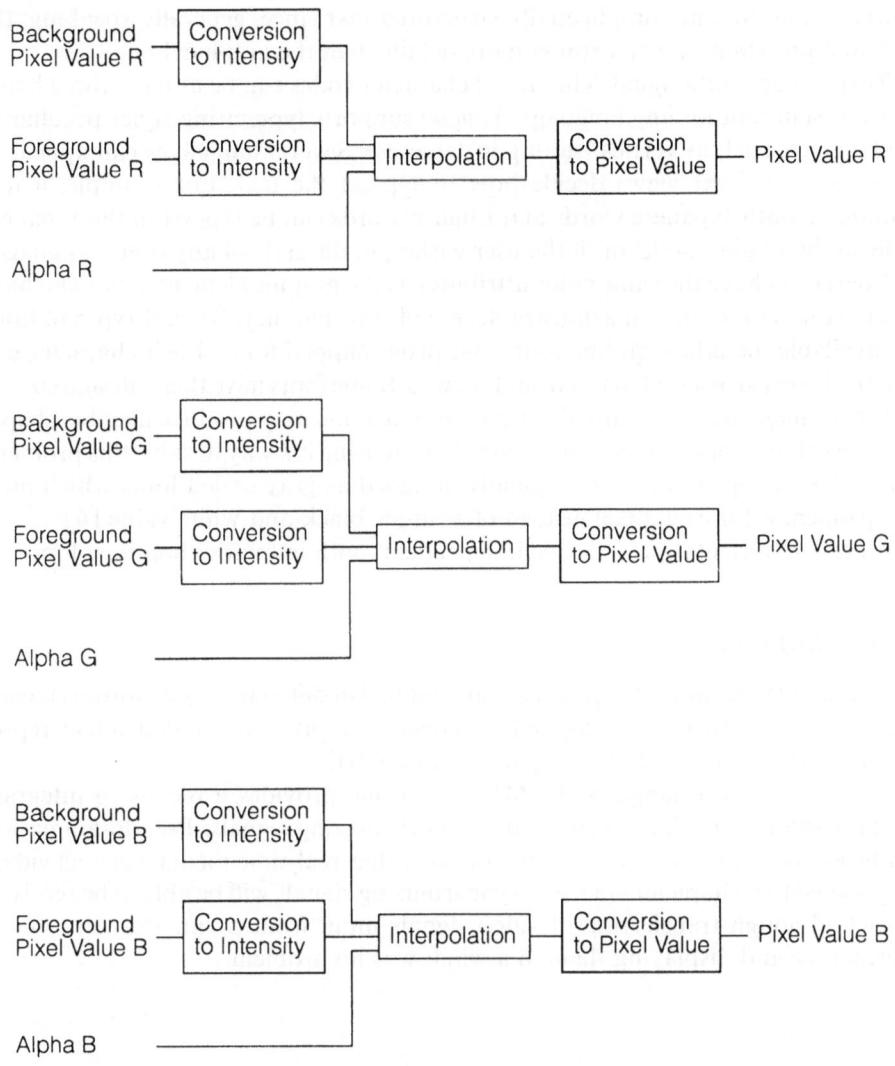

FIG. 17.12. Definition of pixel color

which blocks to emphasize, or whether to apply special character spacing; however, text has no visual form itself. It is the special rendering view called "text view" that determines how to show the text. The text view decides which font to use for each block, determines how to emphasize the block, provides document metrics such as margins and line pitches, etc. This separation of text and format makes abstraction of text possible [5].

Multiple views can be applied to a single text object and it can be edited in several ways at the same time. For example, one text view shows the textual representation of the text, say, in a mark-up language, and another text view shows the WYSIWYG-style image of the whole document containing the same text. It is a powerful way to edit complicatedly structured text since, generally speaking, the textual representation can express more details than the graphical one.

Text can be multilingual. The size of character codes can be at most three bytes, which is sufficient for any language. *Yougao* supports typesetting styles peculiar to the language such as vertical setting in Japanese. Several languages can appear in the same text. Text views decide how to typeset the text. For example, a text containing both Japanese words and English words can be typeset in the Japanese style, in the English style, or, if the user wishes, in the style of any other language.

Characters have the same color attributes as the graphic elements; they can have an arbitrary color, and an arbitrary degree of transparency. Several types of fonts are available including outline fonts and pixel-mapped fonts. Each character can be flexibly scaled, rotated, slanted, and skewed. Some fonts have their "design size."

When small characters are displayed, outline fonts may produce illegible shapes because of the errors of scan-conversion. Anti-aliasing is a way to solve this problem. Some pixel-mapped fonts are originally designed as gray-scaled fonts which have an opaqueness for each pixel instead of a simple black-and-white value [6].

All text representation is device independent, both in metrics and in colors.

17.3.3 Sounds

Music, sampled sound, and speech are all handled in different ways; moreover, each can be either synthetic or analytic [7]. *Yougao* adopts device-independent representation of sound, whether it is synthetic or analytic.

The music macro language (MML) of *Yougao* provides a means to integrate sound with other media; it can produce synchronizing signals. Pseudo-animation can be easily achieved by this. In the future, other real-time media, such as video, are planned to be implemented, and synchronizing signals will be able to be received as well, although transferring of video signals input from a video camera and a microphone and displaying them in a window is no problem.

17.3.3.1 Music

Synthetic music is represented on two different levels. On the higher level, music itself is described in scores, MML, or a standard musical instrument digital interface (MIDI) file. On the lower level, notes in the music are described by the wave form and the intensity of the wave, or *envelope*. Sounds are synthesized in various ways: additive synthesis, subtractive synthesis, frequency modulation (FM) synthesis, etc. In additive synthesis, sine waves are simply added. Subtractive synthesis is frequently adopted by commercial music synthesizers; in subtractive synthesis, some of the harmonic overtones of a sound are cut. Each of the three kinds of synthesis is, of course, device-independent because of its nature.

Analytic sound representation is pulse code modulation (PCM) sampling data. Usually a note is considered to be a unit datum. *Yougao* adopts the MIDI Sample Dump Standard for the sake of device-independency.

A note is used as a primitive component in MML. Notes in synthetic representation and notes in analytic representation can be mixed.

Yougao fully supports MIDI. MIDI signals for output are obtained by converting the music description in MML. In this case, note data can be either simply ignored (instead, external sound sources are used); partially used, i.e., only envelope data are used; or made use of fully, by sending them to sound sources on the MIDI Sample Data Standard.

Yougao can produce sounds on its own without the help of MIDI musical instruments. In such a case, note representation is put through a digital-to-analog converter after sampling, if necessary. To maintain quality of sound, sound is anti-aliased. When the MIDI Sample Dump Standard is adopted, if notes in synthetic representation are sampled, or the sampling rate is changed to that of the receiver of the data, sound is also anti-aliased.

17.3.3.2 Voice and Speech

Currently only sampled voice can be handled. Recognition of human speech remains as a future implementation issue in *Yougao*.

17.4 Operations

The screen of the prototype of *Yougao* is shown in Fig. 17.13. Usually such a screen is called a "desk top," but in *Yougao*'s case, it is called a "wall face" Objects are allocated on the screen by the "post" operation onto the "wall" or another object. When compared with a "desk top," "wall face" faithfully reflects the physical fact that the display screen is usually upright. Even when the model of objects is enhanced to three dimensions in the future, "wall face" can easily accommodate it, while "desk top" cannot as it is, i.e., being raised by 90°. *Yougao* supports projective transformation, and therefore users, if they want, can use a "desk top," which cannot be even seen because it is perpendicular to the screen, by raising it by arbitrary degrees.

Almost all the operations to the "wall face" are given via a mouse. Standard operations of a mouse are: move (of the mouse), press, release, click (of the mouse button), and drag (move while pressing a mouse button). They are not enough in number for the necessary operations; therefore, on existing window systems, function keys on the keyboard such as the shift key are also used. This combination of a key on the keyboard and the mouse operations is against the intuition towards mice and thus unnatural.

Yougao, for this reason, does not use function keys for mouse operations. Instead, more kinds of operations are achieved by the combination of operations on more than one mouse button, especially press and click. For example, an object is opened when the left button is pressed and right button is clicked at the same time. Currently, the mouse of *Yougao* has two buttons, but mice with a different number of buttons can also be used.

The following are primitive operations and how they can be invoked from a mouse. Here, the use of the two-button mouse is assumed:

1. *Menu operations*: clicking right button. A menu is displayed and then the user selects an appropriate command from the menu. Usually menus include commands which can also be invoked without the help of a menu, such as the open command.
2. *Open/close (/metamorphose) operations*: clicking the right button while pressing the left button. The selected object is opened from an iconified state, or the other way round. Generally, an object has two states: iconified state and opened state (usual state). The shape on the screen and available operations differ from one state to the other. This open/close operation is to switch between these two states.

    The number of possible states of an object, which is usually two, is defined within the definition of the object, and the system does not assume objects always have two states. Therefore, some objects may have only one state, and others may have more than two states. In the latter case, states may be changed cyclically by this operation.
3. *Move operation*: pressing the right button. The bounding box of the object on which the mouse cursor is, is shown. Then the user drags it to the desired place, and releases the button. Objects can be moved only within the scene.
4. *Post operation*: clicking the left button while pressing the right button. As in the move operation, the bounding box of the object on which the mouse cursor is, is shown, and the user drags it to the desired position. If the user, however, does not release the right button and clicks the left button after dragging the object to the desired place, the moved object is posted to the object or scene on which the mouse cursor was at that time. This operation is provided to move objects between scenes.

    The post operation, however, is also used in a different connotation. When an operational object such as an editor or a magnifier, which represents an operation rather than an entity, is posted to another object, it means that the operation of the operational object is applied to the object on which the operational object is posted (Figs. 17.14, 17.15).
5. *Select operation*: clicking the left button. The selected object can be "edited" from then on. "Editing" means text editing such as inserting characters from the keyboard if the selected object is a text object, or graphics editing such as drawing a picture if the selected object is a graphics object.

    The difference between the post operation and the select operation is that the post operation declares which editor to use, just like opening a file in a multi-file editor on a traditional operating system, while the select operation really starts editing. In most cases, if an operational object is posted to another object, the latter is selected at the same time. If the selected object is an operational object, the shape of the mouse cursor changes, and then the user can have the same effect with the post operation by selecting the object to which he or she wants to apply the operation.

In this section, the operations of *Yougao* were described. The most fundamental operation in *Yougao* is the post operation. Mouse operations do not use function keys on the keyboard because it is against ordinary intuition towards mice. Instead, combinations of mouse button operations are introduced to provide more kinds of

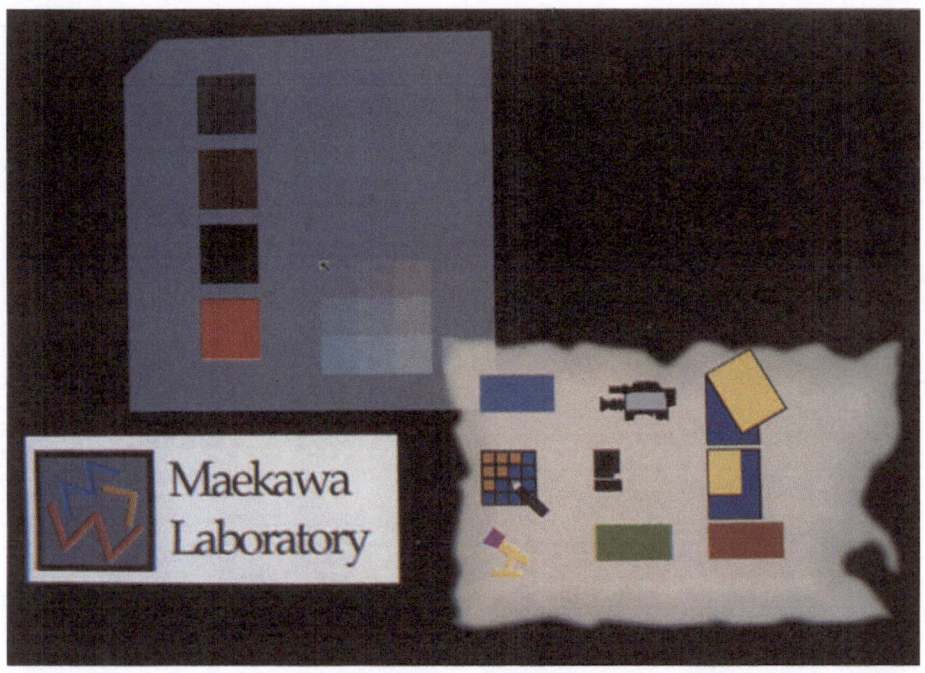

Fig. 17.2. Photo of screen 1

Fig. 17.13. Screen of the prototype of *Yougao*

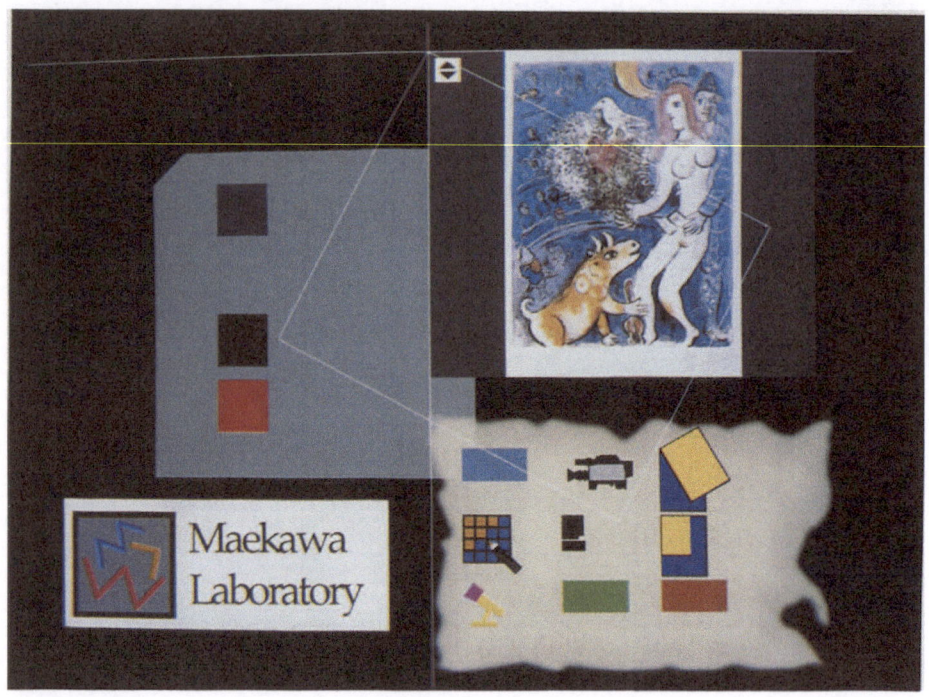

FIG. 17.14. Rotating a picture by posting *Rotator*

FIG. 17.15. The picture rotated

mouse operations. How to do short cuts of menu-driven operations and those of operational objects remains to be studied. The operations discussed so far are the default ones, but a totally different operation environment can be constructed because almost all the operations are programmable.

17.5 Implementation

17.5.1 Hardware Configurations

Yougao's hardware consists of two major components: the Image Communication Processor (ICP) and Image Display Processor (IDP).

ICP is a multi-processor unit for such communications as motion pictures between *Yougaos* through public telephone lines or ISDN lines. ICP compresses image data on a real-time basis, and sends the data to another ICP on another *Yougao*. The ICP which received compressed image data decompresses it also on a real time basis.

IDP is a multi-processor system. As CPUs, transputers of Inmos and TMS34010s, or Graphic System Processors (GSPs) of Texas Instruments are used. Currently, the *Yougao* prototype has six transputers and two GSPs. Each processor is linked to a bus called the G Bus. Besides the G Bus, transputers can communicate with one another by the transputer's standard Inmos Link. Each GSP is controlled by a respective transputer.

As to the memory of IDP, each processor has its local memory of 1–4 Mbytes; moreover, 32 Mbytes of general-purpose shared memory and 16 Mbytes of frame memory (which can be expanded up to 128 Mbytes) are linked to the G Bus. Between the frame memory and CPUs are the G Bus and a local bus to access exclusively the frame memory, which can accelerate frame memory access.

Dedicated hardware for raster processing is linked to these kinds of memory by the H Bus, a high-speed ring-structured bus. This raster-processing hardware includes: video output devices, video input devices (A/D), raster operation ALUs, multi-window controllers, etc. Currently, only video input/output (I/O) devices are linked.

IDP has various kinds of I/O interfaces necessary for multimedia processing, such as: video I/O, sound I/O; connectors for mice, keyboards, scanners, CD-ROMs, MO Disks, etc; and digital I/O of standard I/O ports such as SCSI, GPIB, DMA, RS232C (these are connected to the G Bus or I/O Bus exclusively for I/O).

For output of pictures, standard signals of NTSC, PAL, and Hi-Vision (High-Definition Television or HDTV standard in Japan) standards other than standard high-resolution signals for ordinary workstations, can be switched by software. The input port and the output port of video signals in IDP are linked to the H Bus separately, and video data is transferred as digital raster images. This makes the use of different standards for input and output possible.

As to sound I/O, sound or voice can be inputted and outputted by PCM through a microphone and a speaker directly connected to IDP. IDP also has a MIDI interface.

Currently, IDP supports such devices as mice, keyboards, and scanners. Of course, printers can be connected to IDP easily; however, those with sufficiently good colors, gradations, resolutions, etc., for multimedia processing are not widespread yet, and to what degree low-quality printers should be supported remains to be studied.

IDP is usually connected to a host computer and is used as an intelligent multimedia terminal. IDP and the host computer usually communicate with each other by the Inmos Link and DMA channel. For secondary storage, IDP has an internal hard disk, and supplementary disks can be added through interfaces such as SCSI. Thus, the burden on the host computer is minimized.

As seen so far, *Yougao* has many kinds of multimedia interfaces as its standard interfaces. Other interfaces can be added by connecting them to the G Bus or H Bus.

17.5.2 Software Organization

Yougao is an *R* language machine. Every piece of software inside *Yougao* is described in the *R* language, as in the Smalltalk environment. The *R* language is a concurrent object-oriented language. It not only has features of ordinary object-oriented languages, but also has powerful primitives for multimedia handling. Actions of objects are described in the *R* language in principle, but in actual use most of the operations can be achieved through direct manipulation, as in the NeXT system, and therefore the users usually do not have to write scripts in the *R* language.

The run-time environment of the *R* language, especially for multimedia handling, can be roughly divided into three levels: user interface managers, media drivers, and device drivers.

User-interface drivers play the main role in the human interface. Currently they consist of an event manager and a space manager. The space manager controls visual output such as display or print-out following the view-scene model. The event manager controls input from users for manipulation of objects.

Media drivers handle processings specific to each media. They also help the space manager and the event manager do their work when necessary. These media drivers can be classified into two kinds: output media drivers and input media drivers.

Output media drivers pass the outputs from the space manager and the sound driver, to the relevant devices. Input media drivers make events from inputs of the user.

There are the following five strategies to implement the managers, drivers, and other special functions in the *R* language:

1. Define them as ordinary objects in the *R* language. This is the most flexible way, though it is hard to obtain high performance.
2. Make them *pseudo-object*. Pseudo-objects are such that look like ordinary objects but are actually implemented in a low-level language such as the machine language, or by dedicated hardware. They run fast but the overhead of a remote procedure call (RPC) cannot be avoided, just as is the case with ordinary objects. Even when a new manager is made or an existing manager is modified, pseudo-objects do not have to be compiled again. Also, changes in the actual implementation of a pseudo-object do not affect other objects at all. Pseudo-objects can be prototyped using Strategy 1.

3. Make them a group of functions in an object, with specific names. Such an implementation can be found in (a) read/write in Pascal or in (b) the special form in Lisp. When function calls are actually executed as in (a), they can be defined in the super class by way of the *R* language's inheritance mechanism. This looks similar to Strategy 2 but the overhead of an RPC does not arise. If realized as in (b), higher performance can be expected, but if the implementation of such a function is altered, all the objects calling it have to be recompiled.

4. Embed them in the language structure. When the logical structure can be clearly stated, this way eases a programmer's burden because logical inconsistency in the use can be detected to a certain degree at the stage of parsing.

5. Make them "principles" which may not apparently appear in source codes. For example, if a principle that 'deadlock should be detected and recovered' is strictly obeyed, it looks as though there existed a deadlock manager.

Of course, if Strategies 4 or 5 are employed, frequent modifications of structures should be avoided because they require reprogramming.

In *Yougao*'s case, a manager or a driver adopts a combination of more than one of the strategies listed. *Dogra* (Section 17.5.4) and *Temali* adopt Strategy 3 as do the primitives of Display Postscript [Sun News]. The space manager adopts Strategies 3, 4, and 5. The event manager adopts 2, 4, and 5 because events inherently come asynchronously from outside of the object.

17.5.3 Space Manager

The primary role of the space manager is to manage the views and scenes. It has the following three major functions:

1. Managing the view-scene structure
   Views and scenes are represented in the large single table named space allocation table (SAT) within the space manager. When the space manager is requested to modify the view-scene structure, it first checks the parameter error, then, it asks the relevant objects whether the request may be accepted or not, and finally, if acceptable, updates the SAT.

2. Rendering of the current view
   The space manager draws the current view on the screen. It decides the order, position, and shape to draw views contained in the current views. Objects inform the space manager that they appear, disappear, and transform. Then the space manager updates the SAT and redraws the screen. The rendering process is optimized to reduce the time required to draw views. This process requires a lot of image operations on the views' shapes. The shape is separated into three parts to help the optimization: the completely transparent region, the half-transparent region, and the opaque region. They are compressed and cached by the space managers.

   Views can have a transform matrix. The objects in a lower level of a view-scene hierarchy may be transformed many times, since every scene-view has its own transform matrix.

3. Getting spatial information of views

A user usually manipulates virtual spaces by pointing devices such as a mouse or stylus pen. It is essential to know what objects the user would like to operate. In order to know what objects the mouse pointer lies on, the coordinates of the screen should be converted to the scene's local coordinates. This is the space manager's job. In addition to that, the space manager gives certain spatial information, such as the views located in the specific scene, the view's transform matrix, conversion of the screen coordinates to the view's (not scene's) local coordinates, and the opposite.

17.5.4 Dogra

17.5.4.1 Overview

The name *Dogra* comes from Dynamic Objects' GRAphics library. *Dogra* is a standard graphics library of *Yougao* and almost all drawing operations are executed through *Dogra*.

Dogra consists of five sub-libraries: *Matisse, Renge, Showgi, Gento,* and *Sui*. Matisse does the modeling; it converts the graphics specification expressed in paths or graphs into the device-independent vector graphics primitives.

Renge and *Gento* are both graphic renderers; they actually draw device-independent graphics primitives at a resolution appropriate to the hardware according to the rendering parameters. In this stage, therefore, device independency is lost. *Renge* draws graphic primitives. There are two modes of drawing. One is binary mode, in which only shapes are drawn, and pixel values such as color or gray scale are not considered. The other is real mode, in which pixel values are written. Gradation is also supported.

Gento is the library for rendering images. It magnifies or shrinks images while interpolating or anti-aliasing, does geometric mapping to them, passes them through spatial filters, or does some other kinds of operations just as paint tools do. It also converts the image derived from *Renge* into pixel values to write into RGB frame memories, considering the background on which the image is to be drawn. This is when real pixel values are calculated, i.e., this is when device independency as to color is lost.

Showgi displays the images renderers have drawn on the hidden frame memories onto the real display. It displays the images from *Renge, Gento,* etc., after applying various kinds of visual effects on them.

Sui provides primitive device-dependent two-dimensional graphics functions. This is used to display the mouse cursor, or the "rubber band" while dragging.

17.5.4.2 Matisse

Matisse is a library of shape modeling which produces graphics primitives out of various kinds of two-dimensional (2D) shape expressions. Some of its functions resemble certain kinds of operators of PostScript [8]. It is named after that great artist, Henri *Matisse*. Henri Matisse adopted the manner of paper-cutout and pasting, for drawing pictures by colors themselves. Our modeling library is named after him to capture the image of his skilled scissors.

For the description of 2D graphics, "graphs" are used. Some points are first defined, and then they are linked by lines which have various kinds of attributes to specify how they are drawn. Such a description forms a graphics primitive.

17.5.4.3 *Renge*

Renge "draws" the graphics primitives in the work frame memories which are not actually displayed. Graphics primitives are in most cases, regions enclosed by lines or Bezier curves.

The work frame memory does not necessarily correspond with the RGB planes for final output. Instead, it expresses various abstract concepts. Later, *Showgi* interprets its meaning and translates it to RGB colors. In some cases, not even one frame is used, while in other cases, as many as six planes are used. This work frame is called the abstract graphics plane (Fig. 17.16).

The advantage of the abstract graphics plane is best illustrated by the use of a color model other than the RGB model. For example, in cases where the HSV (hue, saturation, and value) model is more appropriate, three planes will be used for H, S, and V values. *Showgi* later converts these values to RGB values. In this case, *Showgi* has to be told which plane represents which parameter of which color model. Of course, only color models supported by *Showgi* can be used here. Other advantages of the abstract graphics plane are discussed later, in *Showgi* section.

Renge can specify the bit depth of a plane, or the parameter to write in a plane. It also supports gradation of various kinds. If gradation of color and transparency is well exploited, then "soft" displays can be obtained which have not yet been seen widely, and they will give great visual effects.

17.5.4.4 *Gento*

Gento processes images in various ways. It has three major functions: image transformation, raster-image operation, and painting functions.

As to image transformation, *Gento* supports projective transformation (scaling, rotation, distortion, etc.) and other functional mappings. In order to keep the device-independent metrics, these functions are often used when rendering images. Since an image consists of sampled pixels, the resolution of the image cannot be device-independent. *Gento* provides interpolation and anti-aliasing facilities to get better images.

Raster-image operation contains spatial filtering and inter-image operations, which are mainly used for image analysis. For drawing pictures as in so-called paint-tools, painting functions such as making gradation masks, mixing of colors, and pen-drawing facilities are provided.

17.5.4.5 *Showgi*

Showgi shows pictures on the screen. *Showgi*'s major features are: to determine pixel values which are to be actually written into the physical frame memory, and to apply visual effects while showing a picture.

A. Full Color with Fixed Alpha

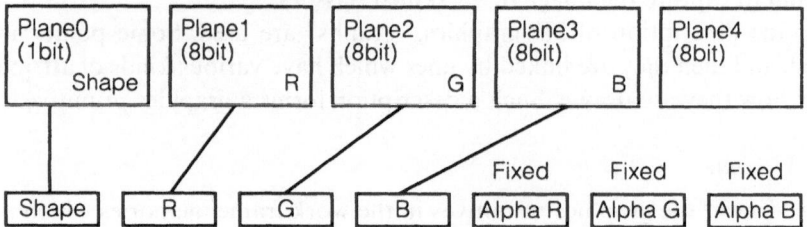

B. 8bit Black and White with Varying Alpha

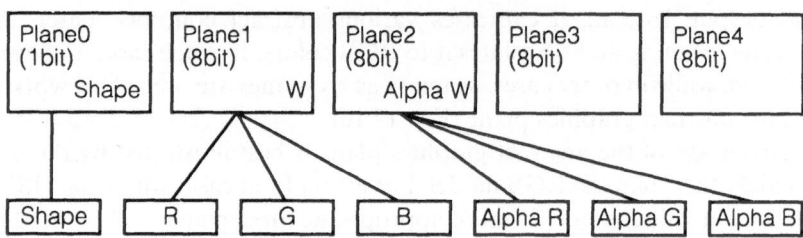

C. Monochrome (Shape Only)

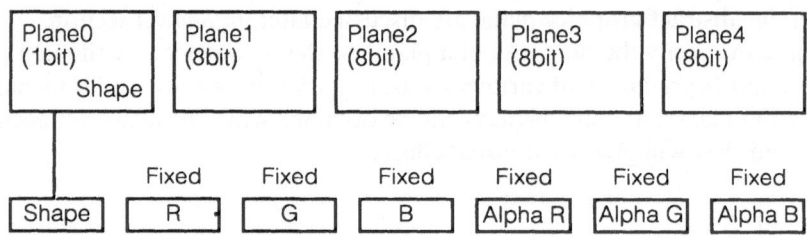

D. HSV Full Color with Varying Alpha

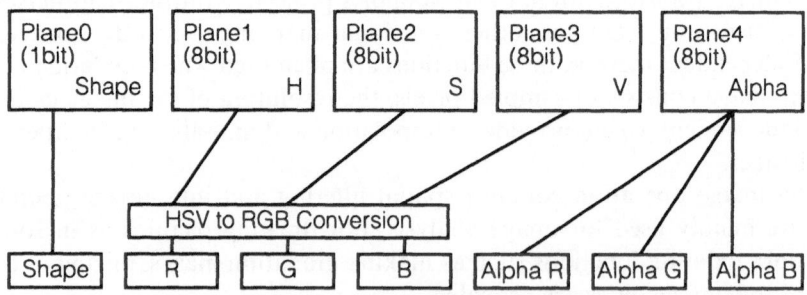

FIG. 17.16. Abstract graphics plane

To get "physical" pixel values, half transparency should be considered. *Showgi* currently supports alpha operation and several abstract half-transparency functions: magnifying, smoothing, edge-enhancing, and edge-extracting of the underlying image.

Visual effects determine how to display the picture. Besides the normal quick appearance, wipe, dissolve, roll, and explosion are currently implemented.

17.5.4.6 *Sui*

Sui provides simple device-dependent two-dimensional graphic functions. It draws lines, curves, circles, ovals, rectangles, and polygons quickly. *Sui* is mainly used for interactive operations such as dragging or posting which require high-speed drawing. Mouse pointers are also drawn by *Sui*.

17.5.5 Event Manager

As in most window systems, user inputs are sent to *Yougao* as events. Events include: movement of mice or other pointing devices, pressing/release of mouse buttons, pressing/release of keys on the keyboard, and a note on/note off message from the MIDI channel. Voices inputted through a microphone or motion pictures through a video camera (which may be some kind of action of the user) can be used as events as they are, or after they are pattern-recognized.

All events are sent to the event manager from their sources. The sources of events are usually device drivers, or media drivers, but arbitrary objects can produce events. The event manager puts all the events into the one and only event queue in the system in the order of occurrence. The time of occurrence of an event is indicated by the time field in the event data, and it is usually the time at which the input occurred to the device driver; however, it can be changed through course of transfer of the event.

An object can freely set the time field of the event it produces. If the current time has not reached the time field of an event received, i.e., if the event claims to happen in the future, the event manager, does not queue it till the specified time comes.

An event in the event queue is sent to the object focused when the event occurred. Focus in *Yougao* is common to all events and is set to an object by the focus cursor. The focus cursor is usually one of the mouse cursors. If the focus cursor is on the unclipped and actually displayed portion of an object, the object is said to be focused. In *Yougao*, transparent objects are supported and therefore there could be more than one such object. In such cases, focus is set on the object which is displayed in the foremost position.

When the focus is changed, an *enter* event is produced to the newly focused object, and the event manager notifies it by way of an RPC. This indicates that the object now has the right to access a certain portion of the event queue. The portion of the queue it can access is from the *enter* event to the *leave* event, which is produced when the focus is again changed; however, the objects are not allowed to change the structure of the queue. The event manager cannot change the data of events either, and therefore mutual exclusion is not necessary.

In most of the existing window systems, a client process, not the window system, has to check whether the relevant events have been issued or not. Consequently, other processings may be blocked by the procedure call for checking events, or time is wasted by repeatedly calling the procedure. By contrast, this loss is avoided in *Yougao* because the event manager notifies objects. As the object directly accesses the event queue, the overhead of the client's requesting access to event data one by one by RPC and of copying the data is avoided. If event data are shared without being copied, usually mutual exclusion is necessary; in the *Yougao* system, it is not, as mentioned before.

These advantages are gained by making the event manager work exclusively for processing user input. (On the other hand, other window systems often use events for general-purpose synchronization among processes.) Any object can produce events, but an event is always sent to the focused object, which limits the use of events.

The explanation which has been presented so far assumes that all objects can receive events; however, in reality some objects do not have to receive events at all, or there may be cases where by use of a scene the programmer wants to process totally all the inputs to more than one object. For such cases as these, objects which want to receive events, have to register at the event manager. Events to objects which did not register are forwarded by the event manager to the parent objects in the view-scene structure. For example, to express an ordinary window which is made up of several components such as a scroll bar, define the window as a scene, and then place all the components in the scene, and register at the event manager that all the relevant events only go to the scene. The scene which received an event decides in which component the event occurred, which is easily done with the space manager; then, it invokes an RPC to the component. As is illustrated here, how to react to events can be described only in the root scene in the most appropriate way which fits the view-scene structure within the scene. Scenes can be said to serve as local event managers in this sense. These scenes can be defined as pseudo-objects, as in the event manager of the system.

17.6 Conclusions

A lot of so-called multimedia-oriented products have been introduced over the past several years. Actually, many of them have new and attractive functions, which reminds us of the arrival of a new era. Many of them, however, deal with each type of media separately. The primary goal of the *Yougao* multimedia workstation is to find a way of integrating these various media in a simple set of equations.

Virtual work space is designed for this purpose. The view-scene model supports this space. It enables mapping of the space onto the object in another space. Users can walk around this "hyperspace," which allows realistic and surrealistic modeling. They can move to different worlds, and see several worlds in a single screen. Views and scenes can also model conventional multi-windows and interactive graphics environments on which many systems already run.

The *Yougao* system is designed in three layers: the media handling layer, the integration layer, and the manipulation layer.

The media handling layer requires sophisticated media handling functions. Graphics, text, and sound handling facilities are then designed in order to keep modeling ability of views and scenes. They provide the state-of-the-art visual/audio environment. For example, *Yougao*'s 2D-graphics abilities cover the arbitrary transparency and abstract color frames. All media expressions including metrics, colors, and times are device-independent.

For the integration layer, the *R* language is designed to describe the action of each object. This layer integrates the various media. A user or programmer can write a scenario of the virtual world using the *R* language. Applications can also be composed by defining new objects in the *R* language.

Finally, as the manipulation layer, the interactive graphical human interface is implemented to provide a sophisticated way to use the system. In addition to conventional mouse-and-icon operations, it can manipulate view and scene structure directly. Switches, sliders and many active objects can be located, posted, and created in the virtual space. Users can then open a box, move to another world, or start the play by using these objects.

Our experience shows that an integrated multimedia workstation provides useful and powerful platforms for building interfaces in many applications including engineering, business, design, publishing, and various forms of simulations.

References

1. Maekawa M, Sakamura K, Ishikawa C, Shimizu T (1983) Multimedia machine. Information processing 83 (IFIP). Elsevier, North-Holland, pp 71–77
2. Ohta M, Maekawa M, Arano T, Kawachiya K (1986) Multimedia information processing based on a general media model. Information processing 86 (IFIP). Elsevier, North-Holland, pp 957–962
3. Foley JD, van Dam A (1982) Fundamentals of interactive computer graphics. Addison-Wesley, Massachusetts
4. Foley JD, van Dam A, Feiner SK, Hughes JF (1990) Computer graphics: Principles and practice. Addison-Wesley, Massachusetts
5. Rubinstein R (1988) Digital typography. Addison-Wesley, Massachusetts
6. Abe S, Maekawa M, Shimizu K, Kato T (1989) Fast display of high-quality anti-aliased Japanese characters. Raster imaging and digital typography (RIDT89). Cambridge University Press, Cambridge
7. Moore FR (1990) Elements of computer music. Prentice Hall, Englewood Cliffs
8. Adobe Systems Incorporated (1985) PostScript language reference manual. Addison-Wesley, Massachusetts

Index